AYAHUASCA, RITUAL AND RELIGION IN BRAZIL

D0143775

Ayahuasca, Ritual and
Religion in Brazil

Edited by
Beatriz Caiuby Labate and Edward MacRae

LONDON   OAKVILLE

Published by

UK: Equinox Publishing Ltd., 1 Chelsea Manor Studios
Flood Street, London SW3 5SR

USA: DBBC, 28 Main Street, Oakville, CT 06779

www.equinoxpub.com

First published 2010

British Library Cataloguing-in-Publication Data

A catalogue record for this book is available from the British Library.

ISBN-13   978 1 84553 679 4   (paperback)

Library of Congress Cataloging-in-Publication Data

Ayahuasca, ritual and religion in Brazil / Edited by Beatriz Caiuby
Labate and Edward MacRae.
    p. cm.
Includes bibliographical references and index.
ISBN 978-1-84553-679-4 (pbk.)
1. Indians of South America--Brazil--Religion. 2. Indians of South
America--Brazil--Rites and ceremonies. 3. Indians of South
America--Brazil--Drug use. 4. Ayahuasca ceremony--Brazil. 5.
Hallucinogenic drugs and religious experience--Brazil 6. Brazil--Social
life and customs. 7. Brazil--Religious life and customs. I. Labate,
Beatriz Caiuby. II. Macrae, Edward John Baptista das Neves. F2519.3.R3A93 2010
    299.8--dc22
                            2009035243

The publication of this book has been supported by the German Research Council (Deutsche Forschungsgemeinschaft – DFG) and the Collaborative Research Center 'Ritual Dynamics – Socio-Cultural Processes from a Historical and Culturally Comparative Perspective' (Sonderforschungsbereich 'Ritualdynamik – Soziokulturelle und historische Prozesse im Kulturvergleich').

Typeset by ISB Typesetting, Sheffield, UK
Printed and bound in Great Britain by

Contents

Acknowledgements

Bringing out this collection of articles was quite a difficult process and was only possible because we counted on the help of many friends and supporters. It would be impossible to mention all and inevitably our acknowledgements will leave out names that should have been remembered for which we apologise.

First of all we would like to thank Christian Frenopoulo and Matthew Meyer for their great help in translating and revising many of the articles that make up this collection, as well as for their comments on the Introduction. They were present and accompanied all the different stages of compiling and editing, always willing to collaborate in any way they could. Their voluntary work during these seven years were a generous donation and, above all, we thank them for their great patience in putting up with us and our anxiety.

Special thanks must also be extended to all the authors who trusted us in the adventure of getting Brazilian texts published in English and were willing to provide for the translation of their work.

Robin Wright gave us the much needed initial encouragement and support to carry out this project, translated several articles and wrote the article 'The Brazilian Ayahuasca Religions', which was published as part of the journal *Fieldwork in Religion* Volume 2.2 (2006).

Sandra Goulart helped by collaborating in the writing of the Introduction and for many years has been exchanging ideas with us, offering many precious opinions and insights. But above all we thank her for her constant friendship and companionship.

We also thank Isabel de Rose and Renato Sztutman for their important comments on the Introduction.

Andrew Dawson´s help was crucial in putting us in contact with Equinox, and in offering many friendly suggestions. We also thank him for writing the foreword to this book.

Editora Mercado de Letras, Editora da Universidade Federal da Bahia and the journal *Discursos Sediciosos, Crime, Direito e Sociedade*, graciously waived their translation rights over some of the articles in this collection.

Flavio Lopes, Evelyn Ruman, Débora Carvalho Pereira, Department of Memory and Documentation of the Centro Espírita Beneficente União do Vegetal, Bento Viana, Mariana Pantoja and João Guedes Filho allowed us to publish pictures of theirs.

Vagner Gonçalves da Silva, Débora Carvalho Pereira, and José Murilo Jr., generously collaborated in researching Internet publishing options.

Sérgio Vidal has been a permanent companion and gave us much help in innumerable tasks as well as having shared with us intellectual and activist exchanges in the last years.

José Carlos Bouso, Rick Doblin, Jeremy Narby, Tom Roberts, Michael Winkelman, Jimmy Weiskopf, Manuel Velásquez, Alberto Groisman, Jag Davies and, especially, Joseph Hobbes and Mark Hoffmann offered us important suggestions on possible editorial options for this collection.

We thank our colleagues at the Institute of Medical Psychology, Heidelberg University, especially Rolf Verres, Henrik Jungaberle and Jan Weinhold for their comments and exchanges on the field of drug research.

Our colleagues of the Interdisciplinary Group for Psychoactive Studies (*Núcleo de Estudos Interdisciplinares sobre Psicoativos – NEIP*, www.neip.info) and especially Henrique Carneiro, Maurício Fiore, Rafael Guimarães dos Santos, Denizar Missawa Camurça, Brian Anderson and Stelio Marras have been constantly exchanging ideas with us and making important suggestions.

We also thank the collaborators of Interdisciplinary Group for the Study of Psychoactive Substances (Grupo de Estudos sobre Psicoativos – GIESP, http://www.giesp.ffch.ufba.br) and the site http://bialabate.net.

We thank Marc Blainey for his help in revising the proofs of this book.

Last, but not least, we wish to thank the journal *Fieldwork in Religion* and its editors Ron Geaves and Andrew Dawson for their interest and trust in offering us the possibility of producing the special edition *The Light From the Forest: The Ritual Use of Ayahuasca in Brazil* (Volume 2.3, 2006 – issued belatedly in 2008), part of which originated this book.

About the contributors

Translated by Matthew Meyer and Christian Frenopoulo

Brian Anderson was born in Manila, Philippines; he is a citizen of the USA. He obtained his BA in Biochemistry with a minor in Latin American and Latino Studies from the University of Pennsylvania in 2007. Currently, he is an MD Candidate at the Stanford University School of Medicine. His anthropologic fieldwork experience includes working with the undocumented Mexican immigrant population in Philadelphia, Pennsylvania, and with the União do Vegetal in Bahia, Brazil. Brian intends to specialize in psychiatry and to conduct research on mood disorders, substance abuse and the therapeutic uses of psychedelic substances.

Wladimyr Sena Araújo was born in Cuiabá (Mato Grosso) in 1967 and moved, at the age of five, to Rio Branco, Acre state, where he currently lives. In 1991 he graduated from the history program at the Federal University of Acre (UFAC). He subsequently majored in dramatic arts at the Paraná College of the Arts (1993). In 1997 he earned a master's degree in social anthropology at UNICAMP. He is currently a professor at UNINORTE in Rio Branco. He also works as an anthropologist for the Acre State Secretariat of the Environment and Natural Resources (SEMA). He is the author of *Navegando Sobre as Ondas do Daime: história, cosmologia e ritual da Barquinha* (1999: Editora da Unicamp) and co-editor, with Beatriz Caiuby Labate, of *O Uso Ritual da Ayahuasca* (2002: Mercado de Letras).

Paulo Cesar Ribeiro Barbosa was born in São Paulo in 1968, studied Social Sciences at the Faculty of Philosophy and Human Sciences of the University of São Paulo and obtained a Masters in Medical Sciences at the State University of Campinas in 2001. He currently works as an Assistant Professor at the State University of Santa Cruz, where he carries out studies of the interface between anthropology and psychiatry and the use of psychoactive substances. He obtained his PhD in Medical Sciences at the State University of Campinas, with a longitudinal study which evaluated the mental health of users of ayahuasca.

Sérgio Brissac was born in Rio de Janeiro in 1967. At 18 he entered the Society of Jesus and was ordained as a priest of this Catholic order in 1996. He earned a bachelor's degree in philosophy and theology from the Jesuit Center for Higher Studies in Belo Horizonte, Minas Gerais state, and was licensed in philosophy by PUC/SP. In 1997 he began his anthropology training at the National Museum, UFRJ, where he obtained a master's degree in social anthropology with a thesis on the União do Vegetal: 'The North Star Illuminating across the South: An ethnography of the União do Vegetal in an urban context', under the guidance of Professor Otávio Velho; and in 2008 he obtained his PhD's degree in social anthropology on the religious experience of Mazatec Indians: '*Table of flowers, mass of flowers: the mazatatecs and Catholicism in contemporary Mexico*', under the guidance of professor Antonio Carlos de Souza Lima. He published a chapter of his master thesis in the edited volume *O Uso Ritual da Ayahuasca* (Labate and Araújo 2002). In 2006 he left Society of Jesus and renounced being a priest. In 2004 he entered the Brazilian Federal Prosecution Office (Ministério Público Federal), where he works as an expert analyst in anthropology to defend the rights of indigenous peoples in Ceará state, where he currently resides.

Arneide Bandeira Cemin was born in Guajará-Mirim, Rondônia (near the Brazil-Bolivia border). A graduate of the history program at the Federal University of Rondônia (UNIR), she earned a master's degree in sociology from the Federal University of Rio Grande do Sul (UFRGS) with her thesis 'Colonization and Nature: An analysis of the social relations of man with nature in the agricultural colonization of Rondônia'. She took her doctorate in social anthropology at the University of São Paulo (USP) with a dissertation called 'Order, Shamanism, and the Gift: The power of Santo Daime'. She is currently a professor in the Department of Sociology and Philosophy at UNIR, and a researcher for the Center for Studies of the Social Imaginary (CEIUNIR), which develops theories and methods for the study of the social imaginary and sponsors research on Amazonian culture and social conflict.

Osmildo Silva da Conceição, sixth of ten children of Milton Gomes da Conceição and Mariana Feitosa do Nascimento, both descendents of indigenous ethnicities of the Pano group. Osmildo was born in 1962 in the place known as the *colocação Vista Alegre* on the upper Tejo river, an affluent of the Juruá river in the far west of Acre state, an historically important rubber producing region. Osmildo grew up on the Tejo river, where he learned the rubber-tapper's trade from his father. In the 1980s he produced rubber with his father and cousins on the *colocação Degredo* on Riozinho creek, a tributary of the Tejo. In these youthful years, as was common for young men of his age, he went to parties, played in soccer tournaments and enjoyed other pastimes. Later, with the involvement of his father in the struggle against the *patrões* and the creation of a rubber-tappers' cooperative, he worked as a pilot on the boats of the National Rubber-tappers' Council and assisted the efforts of the cooperative. In 1989 he married his cousin Rocilda, with whom he has six children. In the 1990s he participated in a pilot program for the production of *couro vegetal* ('vegetal leather'). He was initiated in the science of Ayahuasca in 1989 at the hands of indigenous shamans (Ashaninka and Kaxinawá), later having contact with the Doctrine of Santo Daime. Osmildo affirms his Kontanawa indigenous heritage with pride, and is currently leading a tribal appeal for demarcation of its own Indigenous Lands.

Mariana Ciavatta Pantoja Franco is a native of Ribeirão Preto (São Paulo) and was raised in Rio de Janeiro, where she graduated from the social sciences program at UFRJ. She entered the master's program in sociology at the same institution, and in 1992 defended a thesis on processes of social identity construction among landless groups in southern Brazil. Her fieldwork, anthropological in nature, was conducted at a settlement in Paraná while Mariana participated in consulting and technical fact-finding about associational forms promoted by Landless Workers' Movement (MST) as a member of the Ecumenical Center for Documentation and Information (CEDI). In 1991, also through CEDI, she participated in a census of rubber-tapper populations in the Alto Juruá Extractivist Reserve in Acre state, where she had her first contact with the Amazon. After leaving CEDI, in 1993 she moved to Acre to participate in a broad research project jointly sponsored by USP and UNICAMP and financed by the MacArthur Foundation, spending two years in the Alto Juruá Extractivist Reserve engaged in political consulting and academic research. In 1996 she entered the PhD program in social sciences at UNICAMP and in 2001 defended her dissertation, which won an award from the Joaquim Nabuco Foundation and was published, in 2004, as *Os Milton: Cem anos de história nos seringais* (Recife: Editora Massangana; second edition Rio Branco, EDUFAC, 2008). The book tells the story of a century in the life of a family of rubber-tappers, from the initial occupation of the rubber camps and the persecution of indigenous peoples through the rubber crisis, the end of the *patrão* system and the ascension of the rubber-tappers' social movement for the creation of the Extractivist Reserve. She published a series of articles on her experiences in the Alto Juruá, worked as a consultant in development projects in Acre and beyond and was a fellow at the CNPq, pursuing a project on community resource management among extractivist populations. She lectures at the Federal University of Acre.

Christian Frenopoulo is currently an Anthropology PhD candidate at the University of Pittsburgh, USA. He has a master's degree in anthropology from the University of Regina, Canada. His research was concerned with the use of spirit-possession in the Barquinha religion of Acre, Brazil. He has written and presented texts on different aspects of the Barquinha religion, and also a book review of Labate and Araújo (2002), published in the *Journal of Psychoactive Drugs*. Before this, he had a post-graduate certificate from the Universidad de la República, Uruguay, on Drugs and Intervention Strategies. He obtained two undergraduate degrees: anthropology, from the Universidad de la República, and philosophy, from the Catholic University of Uruguay. He has also worked for the International Baccalaureate in varying contexts.

Sandra Lucia Goulart – PhD in social science from UNICAMP, her dissertation was titled 'Contrasts and Continuities in an Amazonian Tradition: The ayahuasca religions', and comprises a comparative study of the three principal Brazilian religions that use the psychoactive drink long known by the Quechua name ayahuasca and by other, more recent denominations, such as Daime and Vegetal. She holds a master's degree in social anthropology from USP, where she defended a thesis on 'The Cultural Roots of Santo Daime'. She contributed a chapter to, and helped organize, the edited volume *O Uso Ritual da Ayahuasca* (Labate and Araújo 2002). A specialist in ayahuasca studies, in recent years she has widened her focus, as exemplified in the book she edited with Beatriz C. Labate, *O Uso Ritual das Plantas* *de Poder* (Mercado de Letras: 2005). The book brings together work on the consumption of sundry psychoactive substances in various cultural contexts, such as tobacco, coca leaf, the jurema of Brazil's Northeastern Indians, and Cannabis sativa. She also co-edited (with Labate, Fiore, MacRae and Carneiro) the book *Drogas e Cultura: Novas Perspectivas* (Edufba, 2008). Goulart has also done research on the use and traffic of illicit drugs, most recently on crack consumption in São Paulo, and was sponsored by the United Nations' Latin American Institute for Crime Prevention and the Treatment of Delinquents (ILANUD) (see Mingardi and Goulart, *Revista do ILANUD*, no. 15, 2001). The research was part of a wider UNESCO study aimed at comparing contexts of illicit drug use and traffic in four countries, including Brazil. Currently she is assistant professor at Cásper Líbero College.

Beatriz Caiuby Labate was born in São Paulo, in 1971. She earned a bachelor's degree in social science from the State University of Campinas (UNICAMP) in 1996. In 2000 she obtained a Master's degree in social anthropology from the same university, receiving the Prize for Best Master's Thesis from the National Association for Graduate Studies in Social Science (ANPOCS). Her current doctoral research in social anthropology at UNICAMP focuses on the internationalization of Peruvian ayahuasca 'vegetalismo'. She is co-editor of the books *O uso ritual da ayahuasca* (Mercado de Letras 2002, 2004 2º ed.), *O uso ritual das plantas de poder* (Mercado de Letras, 2005), *Drogas e cultura: novas perspectivas* (Edufba 2008) and co-editor of the special edition *Light from the forest: The ritual use of ayahuasca in Brazil* (Journal *Fieldwork in Religion* 2.3, 2006 – published in 2008), author of the book *A reinvenção do uso da ayahuasca nos centros urbanos* (Mercado de Letras, 2004), co-author of the books *Religiões ayahuasqueiras: um balanço bibliográfico* (Mercado de Letras, 2008) translated into English as *Ayahuasca religions: A comprehensive bibliography and critical essays* (MAPS, 2009) and *Música Brasileira de Ayahuasca* (Mercado de Letras, 2009). She is a researcher with the Nucleus for Interdisciplinary Studies of Psychoactives (NEIP) and editor of its site (http://www.neip.info). Currently she is Member of Research Staff at the Institute of Medical Psychology, Heidelberg University and a Member of the Collaborative Research Center (SFB 619) 'Ritual Dynamics – Socio-Cultural Processes from a Historical and Culturally Comparative Perspective' (http://www.ritualdynamik.de) .

Edward MacRae was born in São Paulo in 1946, son of a Scotsman and a Brazilian mother. He was educated in Great Britain, where he earned a degree in Social Psychology from the University of Sussex and received his master's degree in Sociology of Latin America at the University of Essex. Returning to Brazil he studied Anthropology at the State University of Campinas-UNICAMP and at the University of São Paulo-USP, where he earned a doctorate in Social Anthropology. Since then he has researched drug issues, working first in the São Paulo State Institute of Social Medicine and Criminology (IMESC) and in the Drug Dependence Education and Treatment Program (PROAD/EPM), and later as a member of the São Paulo State Drug Council. He currently resides in Salvador (Bahia state), where he lectures in Anthropology at the Federal University of Bahia (UFBA). He is also an associate researcher at the Center for Drug Abuse Studies and Therapy (CETAD/UFBA) and leader of the Interdisciplinary Group for the Study of Psychoactive Substances (GIESP). His main teaching and research interests at the moment deal with themes related to the social anthropology of drug use in general with a special emphasis on the ritual use of ayahuasca in the Santo Daime religion.

Between 2003 and 2006 he represented the Brazilian Ministry of Culture on the National Drug Policy Council (CONAD) and acted for a time as vice coordinator of that Council's 'Technical-scientific Advisory Chamber'. He was also a member of the Multi-disciplinary Work Group (GMT) set up by CONAD to regulate the religious use of aya-huasca in Brazil. Presently he occupies the seat reserved at CONAD for an anthropologist. Dr MacRae has written books about sexuality, social movements, the socially integrated use of psychoactive substances, and the reduction of harm associated with drug use.

Marcelo Simão Mercante was born in Rio de Janeiro in 1970. He has an undergraduate degree in Biology, by the Federal University of Rio de Janeiro (1994), Masters degree in Social Anthropology by the Federal University of Santa Catarina (2000), and PhD in Human Sciences/Consciousness and Spirituality by the Saybrook Graduate School and Research Center (2006). He is a member of the Interdisciplinary Group for Psychoac-tive Studies (Núcleo de Estudos Interdisciplinares sobre Psicoativos – NEIP). Marcelo has been working with Anthropology of Religion, with Medical Anthropology, and Anthropology of Consciousness. He is currently linked to the Post-Doctoral program on Anthropology of the University of São Paulo (USP), where he is investigating the use of Ayahuasca for treating drug addiction and alcoholism. He is the author of *Healing: Spontaneous Mental Imagery and Healing Process of the Barquinha, a Brazilian Ayahuasca Religious System*. Saarbrücken: Lambert Academic Publishing House, 2010.

Domingos Bernardo Gialluisi da Silva Sá was born in Rio de Janeiro in 1941. He earned a law degree in 1966 from the National Law School of the University of Brazil, (currently the Federal University of Rio de Janeiro – UFRJ). His civil law practice is located in Rio de Janeiro. He is a member of the Brazilian Institute of Lawyers (IAB). In 1986, he was the president of committee of the federal narcotics board, formerly known as CONFEN (*Con-selho Federal de Entorpecentes*), which proposed the withdrawal of ayahuasca and its plant ingredients from the Health Ministry's schedule of prohibited substances, thus permitting its ritual and religious use in Brazil. In 1992, CONFEN unanimously reconfirmed the main-tenance of ayahuasca's exemption from the schedule, following his recommendation. He currently belongs to the national anti-drug board, CONAD (*Conselho Nacional de Política sobre Drogas*), and also works for its technical-scientific advisory committee. The CONAD approved a further recommendation that he authored in 2004, which led to CONAD's Reso-lution No. 5 on November 24, 2004. This resolution consolidates CONFEN's and CONAD's prior legitimation of ayahuasca use and implements measures to investigate and explore the therapeutic use of ayahuasca and become acquainted with its universe of users. He offered an inaugural conference on the Ethical Principles of Ayahuasca Use during the Ayahuasca Seminar, organized by the CONAD from March 8–9, 2006, in Rio Branco, state of Acre. He served on CONFEN from 1985–87, 1990–93, and 1996. He has also served as president of Rio de Janeiro's state narcotics board, CONEN-RJ (*Conselho Estadual de Entorpecentes do Rio de Janeiro*), and was deputy secretary of Justice for the state of Rio de Janeiro from 1987–90. He has represented Brazil in international conferences on drugs and has authored several articles on psychoactives, citizenship and legality.

Rafael Guimarães dos Santos was born in 1980 in Brasília. In his undergraduate senior thesis in Biology (UniCEUB, Brasília) he analysed the biological and behavioral aspects of ayahuasca in rats. He has a Masters in Psychology (Behavioral Processes) (UnB, Brasília), where he conducted research with Santo Daime members on the possible relationships between the ritual use of ayahuasca and hopelessness, anxiety and panic states. He has a Diplome in Specialized Superior Studies in Pharmacology (UAB, Barcelona), a Masters in Initiation of Research in Pharmacology (UAB) and is currently a PhD candidate in Pharmacology (UAB), investigating the human pharmacology of repeated doses of ayahuasca, under the direction of Dr Jordi Riba. Rafael has experience in the fields of General Biology, Ethnobotany, Pharmacology, Ethnopharmacology, Psychopharmacology and Neuropsychopharmacology, with an emphasis in the investigation of hallucinogenic compounds. He works mainly on the following topics: psychoactive substances, hallucinogens, psychopharmacology.

Luiz Eduardo Soares, born in 1954, holds a master's degree in social anthropology, a PhD in political science, and has done post-doctoral work in political philosophy. He is a Professor at the Department of Social Sciences of the State University of Rio de Janeiro (UERJ) and has been Professor at IUPERJ (Graduate Institute for the Social Research of Rio de Janeiro) and UNICAMP (University of Campinas). He has been a Visiting Scholar at Harvard University, Columbia University, the University of Virginia, the University of Pittsburgh, and the Vera Institute of Justice in New York. He has written 17 books and co-authored another 30. His most recent book is *Espírito Santo*, written with Carlos Eduardo Lemos and Rodney Miranda (Objetiva: 2009). Professor Soares has been Undersecretary of Public Security of the State of Rio de Janeiro (1999–2000); Coordinator of Public Security, Justice, and Citizenship of the State of Rio de Janeiro (1999–2000); and National Secretary of Public Security (2003).

Foreword

Andrew Dawson

At the end of April 2008, the Brazilian musical legend, Gilberto Gil, visited the community of Alto Santo situated in the Amazonian state of Acre. Alto Santo is the spiritual headquarters of the originating branch of the religion of Santo Daime. Along with Barquinha and the União do Vegetal (literally, Union of the Vegetable), Santo Daime is one of Brazil's official ayahuasca religions. Gilberto Gil's visit, however, was not a private pilgrimage, for he was here in his official capacity as Brazilian Minister of Culture. Whilst visiting the Governor of Acre, Binho Marques, Gil made time in his otherwise hectic schedule to attend a ceremony at Alto Santo where he received a petition presented by representatives of Brazil's three ayahuasca religions. The petition comprised a formal request that ayahuasca be recognized by the Brazilian State as an integral part of its cultural heritage. Upon receiving the application, the Minister of Culture replied that 'I hope that we can soon celebrate the registration of ayahuasca as a cultural legacy of the Brazilian nation'.

The visit of Gilberto Gil to Alto Santo stands at the end of a long road and is clear indication of how far the struggle has come to have the ritual consumption of ayahuasca recognized as a legal right. From the early days of religious persecution and police prosecution, the religious use of ayahuasca has survived and ultimately been endorsed by the latest of a long series of State enquiries. Today, the argument in favour of the ritual consumption of ayahuasca is increasingly winning over a once sceptical, if not suspicious, Brazilian public. Spreading beyond the Amazonian states to the big cities of Brazil in the latter part of the twentieth century, the denominations of the Vegetable Union and Santo Daime are increasingly assuming an international identity with communities now established throughout Europe, the Americas and Australasia.

The spread of ayahuasca religiosity beyond its traditional homeland, however, has not been free from the same trials and tribulations which first met its move beyond the geographical confines of Amazonia in late twentieth-century Brazil. Across Europe, for example, the founding of Santo Daime communities has been met with official suspicion which in a large number of cases has resulted in judicial prosecutions being undertaken on the charge of narcotics consumption or trafficking. Although in a growing number of European countries legal proceedings have not resulted in the wholesale criminalization of Santo Daime members and their religious practices, at best (and excluding Holland) the legal status of the ritual consumption of ayahuasca remains something of a juridical grey area. For now, at least, clandestinity continues to be the order of the day for *ayahuasqueiros* across Europe. In the United States the struggle to establish the legal right to consume ayahuasca in ritual practices has been led by the União do Vegetal. Commencing with a police raid and the confiscation of the sacred beverage being used by a local UDV community, the fight to establish the legal right to the religious use of ayahuasca eventually led to the United States' Supreme Court. Although subject to appeal and further clarification, the 2006 findings of the court upheld the UDV's right to ritually consume ayahuasca on the grounds of the freedom of religious practice (in this instance, weighed against the duties of the State in respect of policing narcotics). The Santo Daime church has also enjoyed a recent success in the State Court of Oregon. As evidenced, however, by the use of bureaucratic delaying tactics in response to the UDV's victory in the Supreme Court and the possibility of the State of Oregon appealing to a Higher Court in the Santo Daime case, the battle is not yet fully won.

In its own way, each of the chapters collected here contributes to the ongoing journey of ayahuasca religiosity toward full and equal recognition as a legitimate mode of religious expression. Some of what follows has already been published in English as a special edition of the Equinox journal *Fieldwork in Religion* (Volume 2.3, 2006), *The Light from the Forest: The Ritual Use of Ayahuasca in Brazil*. With the continuing international spread of ayahuasca religion and the resulting attention generated by its growing presence in contexts previously unaccustomed to its varied institutional and ritual manifestations, it was decided that a broader audience should be sought than that normally reached by an academic journal such as *Fieldwork in Religion*. Hence, the book that is before you now. Here, however, two of the journal articles have been removed, the order of the pieces published by *Fieldwork in Religion* changed and the contents augmented by the addition of an introductory overview. Furthermore, three previously untranslated pieces – by Domingos Bernardo de Sá, Luis Eduardo Soares and Edward MacRae – have been included and a new article by Bia Labate, Rafael Santos, Brian Anderson, Marcelo Mercante and Paulo Barbosa added.

Whether treating Barquinha, Santo Daime or the Vegetable Union, what follows represents a further step in the direction of enhancing public understanding, both academic and lay, of what the ayahuasca religions of Brazil stand for and how they celebrate their beliefs in word and deed. As a fellow traveller on this road to understanding, I am, and have been for some time, deeply appreciative of the guidance offered by the individual and joint works of the editors of this book. Although writing and researching a variety of issues at play in contemporary Brazilian society, Bia Labate and Edward MacRae has each earned an academic reputation as insightful commentators upon one or more aspects relating to the emergence, spread and consolidation of ayahuasca religion in Brazil. Through edited collections, monographs, chapters, and articles, Bia Labate and Edward MacRae have established reputations as scholars worthy to be listened to. What follows serves to reinforce this reputation. I congratulate Equinox for bringing their work to the attention of the English speaking world and commend this book to you.

Brazilian ayahuasca religions in perspective

Beatriz Caiuby Labate, Edward MacRae and Sandra Lucia Goulart

Translated by Christian Frenopoulo, revised by Matthew Meyer

The central theme of this selection of articles is a phenomenon that involves the emergence of religious groups in the Brazilian Amazon that build their systems of ritual, myth and principles around the use of a psychoactive brew known by several different names, one of which is the Quechua term 'ayahuasca'.[1] These religions – Santo Daime (in its Alto Santo and CEFLURIS branches), Barquinha and the União do Vegetal – are generically labelled as 'Brazilian ayahuasca religions' in anthropological writings.

Although the field of studies of these religious movements has seen much development in recent decades, there are still very few publications in English, especially in the area of anthropology.[2] This collection seeks to address this absence and offer visibility to the research conducted in Brazil, most of which has been carried out by Brazilian researchers. The current collection has attempted to select a representative sample of the main types of approaches that have been used. It also offers a view of the historical development of this field of research in Brazil, especially from the perspective of the human sciences, particularly anthropology. We have included articles previously published only in Portuguese, in compilations that one of us has also organized (Labate and Araújo 2004; Labate *et al.* 2008). This is the case of the articles by Mariana Pantoja Franco and Osmildo Silva da

---

1. Luis Eduardo Luna explains the etymology of this name as: *Aya – person, soul, dead spirit*; *Wasca – rope, vine, liana*. According to Luna (1986: 73–74), this name is one of the most used for the brew as well as for one of the plants that compose it: the vine *Banisteriopsis caapi*. Ayahuasca can be literally translated into English as 'rope of the spirits' or 'rope of the dead' and even 'vine/liana of the spirits/dead'. In all the ayahuasca religions discussed in this collection, the vine *Banisteriopsis caapi* is combined with the leaves of the bush called *Psychotria viridis,* which contain the active principle DMT (*N-dimethyltryptamine*). The vine and leaves are boiled together, following certain ritual prescriptions. The final result is a plant preparation that is considered sacred and consumed in religious ceremonies. The brew has different names in each of these religions and in their several sub-groups.
2. For a bibliographic survey on this field of studies see Labate, Rose and Santos (2009).

1

Conceição, Arneide Bandeira Cemin, Edward MacRae, and Wladimyr Sena Araújo. Some of the other articles were previously published in Portuguese in other books and Brazilian journals, such as the articles by Luiz Eduardo Soares and Domingos Bernardo Gialluisi da Silva Sá. The compilation also contains original contributions written by researchers dedicated to these topics, such as the texts by Christian Frenopoulo, Sérgio Brissac, Sandra Lucia Goulart, and Labate *et al.*

We hope that this selection will make explicit what the study of the ayahuasca religions has to say on classical and contemporary issues in anthropology. The compilation presents a broad and varied set of ethnographic approaches employed in the initial mapping out of this phenomenon, thus establishing its historical and cultural origins. This book should provide a basis for the development of future work on these religions both in their original contexts and in their expansion throughout Brazil and the world. Their expansion and diversification throughout Brazil and the world may be related to modern projects of religious transit, the construction of national identities by the reappropriation of Indian and popular elements in transnational circuits, migrations and religious diasporas, cultural hybridism, and so on.

Although there is a tradition of ayahuasca consumption by shamans, rubber tappers, and mestizo healers in several countries of South America, such as Colombia, Bolivia, Peru, Venezuela and Ecuador, the formalization of churches that use the brew only occurs in Brazil. As in the cases of Bwiti in Gabon (who use iboga, *Tabernanthe iboga*) and the Native American Church in the USA and in Canada (who use peyote, *Lophophora williamsii*), these religions re-elaborate the use of psychoactive preparations, inserting them into local belief systems through a reading influenced by Christianity. In the Brazilian case, there is a manifest combination of the Amazonian ayahuasca folk healer (*curandeirismo*) heritage with popular Catholicism and with the African-Brazilian tradition, Kardecist spiritism, and European esoterism (especially via the Esoteric Circle for the Communion of Thought *[Círculo Esotérico da Comunhão do Pensamento]* and Rosacrucianism. We turn to a brief history of the groups.

The first Brazilian ayahuasca religion was the one known as Daime or Santo Daime, created in the 1920s and 1930s by Raimundo Irineu Serra – or Mestre Irineu, as he is known by followers – in Rio Branco, the capital of Acre state, in the north of Brazil.[3] Of African descent, Mestre Irineu was born in the state of Maranhão (in Northeastern Brazil) and arrived in Acre (in Western Amazonia) during the second decade of the twentieth century to work as a rubber tapper (*seringueiro*), that is, in the extraction of latex rubber. During this period, Mestre Irineu came into contact with the brew, probably used by indigenous, mixed-race (*mestizo, caboclo*) and riverine (*ribeirinhos*) populations since time immemorial, and which would become fundamental in the religion he founded in the frontier zone between Brazil and Bolivia. In the 1930s, he moved to Rio Branco and began to organize his new religion. Here, ayahuasca came to be called Daime. The name Daime, which has also come to identify the religion, is derived from the invocations made by the users of the brew during its consumption and ensuing religious ceremonies. 'Daime' is derived from the verb 'to give' (*dar*), and remits to the notion of

---

3. For a history of the Santo Daime, see: MacRae (1992), Goulart (1996), Groisman (1999), Cemin (2001) and Labate and Araújo (2004), among others.

grace received (health, healing, knowledge, revelation, peace, love, etc.) from a divinity or spiritual entity. Mestre Irineu developed his religion in a place known as *Alto Santo* [Holy Rise]. This name refers to the fact that the spot where he installed his church in 1945, in a peripheral rural area of Rio Branco, was at the top of a hill. The name has also come to designate his group of followers. Mestre Irineu registered his religious group in the government registry just three months before his death in July, 1971, after which it came to be officially called Universal Light Christian Enlightenment Center [*Centro de Iluminação Cristã Luz Universal*] or CICLU.

In 1945, another ayahuasca religion emerged in Rio Branco, created by Daniel Pereira de Mattos, who also came to be known as Mestre or Frei Daniel[4] Just like Mestre Irineu, Mestre Daniel was of Afro-Brazilian heritage. He also arrived in Acre early in the twentieth century; probably some years before Mestre Irineu.They were friends and Mestre Irineu initiated him into the use of Daime, and he joined Mestre Irineu's religion in the 1930s. However, with time, his experiences with Daime led him to the revelation that he had his own 'religious mission', which would only be fully accomplished with the creation of a new religion. It is said that, initially, Mestre Daniel was known in the region as a *rezador* (prayer specialist).[5] He would help travellers, hunters, or rubber tappers who passed through the area in the forest where he built his house and a little chapel in which he began to develop his spiritual activities. Some of these people became his first followers. With time, Mestre Daniel blended his activities as a *rezador* with the consumption of Daime. The rites gradually became more complex. One of the most striking characteristics of the religious system created by Mestre Daniel is its ostensible closeness to practices and beliefs from Afro-Brazilian religions, such as Umbanda.

Initially, Mestre Daniel's religion was known in Rio Branco as the *Capelinha de São Francisco* (Little Chapel of St Francis), because of his devotion to this Catholic saint. Later, the groups who identify and are affiliated with the religious tradition founded by Mestre Daniel became known – mostly by people who did not participate in the religion – as *Barquinha* (Little Boat). There are several explanations for this name. One of these harks back to Mestre Daniel's period as a sailor, before he came into contact with Daime and took residence in Acre. In fact, as Araújo and Frenopoulo both explain in this collection, images and meanings linked with the sea and with sailors are abundant in Mestre Daniel's religion.

The União do Vegetal – or UDV, as it is also known – emerged in 1961. The official name of this religious group – also registered with the government shortly before its founder passed away – is Union of the Vegetal Beneficent Spiritist Center (*Centro Espírita Beneficente União do Vegetal*) or CEBUDV. Chronologically, this is the third ayahuasca religion in Brasil.[6] It was founded by José Gabriel da Costa, also known as Mestre. Mestre Gabriel was born in the countryside in the state of Bahia and arrived in Amazonia in 1943, where he worked in various rubber camps (*seringais*) for several years. While both the

---

4. For a history of the Barquinha, see: Araújo (1999), Goulart (2004), Frenopoulo (2005) and Mercante (2006), among others.

5. 'Rezadores' were, and continue to be in some places, important persons in the Brazilian rural milieu, agents of popular Catholicism in areas where the reach of the Catholic Church and its official representatives was rather limited. These people have been the bearers and executers of a whole body of knowledge of prayers, cult of the saints, ceremonies, festivities, etc. linked with the Catholic tradition.

6. For a history of the UDV, see: Andrade (1995), Brissac (1999) and Goulart (2004), among others.

Santo Daime of Mestre Irineu and the Barquinha of Mestre Daniel emerged in Rio Branco, the UDV was shaped in Porto Velho, Rondônia (a neighbor state of Acre). It seems as if Mestre Gabriel never met the founders of the other two ayahuasca religions and while they called the brew by the same name (Daime), in the UDV it was called Vegetal or Hoasca.

These three religious groups and the mythical, doctrinal and ritual constituents installed by each of their creators – Mestre Irineu, Mestre Daniel and Mestre Gabriel – are to this day the main sources for the formation of other groups of ayahuasca users in Brazil, even those who do not immediately define themselves as religious (Labate 2004). Some of the first researchers of this religious phenomenon (Monteiro da Silva 1983; La Rocque Couto 1989) adopted the Santo Daime term *linha* (line or thread) to designate the Santo Daime, União do Vegetal and Barquinha groups, understanding that the distinction between 'lines' occurs in their mythical narratives, ritual forms and the collection of entities that populate each of their pantheons. In a comparative analysis of these three religions, Goulart (2004) attempts to detect their contrasts, continuities and fragmentation processes. She argues that the distinctions between Santo Daime, Barquinha and UDV express particular developments of a single set of beliefs and practices, that is, a tradition that is common to these different religions (Goulart 2004).

In all three religions, the passing away of the founders stimulated a process of ruptures and formation of new groups. A succession dispute began after the death of Mestre Irineu in 1971 and led to the emergence of segmentations in the group he originally created in Rio Branco. The largest of these, in numerical terms, and the most expressive, regarding the intensification of internal differences in this religious tradition, is the *Centro Eclético da Fluente Luz Universal Raimundo Irineu Serra* [Raimundo Irineu Serra Eclectic Center of the Universal Flowing Light] or CEFLURIS, which was created by Sebastião Mota de Melo – known as Padrinho Sebastião – in 1974, also in Rio Branco. CEFLURIS has been one of the groups most responsible for the expansion of this religious phenomenon, both in Brazil and abroad.

Mestre Gabriel, founder of the UDV, passed away in 1971, the same year as Mestre Irineu. From that moment his religion also suffered a series of fragmentations and the creation of new groups. It is not easy to classify all these groups. We wish to explicitly avoid the term 'dissidence'. Besides being derogatory for some, the idea of 'original purity' cannot be sustained from an anthropological standpoint, since all groups are under constant processes of transformation and cultural re-creation.

Toward the end of the 1970s these religions began to expand, triggered by the creation of groups linked to the União do Vegetal and CEFLURIS in the large metropolises of southeastern Brazil. In fact, among the ayahuasca religions, the UDV and CEFLURIS are the largest groups in terms of membership[7] and the most expansive. The Barquinha, whose founder died in 1958, is represented by different groups (called 'centers'), which are autonomous and have idiosyncratic particularities. All have modest membership numbers, and most remain confined to the Acre region – as also occurs with Alto Santo.

As Goulart (2004) and Labate (2004) have observed, the expansion of these religions seems to be driven by their intense secession processes. In this way, segmentations led to expansion, expansion to diversification and, again, segmentation. This circular movement

---

7. The UDV counts some 15,000 members and CEFLURIS has about 4000 (Labate, Rose and Santos 2009).

of fabrication and constant multiplication of ritual practices and symbolic systems marks this religious universe. The current volume seeks in part to deal with this diversity, offering a panorama of the Brazilian ayahuasca domain.

The expansion of these groups was accompanied by an intensification of the debate over the juridical and social legitimacy of the consumption of ayahuasca, in the complex and polemical intersection between state and religion. In 1985, the Brazilian *Divisão de Medicamentos* [Medications Division] (DIMED), a former agency of the Ministry of Health, included the *Banisteriopsis caapi* vine in the list of products prohibited for use in the Brazilian territory. Shortly thereafter, the *Conselho Federal de Entorpecentes* [Federal Narcotics Board] (CONFEN) assembled a multidisciplinary team to investigate the ritual use of ayahuasca in the Santo Daime and the União do Vegetal. Domingos Bernardo de Sá (see this volume) was head of the team comprised by professionals from several fields. The investigation lasted for two years and, in 1987, ayahuasca was removed from the DIMED's list of prohibited products and was authorized for ritual use, partly because DIMED had prohibited the vine without consulting the opinion of CONFEN as procedure required.[8] Ayahuasca's legality was questioned again in 1988 and 1992, but CONFEN consistently confirmed its decision to allow the use of ayahuasca in ritual contexts, incorporating however a new recommendation that it be withheld from people with psychiatric problems, pregnant women, and minors.

A digression is in order here: one of the most polemical issues in the history of the legalization of ayahuasca use in Brazil and one which involves a genuine clash between the several ayahuasca groups in the country concerns the ritual consumption of another psychoactive plant, *Cannabis sativa*, by CEFLURIS – the most eclectic and experimentalist Santo Daime group – which refers to this plant as *Santa Maria* [Saint Mary or Holy Mary]. The practice was influenced by the arrival of backpackers and other young people in Acre in the mid-1970s. Although the other ayahuasca-using groups frequently argued that the use of Santa Maria by CEFLURIS would jeopardize the whole legalization process of ayahuasca in Brazil, this did not happen. This topic which unfortunately had to be left out of this volume, except for a brief mention in the article by Labate *et al.*; poses interesting theoretical and political questions, which still remain to be studied.[9]

On November 4, 2004, a resolution from the National Drug Policy Council (*Conselho Nacional de Politicas sobre Drogas*) – CONAD [the successor agency to CONFEN] recognized definitively the right to the free exercise of the religious use of ayahuasca, thus

---

8. For a history of the process of legalization of the use of ayahuasca in Brazil see MacRae (1992), Goulart (2004) and Labate (2005), among others.

9. We suggest that the reader see MacRae (2008) for further information. He compares the use of Daime with that of Santa Maria, especially in reference to the efforts to ritualize the consumption of these substances. The author argues that the favourable social learning and cultural conditions regarding the use of Daime – which as we said has been legally permitted since the mid-1980s – have allowed for the development of effective internal social controls by the group. The use of *Cannabis*, on the other hand, remains legally prohibited. According to the author, this encumbers the institutionalization of local norms and rituals regarding its use, eroding the culture's capacity to exercise control and hampering its ability to prevent eventual undesirable effects of use of the substance. This empirical example is used in support of the broader argument that the development of social and cultural control mechanisms by local communities is a more efficient process than is the imposition of coercive legal controls by external institutions.

reinforcing the social legitimacy of these groups. This resolution removed the prior restrictions on the use of ayahuasca by pregnant women and minors. It also instituted a multidisciplinary working group (*Grupo Multidisciplinar de Trabalho, GMT*) charged with conducting a nationwide registry of all ayahuasca using groups, attending to its religious use, and experimentally investigating the therapeutic use of ayahuasca. The working group was constituted in 2005, with six representatives from the ayahuasca-using groups and six researchers from various fields. Domingos Bernardo de Sá and Edward MacRae once again were included in the team.

The working group (GMT) released its report, presenting a 'deontology' for the use of the brew – that is, a charter of ethical orientations to regulate consumption and prevent inappropriate usage (see also MacRae in this volume). The final report condemns the commercialization of the brew, recommends that the groups avoid promoting ayahuasca tourism, encouraged ecological self-sustainability of the groups through the plantation and management of the plant specimens that compose the brew, and criticizes the promotion of ayahuasca as a panacea or as a form of therapy, explicitly rejecting *curandeirismo* (folk healing or quackery).

Hence, whereas it was questioned in the past, the legitimacy of the use of ayahuasca in religious contexts currently appears to be reasonably well accepted in Brazil, despite continuing to face some resistance at the level of the state as well as in some of the more conservative sectors of society, such as certain religious or political groups. Generally speaking, the regulation of the use of ayahuasca in Brazil, though not wholly impervious to the restrictive influences of scientific medicine, is exceptional in the history of global drug legislation in that it has combined biomedical knowledge with the discourse of social scientists and the voice of representatives of the ayahuasca religions. This helps in the development and strengthening of mechanisms of cultural regulation within the user groups of this particular psychoactive substance, a process that is usually hindered by repressive drug policy.

****

The article by Mariana Pantoja and Osmildo Silva da Conceição opens this collection. Though not directly focused on the ayahuasca religions, it provides important details and reflections on the wider context of their emergence. The authors – an anthropologist and an Amazonian rubber tapper – offer a historical report on the use of ayahuasca among laborers engaged in the extraction of rubber from the tree *Hevea brasiliensis* in the valley of the Upper Juruá river, an affluent of the Amazon located in western Acre. Although the relationship of the Santo Daime, Barquinha and UDV with rubber tapper culture has been emphasized since the first studies of these religious traditions (Monteiro da Silva 1983 and Goulart 1996), up to now the literature has barely explored the consumption of the brew among rubber tappers themselves. Examining salient events and individuals who, from the end of the nineteenth century to the present, forged the history of the occupation of the Upper Juruá, this article, with its flowing style, broadens our understanding of the historical processes which constituted the cultural, political and economic basis of the emergence of the ayahuasca religions. The uses of ayahuasca in the Upper Juruá described by Franco and Conceição embrace practices that combine diverse strands of Christianity – from popular Catholicism to more recent Evangelical Protestant groups – with the Indian and riverine (*caboclo*) traditions of Amazonia. The rubber tappers' perspectives express

6

not only a religious ethos, but also their political struggles, pointing to the fine intersection between politics and religion.

Moving away from the earlier uses of ayahuasca, the next article, by Arneide Bandeira Cemin, analyses the main rituals of the Daime or Santo Daime. Cemin's reflections largely stem from her fieldwork with a group located in the city of Porto Velho, state of Rondônia, known as CECLU (*Centro Eclético de Correntes da Luz Universal*) [Currents of the Universal Light Eclectic Center], closely associated to the more orthodox group commonly known as 'Alto Santo'.[10] In her ethnography of the rituals, the author investigates the central notions of the 'Daime system', such as the category of 'spiritual works', and the way in which doctrinal principles are assimilated by followers during ritual experiences. Cemin supports much of her analysis on Marcel Mauss' classical concept of 'corporal techniques', combining analytical and native categories in a productive way.

The article by Luis Eduardo Soares moves on to unravel issues raised by the expansion of these religions into the large metropolises of Brazil, a process that began in the early 1980s. Soares reflects on the presence of the CEFLURIS branch of the Santo Daime in the city of Rio de Janeiro, attempting to place Santo Daime in the context of what he labels the 'new religious consciousness'. This term embraces an array of attitudes and cultural and religious interests characterized by a taste for experimentation and constant nomadism based on the principle of individual freedom, as opposed to unconditional and exclusive faith. In this sense, the dissemination of Santo Daime beyond Amazonia is seen to be part of a wider and deeper movement that is related to the development of modern values. Although he considers the adhesion of members of the Brazilian urban middle class to Santo Daime in particular, and to an alternative, shifting mysticism in general, pointing to a persistence of modern values (and to the modern emphasis on subjectivity), the author also argues that the case of Santo Daime expresses a cultural critique of modernity. The attraction felt by members of the urban middle-class to a religion born in the remote Amazonian rainforest – the fringes of archaic Brazil – are seen to be a strong indication of this critique. According to Soares' argument, Santo Daime proposes a reinvention of Brazilian national identity in which Amazonia and the underdeveloped riverine peoples (*caboclos*) are valued as profound and essential. Although short and written in the journalistic genre, this article has been of great importance in influencing and stimulating a number of Brazilian researchers.

There are two articles in this collection dedicated to the religion that has come to be known as Barquinha. The first, by Wladimyr Sena Araújo – author of a pioneering study of this religion (Araújo 1999) – provides a rich ethnography of the ritual spaces of one of the principal Barquinha groups, the *Centro Espírita e Culto de Oração 'Casa de Jesus – Fonte de Luz'* ['House of Jesus, Source of Light' Spiritist Center and Cult of Prayer]. Araújo elucidates key meanings in Barquinha cosmology by analyzing these different spaces. The author identifies an intense spatial mobility in this religious universe in a process whereby ritual performances dynamically activate cosmological elements. Thus Araujo considers the Barquinha cosmology to be mobile and open, a 'cosmology-in-the-making'

---

10. It is important to remember that the manner of classifying these groups varies considerably and there is no consensus regarding this. In other words, although some groups may define themselves as 'Alto Santo', others may not recognize them in the same way.

that is composed or dissolved through the constant movement of elements through the ritual spaces and performances. According to the author, this also makes the cosmology change continuously and with great speed.

The second article on the Barquinha is by Christian Frenopoulo. The author studies another Barquinha group, also located in Rio Branco, focusing on healing practices understood by followers as 'charity works' (*obras de caridade*). These activities are directed toward members of the local community who come to the center in search of treatment for diverse ills and who are attended by spirit-mediums, without necessarily consuming Daime. Frenopoulo provides a dense ethnographic description of the different kinds of ritual practised here, the corresponding trance forms elicited, such as 'incorporation' (*incorporação*) and 'irradiation' (*irradiação*), without leaving out a study of the participants themselves. In so doing, he outlines the intricate symbolic network that draws on elements from the Christian, Indian and Afro-Brazilian universes, including the *Encantaria* from Maranhão. The author places his analytical emphasis on the social interactions that occur between patients and healer spirits incorporated into spirit-mediums during healing encounters. These encounters are seen as patterned performances which, it is argued, are conveyed through idioms that thematically signal cultural alterity. The article concludes by suggesting that the healing services echo symbolic motifs associated with the historical experience of immigration into Acre and the unstable and changing life circumstances shared by the local community.

This collection also carries two articles on the União do Vegetal. Sandra Goulart's article is a wide-ranging analysis of the UDV's formative process and provides important details about its history and its founder. By examining narratives of early followers and the concepts, rituals, and mythology of the UDV, Goulart's article reveals important relations between the UDV and other religious and cultural traditions, such as the universe of beliefs and practices of indigenous and mestizo peoples of Amazonia, Afro-Brazilian religions, Alan Kardec's spiritism, and masonry, as well as the Judeo-Christian biblical tradition, in addition to Brazilian popular Catholicism. In this hefty contribution on this least-studied of the Brazilian ayahuasca religions, the reader is transported to a rich universe where there is an interaction of personages and elements stemming from the different belief systems, such as the notion of reincarnation alongside Christian prayers and *benditos* [a type of prayer – trans.], or simultaneous references to the Hebrew king Solomon and Jesus. The text allows for a reflection on not only the syncretic nature of Brazilian popular religiosity, but also, through the specific case of the UDV, on the possibility of articulating popular religious traditions with erudite ones.

The other article on the UDV, by Sérgio Brissac, analyses the religious experience of urban followers of this religion, specifically those of a UDV 'nucleus' located in the industrialized southeastern region of Brazil. Brissac describes these followers' experience, considering aspects that range from the moment of their conversion to the process of adoption of doctrinal elements in their daily lives. Through the narratives and interpretations of followers, the author reveals the meanings and native exegesis of doctrinal values and concepts of the UDV religion, such as the notion of *mestre* (master or teacher), *memória* (memory), *merecimento* (merit), *evolução espiritual* (spiritual evolution), *peia* (punishment), and *luz* (light), among others. Brissac's article is also an ethnography of the altered state of perception and embodiment induced by the ingestion of ayahuasca, called *burracheira* in the UDV. By analyzing the meanings attributed to them, the author offers provocative analytical suggestions, such as the notion of '*englobamento na força da burracheira*' (encompassment in the force of the *burracheira*), which is also useful for thinking about the other ayahuasca religions, as well as shedding light on the pertinence of concepts frequently used in the general field of studies of Brazilian religiosity, such as 'syncretism'.

The next article is by the lawyer Domingos Bernardo Gialluisi da Silva Sá. Since the beginning , this author has played a fundamental role in the process that has led to the present legal regulation of the use of ayahuasca in Brazil. Sá recounts some episodes that led to the first initiatives of the Brazilian government to regulate the use of ayahuasca, revealing the main ideas, arguments and people involved in the debate from the mid-1980s until the end of that decade. As mentioned before, this was the period in which the ayahuasca religions began to spread to other regions of the country, becoming more widely known in the broader society and emerging as an issue that demanded the state's attention. Notions such as 'structured use' or 'ritual use' of psychoactives and concepts such as 'entheogen' appear in the documents discussed by the author, and are shown to become more consolidated with the advancement of state regulation. Thus Sá's article, originally published over a decade ago, is of inestimable historical value. The article describes the process of institutionalization of the use of ayahuasca in Brazil, which thenceforth became a model for such debates in other countries.

Next, MacRae, who has also played an important role in the processes of state regulation of the use of ayahuasca in Brazil, draws an analogy between the manner in which the Afro-Brazilian religions (such as Umbanda) and the ayahuasca religions have been classified and regulated for purposes of political control during the last century and the beginning of the present one. Albeit in different ways, both religious practices have been or continue to be seen with suspicion both by the ruling groups and by the bulk of the traditionally Christian and/or white population in Brazil. Reservations have often been expressed in medical terms, referring to alleged threats to mental health either posed by possession trances or by the psychoactive nature of ayahuasca. A number of similarities between both processes are highlighted, including the role played by anthropologists sympathetic to these religions. MacRae maintains that both processes were marked by an attempt to exercise 'scientific control' where 'science' was equated almost exclusively to biomedicine. However, he argues that at present anthropological perspectives have been receiving more attention and have been more successful in ensuring the official adoption of a broader approach which emphasizes the equal importance of the socio-cultural aspects alongside the medical considerations on the issue. The author concludes by analysing the 2006 report by the official multidisciplinary working team set up by the National Office for Policies on Drugs (SENAD) which was commissioned to regulate the now officially recognized right to religious use of ayahuasca in Brazil.

Finally, the collection closes with a last article by Beatriz Caiuby Labate, Rafael Guimarães dos Santos, Brian Anderson, Marcelo Mercante and Paulo Barbosa. In recognition of the complex nature of the effects of ayahuasca use, this text attempts an interdisciplinary dialogue, incorporating notions derived from anthropology, cultural psychology, medicine and pharmacology. It was included here with the intent of relating the ayahuasca religions to a broader body of knowledge about other ayahuasca-using contexts, as well as to the larger debates on the therapeutic uses of psychedelic substances and harm reduction. The text examines evidence for the therapeutic value of using ayahuasca in ritual contexts to treat substance dependence – these ritual contexts include both the Brazilian ayahuasca religions as well as two psychotherapeutic centers located in South America. The medical focus of the authors' inquiry into this specific type of ayahuasca use is balanced out with a list of suggestions for methodological, ethical and political considerations that could be developed in future research on the therapeutic effects claimed by practically all ayahuasca-using groups.

****

Some reflection on central concepts that permeate this collection is necessary. One of them is the term, 'ayahuasca religions' (*religiões ayahuasqueiras*). This expression should not be naturalized. Historically, we observe that some researchers have used the term 'sect' to refer to these groups, such as Andrade (1995), Gentil and Gentil (2004); Brito (2004), Grob *et al.* (1996), Sá (this volume), among others. As this term has increasingly acquired pejorative connotations, the expression 'ayahuasca religions', has been gaining increasingly more currency, and is now widely adopted in the specialized anthropological literature. According to Labate *et al.* (2009), the expression seems to have first appeared in Portuguese as '*religiões ayahuasqueiras*' in the book *O uso ritual da ayahuasca* [The Ritual Use of Ayahuasca] (Labate and Araújo 2002, 2004; see esp. Labate *et al.* 2004). Although the authors have not justified their choice of terminology, it seems possible to suggest that the term is an adaptation from the Spanish '*vegetalismo ayahuasquero*' used by Luis Eduardo Luna (1986) to refer to a form of folk medicine based on the use of plant hallucinogens, chants and diets. *Vegetalistas*, according to Luna, are *curandeiros* (folk healers) from popular rural parts of Peru and Colombia who maintain elements of the old indigenous knowledge of plants, simultaneous to their absorption of influences from European esotericism and the urban milieu.

Two issues have to be highlighted regarding the expression 'ayahuasca religions': firstly, it can be questioned for its excessive emphasis on the pharmacological dimension, since religious experience cannot be reduced to mere contact with the active principles present in ayahuasca. To what extent is the consumption of ayahuasca central to the activity of these groups? Frenopoulo, in this collection, for instance, shows us how certain ceremonies in one of the Barquinha groups forgo the use of Daime for some types of participants. Analogously, it is common to hear *Daimistas* assert that, according to Mestre Irineu, 'his Doctrine is independent of Daime' ('*a Doutrina dele prescinde do Daime*'), that is, the religion goes beyond the consumption of Daime *per se* and cannot be reduced to a substance. Further, it is interesting to remember that during the long period in which the UDV practices were prohibited in the USA, while the juridical process was ongoing, followers continued to carry out their sessions drinking water instead of Vegetal (see below).[11] Secondly, to what extent are the different religious groups drawn together simply by the fact that they consume the same psychoactive substance? As is known, several of these groups see themselves as manifestations of independent origins that should not necessarily be linked.

While acknowledging its possible limitations, we affirm the pertinence of the term 'ayahuasca religions'. As authors such as Labate (2004) and Goulart (2004) have shown,

---

11. Some people allegedly even vomited from drinking just water.

there are several similarities and continuities among these groups; in fact, their points of dissension and rupture indicate a shared semantic field. We argue that the practice of the consumption of Daime or Vegetal *is* foundational to these groups – which does not imply an equation of their activities or their religious ethos with the consumption of this psycho-active. The idea that Daime and Vegetal are central to the religions is not only a product of intellectual representation of the phenomenon, but is also supported by empirical reality. From the emic perspective, there is an important valorization of the spiritual, divinatory, therapeutic, pedagogical, and other properties of the brew. The consumption of ayahuasca also appears to function as a form of diacritical sign of the identity for these groups *vis-à-vis* its other religious manifestations (such as Catholicism, Protestantism, Umbanda, Spiritism, religions of Oriental orientation, etc.). At the same time, despite the ruptures and rivalries among the groups, the consumption of ayahuasca marks their collective identity, 'us' as opposed to 'them' – in this case the broader social milieu of non-users of the substance. Indeed, historically, strategic political needs have at certain moments drawn these groups closer to one another at certain moments, especially during the process of legalization.[12]

In our view, it is also valid to conceive of the existence of a field of research on the aya-huasca religions. The idea of a field assumes that it is difficult to speak about any of these groups without somehow considering the others, given the process of continual exchanges and dialogues among them – that is, a system of differences in which the identity of each is constructed in a large part in opposition to the others (see Goulart 2004). We hope with this collection, then, to contribute to the consolidation of this emergent field of research.

Another aspect of the expression 'ayahuasca religions' that deserves attention is the notion of 'religion'. Should these groups be characterized as 'religious'? We have observed that, while a large part of the anthropological literature has referred to the Santo Daime, Barquinha and UDV as 'religious' organizations, in the realm of media and public debate – and even in the internal discourse of the groups – it is common to refer to them as 'sects'. According to a widespread commonsense understanding, 'religions' are established institu-tions in a society, while 'sects' are numerically small voluntary associations that have gener-ally separated from 'official churches'. Further, especially in Europe and the US, the notion of 'sect' frequently evokes a pejorative image, related to fanatical behaviors that border on madness, and which should be prohibited by the state in the interest of the common good. From the sociological point of view, however, we know that the limits between 'sect' and 'religion' are unstable, and that their definition depends on criteria of power, based on an ethnocentric tendency to confer higher status to one's own religion, while the *other's* is, as a rule, considered inferior or less legitimate. Thus, although it is true that the major mono-theistic religions – such as Islam, Christianity, and Judaism – vie among themselves for space and may circumstantially be questioned, it can generally be affirmed that they have

---

12. This process is rather complex, involving circumstantial approximations and distances between the various groups. Recently, for example, a certain polarization appears to have consolidated itself in the context of Acre state where Alto Santo, Barquinha, and the UDV have been in opposition to Cefluris, considered less legitimate by the former. From another perspective, Cefluris and UDV are drawn closer to each other due to their shared expansionist interests and the institutional challenges both must overcome in this process. This does not occur with Alto Santo and Barquinha, which basically remain regional phenomena and whose local legitimacy is being increasingly consolidated – even to the point of their becoming progressively incor-porated as cultural and religious symbols of Acre by the state government.

achieved a certain degree of stable 'religious' legitimacy as 'transcendent' and 'institutionalized' religions. Other religious manifestations struggle to achieve the same. The groups that use ayahuasca are located in the lower echelons of this ranking, given their association with exotic practices, trances and the consumption of 'drugs' or 'hallucinogens'.

Given the limited scope of this book, it is not possible for us to conduct a detailed reflection on the concept of 'religion' – a central issue in anthropology, which has already been much discussed. For now, it suffices to stress that within a political context in which special rights are granted to particular groups involving the 'religious' use of certain 'drugs', formal state classification as a 'religion' is especially important. In such a situation, other groups with other consumption practices may claim a religious basis for their acts – as in the consumption of *Cannabis* by some groups in the US – but ultimately be denied legitimacy and labelled criminal because they have not been recognized as such by the state (see Meyer 2006). In this process we observe, for example, that even though many aspects of the União do Vegetal were questioned during the juridical process the group faced for years in the United States, they were able to satisfy the North American courts that they were a *bona fide* religion (ibid.).

In this sense, we see no problem in acknowledging that our decision to use the term 'religion' is also linked to an attempt to confer legitimate status to practices that otherwise would remain persecuted and stigmatized. On the other hand, by attributing to the activities of diverse ayahuasca-using groups an analogous status to that of Catholics, Spiritists, Umbanda practitioners, and others, we have the goal of making explicit that these manifestations effectively possess a series of shared elements with Brazilian religiosity, displaying continuities, and also ruptures and reinventions.

While not pretending to settle the issue, we suggest here that in their classificatory impulse, researchers sometimes forget to consider what natives themselves say or, conversely, may uncritically transport native categories to academic texts. Consequently, we should ask: how do the groups tend to think of themselves? In the UDV, a recurrent native term is 'religious society'. Official representatives of the UDV appear to adopt, occasionally, the term 'sect' in their public discourses – though more research is necessary to determine the extent of this.[13] In case of the Santo Daime, followers appear to refer most frequently to the notion of 'doctrine', rather than 'religion' proper, to classify their spiritual affiliation. The notion of 'doctrine' can be used to refer to the dimension of beliefs themselves or, metonymically, to the Santo Daime.[14]

Simultaneously, followers of the different groups frequently appeal to the notion of 'religion' to classify their activities in a number of contexts and situations, especially when directing discourses or demands to people outside this religious universe. It is common, for example, to emphasize to a newcomer intending to participate in a ritual for the first time, that this is a 'religious' experience and not a 'trip', 'kick', or 'mere curiosity'. (In this,

---

13. Goulart (2004), for example, during her dissertation research, heard a member of one of the two groups that separated from CEBUDV, that the UDV 'is a sect, because it accepts all people' (*'é uma seita, pois ela aceita todo mundo'*) [Trans. – the word for 'sect' and 'accept' sound very similar in Portuguese]. This notion is somewhat consistent with the 'mystery of the word' (*'mistério da palavra'*) perspective that is current in the UDV, in which words carry certain intrinsic powers (see Goulart, this collection). However, we do not know to what extent this interpretation represents a homogeneous view within this ayahuasca religion.

14. For a discussion on the concept of 'doctrine' (*doutrina*) in the Santo Daime, see Groisman and Sell (1996).

ear to echo Durkeim's (1996) distinction between the 'religious' and that
ly 'magical'; the first being something involving 'collective' and 'social'
the latter being 'individual', and less subordinated to controls, and thus
. This view is linked to the historical expansion of the groups beyond the
rs of Amazonia, where these religions are often bracketed alongside latter-day man-
ations of the counter culture and its psychedelic experiences involving the free use
of various 'drugs', such as LSD, mushrooms, *Cannabis,* and others. Finally, the definition
of these groups as 'religious' is probably related, to a considerable degree, to the process
of legalization of ayahuasca use in Brazil (understood to be religious) which involved the
interaction of a variety of agents and discourse types.

Another native concept deserving our attention is that of 'sacrament'. It may have been
intellectuals from the Santo Daime, such as Alex Polari de Alverga (1984, 1992) or academics, such as Edward MacRae (1992), among others, who first adopted this term, now
widely used by the anthropological literature, as well as by followers of some of these
groups to refer to the Daime or the Vegetal. While in the Santo Daime it is common to
speak of 'our sacrament' (the Daime), in the União do Vegetal the expression 'communion of the Vegetal' is regularly used. The notion of 'sacrament' has been used by several
researchers of the religious use of psychoactive substances (for a history see Baker 2005).[15]
The term has an explicit relationship with practices and concepts of Christianity, especially the Holy Communion of the Roman Catholic Church, the largest religion in Brazil.
It is also consistent with the idea of a structured and ritualized use of 'sacred' substances,
ideologically deserving legal protection, as opposed to the profane and unregulated use
of 'drugs'. Consequently, in this far from neutral domain, the notion of 'religion' is politi-
cized and a distinction is drawn between substances that are 'sacred' from those that are
'drugs', according to the inscription given by moral discourse. It is necessary, therefore, to
investigate the genesis of certain concepts, making explicit how they are constructed, how
they migrate and how they mutually affect one another, in an intense dynamics of cultural
creation where religion, politics and academic research interact.

There are several other expressions and concepts that have migrated between the
academy and the field that should also be reconsidered. Some authors, for example, refer
to ayahuasca as 'the tea' (*chá*), an expression that should not be naturalized since, although
it is abundantly used in the UDV milieu, it is not frequently heard in the context of the
Santo Daime or the Barquinha. Given that the nature of the preparation of ayahuasca is
much more complex than the simple infusions that normally go under the name of teas,
some authors, like MacRae, believe a different name is needed and so he proposes that in
English, for instance, the expression 'brew' might be more appropriate. Similarly, the designation 'psychoactive substance' has occasionally been used in native discourses oriented
to outsiders, but we must not forget that – despite being preferable to the pejorative term

---

15. An exploration of the concept of 'sacrament' in the context of these religious groups is still needed. We know
that among Roman Catholics the Christian Eucharist is conceived of as implying the 'transubstantiation of
the body and blood of Christ, an act that leads to a sort of sacred banquet'. Note that the word 'Host' derives
from a Latin term that designates 'a victim offered to the deities' (see Sztutman 2005). Can we speak of
transubstantiation in the case of the ayahuasca religions? And, in what sense does the idea of transubstantiation reflect the encounter between Christian and Amerindian religions? These are questions that merit
investigation.

'drug' – it is also not a native expression, as it is has a pharmacological-scientific origin and is, consequently, foreign to certain regional contexts of ayahuasca consumption. Additionally, these reflections should not lead us to the reductionism of particularizing or singularizing all the dimensions of the experience, falling into immobility when designating and classifying the phenomena we study.

The collection has some gaps that need to be mentioned. One of these concerns the absence of an article about the groups of users that Labate (2004) has labelled 'urban neo-ayahuasqueiros' – an important development of the arrival of the ayahuasca religions to the central and southern regions of Brazil – which are undergoing outright expansion, although the groups are still restricted in terms of followers.[16] Neo-ayahuasqueiros oblige us to reconsider the limits between 'ritual' or 'religious' uses and 'therapeutic', 'artistic' and other uses, generating interesting questions about the juridical status of 'drug' consumption. Additionally, these subjects, as well as urban members of the Santo Daime and UDV, exemplify that which Giddens (1991) has called the 'quest for a reflexive project of the self'. Ayahuasca use has become progressively linked with a project of 'self-knowledge' (which is different, for instance, from the orientation that it acquires among diverse Indian and mestizo contexts, or even among other followers of the Santo Daime and UDV), consistent with the contemporary – almost obsessive – emphasis on the 'search for one's self' and 'self-realization' that has been identified by various thinkers. More needs to be known about the contemporary therapeutization of ayahuasca use, which involves its own mechanisms of legitimacy.

Another process that is underway in several parts of Brazil – though still quite incipient – and which has not been much explored in this collection, refers to the diverse groups of indigenous and mestizo peoples who have been becoming increasingly influenced through exchanges with the União do Vegetal and especially with the Santo Daime, such as the case of the rubber tappers of the Upper Juruá region discussed by Franco and Conceição in this collection, and also the Kaxinawá (Cashinahua) Indians of the Jordão river (in Acre state). In some cases, groups have begun to consume ayahuasca as a result of their contact with the ayahuasca religions, as has occurred, for instance, with the Apuriná Indians of the Boca do Acre region (Amazonas state) and the Guarani Indians from the coast of Santa Catarina state, among others.[17] Contemplating the phenomenon of the 'Brazilian ayahuasca

---

16. These are groups that splintered off from the three major religions, inaugurating new urban modalities of ayahuasca consumption, related to the New Age movement, holistic therapies, various orientalisms, different fields of the arts (painting, theatre, music) and even drug treatment for homeless street-dwellers, composing what the author has called an 'urban ayahuasca network'. These groups usually have an ambiguous relationship with the historical matrices from whence they derive: the Santo Daime and the União do Vegetal. On the one hand, they claim a historical and symbolic link with them – a connection which evidently provides them with legitimacy, as it implies an uninterrupted continuity which spans from what is represented as the 'ancestral indigenous use of ayahuasca', to 'traditional religious use' and new urban uses. On the other hand, these groups tend to be critical and reject the religious models of the use of ayahuasca, labelled as 'traditional'. Thus they develop new rituals and sets of doctrinal references, affirming their difference and striving, simultaneously, to avoid falling into what is represented as 'profane' use of 'drugs' (Labate 2004).

17. In this regard, Isabel Santana de Rose (2007) is carrying out research on a movement known as the Alliance of the Medicines (Aliança das Medicinas) headquartered in Florianópolis (state of Santa Catarina, in the southernmost part of Brazil), which mainly articulates three groups: the Santo Daime community Céu do Patriarca (Cefluris line), the Sacred Fire of Itzachilatlan (Fogo Sagrado de Itzachilatlan) – also known as the Red Path (Caminho Vermelho) – and the Guarani village Yynn Moroti Wherá, located in the Biguaçu municipality, on

religions' implies recognizing these mutual connections, these multiple rural and urban ramifications. Once again, what is at play here is the migration of people and symbols on a local and global scale, the transit among diverse religious practices, and the construction of hybrid religiosities and identities in a post-colonial context.

Another dimension that has not received attention in this collection refers to the expansion of the UDV and the Santo Daime abroad from Brazil, which began in the late 1980s and early 1990s. According to a preliminary survey conducted by Beatriz Caiuby Labate in 2005 (www.neip.info/simposio_audio), CEFLURIS has centres in the United States, Canada, Mexico, one in Central America, three in South America, 14 in Europe (the groups in Holland and Spain being the largest), two in Asia and two in Africa, totalling at least 23 countries in which there are fully operative centres. The UDV, on the other hand, has 'nuclei' in the American states of New Mexico, California, Colorado, Washington, Texas and Florida, with a total of around 140 members. It also has a nucleus in Madrid and nuclei in formation in Italy, Portugal, Switzerland and England (Labate *et al.* 2009). The most important of the very few works on the expansion of these groups abroad is an ethnography of Santo Daime groups in Holland carried out by Groisman (2000).

The Santo Daime and the UDV have essayed diverse political strategies to survive within the contemporary global prohibitionist regime. The legal status of these groups varies from country to country. Holland appears to be the place where the legality of the religious use of ayahuasca appears to be most well-established. The United States has recently taken a favourable position in regards the UDV, though the legal process has not yet been concluded. In Spain, the Santo Daime is included in the Ministry of the Interior's (Home Office/Department of Justice) registry of religions. However, despite its being tolerated, the consumption of ayahuasca is not officially legal. In France, French and Brazilian Santo Daime followers were absolved from the charges of drug use and trafficking after a pharmacological-juridical-political dispute that lasted more than five years (1999–2005). They obtained the right to free religious practice only to see, in the same year (2005), a commission of the Ministry of Health schedule the principal components of ayahuasca (*Banisteriopsis caapi* and *Psychotria viridis*) in the list of prohibited products. Juridical processes are still underway in Canada, Australia, Germany, Italy, and other countries.

The expansion of these groups carries important implications, not only in Brazil, but also abroad. In the case of Santo Daime, international expansion has had a significant impact on Vila Céu do Mapiá, CEFLURIS' flagship community in Amazonia. In general, CEFLURIS churches in foreign countries customarily receive periodic visits by 'entourages' (*comitivas*), which are groups of senior members, musicians and singers who conduct spiritual works and teach the ritual performance to the locals. Generally, the entourage members receive favours, and even money, in exchange for their visit. This has generated opportunities both for members native of Amazonia and for Mapiá residents who come originally from the intellectualized urban middle class of other parts of the country. It has contributed to generating income and decreasing a series of hardships which are common

---

the coast of Santa Catarina. According to Rose, the Red Path is a group that carries out original rituals from several indigenous ethnic groups of the Americas, chiefly North American indigenous groups, frequently involving the consumption of psychoactive substances, such as tobacco, peyote, ayahuasca, mushrooms and others.

among the deprived Amazonian communities. Paradoxically, this also leads to accentu-ating local social inequalities. Santo Daime members who are able to communicate in English tend to acquire a fundamental role in this expansion and may ascend within the group's internal hierarchy. A new social category emerges: the Santo Daime follower who goes away to live abroad, or who returns to Mapiá after spending a period outside.

With the expansion of the line of Padrinho Sebastião to the rest of Brazil and abroad, the socialization process of Mapiá's youth, in turn, begins to suffer the influence of these new references. Knowledge that was previously an integral and naturalized part of 'being a *Daimista*' (singing, dancing, playing instruments, knowing the hymns by heart) is increas-ingly valued as a 'specialized knowledge', a type of expertise. In other words, the 'foreigner Other's' interest in everyday Santo Daime practices influences the natives'perception of these practices, as well as their way of carrying them out. New methods of teaching and performing religious activities begin to be developed, such as 'classes' or 'workshops' to learn to make Daime and to incorporate spirit entities;[18] the hymnals are translated into other languages, and with these appear new exegeses of the hymns and leaders' teach-ings (*preleições* – types of patterned discourses with diverse esoteric teachings), and so on. Service and religion are thus interlinked, in an equation characteristic of the urban religiosity of the contemporary New Age style.

However, it is rather limiting to adopt a perspective that reduces the expansion of the Santo Daime to a merely economical dimension or to the promotion of 'religious tourism' or 'drug tourism' – an accusation frequently levelled against CEFLURIS in the ayahuasca arena, or even by not fully informed researchers. It is quite common to come across epi-sodes of religious conversion to the ayahuasca religions occurring at present in many parts of the world , and these may at times cause radical transformations in the lives of the new converts. Foreigners commonly move to Mapiá, or build houses in Juruá (the new community in the middle of the forest founded by the current president of CEFLURIS, Alfredo Gregório de Melo, or Padrinho Alfredo). They learn to speak Portuguese, or begin to receive hymns in their own languages. Some foreign leaders of the Santo Daime have even achieved recognition within Mapiá itself. A series of transnational, inter-ethnic and inter-class marriages seal these new relationships and spiritual and political hierarchies. In addition, this international expansion is a product, and further inspires, a certain 'sal-vationist' or 'millenarian' mission or vocation of CEFLURIS, marking its identity *vis-à-vis* the other ayahuasca groups.

Alongside the valorisation of native knowledge, stemming from Indian and mestizo traditions – which in the context of broader Brazilian society are usually held in little regard – the topic of ecology has also achieved a central position in the expansion of the Santo Daime and UDV abroad, in the same way as it did during their process of expansion into the large metropolises of Brazil (see Soares, this collection; MacRae 1992; Goulart 1996). For some foreigners, adherence to Santo Daime or the UDV is a form of support for the Amazonia forest and for the preservation of 'nature'. Both groups come to repre-sent themselves more and more as 'ecological religions'. Groisman (2000) suggests that

---

18. It is worth remembering that some Cefluris groups have a set of rituals characterized by the ostensible influ-ence of the beliefs of Afro-Brazilian religions, such as Umbanda. During these rituals, spirit entities may manifest themselves through possession or incorporation trance.

some Dutch Santo Daime members join in part to sustain a kind of nostalgia or idealization of pre-industrial communities. Adherence to Santo Daime is also considered, at times, as a means of reparation for colonialism. Little research has been conducted on the interests of North Americans and Spaniards in the UDV, though it is known that part of the expansion of this religion abroad is related to a conservationist appeal. According to informal accounts by some UDV members, North American members of the group have been responsible for exporting part of the ecological movement of 'permaculture' from the USA to Brazil and, additionally, have enthusiastically joined a conservationist Brazilian NGO founded and composed mainly of UDV members: the New Enchantment Ecological Development Association (*Associação de Desenvolvimento Ecológico Novo Encanto*).

In the case of the Santo Daime abroad, alongside the quest for 'untamed nature' and for knowledge that is deemed ancestral, there is also a valorization of the integration of new forms of therapy and diverse cultural, esoteric and philosophical tendencies, such as New Age neo-shamanic movements, holistic and psychedelic therapies, and the *sannyasin* movement (followers of the guru Rajneesh or Osho), among others. CEFLURIS, above all, dynamically incorporates local differences, composing infinite combinations that do not cease to multiply and diversify in a process of continual reinvention. All this remains largely unknown by the broader public, and is barely documented.

Finally, another matter that has not yet received much national and international attention, and which is also absent from this collection, is the juridical process of the UDV in the United States. For seven years the União do Vegetal maintained a scheme whereby ayahuasca was shipped from Brazil to Los Angeles to be distributed among its chapters in the United States. However, in May, 1999, the US Customs Office finally decided to examine the substance and when the lab tests detected dimethyltryptamine (DMT) a long judicial confrontation began between the US Government and the local UDV religious leaders. Their first reaction was to cease their ceremonial use of ayahuasca, substituting it for water and engaging in a fight for their constitutionally guaranteed rights to religious freedom. In the lengthy court battles that ensued the UDV focused much of its arguments on demanding the same treatment accorded to the Native American Church and its ceremonial use of peyote. Another line of argument was developed questioning whether or not ayahuasca could be included among the substances forbidden by the 1971 Convention on Psychotropic Substances.

A federal district court issued a preliminary injunction in 2002 allowing the UDV to resume importing and using ayahuasca, but this was blocked on appeal by the US Government until November, 2004, when the UDV was finally able to resume its rituals in the United States. Subsequently the federal government took its case to the US Supreme Court, which concluded in February, 2006 that the government had failed to present enough evidence that the use made of ayahuasca by the UDV was dangerous enough to merit legal repression. This means that the UDV is free to perform its rituals in the USA, pending conclusion of the case in the district court. Some optimistic psychedelic activists consider this decision to be a watershed in the campaign for the liberation of entheogen use. It also marked a moment of unusual solidarity between a wide range of different religious groups (including Christian Fundamentalists) who were willing to give their collective support on the grounds of the protection of religious freedom, though maintaining strong doctrinal objections to the sacramental use of entheogens.

Other ayahuasca religions, like the CEFLURIS branch of Santo Daime, which is also active in the USA, were not covered by the Supreme Court's decision, which was specific for the UDV. More recently, in March 2009, district court Judge Owen Panner set out the terms of a permanent injunction allowing the Oregon-based Santo Daime group Church of the Holy Light of the Queen to import and use Daime in its religious rituals. Even though the government can still appeal, and the terms of the injunction are to be negotiated, this represents an important step in the discussion about the legalization of the uses of ayahuasca around the world. Thus, it seems likely that the precedent will lead to a lessening of the American cultural and political resistances against the religious use of psychoactive substances.

Among the topics that deserve further examination within the analysis of the expansion movement of these groups to the Old World is the way in which scientific knowledge, produced by ethnographers on the ayahuasca religions, has been incorporated into ongoing juridical processes against these groups in several countries. It would also be interesting to learn more about the influence that the state may exert in the configuration of religious practices in the context of such litigation (Groisman and Dobkin de Rios 2007). We hope that this book may awaken interest in these and other issues, as well as stimulate more research on Santo Daime, Barquinha and União do Vegetal, and their multiple strands, contributing to the broadening of our knowledge about this fascinating cultural phenomenon.

Bibliography

Alverga, Alex Polari de. 1984. *O Livro das Mirações – Viagem ao Santo Daime*. Rio de Janeiro: Editora Rocco
Alverga, Alex Polari de. 1992. *O Guia da Floresta*. 2nd ed. Rio de Janeiro: Editora Record..
Andrade, Afrânio Patrocínio de. 1995. 'O Fenômeno do Chá e a Religiosidade Cabocla'. Master's thesis, Religious Sciences, Instituto Metodista de Ensino Superior.
Araújo, Wladimyr Sena. 1999. *Navegando sobre as ondas do daime: história, cosmologia e ritual da Barquinha*. Campinas: Editora da Unicamp.
Baker, John. 2005. 'Psychedelic Sacraments'. *Journal of Psychoactive Drugs* 37(2): 179–87.
Brissac, Sérgio. 1999. 'A Estrela do Norte iluminando até o sul: uma etnografia da União do Vegetal em um contexto urbano'. Master's thesis, Anthropology. Museu Nacional/ UFRJ.
Alverga, Alex Polari de. 1984. *O Livro das Mirações – Viagem ao Santo Daime*. Rio de Janeiro: Editora Rocco
Alverga, Alex Polari de. 1992. *O Guia da Floresta*, 2nd ed. Rio de Janeiro: Editora Record.
Andrade, Afrânio Patrocínio de. 1995.'O Fenômeno do Chá e a Religiosidade Cabocla'. Master's thesis, Religious Sciences, Instituto Metodista de Ensino Superior.
Araújo, Wladimyr Sena. 1999. *Navegando sobre as ondas do daime: história, cosmologia e ritual da Barquinha*. Campinas: Editora da Unicamp.
Baker, John. 2005. 'Psychedelic Sacraments'. *Journal of Psychoactive Drugs* 37(2): 179–87.
Brissac, Sérgio. 1999. 'A Estrela do Norte iluminando até o sul: uma etnografia da União do Vegetal em um contexto urbano'. Master's thesis, Anthropology. Museu Nacional/UFRJ.
Brito, Glacus de Souza. 2004. 'Farmacologia Humana da Hoasca. Chá preparado de plantas alucinógenas usado em contexto ritual no Brasil'. In Beatriz Caiuby Labate and Wladimyr Sena Araújo, eds, *O uso ritual da ayahuasca* (2nd edn), 623–51. Campinas: Mercado de Letras.
Cemin, Arneide Bandeira. 2001. *O poder do Santo Daime – ordem, xamanismo e dádiva*. São Paulo: Terceira Margem.

Durkheim, Emile. 1996. *As Formas Elementares da Vida Religiosa*. São Paulo: Martins Fontes.

Frenopoulo, Christian. 2005. 'Charity and Spirits in the Amazonian navy: the Barquinha mission of the Brazilian Amazon'. Master's thesis, Anthropology Department, University of Regina.

Gentil, Lucia Regina Brocanelo and Henrique Salles Gentil, 2004, 'O Uso de Psicoativos em um Contexto Religioso: a União do Vegetal'. In Beatriz Caiuby Labate and Wladimyr Sena Araújo, eds, *O uso ritual da ayahuasca* (2nd edn), 559–69. Campinas: Mercado de Letras.

Giddens, Anthony. 1991. *Modernity and Self-identity: Self and Society in the Late Modern Age*. London: Polity.

Goulart, Sandra Lucia. 1996. 'Raízes culturais do Santo Daime'. Master's thesis, Anthropology, USP.

Goulart, Sandra Lucia. 2004. 'Contrastes e continuidades em uma tradição amazônica: as religiões da ayahuasca'. Doctoral thesis, Social Sciences, Unicamp.

Grob, C. S., D. J. McKenna, J. C. Callaway, G. S. Brito, E. S. Neves, G. Oberlender, O. L. Saide, E. Labigalini, C. Tacla, C. T. Miranda, R. J. Strassman and K. B. Boone. 1996. 'Human psychopharmacology of hoasca, a plant hallucinogen used in ritual context in Brazil'. *Journal of Nervous & Mental Disease* 184(2): 86–94.

Groisman, Alberto. 1999. *Eu venho da floresta. Um estudo sobre o contexto simbólico do uso do Santo Daime*. Florianópolis: Editora da UFSC.

Groisman, Alberto. 2000. 'Santo Daime in the Netherlands: An Anthropological Study of a New World Religion in a European Setting'. PhD dissertation, Social Anthropology, University of London.

Groisman, Alberto and Marlene Dobkin de Rios. 2007. 'Ayahuasca, the US Supreme Court and the UDV-US Government case: culture, religion and implications of a legal dispute'. In Michael Winkelman and Thomas Roberts, eds, *Psychedelic Medicine: Social, Clinical and Legal Perspectives*, 251–69. Westport: Praeger.

Groisman, Alberto and Ari Sell. 1996. 'Healing Power: Cultural-neurophenomenological Therapy of Santo Daime'. In M. Winkelman and W. Andritzky, eds, *Yearbook of Cross-cultural Medicine and Psychotherapy*. Berlin: Verlag.

Labate, Beatriz Caiuby. 2005. 'Dimensões legais, éticas e políticas da expansão do consumo da ayahuasca'. In Beatriz Caiuby Labate and Sandra Lúcia Goulart, eds, *O Uso ritual das plantas de poder*, 397–457. Campinas: Mercado de Letras.

Labate, Beatriz Caiuby. 2004. *A reinvenção do uso da ayahuasca nos centros urbanos*. Campinas: Mercado de Letras.

Labate, Beatriz Caiuby and Wladimyr Sena Araújo, eds. 2002. *O uso ritual da ayahuasca*. Campinas: Mercado de Letras.

Labate, Beatriz Caiuby and Wladimyr Sena Araújo, eds. 2004, *O uso ritual da ayahuasca*, 2nd edn. Campinas: Mercado de Letras.

Labate, Beatriz Caiuby and Sandra Lucia Goulart, eds. 2005. *O uso ritual das plantas de poder*. Campinas: Mercado de Letras.

Labate, Beatriz Caiuby, Sandra Lucia Goulart and Wladimyr Sena Araújo. 2004. 'Introdução'. In Beatriz Caiuby Labate and Wladimyr Sena Araújo, eds, *O uso ritual da ayahuasca* (2nd edn), 21–33. Campinas: Mercado de Letras.

Labate, Beatriz Caiuby, Sandra Goulart, Maurício Fiore, Edward MacRae and Hernriqqe Carneiro, eds. 2008. *Drogas e cultura: novas perspectivas*. Salvador: Edufba.

Labate, Beatriz Caiuby, Isabel Santana de Rose and Rafael Guimarães dos Santos. 2009. *Ayahuasca Religions: A Comprehensive Bibliography and Critical Essays*. Santa Cruz, CA: MAPS.

La Rocque Couto, Fernando. 1989. 'Santos e Xamãs'. Master's thesis, Anthropology, UnB.

Luna, Luis Eduardo. 1986. *Vegetalismo: Shamanism among the Mestizo Population of the Peruvian Amazon*. Stockholm: Almquist and Wiksell International.

MacRae, Edward. 1992. *Guiado Pela Lua – Xamanismo e uso da ayahuasca no culto do Santo Daime*. São Paulo: Editora Brasiliense [An English on-line version was published as: *Guided by the Moon: Shamanism and the Ritual use of Ayahuasca in the Santo Daime religion in Brazil*. Interdisciplinary Group for Psychoactive Studies, *Neip* 2006, available at: http://www.neip.info/downloads/edward/ebook.htm].

MacRae, Edward. 2008. 'The religious uses of licit and illicit psychoactive substances in a branch of the Santo Daime Religion'. In Beatriz Caiuby Labate and Edward MacRae, eds, *The Light from the Forest: the Ritual use of Ayahuasca in Brazil. Fieldwork in Religion* 2(3): 393–414.

Mercante, Marcelo Simão. 2006. 'Images of healing: spontaneous mental imagery and healing process of the Barquinha, a Brazilian ayahuasca religious system'. PhD dissertation, Human Sciences, Saybrook Graduate School and Research Center.

Meyer, Matthew. 2006. 'Religious Freedom and United States Drug Laws: Notes on the UDV-USA legal case'. Núcleo de Estudos Interdisciplinares sobre Psicoativos – NEIP. Electronic document, http://www.neip.info/downloads/Matthew%20UDV-USA%20case.pdf. Accessed July 2007.

Monteiro da Silva, Clodomir. 1983. 'O Palácio Juramidam – Santo Daime: um ritual de transcendência e despoluição'. Master's thesis, Cultural Anthropology, UFPE. Electronic document, http://www.neip.info/downloads/clodomir/teseClodomir.pdf. Accessed July 2007.

Rose, Isabel Santana de. 2007. 'Aliança das medicinas: um (re)encontro entre os índios Guarani, o Santo Daime e o Caminho Vermelho'. Doctoral work-in-progress, Social Anthropology, UFSC.

Sztutman, Renato, 2005, 'O sacrifício, ontem e hoje'. Electronic document, http://pphp.uol.com.br/tropico/html/textos/2685,1.shl. Accessed July 2007.

1

The use of ayahuasca among rubber tappers of the Upper Juruá[*]

Mariana Ciavatta Pantoja and Osmildo Silva da Conceição

Translated by Robin Wright, revised by Matthew Meyer

Testimony of Osmildo Silva Da Conceição (taped in January, 1996)

I came to hear about this brew from the oldest people, I was about nine years old. I was always curious to get to know it, but it wasn't easy to find. But when God promises, He may be late but He never fails. So there were many friends who I got to know, of those who are still alive, those who have died, and they were adults like I am today and they were already taking this brew, called ayahuasca, the name used by the rubber tappers and the Indians too. I came to know a fellow named Crispim, he was one of the strong shamans who lived here on the Extractivist Reserve, and Sebastião Pereira, who was also one of the most experienced, who came out of this rubber camp before it became a Reserve, and they didn't forget to pass on the teachings they had to other people.

I wanted to know this brew, I wanted to drink it, but I was a kid and my Dad was still the boss. When I got to be 14 years old, I was able to see the brew, but I still didn't have the power to drink it. The first person who I saw preparing it was Major. So that was

[*] First published in *Fieldwork in Religion* (2006) 2.3: 235–55. This translation is of an article in Labate and Araújo, 2004: 201–27. The first version of this text was finished in 1996, and it had the decisive collaboration – in the form of testimonies, information and impressions – of Milton Gomes da Conceição, Pedro Gomes do Nascimento, Damião Silva da Conceição, Pedro Gomes da Conceição, Francisco Edir França da Costa, Francisco Nogueira de Queiroz, Jorge Feitosa do Nascimento (in memoriam) and the anthropologists Mauro Almeida and Gabriela Jahnel Araújo. At that time, the objective of the research was to record systematically the use that rubber tappers made of ayahuasca, for the purpose of publication in the 'Encyclopedia of the Forest' (organized by Manuela Carneiro da Cunha e Mauro Almeida; São Paulo: Cia. das Letras, 2002). The non-inclusion of the complete article, for editorial reasons, in the Encyclopedia and Beatriz Labate's invitation were responsible for its inclusion in this publication. Thus, in 1999, the text went through small alterations, including an historical part on the Juruá Valley and bibliographical citations, giving it more the character of an article. However, the spirit and original form are the same.

something that wakened my ideas. People said that they drank and that they saw another life, so I wanted to drink this brew, but things didn't happen so quickly as I wanted. I was only able to have the pleasure of drinking after I got to be of age, that was in 1988, when I got to know Macedo, the first time that he came here on the Tejo River. He prepared it but we didn't get to see [have visions]. We got to feel the effects, the force, of the brew well, but there were no visions. I drank and I was curious to know, but unfortunately it didn't work out.

I really only got to see, to find myself on this brew so I could see what people were talking about, and also to believe whether it was true or not, when Macedo went to the indigenous area of the Breu River and brought it from there, prepared by the indigenous shamans, by Davi Lopes Kampa, an Ashaninka Indian, and a very powerful shaman who today no longer lives on the face of this Earth. It was also really good, but since there was little, I didn't get to see a whole lot, he only gave a little bit to each one of us. But I was pleased, I wasn't able to see anyone, but I saw many beautiful things, a lot of beauty, I felt a great deal of happiness.

After 1990, it was at the time that we were at the beginning of the creation of the Reserve, the proposal was already a strong proposal, the National Council of Rubber tappers was already in operation, and they made a proposal for Milton Nascimento to come here to get to know the rubber tappers, to get to know the Ashaninka people of the Amônea River, and I was also one of the people who was invited. And it seems to me that on that trip, I was already being guided by God. It was when I came to meet the shaman Antonio Pianko, his sons also, and I didn't have the least idea how these things were. At the time I was living another life: I drank a lot of alcohol, I didn't have the least idea of what I wanted to be, of what I wanted to make of my life. And when we came to Antonio Pianko's house, we were received very well with a lot of fireworks, I felt that there was a power there. And at night, Antonio Pianko invited us to drink kamarãpi, as they say, and I was also invited. That was when I began to see how spiritual life is.

The first time I drank, nothing happened, after an hour I hadn't even felt the effects of the brew. I asked to drink more, people brought it to me, and I drank.

After another half an hour, I still felt nothing. Then I asked to repeat the dose for the third time. That was when I came to receive the energies of the divine light. That was on August 14, 1990. I went on to really see, see the light, see and experience the vision, the beauty of life. I asked God that if this brew was from God, that He make me stay with this brew, that if it wasn't part of Him, then I would prefer to stay in the life that I was living. Because on many occasions I heard that the brew could show the reality of life, and that the person could see another life as well. Many people also said that this brew was not from God, that it was a brew from another spiritual line. So I drank it more with that intention to see if it was true, I asked God, I think with a lot of love, with a lot of worthiness also, I think that for that reason I got to see a lot of things I didn't expect to see.

The first thing I came to see was from when I was a kid, playing canoe in the rivers, running around on the grounds, playing with my brothers, my life as I was growing up and living, I saw myself in a school studying. It seemed to me that I was dreaming with life, that the brew came with such a force that I couldn't even get up to walk, but I knew that I was comfortable lying in a hammock. To me, at that moment, if God had come to take me out of where I was it would have been better. Because the visionary experience was good, I was seeing all that was beautiful and I even asked God to not take me out of that life, and so, it was because of that that I am leading the life I live today. And I also got to see even the point of being grown up, the man that I feel I am today. It was then that I also asked God to give me the capacity and the worthiness to learn to work with this brew, I wanted more and more to stay on that line.

When I came back from that trip, the indigenous people gave me some guidance. They said that one had to drink that brew with someone who had a good knowledge of it, who was used to drinking it. So it was in that sense that I too was very satisfied, knowing that these things didn't just happen, that it was something that you had to have respect for, and be really secure about. And then I went back with Milton Nascimento's people. Travelling on the Amônea River, we drank the brew on a beach, it was fantastic, and we listened to some hymns of Mestre Irineu. So it was in that sense that I saw that each person has a way of watching over this brew, each one has a way of respecting this brew, which is found not only here on the Extractivist Reserve, but in various other places as well.

At the time I went downriver with Milton Nascimento, I spent the months of August, September and October with them so as to be able to go back to the area where my people, my family was. And when I arrived, I met a brother who was already working, who had already taken cipó for the first time, and who had been taken out by a person who knew the cipó, who knew the leaf and who showed it to him. My coming back to the Reserve was more for the purpose of being together with my family, because I knew that in the city, life wasn't good for me. And when I got to my brother's house, I drank the brew he had prepared. It was good, for me, I was glad to be coming back home, meeting up with my family and with that light that was already there within as well.

So then I went on to drink ayahuasca for three more months, seeing if there was a place for me to work as well. I was following the advice of the indigenous shamans, I didn't want to make a ritual drink that I didn't have the permission to do so. Every time I drank, I was asking to work, but I still didn't have an answer, so I couldn't get into something if I wasn't certain that it was really that, that I wanted to follow. I only came to make this brew when one day I met up with shamans in my visions and they came and showed me what was the type of leaf that was right one to use, how they did it, and what was the cipó. It was then I talked with my brother, he went there, he took me along, he showed me a cipó, but he didn't tell me how to make it, but I had already seen how through a vision. So it was then that I began to prepare, really preparing ayahuasca, kamarãpi. It was then that I began my story with ayahuasca.

I had heard Macedo sing hymns of Mestre Irineu, which were the things that pulled me into this life. There were hymns that I learned quickly, watching Macedo sing twice and from that I also had the power to sing because, thank God, I've always had a very good memory. After 1991, at the time of the registering of the Extractivist Reserve, I had the pleasure and satisfaction of meeting Toinho Alves, who is an adept of Mestre Irineu's church from way back when, it was he who told me the name of the brew that is being administered in the churches today, Santo Daime. So I can't forget the people of the indigenous traditions, because it was through them that I got to know it for the first time, but I also can't forget to thank the people who are in these churches, taking care of the same ritual beverage but in a different way. They have the same respect, also, as the indigenous traditions. It was more or less because of that that I decided to stay with the tradition.

My life changed a great deal, I became more obedient, I came to respect the Divine Being, all the beings that inhabit the Earth and that have to be respected as well, in the same way that I respect myself. Because I know that all beings who live have a life like I have, they have to live as well. So it's not easy to learn to work with this brew, but whoever wants to learn has to do so by being worthy. So, for that reason, I feel very honored to be in this life that I am living today.

Introduction

The use of the vine called Jagube (*Banisteriopsis caapi*) and the leaf called Chacrona, or Rainha (lit. 'Queen') (*Psychotria viridis*), which is quite common in the forests of the Juruá River valley, in the preparation of a beverage for ritual use, is inscribed in the tradition of Arawak and Panoan-speaking indigenous peoples who have, from time immemorial, inhabited the region. In this text, however, we intend to explore the history, forms of use and meaning of this ritual beverage among non-indigenous groups, more specifically the rubber tappers of the Extractivist Reserve of the Upper Juruá.

We prefer to use the name 'ayahuasca' throughout this text, although we also mention other names used by rubber tappers to refer to the beverage.[1] This choice of terms was made, on the one hand, because this term is sufficiently well-known and allows us to discuss the case that is narrated in this article in the context of a larger tradition. The vastness of this tradition, on the other hand, allows us to highlight the singularity of the case of the rubber tappers of the Extractivist Reserve of the Upper Juruá.

The following text is divided into four main parts: the first introduces the reader briefly to the history of occupation of the Juruá Valley by northeastern migrants who became its future rubber tappers, and their conflicts with the native populations; the second deals with the history of ayahuasca among the rubber-gathering population of the Upper Juruá; the third, the preparation of the brew; and finally, the last part is on its ritual consumption. The text also includes a statement by one of the authors on his initiation to the use of ayahuasca. The culture of ayahuasca has always spread amongst rubber tappers in the midst of great secrecy, and we shall seek to respect this spirit here.

Brief history of the recent occupation of the Juruá valley

The Juruá Valley, a vast area of rivers and forests with a large number of rubber trees, *Hevea brasiliensis*, is located in the far west of the state of Acre. Until 1870 exploratory expeditions were occasional and for commercial purposes, concentrating on the extraction of sarsaparilla, vanilla, copaiba balsam, rubber and other similar products, by the

---

1. This same name is used by native populations of the neighboring countries of Peru and Colombia, who also use the term yagé. See, for example, Taussig (1993).

indigenous peoples. These products were traded for merchandise[2] with Panoan and Arawak-speaking indigenous peoples, traditional inhabitants of this region, and with the 'caboclos', a name which was used to refer to the non-indigenous regional population. In the case of the Indians, many groups had been, by that time, persecuted and enslaved (see Aquino and Iglesias, 1994).

In the last decades of the nineteenth century, the continuing increase of the international demand for rubber was responsible for the opening-up of the majority of the rubber camps existing in the Juruá Valley, and for the structuring of an economy that marked the region in a decisive way. In 1870, a steamboat went up the Juruá River for the first time, marking the beginning of a new era. This expansion took place through the penetration and exploration of new lands located along the courses of the rivers, claims made to their ownership, and speculation based on illegal titles (see Almeida, 1992).

The first problem to be settled was the scarcity of labor for work in the extraction of latex. The indigenous population resisted, and the conflicts were violent. Armed expeditions – called 'correrias' (incursions) – were organized which sought to decimate and expel the indigenous populations from their traditional territories, and were responsible for the extermination of several groups, or for their flight to areas in Peru where there were no rubber trees. In several cases, indigenous groups were absorbed by the rubber industry, as was the case of the Panoan-speaking Kaxinawá of the Jordão River.[3] Their traditional Arawak-speaking enemies, whose population was concentrated predominantly in Peru, were at first enslaved by the 'caucheiros'[4] and, after 1870, they were used by Brazilian bosses as a fighting force against the isolated Pano (Mendes, 1991).

The solution to the problem of lack of labor was the importation of workers from the Brazilian Northeast, ravaged by the drought at the end of the nineteenth century. Transportation of the immigrants to the newly-formed rubber camps was financed by the supply-houses of Belém and Manaus, which were responsible for the exportation of the rubber. It is estimated that between 25,000 and 50,000 new rubber tappers migrated to Amazonia in each decade since this first rubber boom. The Juruá Valley then became one of the principal areas for native rubber production in Amazonia (see Almeida, 1992).

The Tejo River basin, where the main characters of this text lived and live today, was the jewel of the Upper Juruá. It was first occupied by rubber tappers in the last decade of the nineteenth century, and in 1900 it was being exploited up to the headwaters of the Manteiga and Riozinho streams. The opening of the Restauração rubber camp also dates to this time. In 1907, the Tejo was described as a river that was already much inhabited by rubber tappers, from its mouth, passing the Paraná do Gomes (today, the Bagé River), the Riozinho, Camaleão, Tamisa and Machadinho, and up to the Boa Hora, one of its last tributaries (Mendonça, 1989). The labor system that was then established and which

---

2. Here generically conceived as manufactured goods (such as knives, mirrors, beads, etc.) which were offered to the local populations. It should be clear that, at that time, commerce wasn't an economic enterprise that demanded investment and involved permanent occupation, as was the case with the rubber-gathering industry. See below, note on 'merchandise' in the time of the rubber camps.

3. On the 'correrias' and the case of the Kaxinawá of the Jordão River, see Aquino and Iglesias, 1994.

4. *Castilloa elastica*, or 'caucho', also produces latex, but it's necessary to fell the tree in order to extract the latex, which implies a system of labor that is different from that of the rubber camps, where the network of relations that is established is more permanent.

made the economic exploitation of the rubber trees viable was based on the subordination of the rubber tappers to the 'bosses',[5] who exercised a supposedly absolute commercial monopoly over all the rubber produced by the rubber tappers.[6] Besides that, the rubber tappers paid the bosses 'renda' (rent): an annual amount, in rubber, for the use of the 'rubber trails'.[7]

Descriptions by travellers from the beginning of the twentieth century suggest a great vitality of economic life in the rubber camps: the center of the camps with 'barracões' (trading posts owned by the bosses) abundantly stocked with basic necessity and 'luxury' items for domestic consumption,[8] well-kept roads, open trails to allow the passage of wagon trains ('ramais'), and bustling 'colocações'[9] in full operation. In 1912, however, there was an almost total collapse as a result of the introduction onto the market of latex production from the rubber plantations of the Far East, which were far more productive and at considerably lower production costs. But, in this first crisis and in the following crises, the rubber camps were not abandoned en masse, but rather the inhabitants adopted a strategy of diversification of agricultural and extractivist activities (Almeida, 1992)

Thus, the rubber camps continued to be active throughout the century, inhabited by successive generations of descendants of the first Northeastern migrants, many of whom established families through marital unions with Indian women captured in the 'correrias' and/or their daughters (Pantoja, 2004; Wolff, 1999). It is almost certain that the rubber tappers' introduction to ayahuasca took place in the context of the nearness and contact with the indigenous populations.

In the 1980s, the rubber camps of the Upper Juruá became surrounded by Indigenous Lands which had been demarcated in the previous decade, producing a situation of land tenure which was quite distinct from previous times. Indians and Whites were now

---

5. The 'patrões' [bosses] are the owners or leaseholders of the rubber camps, who retained total control over access to the land, production and commerce.

6. For an ethnographic and original analysis of the relations of domination on the rubber camps, see Almeida, 1992.

7. Trails cleared through the forest that follow the spatial distribution of the native rubber trees, and which are traversed by the rubber-gatherers during their work of extracting latex. In this work, the rubber-gatherer goes over each trail twice in the same day: on the first trip he will make an incision on the bark of the tree, then fitting a small cup to gather the latex. The second trip is called the 'colha', when the latex is poured into a single recipient (the 'bucket') and carried home. A rubber-gatherer on the average will occupy two rubber-trails, each of which is travelled over twice a week. A standard rubber-trail will have 120 rubber trees, and can include an area of up to 500 hectares. Thus, the workday of the rubber-gatherer should start before dawn, if not at night, and only in the late afternoon does he come back home with the product of his work. The latex will then be 'pressed' or 'smoked', which refers to crafting techniques that increase the value of the product.

8. These articles are locally called 'mercadorias' [merchandise, goods], which can be 'estiva' [basic goods] or 'luxury' items. Among the first are included the items considered essential for life on the rubber camps (salt, ammunition, oil, soap, among other things), and in the second category are non-durable articles the consumption of which is not considered to be absolutely necessary as, for example, perfumes, mirrors, powdered chocolate and juices. There is yet another type of merchandise, which we shall classify here as items of worth: shotguns, motors, sewing machines and battery-operated radios.

9. Social, economic and spatial unit that constitutes the rubber camps. A rubber camp is formed by a group of 'colocações', and in each one of them we find the houses of one or more resident domestic groups, generally related by kinship, besides the rubber-roads, gardens and hunting and gathering areas.

neighbors, although the tensions inherited from the past were still present, as in the case of the use of the mildly pejorative term 'caboclo' to refer to the now-'tame' Indians, as well as to the rubber tappers of mixed blood. But, in their relations as neighbors, positive exchanges also took place. In the struggles against the bosses at the end of the 1980s, the Indians always cited the conquest of their lands, an independent economy in relation to the bosses, and rights such as to health and education. The creation of the Extractivist Reserve of the Upper Juruá, in 1990, always had the support and participation of Kaxinawá and Ashaninka leaders. These populations had their rituals of ayahuasca – 'kamarāpi' and 'nixi pëi', respectively – and we shall see that they were important in the more recent initiation and apprenticeship of the rubber tappers into the ways of ayahuasca.

Ayahuasca among the rubber tappers

In tracking down the history of the uses of ayahuasca among the rubber tappers of the Tejo River basin, one name is always mentioned: Crispim. According to the oral tradition, this well-known curer was the son of Indians of the Envira River, and was separated from his people when he was captured in a 'correria'. Adopted by the Whites, Crispim, it is said, went to live in Rio de Janeiro. After five years of military service, 'he thought it better to go back to the village'.[10] A rubber tapper told us that, as a boy, living in his grandfather's house in the Restauração rubber camp, he remembers Crispim telling of his return to the Envira to live with 'wild' (isolated) Indians. The reasons that would have led him to decide to return to his origins remain unexplained, but it was during this time when he stayed with his 'kin'[11] that, it is said, he learned the 'science' (see n. 15) of curing.

Crispim is supposed to have arrived in the Tejo river basin in the 1950s. He lived for several years on the stream called Dourado, where he set up a family, but today his name is associated with the Yaminawa people who lived on the upper Bagé River. Those who knew him say that he used to take long walks through the rubber camps, visiting friends and 'kin', such as those who lived on the Camaleão stream. Crispim was also much sought out, and quite a few people went to his house to be cured. 'He was the best curer inside our Reserve', a retired rubber tapper remembers today, who had his wife cured from an 'encosto' (harmful spirit). Reports of people who were benefited by his power and knowledge reveal that in his curing work, Crispim made use of an infinite variety of 'forest remedies', and resorted to ayahuasca when necessary. It is even said that Crispim recorded in writing, in notebooks, the properties of the plants that he used as remedies.[12]

The testimonies lead us to believe that there were rituals that he led, and that he was the one who prepared the brew. Although not all of the participants were necessarily

---

10. The oral tradition on Crispim does not seem to be consensual or homogeneous. It is possible to find a variation of the life history described above in Carneiro da Cunha (1998). Information on Crispim can also be found in Araújo (1998).

11. Here synonymous for highly inclusive kinship: all the Indians or, at least, the Pano.

12. See Araújo, 1998. According to the author, Crispim's belongings, including his notebooks, were burned after his death, following the tradition of the Yaminawa among whom he lived.

looking for a cure for physical ailments, reports allow us to suppose that Crispim made use of ayahuasca in order to make diagnoses, prescribe remedies and even to effect cures: 'I heard him say to my grandfather that when he took ayahuasca, he could operate on people. He performed operations, using ayahuasca'.

The rubber tappers' mythology on the origin of the 'science'[13] of ayahuasca among the rubber tappers of the Upper Juruá goes back, then, to this man, an Indian named Crispim. It was after him, and from the contact he had with other rubber tappers, that knowledge about ayahuasca expanded to the rubber camps of the Tejo.

In this sense, oral history speaks of another man, named Sebastião Pereira, who came to the Restauração rubber camp at the end of 1966. According to those who knew him, Sebastião made contacts with Crispim and it was through him that Sebastião learned a great deal about the use of ayahuasca. But, everything indicates that Sebastião ended up finding his own way, both within and outside the context of the sacred brew. He became known as a good prayer-maker – that is, prayers, not 'forest remedies', were his tools in the curing process – and over time, he got the nickname 'of the cipó' [ayahuasca vine] tacked on to his first name.

The reports of the use of ayahuasca, now baptized as 'cipó', in a group led by a white rubber tapper, are more detailed, perhaps because of the nearness in time and also culture. Sebastião of the Cipó held nightly meetings with neighboring rubber tappers, with the presence of women, in order to drink bottles of cipó which he himself prepared. 'He used that kind of music of Texeirinha (a popular singer), that speaks of God. His rattle was made of coité, the kind that has a little point.' It is said that this man manifested extraordinary powers during those nightly sessions. 'The guy could be as he was, but when he [Sebastião] put his hand on his head, he got well.' It is also said that he sang and danced with the maracá to help those present to have visions while under the effects of the brew. 'When it was time for the force to come, he would go out singing, and he would come back whistling. Then he began.'

During this same period, in the midst of the white rubber-tapper population, several members of the Cunha family group, known for their skills as curers and prayer-makers, also would take part in, or hold, sessions with cipó. João Cunha, today one of the most well-known curers of the Extractivist Reserve, still has fond memories of this group, of the night sessions with cipó, and the teachings he received from Crispim.

The career of João Cunha is by itself very interesting, including extraordinary previous experiences with the cipó.[14] Still a boy, he learned prayers from his grandmother who was from Ceará, but at 17 years of age, he began to suffer inexplicable falls, which were diagnosed at that time as manifestations of a curing spirit which was searching for a partner in whom it could incarnate and through whom it could act. This spirit, named Manoel Pinheiro, has since then become João Cunha's teacher in the arts of curing, from sicknesses to

---

13. The term 'science' is used among rubber-gatherers to designate specific knowledge about the environment and the cultural forms of appropriation of the natural resources. This knowledge is organized according to rules of observation and classification which are different from those that hold in modern Western science. In this sense, the science of ayahuasca includes the acquisition and development of knowledge about the Jagube cipó and the Chacrona leaf, about the preparation of the brew and its ritual consumption, besides the forms and criteria for transmission of this knowledge.

14. All information about João Cunha was taken from Araújo, 1998.

spells. Now more than 70-years old, the curer is seeking to pass on his function of serving as an instrument for Manoel Pinheiro to his children. He doesn't use cipó anymore, the brew that he respects for the mysteries into which he was introduced, although he does not reveal their contents.

Few people seem to have been gifted with the power to hold command over an ayahuasca session and, especially, with the gift of curing. People like Sebastião of the cipó and João Cunha, for example, achieved some leadership. It was not possible to discover the presence, or lack, of an *ayahuasqueiro* mysticism among them. On the other hand, the motivations that led many rubber tappers to seek them out to participate in rituals with the brew were quite different from the cures done by Crispim. To discover theft in the calculation of debts of the rubber tappers to their bosses, to check on the moral behavior of wives who went to the city, to know the river conditions on the day before a trip, or the loyalty of friends, and to know new and inaccessible places, were all part of the repertoire of expectations of those who at that time drank the brew.

Testimonies reveal that in the 1970s, the rubber bosses themselves even prohibited the preparation and consumption of the brew, claiming that it caused an indifference to work. But the rubber tappers understand the motives for that attitude differently: the fear that the visions resulting from drinking the brew would allow the rubber tappers to witness the theft that the rubber bosses were making on their accounts at the trading post. In view of the persistence of the sessions, police forces were even called to intimidate the rubber tappers who frequented them. Everything indicates that the meetings to drink the brew continued, even though in secret. Not even the condemnation of Brother José, a holy man who passed through the Juruá at the end of the 1960s and who is venerated even today, against those who drank 'things of the Devil' was capable of restraining its use among the rubber tappers (Araújo, 1998).

Ayahuasca and its more recent use

The first anthropological observations of the use of this sacred drink among the rubber tappers of the Extractivist Reserve go back to the beginning of the 1980s.

In November, 1983, the anthropologist Mauro Almeida was waiting for the first high-water to go downriver in his canoe to Cruzeiro do Sul, ending a period of 14 months of fieldwork on the Riozinho of the Restauração. One day before he finally was able to make his trip, he received the following message from a fellow named Rui,[15] who was a rubber tapper who lived on the Cachoeirinha 'colocação': 'Let's drink some brew in the house of Major', which was next to the Rapids of the Jarana. The researcher traveled the next day without being able to accept the invitation, but he remembered the invitation which was from someone who, even having stayed for such a long time in the field, had remained so hidden to him until then (Mauro Almeida, personal communication).

In 1987, on returning to the Riozinho of the Restauração, the anthropologist looked for Major saying that he was interested in trying the brew. Despite Major's initial distrust,

---

15. Or maybe Evilásio (Vila), Mr. i.

a session was held with his son Tonho: after drinking the cipó, the participants laid back in their hammocks, over which a palm-leaf of jarina (*Phytelephas* spp.) was put, to 'give a direction to the trip'. In the absence of a guitar, 'forró' (music of the Northeast) was put on the record-player. The place set aside for the session was a room, separate from the house, with a hole in its floor, which everything indicates was for alleviating an occasional nausea. They stayed in this place, in the dark, until all the symptoms of the brew had ended.[16]

Thus we see that the use of the cipó was not public. Probably there was a reference group, and for sure many rubber tappers, including non-adepts, know of the sessions. But all of this remained inaccessible to the outside researcher, and was only revealed at the end of a long period of living together.

In retrospect, another landmark in the history of the use of ayahuasca among the non-Indian rubber tappers of the Upper Juruá occurred in 1988, when the process of mobilizing for the creation of the Extractivist Reserve began. During the first trips of Antonio Macedo, who was then Regional Coordinator of the Juruá Valley for the National Rubber Tappers' Council, rubber tappers were invited to try out the brew that he came to know when he was still young and, for many years as a backwoodsman of the FUNAI (National Foundation of the Indian), he had the chance to learn and find out more about in his trips through the indigenous villages of the State of Acre. At this time, it is possible to perceive the formation of another reference group.

During the nightly sessions with the cipó, or Daime (see below), generally in the open air, in the area in front of the houses, rubber tappers who were participating in the meetings of the Council and the initiative for creating the cooperative nuclei to break the rubber bosses' monopoly had their first contacts with the brew. In this period, there were occasions when contacts occurred through visits to the neighboring Indians, like the Ashaninka of the Breu river, whose memorable shaman Lopes Davi Kampa actually led rituals of 'kamarãpi' during the assemblies of the newly-formed Association of Rubber Tappers of the Reserve.

It is intriguing to ask how much and how *ayahuasqueiro* mysticism was a part of the struggles and victories that resulted in the creation of the Extractivist Reserve of the Upper Juruá, and which resulted in the end of the rubber bosses. No doubt it created loyalties and reinforced faith in life and justice, which was after all what the rubber tappers wanted. Practically all the leaders who, at one moment or other and in different ways, participated in this period of struggles took part in rituals of the sacred brew. But, in this process of forming a new reference group in the use of ayahuasca, one kin group of father and sons, which became known locally as 'the Miltons' (referring to the leadership of the patriarch)[17] stood out for its involvement in the creation of the Extractivist Reserve.

Resident on the Restauração rubber camp, rubber tappers by tradition and with indigenous ancestry, this family group came to dedicate itself to cultivating and studying the ritual brew. Reconstructing the history of their contact with ayahuasca, they mixed elements from indigenous and Christian cultures. As one of them said, 'we already consid-

---

16. Tonho declared, after taking ayahuasca, that he would go to São Paulo to get to know the house of the anthropologist. In the end, he confirmed that he was in the capital city, but he never was able to get to the anthropologist's house, he got lost on the way (Mauro Almeida, personal communication).

17. See Pantoja (2004).

ered ourselves really indigenously traditional, civilized Indians, you know?' It is in the light of this statement that the initiation of the Miltons to the rituals of ayahuasca should be interpreted.

The first and strongest contacts with the brew were made with the guidance of indigenous groups and leaders – like shamans. The development of apprenticeship in the preparation of ayahuasca was done under the influence of the sacred drink, in which the indigenous presence in visionary experiences was frequent. The reports show the discipline and generosity of the mystical experience provided by ayahuasca, and demonstrate a strong respect for the holders of an age-old tradition and knowledge. 'I took Daime once, and then in my vision an Indian appeared. Now, this Indian was like the king of the empire of the sacred drink', one of the collaborators of this text revealed.[18] Under the effects of ayahuasca, many rubber tappers took geographical and astral trips, which refer to the idea of shamanic flights (Araújo, 1998).

The building of a new worldview based on contact with ayahuasca was also marked by contact with another reading of the sacred, deriving from the Christian tradition. Especially significant in the combination and aggregation of traditions that was being forged were the teachings of an ex-rubber tapper, born in Maranhão and who migrated to the Acre forests in 1912, by the name of Raimundo Irineu Serra, Mestre Irineu.

The origins of this man's mystical experience refer to an encounter – in the forests of the border between Acre and Peru and after having taken ayahuasca – between a man and a female entity who was presented as the Virgin of Conception.[19] In this encounter he was given the mission to receive instructions sent directly from the Astral plane, which were presented to him in the form of hymns 'received' over the years. Altogether, these hymns came to form the founding stone of the Doctrine of Santo Daime, which reworks the Christian tradition based on a reading of it that incorporates the cosmology of the world from which it derives. Thus, there are entities and invocations connected to the forest (such as the Queen of the Forest), to the elements of nature (sun, moon, star, sea, wind, etc.) and to the divine entities of the Christian world (God, Jesus Christ, the Virgin Mary and the pantheon of saints and archangels).

Beyond the teachings of Mestre Irineu, the early period of working with ayahuasca still relied on the words contained in various evangelical and Catholic hymns, which were introduced either by pastors and priests who visited the area, or by those rubber tappers who were accustomed to participating in these churches in the city of Cruzeiro do Sul. Historical figures such as the Brothers of Nova Olinda[20] and Brother José are also present in the visionary experiences of the rubber tappers.

Another specific feature of the sessions with ayahuasca done by these rubber tappers, and which seems to be a cultural heritage of the pioneers, is the use of popular songs, even commercial songs, but with a strong emotional appeal. Singers like the 'memorable

---

18. All the following citations were gathered from rubber tappers who collaborated in the discussion and organization of this text, and whose names are listed in the introductory footnote. The group decided not to mention their names in the body of the text.

19. On the origins of the doctrine of Santo Daime, see, for example, Fróes (1983).

20. They are also known as the Miraculous Brothers of Nova Olinda. These are two brothers from the Northeast, who were killed by Indians at the beginning of the century on the upper Tejo river, Machadinho branch. The brothers are considered miraculous and even today their tomb is visited to 'pay promises' (see Glossary).

Texeirinha' and Gildo de Freitas are often heard in the rubber camps. Their music shows that they are, in the view of their fans, singers who are 'connected to God'. There was, for example, a song by Texeirinha about two truck-drivers whose greatest wish was to become their own bosses, and to stop being subordinate as employees. But, when they attain their objective, one of them dies, and the song tells of the sadness of the other in the absence of his friend.

In the ayahuasca sessions, on hearing this music the rubber tappers perhaps also see themselves in the emotional climate in which they have lived, which has been marked by the end of the system of bosses on the rubber camps. On these same occasions, it was also possible to hear local songs sung in the name of the growing experience of cooperativism, a counterpoint to domination by the bosses.

In this new context of expansion of the use of ayahuasca, the names of the substance have also been diversified: cipó, Daime or Vegetal have come to be used. Besides Antonio Macedo, from this time on, scholars and supporters of the proposal for creating the Extractivist Reserve, and also those familiar with the brew, began to circulate in the Upper Juruá, bringing more information about its use on the neighboring Indigenous Lands, in the churches of Santo Daime and in other centers that perform spiritual sessions with ayahuasca.

The following two parts of the text are based on the more recent use of ayahuasca.

The 'science' of preparation

Ayahuasca cannot be prepared by just anyone. The person who takes responsibility for preparing the brew has to have also acquired knowledge about its 'science' and to have obtained, in a vision, permission to do so. Those on the Extractivist Reserve, today, who take responsibility for such a task, always make reference to the astral permission that they receive in order to do so. There are not many rubber tappers who take on the task of the 'feitio', the occasion when the brew is prepared.[21] One of the people who has this knowledge says that the early times of contact with ayahuasca were dedicated to investigating whether there was 'an opening' so that he could work with it.

After deciding on the preparation, the first step is to find the Jagube vine, which could be hours away from the camp where the ritual drink is to be prepared. Tracking down and finding a 'cipó' could be casual – when the rubber tapper finds a Jagube vine in his hunting-trips or while extracting latex – or not. This is the case of the existence of a vine in the areas indicated by a vision. On finding it, it is up to the specialist to identify what kind of vine it is: Little Rose, Macaw or Caboclo. All of them are appropriate for preparing the brew, the only difference being the quantities that each one requires to be mixed together with the brew (Figure 1).

The gathering of the leaves, thus, is the next step. One must take care, since not all of the leaves are appropriate, there are 'cold' leaves, that is, those which, although they are

---

21. In general, the preparation of ayahuasca involves two or three rubber-gatherers on the average of two days. Only men prepare the brew.

Figure 1. Cut pieces of the *Banisteriopsis caapi* vine (copyright Flavio Lopes).

classified as belonging to the group of 'Chacrona', are not used in the preparation of aya-huasca. Indeed, the cipó and the leaf, when they are mixed together, establish a relation of complementarity. Thus the rubber tappers say it is the 'force' of the cipó, balanced by the power of the leaf, that brings 'light' to the visionary experiences (Figure 2).

The next stage of preparation is 'beating' (mashing) the vine with a wooden club, sepa-rating the pulp from the shell, which will produce different flavors when the brew is drunk. One should then 'choose' the leaves, that is, remove those that are crushed or unhealthy. Having beaten the vine and chosen the leaves, now they have to be put together to boil. This is an important moment, and, like all the stages of preparation, there is 'science': 'It's not just taking it, mixing it altogether and throwing it into a pot, into a bucket and letting it boil'.

After packing the vine and the leaves into a pot exclusively for that purpose, it is then time to demonstrate knowledge in combining two elements: water and fire. Knowing the ideal quantity of water, the right boiling point and the heat which is necessary for the fire, including the right firewood to burn, are all essential. There is special care taken during the boiling, because it is a time when bad words can do damage to the effort of preparing the brew, and sincerity in singing the hymns and songs can prove to be fundamental. Pre-paring the brew also involves knowledge about the boiling and the degree of concentra-tion of the brew. After letting it cool, the correct thing is to put the brew into glass bottles. On the Extractivist Reserve, sporadic acquisition of glass bottles means that the makers of ayahuasca have to take special care of the glass bottles that they have.

Figure 2. A bowl of chacruna leaves (copyright Flavio Lopes).

The ritual

Although there is a minimum fixed group of people who get together to drink the brew, there is no formally established calendar for the ayahuasca sessions. The ideal, for individual and group evolution, is that they hold sessions with some regularity. The rituals for drinking can be scheduled some time ahead, but there is always space for those unprogrammed moments and for individual and convenience decisions. The obligation to show up, indeed, is defined by the profile of the group that is dedicated to the cultivation of ayahuasca on the Extractivist Reserve. Several are neighbors, others live further away; several have a definite residence, others constantly travel. 'Our group is sometimes here, sometimes there.'

A closer look at the present-day composition of the group shows that there is a set of people linked by kinship and friendship ties: fathers and sons, godparents, cousins and friends from some time ago. That is, with rare exceptions, the people who today get together to take ayahuasca have close, prior relations. There are women who participate in the sessions, but the men have a more numerous and avid presence.

Invariably the meeting to drink ayahuasca will take place shortly after nightfall. Open-air sessions can take place, but the preference is for sheltered environments, although

Figure 3. Osmildo Kuntanawa preparing cipó (2007) (copyright Mariana Ciavatta Pantoja).

there is the possibility of going outside to appreciate the starry sky and moon. There are, however, invisible borders demarcating freedom of movement, so it is not considered correct if a person decides on his own account to leave the session before it has come to an end.

A candle or, lacking that, a kerosene lamp, should be kept lit during the whole ritual. Soon after taking ayahuasca, people generally chat a little and smoke a tobacco cigarette. Little by little, the setting begins to get quiet, those present lie down in their hammocks or sit on the floor, benches or chairs.

The ritual always has one, or more than one (in exceptional cases), person responsible for the distribution of the ayahuasca to all those present. This person will have to take care that all goes well in the session, attending to everything that may be asked of him. As it is known, ayahuasca can produce physical effects, such as nausea, besides strong sensory and emotional experiences, many of them unexpected or unknown. Leading a session is thus a task that involves a great deal of responsibility. To qualify for such a task requires apprenticeship with those more experienced and a special understanding of the forces and entities that dwell in the brew.

Music is an element that is always present in the ayahuasca sessions. Practically all the participants of the group today play guitar, and many of them declare that they learned the art under the order and with the help of the brew. If there is a tape-recorder, people can listen to hymns from the Santo Daime, and also Baptist, churches. If there is none (or if there are no batteries to make it work), the guitar is played throughout practically the whole session, accompanied by the voices of those present. Singing under the effects of ayahuasca is a gift which, in principle, is accessible to all. There are singers who stand out more, leading hymns, songs and, occasionally, indigenous chants.

After a few hours, there is a break, during which people are at ease to chat, if they wish to. The sound of the guitar continues, generally with locally and regionally composed songs. There is no established length of time for these breaks, but this will be agreed upon by those present depending on the time for closing the session and its more or less formal character. Sessions that follow the Christian, or Daimist, calendar are considered 'official', and demand greater punctuality and observance of the programming which is established at the beginning. When it is a non-official session, there is greater flexibility for improvising at the last minute, such as in changing the time of closing the session. The ritual formality of the ayahuasca night sessions can vary, but a session always has a beginning, middle and end.

The ritual will always be closed with hymns and, at the very end, prayers – Our Father and Hail Mary. There will still be some time for those present, if they wish, to talk about their experience and the session they held on that night. A snack, or meal, ends the night of communion.

Today, those who participate in a ritual of ayahuasca declare that they are looking for 'hints' that may reveal new realities. 'We take Daime to go looking for something fundamental, something that we don't have knowledge of, something inside our spirit.' Everyone acknowledges that the brew is 'a teacher' and that the 'science' is in knowing how to understand what is experienced under its effects. External knowledge, like scientific knowledge, is worth nothing: 'Nobody ever came to the Daime to research it, and wasn't by the Daime researched.'

This access to depths never before reached, for these people, can provide clarification about their daily, or 'material', life, in a search 'to perfect oneself more and more and to clean out the material (body) to be better adapted, to see what is the meaning of life'. A meaning that takes them back again to the Divine and, in an apparent paradox, to the Inexplicable: things of God.

Ayahuasca can also operate as a guide in the conduct of practical life. This happens when the people who take it seek to know, or 'futurar' (know the future of), their work, trips, or even their friendships. One can also take it in search of a cure for sicknesses or to 'clean' the organism. There are cases of rubber tappers who seek moral changes in their lives, like to stop drinking alcoholic beverages, to stop smoking cigarettes and going to parties or soccer games, which are the main times when fights can break out in the rubber camp.

There are personal testimonies that speak of what is near, but not discerned. Simple things, like family life. 'With this brew I came to know my family, because before I was unknowing about my family', one rubber tapper declared. Others speak of the opportunity they had, through the brew, to make new friendships or catch up on previous ones. The strength of loyalties that comes from ayahuasca is visible, loyalties that are built from the experience of opening up to the unknown. Those who cultivate this fine 'science' make no secret about the break that contact with ayahuasca has meant in their lives – 'I go forward knowing that I'm not what I was'. The sense of the collective so formed comes to be a strong reference point of belonging and reciprocity on various levels. 'So it was that I began to know this group and I'm in this group until today, and I'm hoping not to go out early, or even never more'. Here we end this text, which we fear is already too long. The 'science' of ayahuasca recommends more description and little interpretation.

References

Almeida, Mauro. 1992. 'Rubber Tappers of the Upper Juruá River, Brazil. The Making of a Forest Peasant Economy'. PhD dissertation, Cambridge University.

Aquino, Txai Terri Valle de, and Marcelo Piedrafita Iglesias. 1994. *Kaxinawá do rio Jordão. História, território, economia e desenvolvimento sustentado*. Rio Branco: CPI.

Araújo, Gabriela Jahnel. 1998. 'Entre almas, encantes e cipó'. Master's thesis (Anthropology), Unicamp.

Carneiro da Cunha, Manuela. 1998. 'Pontos de vista sobre a Floresta Amazônica: xamanismo e tradução'. *Mana* 4(1). Rio de Janeiro: PPGAS/MN.

Fróes, Vera. 1983. 'Santo Daime, cultura amazônica'. *História do Povo Juramidam*. Manaus: Suframa.

Labate, Beatriz C., and Wladimyr Sena Araújo, eds. 2004. *O Uso Ritual da ayahuasca (The Ritual Use of Aya-huasca)*. 2nd edn. Campinas, Mercado de Letras.

Mendes, Margarete Kitaka. 1991. 'Etnografia preliminar dos Ashaninka da Amazônia brasileira'. MA thesis (Anthropology), Unicamp.

Mendonça, Gal. Belarmino. 1989. *Reconhecimento do rio Juruá (1905)*. Belo Horizonte: Itatiaia; Rio Branco: Fundação Cultural do Estado do Acre.

Pantoja, Mariana C. 2004. *Os Milton. Cem anos de história nos seringais*. Recife: Fundação Joaquim Nabuco/Editora Massangana.

Taussig, Michael. 1993. 'Xamanismo, colonialismo e o homem selvagem'. *Um estudo sobre o terror e a cura*. Rio de Janeiro: Paz e Terra.

Wolff, Cristina S. 1999. *Mulheres da floresta: uma história. Alto Juruá, Acre (1890-1945)*. São Paulo: Hucitec.

2

The rituals of Santo Daime: systems of symbolic constructions*

Arneide Cemin

Translated by Robin Wright, revised by Matthew Meyer

The 'Ayahuasca Religions' arose in Brazil in the 1930s, and were organized by migrants from the Northeast who came to the Amazon region to work in the extraction of rubber (*Hevea brasiliensis*). Two main branches were formed: the Santo Daime and the União do Vegetal (literally, the Union of the Plants; hereafter UDV). Both religious denominations derive from 'ayahuasca shamanism', the widespread tradition of many Amazonian indigenous groups of contacting the sacred through the use of *ayahuasca* (a psychoactive decoction prepared from the forest vine *Banisteriopsis caapi* and the plant *Psychotria viridis*).

The Santo Daime religion was created in the city of Rio Branco, capital of Acre, by Raimundo Irineu Serra, who migrated from the state of Maranhão to the Amazon region in 1912, working as a rubber tapper, a soldier of the Territorial Guard, and finally, after 1930, as a respected *curandeiro* ('healer'). The UDV was founded by José Gabriel da Costa, a migrant from the state of Bahia and an ex-rubber tapper who established his religious center in the city of Porto Velho, Rondônia state, in the late 1950s.

While working as rubber tappers, Irineu and Gabriel, like many other migrants, came into contact with native peoples of the Peruvian Amazon, and were thus initiated to the ritual use of ayahuasca. With the fall in the price of rubber on the world market, there came a crisis in the Amazonian extractive industry, which forced hundreds of rubber tappers, sick and with no money and belongings, to leave the forests and go to the incipient urban centers of the region. Irineu took up residence in Rio Branco, where he created a religious community, establishing its precepts and rituals.

The rituals in the religion of Santo Daime are called *trabalhos* ('works'). In our understanding, this 'work' is done on the body and thought: symbolic productions, the imagi-

* First published in *Fieldwork in Religion* (2006) 2.3: 256–85. This translation is of an article in Labate and Araújo (2004), 347–82.

nary. The notion of work refers to 'spiritual work' which nevertheless includes the body in its totality as support. Some *trabalhos* are considered 'lighter' and others 'heavier', both from the individual and from the collective points of view. The *trabalhos* done on Good Friday and on the Day of the Dead, for example, are considered 'heavy'. Classified another way, it is said that, normally, the first part of the *trabalho* is 'heavy' due to the disorderly or negative charge of energies that have to be transformed by the ritual into harmonious and positive energies; at that moment, the *trabalho* becomes 'light'. It can even happen that some member of the church is not able to free himself or herself from the negative energies that circulate in the *trabalho*, which remain with him or her for a longer time, provoking symptoms of disharmony which are manifested in various forms, in the individual himself or herself and in the persons around him or her.

Thus it is necessary 'to learn to work with Daime'. This and other related expressions refer to the multiplicity of techniques in which the body serves as support: uniforms, concentration, coordination of movements in the dance steps, the singing of hymns and the rhythm of the maraca rattle, and even the physical effects of the liquid which go from accepting its smell and taste, to the sensations that it can cause: drowsiness, palpitation or quick beating of the heart, vomiting, diarrhea, 'astral journeys' (the sensation of death and rebirth, anxiety, pleasure; beautiful, illuminating and/or terrifying visions), besides acceptance of the codes of conduct within the system, notably 'obedience', 'humility', and 'love' for all members of the church.

Obedience is clearly highlighted in the '*Cruzeiro*', the hymnal of Mestre Irineu, and all other hymnals make reference to it in one way or another, because it is one of the basic components in the process of adapting the follower to the system. So much so that Mestre Virgílio (*in memoriam*) would emphasize that: 'here the main thing is to obey'. Disobedience is called 'rebelliousness'. This has to do with what Mauss (1974a) called 'education in cold blood', referring to response-delaying movements that inhibit movements unauthorized by the system in question; allowing in sequence, coordinated responses in the direction of the desired ends.

We can say that the *trabalhos* actually designate 'corporeal techniques' in the Maussian sense; that is, they have to do with body attitudes, the 'arts of using the body', seeking to realize a specific end: the proper adaptation of the neophyte to the system. This, in turn, has the religious objective of making possible magical flight or passage to the astral plane. For Mauss (1974a), the corporeal techniques, or ways of using the body, are 'facts of education' that are subject to the dictates of space and time, and for that reason are the object of social classifications and learning. In this way, walking, swimming, marching, running, table manners and attitudes toward biological reproduction, birth and death, among other things, are facts of education, that is to say, socially acquired *habitus*. The efficacy of education shows its full potential in the presence of 'social authority'; for education, he says, occurs through 'prestigious imitation'. It is through imitation that the individual learns the series of interconnected movements that make up the technique in question.

'Prestigious imitation' refers to the fact that children and adults imitate successful acts when performed by people whom they trust. It is thus in the 'notion of prestige of the person that makes the act ordered, authorized and tested in relation to the individual imitator, that one finds the entire social element' (1974a: 215). That is, prestigious imitation is the essentially sociological aspect that permits learning and the assimilation of a given corporeal technique. Taking into account the necessary internalization of the imitative act, it is a question that is at the same time relevant to psychology and biology.

Mauss warns that it is wrong to think that technique only exists in the presence of an instrument. Thus, beyond Daime, strictly speaking, which as a sacred beverage is considered an instrument that allows access to the 'spiritual world', one also has to consider the set of body techniques that induce the effects which are embedded in and prescribed by the system. Technique is an 'efficacious traditional act', Mauss says, adding that it 'does not differ from the magical, religious, or symbolic act', for it is necessary that there exists a tradition, or a defined pattern, in order for there to exist technique and transmission of technical knowledge. In general, the transmission of knowledge occurs especially through oral means. The technique for ritually preparing and consuming ayahuasca, as we have said, derives from the shamanic tradition. Through his social actions, and thus his person, Irineu instituted the element of prestige of this practice in the city of Rio Branco, propagating the technique through prestigious imitation and narrative art (Cemin, 1998).

While every traditional act is a technique, not every technique is a religious or moral act, Mauss adds, pointing to the difference between the 'traditional technical act' and the 'traditional act of religious techniques'. The difference, he says, is that the first 'is felt by the author as a mechanical, physical, or physio-chemical act, and it is done with that purpose' (1974a: 217). The traditional act of the religious technique is preceded and accompanied by the belief in the physical, moral, magical and ritual efficacy of certain procedures, many of which are mediated by the body. Thus they are covered with meanings shared by the belief in question. Mauss adds that the body is the first instrument of human beings and that, even before the notion of the instrument, it presents itself as our first object and technical medium. Thus, the 'principle of the corporeal technique' becomes visible when we see the 'constant adaptation' of the body,

> to a physical, mechanical, or chemical (for example, when we drink) purpose pursued in a series of acts assembled on the individual not only by himself, but by all of his education, by the whole society of which he is a member, in the place that he occupies in it (Mauss, 1974a: 218).

Through corporeal techniques, one produces the 'symbolic life of the spirit'. The activity of consciousness is, before all else, 'a system of symbolic constructions' made effective by body techniques; we are dealing with 'physio-psycho-sociological constructions'. A varied series of acts extracted from the stock of habits, some more, others less ancient in the lives of individuals and collectivities. We argue that the 'essence' of Irineu is the fact of his being a 'Mestre Ensinador' (Master Teacher), an educator *par excellence*, the 'greatest professor in the world' and, no doubt, an expert in the 'construction of symbolic systems'. At the same time, a commentary by Mauss in the same text (1974a: 231) elucidates another angle, the way in which the organization founded by Irineu takes on the form of an 'army' (the followers, who are organized into male and female 'battalions', call themselves 'soldiers of the Queen of the Forest'): 'There is in the whole context of group life a kind of education of the movements in closed formation', a standardizing 'example and order' that is the main principle, he concludes.

41

Thanks to the standardizing, that is, ordered example, it becomes possible to intervene in society, including in contexts where the unconscious or chaos could predominate. Having learned the basic pattern of ayahuasca shamanism, Irineu adapted it by recomposing the shamanic system, through a series of defined movements, capable of exercising control over reality experienced in an 'altered state of consciousness', by directing the domain of the conscious person over his emotion and unconsciousness. Mauss attributes this function to society, that is, to social practices; hence, we can agree with the author when he says that 'there really is, behind all our mystic states, corporeal techniques... There are biological means for entering into contact with God' (1974a: 233).

The corporeal techniques obey principles of classification that define the position of bodies in relation to objects. Space, time, and movement are coordinated, which painstakingly demarcate the uses of the body: 'details are essential', Mauss reminds us, because they point to the principles of movements. In this way, body movements are classified in relation to the sexes and not only by the principle of the social division of labor, but also by establishing identities and social positions.

The body techniques even vary with age, and can be classified in terms of how much they produce. The last item mentioned elucidates the *Daimista* corporeal technique as applied to the transmutation of the 'vegetal body' into the 'divine body', that is, into the 'true Daime', in accordance with the 'line of the Mestre'. This is applied even to the bodies of adepts seeking them to make them capable of transporting themselves to the 'realm of the higher astral plane'. That is, it puts them 'inside the power', it makes them 'children of the power'. This is because in order to obtain the 'true' Daime and to transport the adept to the world of the 'astral plane', that is, in order to 'get more' out of the technique, it is necessary that all the prescribed procedures be rigorously obeyed. Another way of classifying the corporeal techniques is to consider the way they are learned and transmitted, which in the *Daimista* system has two vectors: 'drink Daime and pay attention to the hymns'. However, these two vectors demand a set of techniques that establish the religion as a 'way of life', as Mauss (1974a) would say.

On going through the list of the 'biographical recapitulation of corporeal techniques' presented by the author, we perceive how much the *Daimista* system provides the most important techniques, beginning with the 'techniques of birth and obstetrics', as we shall see regarding the use of Daime during pregnancy and birth. 'Techniques of childhood': 'at birth take a little spoonful of Daime', not to mention the 'indoctrination', this, strictly speaking, goes on throughout a lifetime. 'Techniques of adolescence', where perhaps the most important applies to girls, given that control over their sex life is part of the public domain, insofar as the ritual includes a space set aside for the 'virgins'. 'Techniques of dreaming, sleep and wakefulness', for the *Daimista* system, in granting visions the same ontological status as dreams, re-orders attitudes with regard to the act of dreaming which take them into the sphere of sacred, and thus true, experiences.

There are 'Techniques of movement', (to concentrate, to dance) and 'Techniques of body care' (to scrub, to wash, to abstain from sexual relations) in which, in the first two items, we must consider the 'vegetal body' (the ingredients of the tea) and the human body. There are also 'Techniques of consumption', mandating the eating of light foods, and abstention from alcoholic beverages. For example, during the *feitio*, or making of the Daime, to consume only sweet manioc without salt accompanied by lemon balm tea, and, above all, 'to drink Daime'. We could even add corporeal techniques applied to the imagination properly speaking, to control the thoughts, not to think useless thoughts, that is, outside the prescriptions of the doctrine; 'to pay attention to the hymnals', besides allowing oneself to be subjected to frequent and systematic sessions of singing and listening to the hymns, in an 'altered state of consciousness', where the 'hymn is something that is fixed in the memory and never leaves'.

Let us see how these techniques are applied in the group of Daime *trabalhos*. We would like the reader to keep in mind, however, the notion of corporeal technique, without our mentioning it at each point where it appears, since such a procedure would be extremely repetitive and, it seems to us, unnecessary. The following diagram presents the scheme of body techniques applied to the human and plant dimensions seeking to attain or constitute the 'divine body'.

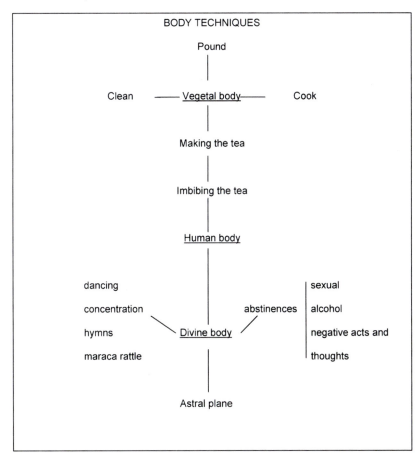

Sacred space: the forest, the hall and the *casa do feitio*

The main sacred space for *Daimistas* is the Amazon forest, the 'woods', source of raw material for the tea they ritually imbibe. Another space is the center (the see) which, in the case of Eclectic Center for Currents of the Universal Light or CECLU, is subdivided into three liturgical spaces: the hall, the *casa do feitio* ('house for making Daime'), and the secondary forest in the back of the center's grounds. Each year the center pays homage to the Queen of the Forest in this space in a *trabalho* celebrated on August 15. It is a *trabalho* of 'concentration' and seeks to recall the 'origin of the doctrine', and for that reason it is done in the woods. In the house for making the tea, only the *trabalhos* related to making the tea take place. In the hall, all the other *trabalhos* and activities are done: dances, concentrations, 'masses', baptisms, delivering the star, wakes, birthday parties, evangelical school for the children, meetings of the Youth Group called 'Messengers of the Queen' and the General Assembly.

The architecture of the hall was defined by Irineu, highlighting two features: it is oriented to the rising sun and has no complete walls. Thus, the walls are about 120 cm high, allowing wide internal and external visibility. The only complete wall is located to the west of the entrance. Let us begin with that. At the front of the temple are the chairs of the leader (north) and his wife (south). Decorating this wall is the Brazilian flag, 2 m × 1.5 m in size, and on either side, are two photos of Mestre Irineu. In one of them, he appears from the waist up, wearing a straw hat and holding a staff almost as tall as him. The other is a retouched photo showing only his face, a technique that is very widespread in the interior of Brazil (reproductions of these photos of Irineu are found in almost all *Daimista* homes). Then there are framed photos of Mestres Regino, Virgílio and Francisca (all of CECLU, all deceased). Behind this wall, there is the 'little house of the Daime', with two side windows, for the purpose of serving the Daime to the line of women, to the south, and the line of men, to the north. To the front of the leader's chair there is the dance square, where the east and south sides are occupied by rows of women, and the west and north sides are occupied by the men. In the center of the square, there is the *mesa* ('table'), the name given to the altar. The place for the *mesa* and the rows are marked off on the floor of the hall.

Elements of the sacred: the *mesa*, the chair, the uniform, the maraca rattle and the *hinário*

The *mesa* is considered the source for receiving and transmitting the energy currents from the astral plane. Along with the leader, it constitutes a mechanism capable of capturing and distributing the power of the astral plane between the brotherhood and the cosmos. The set comprised of table-leader-brotherhood is one of the ritual mechanisms which generate power.

During the dancing rituals, the table is not physically occupied by anyone. In the case of CECLU, three chairs are placed around it. The one with the highest back is considered to be spiritually occupied by Mestre Irineu, and the other two, by Mestres Virgílio and Francisca. In concentration *trabalhos*, eight chairs are placed around the table and occupied by male disciples, chosen by the leader. In the 'masses', four chairs are placed around the table, and occupied to the east and south by women and to the west and north by men.

The *ritual objects* that are on the table are: at the center, the *Santo Cruzeiro* ('Holy Cross'), also known as the 'Caravaca Cross'. Next to the *Santo Cruzeiro*, there is an image of Our Lady of the Immaculate Conception and a jar of flowers, symbolizing the mission, which is considered a garden, whose flowers are the followers of the religion. On the altar, there is also the Holy Bible, and a glass of water symbolizing aid to spirits in need, and three lit candles that represent the Holy Trinity.

The *chair* is the symbol of power of the leader. Expressions such as 'to take the chair of the Mestre' refer to conflicts of the brotherhood with the leader. There are various chairs that symbolize the power of the chief. In the case of CECLU, three of them stay in their places around the table (physically empty) symbolizing, we repeat, Mestre Irineu and Mestres Virgílio and Francisca. Outside the dance square, there are the chairs of the leader and his wife. It is from this chair that it is expected that the leader will guide the *trabalho*, facilitating the full manifestation of 'light' and 'force'.

The 'uniform' consists of two outfits: the 'official uniform' also called the 'white uniform' and the 'unofficial uniform' or 'blue uniform'. The first consists of a white suit for the men, with the Star of Solomon on the lapel that has a crescent moon in the center over which there is an eagle poised for flight, and, on the shoulder there are several thin, colored ribbons draped, symbolizing the forces of the astral plane.

For the women, the white uniform is composed of pleated skirt, long-sleeved blouse, and, over the white skirt, there is a skirtlet of approximately 60 cm, also pleated and green in color, symbolizing the forest. Wide green ribbons cross the women's chest, forming a Y-shape; on the right side there is the Star of Solomon and to the left, there is a rose for the women who have already been sexually 'initiated', and a palm-leaf for the girls and virgins. On the right shoulder, there are colored ribbons. On the head, a rhinestone crown with white and silver sequins that symbolize the Queen.

The blue uniform used by the men consists of navy-blue pants, long-sleeved white shirt, white socks and shoes, navy-blue tie and the Star of Solomon. The uniform of the women is a pleated navy-blue skirt, short-sleeved white blouse on the pocket of which the initials CRF (in the Center for Christian Illumination Universal Light or CICLU) are embroidered in navy-blue, meaning *Casa da Rainha da Floresta* (House of the Queen of the Forest) and, in CECLU, only the initials of the center over the Star of Solomon, in addition to the 'rose' or the 'palm-leaf'. The blue uniform also includes a navy-blue bowtie, white socks and shoes.

The *maraca rattle* is a musical instrument and a spiritual weapon. It marks the beat and summons up force for the *trabalho*; just like the hymns, through guided human will, it intensifies and makes the force vibrate, potentializing spiritual power. It is used in all the dance rituals (Figure 1).

The *hinário* ('hymnal') is received directly from the *astral* ('astral plane'), for it is considered that in the spiritual world there is a *linha* ('lineage') of *trabalhos* whose teachings are transmitted through hymns, and that this lineage of *trabalhos* was delivered by the Queen of the Forest to Irineu Serra. Not all followers receive hymns. It is possible that not even the leader is the owner of an *hinário*, for example, João Nogueira, President of CECLU and Leôncio Gomes (Irineu's widow's uncle, ex-leader of the CICLU, already deceased).

Figure 1. Dancing with a maraca (copyright Flavio Lopes).

To receive the hymns, the adept does not have to imbibe Daime; however, they say that they feel as if they had 'taken Daime', they feel themselves to be on the astral plane. They could be at home, in the street, and very often, sleeping, when they wake up with the hymn or a dream of having received it, which could be either through hearing or seeing the hymn being delivered by an entity or even visualized as texts 'floating in the air', or printed on a sheet of paper.

A set of hymns received by the same adept constitutes an *hinário*. The pattern of the hymns and the process of 'receiving' them was established by Irineu based on his own experience 'receiving' his book of hymns, the '*Cruzeiro*'. The rhythms of the music are the waltz, the mazurka, and the march. The themes also are modeled on the *hinário* of Irineu. On receiving a hymn, the adept must show it to the leader who evaluates whether the hymn is consistent with – that is, in the lineage of – the *hinários*. The hymn is presented to the brotherhood and tested for later singing in *trabalhos*. This is called 'instructing' or 'educating' the hymn for the process of getting the melody and the words of the hymn right.

As Dona Percília, who was from the time of Irineu, told us, 'in the *hinário* is our life, our sentiments'. Indeed, the institutionalization of the *hinário*, like the entire *Daimista* system, is a collective project. In the specific *trabalho* of the *hinários*, the first followers of Irineu who 'received' hymns stand out in terms of their importance. These first *hinários* were composed in dialogue with the '*Cruzeiro*'. Those which came after, also have their reference in the '*Cruzeiro*' and in the *hinário* of these first followers. They constitute the model, they amplify the multiple senses present in the '*Cruzeiro*', they explain and unfold themes. They construct and reinforce the legitimacy of Irineu as *Mestre Ensinador* ('Master Teacher').

The *hinário* of these first followers is today called the '*Hinário* of the Dead', not only in reference to the fact that their composers are deceased, but also keeping the sense of tradition.

Besides their ritual use, where they summon the astral force, the hymns are part of the everyday life of the followers, keeping them 'connected to the power'. In *Daimista* homes, the hymns are often reproduced through tape recordings or sung live by one of the members of the household. They are highly respected messages in daily life, for if a hymn comes to mind associated to an event or person, the adept is attentive to decipher the meaning of the occurrence. They are copied by hand into notebooks and practiced outside the ritual contexts properly speaking. During *hinário* rehearsals, Daime is often served. The rehearsal is done for the purpose of memorizing the melody and words of the hymn. Singing it constantly in different situations helps to memorize it.

The 'receiving' of hymns usually is accompanied by physical sensations described as 'agony' or the sensation of urgency, a kind of imminence in looking for pen and paper to record it, or even an effort to fix it in the memory. As we have said, the hymn can be received during dreams and the person wakes up right after and 'holds onto' the hymn, that is, keeps it in his memory. It could happen that the person remembers it on waking up the next day, or even that he forgets it and only remembers it days later, usually as the result of processes of association. The hymn also has the function of announcing things to come and guarding against evil. As to their interpretation, it is understood that the hymn speaks for itself, revealing itself fully in the ritual context, that is, within the precepts and under the Force and Light of Daime.

The formulas for opening and closing the *trabalhos* vary according to the ritual: the 'mass', concentration, *feitio* or *bailado* ('dance'). For example, the *bailado* begins with the two hymns of the '*Cruzeiro*' chosen by Irineu for this purpose of 'opening the *trabalhos*'. It can still vary, although within the same pattern, depending on the leader; however, the general pattern is the following for the opening: 'Praying to God the Father that He may Grant us the Redemptive Currents of Goodness and a Spark of His Holy Love, this *trabalho* is considered open: concentrate!'

To close, the leader pronounces the following formula: 'In the name of God the Father, of the Lady Virgin Mother, of Jesus Christ the Redeemer, of All the Divine Beings of the Heavenly Court, and, with the Orders of the Chief Empire King Juramidã, this *trabalho* is now closed. My brothers and my sisters, praise be to God and the Most Holy Virgin Mother, among all us here on earth.' To which all respond: 'So be it' (Figure 2).

The *feitio* of the holy Daime – the gathering, transmutation and the offering

We have said that the rituals of Daime are generically designated as '*trabalhos*'. They may also be called *serviços* ('services') by the veteran *ayahuasqueros* ('ayahuasca users'). The *feitio* ('making') is the process of producing the Daime, which is begun by the '*trabalho* in the forest'. It is where 'everything begins'. It is divided into four main parts: gathering, cleaning, macerating and cooking of the vine.

The forest is essential to Daimista activity: from it the raw material for ayahuasca is collected in its natural state. (The plants are also cultivated, but the production is insufficient

Figure 2. The Daime ritual (copyright Flavio Lopes).

for the center's needs.) Also, the origin of the cult and its cultural traits derive from the forest. The forest is understood as a sacred space populated by spiritual beings that protect all life-forms. In this symbolic, spiritual space, the female figure has major importance: it was the Queen of the Forest who delegated the mission to Mestre Irineu, and the forest was the stage for his initiatory apprenticeship.

To go to the forest takes on a special meaning. More than the encounter of urban activity with rural, it is an encounter with the original source of all *trabalhos*. Thus, to go inside this sacred space, the group must be prepared, mentally, materially, and spiritually; they must know how to invoke the permission and protection of the divine beings that are 'dominant' in that realm, and have the sensibility and the skills necessary to know how to find the leaf and the vine among the many varieties of plants. One's thought must remain on the good and on the activity that they are doing, with focus and joy. There can be no disharmony in thought, words, or actions. The integration of man with himself and with nature in the fullest possible way is what is sought.

The *trabalho* of the forest is directed by the 'Commander of the woods' who, in the case of CECLU is Valdeci Rapcham, also the 'Commander of the pot and the *feitio*',[1] recognized by the group as the best woodsman the center has. The rest of the group is comprised of various members, always men, depending on the availability of each man. The first trip into the forest, as a member of the group, constitutes a *rite of passage*. If successful, the

---

1. The title has to do with the fact that the production of Daime is done under his direction during the whole process from the gathering of the leaf and vine in the forest, through the 'preparation' and bottling of Daime.

person acquires the maturity and the confidence of the group to go further into the secrets of the journey. We thus have the veterans, who are capable of going alone into the forest without getting lost, and the novices, who are always accompanied by a veteran.

For the 'novice' who is normally used to urban life, the activity is not easy: going through the forest off the man-made paths and trails, facing sleepless nights, eating cold meals (sandwiches, fruits, toasted manioc flour), braving thorns, holes, rains, slides and falls, traversing long stretches with heavy sacks on their backs. Confronting one's own fears of animals and the unknown is, in a way, an experience that is totally different from daily urban living. This, in itself, is sufficient to restructure the individual's convictions and turn him into a social being linked to the category in which he is inserted and recognized, a 'man of the Daime'. This self-reconstruction, though very complex, can be illustrated by stories of novices who, after traveling in the forest, find it very strange, for example, to have to sleep on the ground in the bus station of a city of the interior, together with drunks, beggars and dogs; one man refused to eat toasted manioc flour in front of people in a small frontier bar. Such sensations of strangeness are common to the city dweller, but are considered vulgar and improper by a 'man of the Daime' or a 'man of the woods', who require, for their 'work of the woods', simplicity, humility, strength, courage, obedience, purity, joy, and goodwill.

While gathering the material in the forest it is common to sing the hymns that constitute the doctrinal foundation of the Church, particularly those that make reference to ayahuasca, such as 'Jagube Blossom' and 'I will Sing'. The hymn 'Jagube Blossom' is particularly important. While the men are on their journey in the woods, several brothers get together to prepare the *feitio* hall. When the washing and ordering of the '*feitio* house' is complete, the center's main hall is prepared for the cleaning of the leaves. There, improvised tables will be surrounded by the women during the work of leaf cleaning, on the day established for the *feitio* (Figure 3).

The *feitio* takes place on the weekend nearest the last new moon of the month. The cleaning of the Jagube and the Chacrona are done on Saturday afternoon. On Sunday, the pounding and cooking are done, and any remaining leaves are cleaned, either by the women or the men. The leaves are cleaned without water by passing the hand over each one of them, aiming to remove any residue left by insects, as well as material and symbolic impurities, for, as Mestre Virgílio explained, 'the whole process has its secret: in cleaning the leaves the women at the same time separate the good from the bad'. The Jagube is cleaned, also instrumentally and symbolically, exclusively by the men, who use small wooden knives to scrape the earth and other detritus from the vine.

On Sunday, at five in the morning, the men meet at the *feitio* house to begin the pounding and the final preparations for the brewing of the drink. While one man buys sweet cassava – which, cooked without salt, will be the only food of the day – others prepare the lemon balm tea that will be drunk in the course of the *trabalho*, and still others wash the buckets that will be used in the cooking of the Daime. According to Mestre Virgílio,

> The process is to go to the fire three times. Because everything has meaning. Three times because there are entities represented in the heavens by the sun, moon, stars; and on the earth, by the earth, the wind and the sea. These three beget us, raise

Figure 3. The *feitio* (preparation) house (copyright Flavio Lopes).

us, supply us, and provide us with everything: comprehension, understanding, wisdom, reasoning, loyalty, honesty, which are the spiritual gifts.[2]

The ritual of beating begins with the imbibing of Daime and with the hymns used to 'open the *trabalhos*' which are the 'Sun, Moon, Star' and 'I Must Love That Light', both by Mestre Irineu, continuing with hymns from the other *hinários* of the brotherhood. The group begins the pounding while others cook the cassava and prepare to boil the Daime, heating up water. When there is a sufficient quantity of macerated vine, the vine and the leaf are placed in the pot in alternating layers, and the cooking of the ingredients begins. This whole process is done under the 'light of the Daime', for, to participate in the preparation, one must commune with the drink while being under its effect. At the pot remain the 'commander of the pot' and a helper, in a *trabalho* that extends for more than ten hours.

The order of the day is to converse only about subjects which are pertinent to the event, aiming to guarantee a result that depends on the good behavior of all, as Mestre Virgílio, of CECLU, explained:

Here, for us to make a good drink, one must maintain sexual abstinence and mental hygiene, do good, prepare oneself at home… Doing it with this perfection in diet and intention, a divine body comes out. Otherwise, a vegetal body comes out. Daime is not a drug. Made with perfection, that drink contains the divine essence, a spiritual body. When we drink it, the divine body acts in us.

2. All quotations from participants are taken from original fieldwork interviews.

Outside the *feitio* hall, the women accompany the chorus of chants sung by the men, seeking to help them in the exhausting work of the pounding. Although the beating and the cooking are separate, both represent arduous tasks, for the beating goes on for more than seven hours, which makes the mallet get heavier and heavier, blistering the hands of the novices, forming calluses and abrasions of the skin. In the pot, the intense heat of the stove is added to the concentration necessary for there to be no errors or problems whatsoever that might detract from the quality of the Daime. However, despite all the sacrifice, the preparation is presented to the brotherhood as a true festival. Incidentally, all the liturgical rites of the Daime, with the exception of the 'mass', which is a mourning ritual, seem to have a dimension of pleasure and festivity. One interviewee explained to us: 'the doctrine of Mestre Irineu, in my opinion, is a recapitulation of all that Christ taught, but in a way that gives us pleasure, through singing, dancing and having the *"mirações"* [visionary experiences]'.

From the *feitio* comes the 'sacred drink' that is the fundamental basis of the spiritual *trabalhos* done by the center. The happiness and satisfaction are visible in all those participating, and the sacrifices are small in comparison with the meaning represented by the process of preparation.

To those who participate in the work, particularly the men who do the greater part of it, and more so those who are able to stay at their posts, the work represents a conquest. The main and visible goal is obtaining the Daime; however, in the process of producing the Daime 'spiritual gifts' are necessarily produced as well, such as love, humility, honesty, loyalty, firmness, obedience, endurance. When the Daime is 'offered' during the *feitio*, it is an occasion of great rejoicing as the 'new Daime' is presented for appreciation and proof of its quality.

From the internal, personal point of view, each one of the participants 'suffers' or 'enjoys' his own experience of an altered state of consciousness in the form of the *miração*, which carries initiates to the 'spiritual realm'. According to Mestre Virgílio, 'the *miração* is like an illustration, a lesson in pictures. The *miração*, besides being a caress of the spiritual mother to bring happiness to our heart, also, within that happiness, awakens our timeless archive.'

All of this contributes to the satisfaction that the fraternity expresses in finding itself inserted in a specific, virtual world, which however has become concrete, established by a peculiar human grouping, with its own language, ideas, culture and thought complexes, which represent what the group understands as 'divine harmony'. The experience of ecstatic, shamanic flight that authorizes them to pray the 'Our Father' in all the rites, saying: '*let us go* to thy kingdom'. In fact, each finalized *feitio* guarantees the 'vehicle' of transport to the 'astral realm'.

Having finished the work of the *feitio*, one often sees the Daimistas joined together around their leader. There they converse pleasantly like one big family, with games, stories, jokes, and accounts of experiences obtained in the spiritual life. Simplicity structures this social interaction. It is this simplicity which configures social relations amongst all. It marks the social condition and the language, replete with entrances and exits from what is sacred and what is profane, reinforced by the chanting of hymns in the demonstration of some teaching. This connotes a very distinct specificity for the members of the group, and which appears strange and even incomprehensible for those who are not adepts. As the 'Jagube Blossom' hymn says, 'Not being in this line, I will never come to know'. This recognition among equals, 'all simple and humble', reinforces even more the internal sociability of the brotherhood.

The *bailado*, the *concentração* and the *missa*

Another type of *trabalho* is the *bailado* ('dance'), also called the *festejo* ('celebration'). In it, men and women face each other in rows separated by gender, forming a rectangle around the 'table' and dance in movements to the left and to the right to the rhythm of waltzes, marches and *mazurcas*, for, as we said, these are the musical genres corresponding to the hymns. At the same time that they dance, all dressed in uniforms they sing from the *hinário* chosen for the *trabalho* being performed, in sequence from the first to the last hymn. They are accompanied by the sound of the rattles shaken by each participant in the dance.

The *trabalho de bailado* begins with the recitation of the rosary. On the third mystery, there begins the imbibing of the Daime, done in separate lines of men and women. The drink is always served by a man, the 'dispatcher of the Daime'. After drinking the Daime, each one returns to his/her place in the hall. The next act is the dance properly speaking, which is begun by a person who leads the singing of the *hinário*, who might be the 'owner' of the *hinário* or someone who is appointed to do so.

All the dances, we repeat, begin with the two hymns of the 'Cruzeiro' called the 'hymns for opening the *trabalhos*' (the 'Sun, Moon, Star' and 'I Must Love That Light'), unless the *hinário* of the *bailado* is the 'Cruzeiro' itself or features the rituals of 'confession', about which we shall have more to say further on.

In between the singing of the hymns, there are call-and-response cries of 'Viva!' (Hurray!) led by the guide himself or some brother designated for this interjection. The function of the '*viva!*' is varied: exaltation, recognition, vitality, bringing spiritual force, and the possibility of rest for the members of the dance, because they are shouted at each interval of six hymns, which allows for pauses. The '*viva!*' even has a political function in reinforcing the authority of the leaders in the phrase, '*Viva* our President!' This latter function is more evident in periods of crisis, or 'rebelliousness of the brotherhood'. In general, the pronouncements are the following: '*Viva* the Eternal Father, *viva* the Queen of the Forest, *viva* Jesus Christ the Redeemer, *viva* the Patriarch Saint Joseph, *viva* our Empire Chief King Juramidã, *viva* all Divine beings, *viva* the Holy "Cruzeiro", *viva* the whole brotherhood, *viva* our President'. In CECLU three more '*viva*'s are added: '*viva* all of humanity, *viva* the dignitaries of this house', and the saint or person celebrating a birthday; frequently, however, there are two more '*viva*'s – '*viva* our Vice-President! *Viva* our Vice-President!' to which all respond, '*viva!*'

More or less in the middle of the *hinário*, there is an interval where men and women, in the CECLU, mingle in conversation (in the CICLU they stay separated). At the end of the interval, which generally lasts about 30 minutes, there is a call to re-initiate the singing of the hymns, a moment when the dose of the Daime is repeated for those who wish. The dance goes on until the end of the *hinário*. This done, the dance goes on to the singing of the last 13 hymns of the 'Cruzeiro', which were selected by Irineu for this purpose. These hymns are considered a summary of the 'Cruzeiro' and, among the Daimistas, they are called the 'Crown' of the 'Cruzeiro', referring to its apex, its 'crowning'. The *bailado* may also be closed with 'crowns' from other *hinários*, generally of the leaders. The *trabalho de bailado* ends with the praying of three 'Our Father's and three 'Hail Mary's followed by the formula for closing the *trabalhos* which is spoken by the leader.

The time that the *bailado* lasts (generally, it is begun at eight o'clock at night) is determined by the length of the *hinário*, and frequently it goes on for a long time, sometimes until dawn. Its scheduling follows a fixed calendar, which ends in the *Bailado* done on January 5, in the celebration of the Magi Kings; it includes Holy Week, the cycle of June festivals, the day of Our Lady of the Conception, December 8, and Christmas. The opening of the cycle of *trabalhos* takes place during the first *trabalho* of concentration of the year, which occurs on January 15. There are also *bailados* to celebrate the dates of birth and death of the leaders. The dances with fixed dates are also called 'official' *trabalhos* and require the use of the 'white' uniform, also known as the 'official' uniform.

The *trabalho de concentração* ('concentration *trabalho*') is done twice a month, on the 15th and 30th. It begins with the ingestion of Daime and the reading of the Service Decree, which was written by Irineu Serra. The concentration is marked by immobility: men and women in separate rows, facing each other, remain immobile, seated, and with eyes shut for more or less an hour-and-a-half. In this period, often the leader makes use of speech to sermonize, giving instructions for the concentration, admonitions, and counsel of a moral or religious order. The concentration sessions are also used frequently for the purpose of 'adjusting the brotherhood'. During the concentration, as reinforcement to the 'instruction', various hymns are sung which are chosen by the leader 'in accordance with the situation predominating in the brotherhood: sickness, disharmony, rebelliousness'. On those occasions he will then choose hymns of 'comfort, firmness, equilibrium, cure or discipline'. He can lead the hymns himself or put someone in charge to do so. To close, three 'Our Father's, three 'Hail Mary's and one 'Hail Holy Queen' [a Roman Catholic prayer to the Virgin Mary] are recited, and the leader pronounces the formula for closing the *trabalho*. This is followed by announcements of events for the month, requests for help with the operations of the church, or even reminding the tardy to contribute.

The *missa* ('mass') is always held on the first Sunday of each month and irregularly, as on the occasion of a death, the 'passage' of some brother, or on the anniversary of the passage: the seventh day, month and year. The mass is the 'rite of the dead', always held in benefit of all those who have made the passage to the afterlife, principally 'the souls most in need, those who have no-one to pray for them', following the orders of Mestre Irineu. It begins with the reciting of the rosary and the chanting of ten hymns, selected by Irineu for this purpose. The one who leads the prayer is always female, and the one who leads the hymn is considered to be the celebrant of the mass, and can be a man or woman. Each hymn sung is followed by three 'Our Father's and three 'Hail Mary's, besides a small supplication from the Roman Catholic tradition that goes: 'Oh, my Jesus, forgive us our sins, free us from the fires of Hell, take all souls to heaven, and help principally those who are most in need'. Before singing the eighth hymn, 'O My Eternal Father', the four persons seated at the table light the candles and stand up. At the end of the hymn they blow out the candles and sit back down. The mass ends with a 'Hail Holy Queen' and the offering of the 'mass of the month' to all the 'disincarnated', those in need, followed by the reading of the names of dead people, whose kin and friends requested that the mass be offered to them.

Uniforms are not worn, nor is Daime served for the mass. The scene is composed of the 'table' where the *Cruzeiro* is, that is, the 'Caravaca Cross', two jars of flowers, a lit candle, and four more candles placed horizontally in the form of a cross. These candles will be lit and kept in this form during the chanting of the hymn mentioned above. The candles point to the four places at the table that will be occupied by those who will make up the table for the *trabalho*. Two places are occupied by men and two places are set aside for women.

The awarding of the star, the baptism, the pledge, the delivery of the *trabalhos* and confession

The awarding of the star and baptism are ceremonies that take place at the end of the official *bailados*, for example, on the Feast of Saint John, Our Lady of the Conception, and Christmas. The awarding of the star only takes place in CECLU, since it was established by Mestre Virgílio. It consists of delivering the star emblem that those who wear uniforms use on the lapel of the official uniform, also called the white uniform; it is also used on the blue uniform.

The awarding of the star complements the 'receiving of the uniform', an act that commits the follower to the doctrine. In the ceremony of the awarding of the star the emblem is delivered by the leader, while those who are in uniform and the assistants chant a hymn from one of the *hinários* of Mestre Virgílio, 'The Little Branch of my Thought', in which there is the hymn for awarding the star called 'Star'. The second time he says, 'I deliver this star', the one who delivers the star places it on the uniform of the one who is receiving and the assistants continue chanting the hymn without interruption until the last star is delivered. At the end, the people who have received the star are greeted by the leader and by the other people.

The baptism of a child or adult necessarily includes the presence of the godfather and godmother plus the parents, in the case of children. As in the awarding of the star several people can be baptized at the same time. The ritual consists of the leader placing a small quantity of salt in the mouth of the person being baptized, followed by several drops of Daime, and the spilling of a small quantity of water over the head of the neophyte, while saying the following: 'As Saint John baptized Jesus in the waters of the Jordan River, so I baptize you [name of the person being baptized] to be a Christian'. The brotherhood and assistants pray out loud, forming a harmonic background of one Our Father, followed by one Hail Mary, repeated until the end of the ceremony, which is closed with one Hail Holy Queen.

People are not invited to be baptized (it is considered that, having already been baptized in other churches, these baptisms are valid); rather, it only occurs as a function of the spontaneous desire of adults. The children, generally, are brought to be baptized by their parents. Often, then, there is double baptism among the children, in the Catholic Church and in the Daime.

There is no rite for the pledge or delivery and, in this sense, it is very esoteric; nevertheless we think it is important to highlight it, because it has to do with the initiatory passage in which the adept adheres to and deepens his commitment with the power. It is an individual act that affects those who have incorporated the mission, being recognized as 'children of this house', 'children of this power', 'children of Juramidá and the Queen'. One perceives that the system demands the commitment of the follower which is expressed in such terms as firmness, pledge and surrender. Thus, as we become more familiar with them, we perceive that the *hinários* contain pledges, also called surrenders. In our view, this 'passage' in fact keeps the system functioning. It takes place at the beginning of the conversion, shaping it and, after moments of crisis, marking the renewal of the system by the follower, reaffirming him to be 'together with the power'.

The 'delivery of the *trabalhos*' is a ceremony held at the end of the *trabalho de bailado* dedicated to the Three Kings, celebrated on January 5 (generally Daimista celebrations occur on the eve of each holy day). This date closes the calendar of *trabalhos* of the previous year. At the beginning of this dance, there is the 'confession' and at the end, there is the 'delivery of the *trabalhos*' when the followers go in line to the leader (or to someone appointed by him) and 'deliver' the '*trabalho* of the year' through a formula: 'I received the *trabalho* of the year in peace, in peace I deliver it with no alteration in my life. Prayers prayed and counted, or prayers prayed and not counted.' Alteration is a reference to possible suspensions. The prayers are the total amount of prayers recited during the year. These prayers are a 'task' that has the character of penitence that the leader attributes to all on this occasion. The penitence can be to pray 25,000 prayers, for example, with each 'prayer' consisting of one Our Father, one Hail Mary, and one Hail Holy Queen.

The 'confession' is done during the dances of the day of the Kings, the Feast of Saint John, and the Day of Our Lady of the Conception; in the CICLU it also occurs on Christmas because there, on that date, the *hinário* of the dance is the '*Cruzeiro*'. Thus, the ceremony of confession is related to the *hinário* of Mestre Irineu. Specifically, it refers to the hymn number 17, titled 'Hymn of the Confession'. If the '*Cruzeiro*' is sung outside the dates mentioned above, this hymn is suppressed, unless there is an express decision by the leader, if he needs to settle disharmonies among the brotherhood. At the singing of the hymn of confession, all those present, in uniform or not (all participants) hold a lit candle. Whoever wishes may kneel. Confession is done in thought, directly to the divine beings. It is considered that the hymn itself, on being sung, realizes the confession. A veteran *ayahuasquero* told us, 'the hymn of the confession is heavy, it is beautiful, and it is good'. The confession done on the day of Kings, which closes the annual calendar of *trabalhos*, allows the adept to begin the year 'light', purified of his faults.

The healing, birthday, birth and death *trabalhos*

In the healing *trabalhos* at most nine people, chosen by the leader,[3] get together in the center or in the house of the sick person, who may be absent, and the *trabalho* is done on

---

3. Chosen from among the people who are '...firm, well-balanced in order not to vacillate, because the Daime requests firmness, and for the healing *trabalho* it has to be done with a full cup, it may even be necessary to repeat the dose, and even more because generally, the *General* is selected, which is high-degree Daime...'

his behalf. If the sick person is present, he also drinks Daime, preferably a full cup, but if he is not able to take a larger quantity, he should drink at least one spoonful of Daime.

Along with the ill person, those selected for the healing *trabalho* drink Daime. The cure proceeds with the opening formula, followed by a concentration in which they seek through 'shamanic flight' to find the origin of the illness. Meeting up with it, they enter into 'shamanic combat' accompanied by requests and pleas in their thought, for the ill person, seeking the necessary transformation for the cure to be brought about. In this phase, hymns selected by the leader are sung, and the leader may also request that the brothers sing hymns of their choosing which are considered appropriate for the occasion. If someone 'receives' information regarding the sickness, and if the 'power' allows that it be communicated to the ill person, he will be informed; if not, he will only receive guidance on how to proceed in order to be cured, if he has this merit.

The *trabalho de cura* ends with three 'Our Father's, three 'Hail Mary's and one 'Hail Holy Queen'. This *trabalho* is done only once, although another *trabalho* can be scheduled in case of necessity. During the series of illnesses that led to the death of Mestre Virgílio, for example, a *trabalho* of this type was done for nine consecutive days.

Another type of healing *trabalho* is the '*trabalho* of the nine crosses', also called the 'cross *trabalho*' or the 'table *trabalho*'. Unlike the previously described *trabalho*, this is done without Daime. In it, nine people hold a lit candle in the right hand and a small wooden cross in the left hand. This *trabalho* can be done in the presence or not of the sick person. It has the character of exorcism, because it seeks to free the person of bad spirits, of witchcraft and obsessions.

The *trabalho* begins with a request for permission from the Mestre to carry it out, followed by the prayer 'Hail Mary', and the prayer that is specific to the *trabalho* called 'Prayer to free a person from bad spirits', which can be found in several editions of the 'Caravaca Cross Book of Prayers'. The *trabalho* should begin on a Wednesday, and is repeated for three consecutive days, always at the same time, generally at eight o'clock at night. In CECLU this *trabalho* is done very rarely.

The anniversaries of birth and death of the leaders are celebrated with danced *trabalhos*. The anniversaries of the birth and passage of Mestre Irineu are celebrated in all the centers which derive from the mythic system of Juramidã. Besides that, each center celebrates the birth and *passage* of their respective leaders. The anniversaries of other brothers are also celebrated. The most common is for all the anniversaries of the month to be commemorated at the end of the dances which are already scheduled on the calendar.

Depending on the importance of the brother, however, it can happen that his birthday is celebrated in a specific *trabalho*, when his *hinário* is consequently sung. Or, it could even happen that the *hinário* of the birthday celebrant be set aside to be sung on the celebration coinciding with his birthday. Or, that the birthday celebrant is not the owner of the *hinário*, in which case some other *hinário* is set aside for the occasion. On the occasions of birthdays, at the end of the dance, 'happy birthdays' are sung at length, besides scattered hymns. Cakes, juices, and soft drinks are served. Birthdays can also be held at the home of the birthday celebrant, with Daime or without Daime, according to the wish of the person celebrating a birthday and the authorization of the leader. In the same way, in the domestic sphere, one can also inaugurate a home when someone moves into a new home, or when a person believes that a *trabalho* is necessary to transform the negative energies of the house, in which case, a '*trabalho* for the cleansing of the home' is held.

Other uses for the holy Daime: giving birth, burns, wounds, diverse evils, talisman

The Santo Daime, besides being utilized by pregnant women in their normal *trabalhos* of the church, is also used as protection and as a facilitator for giving birth. In general, the Daimista women give birth to children at home, although they can go to the hospital if they prefer. During births, at home or in the hospital, they are advised to take Daime, which they normally do. At birth the children receive a drop of Daime in their mouth, and can continue to receive it during their early lives at the discretion of their parents.

Daime can even be used, in small daily doses, as treatment of some sicknesses, fevers, headaches, and diarrheas, for it is believed that if the person needs to be cleaned out, Daime makes him or her evacuate and vomit and, in the case of vomiting and diarrhea type illnesses, Daime cures them. In addition, it is used on wounds or burns, and, according to witnesses, it has a notable healing power. Moreover, Mestre Irineu counseled that one should take a spoonful of Daime tea every day before breakfast, to prevent sicknesses. When the quantity of Daime to be taken is 'two fingers' deep or more, a 'diet' is required, including abstinence from sex and alcoholic beverages, and preparing oneself physically and mentally through diets, prayers and good thoughts, for three days before and three days after taking Daime. Finally, Daime is even a talisman for personal protection, of the home and while on trips.

Santo Daime as a talisman

Daime constitutes the material basis for the religious life of the group and can be seen as one among numerous products of the Amazon forest. Endowed with peculiar characteristics, in the subsystems that we have investigated, it is far from a profane product or piece of merchandise, and rather is part of a broader and deeper notion concerning 'non-capitalist' forms of production, which are identified by ethnography as an archaic form of contract and exchange. Exchange and contract of men amongst themselves and with the divinities, whose identities in this case are the 'Empire Chief King Juramidã' and his female complement, the 'Queen of the Forest'.

In discussing the notions of archaism to explain the *principle of reciprocity*, Lévi-Strauss (1982) clarifies that we can consider an institution archaic by virtue of its being judged obsolete or by virtue of its essentialness. The 'gift exchange' is an example of the latter. In primitive societies, it is a *total social fact*, in the Maussian sense. It involves objects, and legal, political, economic, aesthetic, and religious values.

Daime is the same ayahuasca used secularly as a psychoactive stimulant, which operates, in our understanding, by accelerating and diversifying the imaginative powers of man, his symbolic production. It thus can be a source of knowledge and creative power. Transformed from a stimulant to a cultural sign, it operates the passage from nature to culture, flourishing institutionally. It is thus one of the products that have come from the forest and gone to the city, along with cashew nuts and rubber latex, but, different from these others, ayahuasca was inserted into another logic of exchange and contract, the gift exchange, while the others were subject to the logic of monetary exchange and barter, the principles of which are the same as those of merchandise. Ayahuasca is inserted into other spheres of application: curing and pleasure of the body and spirit, as well as life-counseling for, as one veteran ayahuasca user explained to us:

> Money is not wealth, money is the movement of things, it's only good for trade and nothing more, only for the coming and going of merchandise. So, for the spiritual life it's worth nothing. Daime is not good for movement, the movement of Daime is you knowing what you want in life… (Chico Granjeiro).

Daime reconciles man with himself, with his social milieu, his history, position and culture, and with the milieu of origin of the product which is essential to the Daimistas: the forest, because 'Daime is from the forest, the doctrine is from the woods', and, for example, Daime harmonizes man with the whole cosmos represented by the woods, the stars, and the visible and invisible, physical and spiritual beings that inhabit them. Daime is a 'natural stimulant' for one of the anthropological functions that is considered the foundation of being human: the symbolic function, in this case, applied to the religious relation of man with society, the cosmos and the gods. In this way, it is a stimulant that is capable of founding codes of ethics and moral conduct. Like the 'women' in the analysis of Lévi-Strauss (1982), Daime shows its broad capacity to operate the passage from 'natural stimulant' to culture. Moreover, spiritually, Daime was given to the man Irineu, by a woman, the Queen of the Forest.

The mythic system of Juramidã can be interpreted as a system of exchange and contract similar to that defined by Mauss (1974b) as a 'system of total prestations'. A system that covers, at the same time, magical, religious, affective, political, and moral relations, involving both kinship relations and aesthetic production.

The principle that is at the basis of the archaic form of contract, according to Mauss, is the social division of labor; however, this exchange relation does not have an essentially economic character and substitutes, in part, the notion of individual interest. This is because we are not dealing with simple exchanges between individuals: 'The persons who participate in the contract are moral persons – clans, tribes, families'; in the case we are studying, the religious brotherhoods founded on kinship relations, on the prescribed relations between parents and godparent and on the moral commitment to 'drink Daime with godmother Peregrina, or with godfather Virgílio, and not to drink Daime from the hand of another person', that is, at another center, unless this is authorized. Thus, one must be faithful to the 'contract' of remaining circumscribed to that circuit of exchanges, strengthening it spiritually and materially.

In adhering to Daime, the individual commits himself to moral persons, the brotherhoods, the Mestres; it is these groupings that establish alliances, and confront each other and are opposed, as groups or through their chiefs, or both ways at the same time. The category 'house', a frequently used metaphor among the Daimistas, designates the 'moral community'. It is common to hear declarations of loyalty of the type, 'I owe everything to this house, I have only received good things from it', so I must be faithful to it.

What they exchange, Mauss tells us, are 'gifts', it is the system of gift and counter-gift, expressed by the obligation 'to give, to receive, and to reciprocate'. The 'thing given' confers honor, prestige, mana (magical power) and wealth. In our case, Daime is considered to be the greatest wealth. It has even happened that people who exercised the profession of gold-prospecting and have come to Rondônia motivated by the search for gold, have said that 'in fact the gold was Daime and that thanks to God' they found it.

Associated with the received gift, there is the counter-gift, that is, the obligation to reciprocate the gift under the penalty of losing its mana, that is, its magical power. Among the Daimistas, there is also a sense of honor and prestige, so much so that they consider themselves 'children of the *poder*'. The hymns and many colloquial expressions indicate that Daime confers power, knowledge and prestige, aesthetic sentiments, or even material skills associated with spiritual protection to those who partake of it, as its adepts recognize: '...all that I have is what Daime has given me. I have a good knowledge of people with authority, I see authorities there that show that they recognize me and I owe that to Daime. Daime has a magnet that makes people see us' (Chico Granjeiro, CICLU).

To go against the precepts and the code of honor incorporated into the system is to run the risk of being 'out of the power', identified with the absence of vision and wholeness, and with psychic and material 'blunders'. In fact, the vision itself and the beatific ecstasy are, according to the native expression, considered a 'gift' of nature, from the Virgin Mary, or from the Daime, from Juramidã, from the Mestres Irineu, Virgílio or Francisca; from the Eternal Father, Jesus Christ or from the Queen of the Forest. Variations on who is the giver, in this case, don't matter; they are all variations on the same theme, the theme of the astral or divine world, or better yet, the theme of the existence of a luminous cosmic force (and the possibility of a gift from the divinity), the astral plane. The astral plane is the creative source of everything that exists, being represented on earth by the leaders and the Sun, Moon, Earth, Wind, and Sea, being the Light of the Heavens, whom one must love, as the hymn 'Sun, Moon, Star' by Mestre Irineu states, as do so many other hymns of the Mestres and followers (Figure 4).

Daime is a 'talisman' product, a relic. To keep it in the home is equivalent to having a special protection, a 'life insurance', as José Dantas, a veteran *ayahuasquero*, explained to us. Today, Dantas is 60 years old, but when he was born in 1936 he '...had the honor of receiving as his first food, two spoonfuls of Daime'. In Rio Branco, in the community of Alto Santo CICLU, we witnessed the custom of taking a spoonful of Daime on leaving the house, as a form of protection. In the house of people who were contemporaries of Mestre Irineu, where we were received as guests, the mother, before going off to work, asked the grandmother of the child not to let the child go to school without 'protection', that is, without taking a spoonful of Daime. The same thing happens on trips: 'whoever knows the power of Daime doesn't travel without taking along a little bottle of Daime'. Not only that, the family that hosted us had a bottle of Daime, containing 200 ml, which is the 'talisman for trips'. Any member of the family, in going on a trip, takes along that little bottle of Daime. The small quantity and the absence of use attest to this character of 'talisman property'. This notion, according to Mauss, connotes everything that makes someone powerful, including such things as treasures, talismans, coats of arms, and the traditions themselves, cults and magical rituals. At the same time, Daime is considered the best remedy of all, and a 'guide' to be used in crucial situations, for it protects and counsels. As José Dantas explained to us, Mestre Irineu recommended keeping Daime as 'a guide, protection, life insurance, a relic; in the hour of need, [it is] necessary to have Daime in the house'.

Figure 4. A Santo Daime church (copyright Flavio Lopes).

In the ritual practice of the group, Daime is an instrument of access to the spiritual world. In this capacity, like any and all instruments, its efficacy depends on its intrinsic qualities, that is, the material elements that comprise it: raw material and technical procedures. It also depends on its spiritual character, established through intentionality and ritual and moral procedures. This set of elements defines the profile, the personality of the 'Daime' product, as Mestre Virgílio (CECLU) said:

> I know five different kinds of leaves, but here only one is used. So, there are those things there [relative to the type and quality of the raw material], but there are other things also. Like they do there, with no rules [he cites other groups as examples] when that tea is ready, do you know what comes out? A vegetal body comes out. Here, until the tea comes out you really have to follow that diet. So then, there's all this perfection [of technical operationalization, also understood in the magical sense] of material hygiene and hygiene of our bodies. On the day of the *feitio*, daily life is left behind, so on that day, you can only sing, pray, not think of useless things and only speak about the *trabalho*. Do you know how that tea comes out? It comes out a *divine body, not a vegetable body* [hence transmutation occurs].

When it is obtained in 'perfection', Daime is connected to the spirit of the forest, from whom one asks for permission and whose protection is invoked to gain access to the raw material. At the same time, the Daime is related to each one of the members of the brotherhood and to the brotherhood as a whole and, particularly with the chief, on whom depends the harmony of the group and the very physical existence of the Daime. In this way, having obeyed the spiritual, moral, ethical, hierarchical and also customary rules, the Daime is obtained, because obedience to the legal precepts, established by custom is as important as the observance of mystical principles. As indicated by Malinowski (1976: 34), it is not correct to suppose that 'primitive man' lives in '...a confused world, where the real and unreal are mixed, where mysticism and reason are interchangeable'.

Having complied with all the legal and mystical precepts, one produces a tea that contains power and force, magical and spiritual force. This seems to us similar to what Mauss tells us regarding the 'spirit of the thing given' among the Maori: '...the *taonga* are connected to the person, to the clan, to the soil; they are the vehicle of its *mana*, its magical, religious and spiritual force' (1974b: 52). Once it is prepared, Daime comes to be the bearer of all the attributes invested in it. As a divine body, it is a spiritual product. Daime is given life by the 'spirit of the things' that comprise it: the leaf, the vine, the water, the fire that participates in its transmutation, and it is particularly animated by the spirit of the men and women who handle and consume it; hence all of the precautions that the brotherhood, the 'people of the Daime', take in its production, circulation and consumption. This care begins from the time that 'going to the woods' to gather the leaf and the vine is announced: '...at that point you can't let the day-to-day problems interfere, and generally you're advised four, five days before, due to the sexual abstinence. It begins there; it's not so much for other things, it's just that with that, we create an aura around us that is so positive, we are cleansed...' (Milton Rapcham, CECLU).

Besides the phase of 'separation' that is necessary for making the ritual of going to the woods effective, and which means suspending daily routines and following the ritual elements of purification, it is fundamental that there be harmony with the forest and its visible and invisible inhabitants. All the precautions have in mind the well-ordered succession of the parts that make up the '*trabalho* of the woods'.

All the rituals of Daime require 'magic'. This magic has its origins in the woods, in this case, it has to do with the sum total of knowledge connected to the 'ayahuasca culture'. The 'magic of the woods' is the formula for the source of power par excellence, the place of the Empire of the Queen of the Forest and the King Juramidá: '...to prepare Daime here [in the city], there it's already in the final stages, the difficult part has already been done. Because everything around it goes on creating that energy, that harmony, the magic, the magic goes on being created...because Daime, to be Daime, has to have that magic, all that I told you, from the woods' (Milton Rapcham, CECLU).

Daime is connected to the woods, whence comes its 'mana', its magical, religious, spiritual force, its 'power', that is connected to the 'power' of the leader and the brotherhood. This magic is also the result of hierogamies: the sacred marriage of the Queen of the Forest and Juramidá, of the leaf with the vine, of the chief with the brotherhood, of nature with culture (or better, of culture with nature):

> The leaf is more on the side of woman...it's more on the side of magic... I felt as though I was on the Virgin Mary's lap... When I went to gather Jagube...it was something different, it's the male side, it's the force... Everything around it goes on creating that harmony, magic – so to speak, the romance between the vine and the leaf; when it is prepared, that's their marriage (Milton Rapcham, CECLU).

61

At the level of circulation and consumption, we can speak of 'restricted circulation' and 'wide circulation'. The first type is circumscribed to the *trabalhos* done in the center and to domestic uses, as medicine and as talisman. The wide circulation has to do with the supplying of other centers. Together with Daime, what circulates is the spirit of Daime, the tie that establishes the physical and spiritual current created and sustained by the brotherhood. Daime establishes a connection with the brotherhood, because as Mauss attests, in archaic systems of exchange and contract, the connection through things is a connection of souls, for the thing itself has a soul, it is soul, and what is traded are not only objects.

Once the circulation of the 'spirit of the object' has begun, the first giver, the spirit 'Taonga' or its 'Hau', which in our case, is represented by the power of the Queen of the Forest, Irineu and Daime – is connected to the user who, in turn, receives 'gifts', 'wonderful things', 'visions', 'teachings', reciprocating these gifts with frequent participation in ritual *trabalhos*, loyalty to the chief and to the system, obedience to the precepts, willingness to help one's brothers. In such a way the adept becomes the last person to whom a gift is given, closing the circle of giving, and at the same time, creating the conditions for the renewal of the movement of giving and receiving, a continuous process, the chain of which cannot be broken unpunished.

This is the key idea that governs the obligatory circulation of wealth, tributes and gifts: a cycle that closes over itself, then is opened in order to close itself once more and reopen in concentric circles that get wider and wider. Entrance to the center is 'free'; to enter, however, implies a moral obligation to keep the circuit of exchange alive and moving: dedication to the mission, obedient work done with good will, payment of tithe (when it occurs), and help to the brothers. For the adept the counterpart of this process of giving is participation in the current, experiencing 'being within the power', to be a 'Child of the Power', which is the same as saying, a 'Child of the Daime', a factor which facilitates receiving the *miração*, 'wonderful things', 'gifts' and 'teachings'. A psychoactive stimulant transmuted by the culture of 'nature' into sign, it is capable of arousing the 'imaginative function' through its symbolic potency, making it a spiritual-magical force capable of transforming 'vegetal body' into 'divine body'. With power and force it can send 'all of us' to the realm of the *astral* through 'shamanic flight'. For that reason, while praying the 'Our Father', Daimistas invert the usual relation established by Christianity: instead of 'Thy Kingdom Come', the adepts affirm: 'Let us go to Thy Kingdom'.

References

Baldus, Herbert. 1965/66. *O xamanismo*. Revista do Museu Paulista, ns 16.

Cemin, Arneide. 1998. 'Ordem, xamanismo e dádiva: o poder do Santo Daime'. Doctoral thesis, Anthropology, University of São Paulo.

Labate, Beatriz C., and Wladimyr Sena Araújo, eds. 2004. *O Uso Ritual da ayahuasca (The Ritual Use of Ayahuasca)*. 2nd edn; Campinas, Mercado de Letras.

Lévi-Strauss, Claude. 1982. *As estruturas elementares do parentesco*. Petrópolis: Vozes. Published in English as *The Elementary Structures of Kinship*. Boston: Beacon Press, 1969.

Malinowski, Bronislaw. 1978. *Argonautas do pacífico occidental: um relato do empreendimento e da aventura dos natives nos arquipélagos na Nova Guiné melanésia.* São Paulo: Abril Cultural. Published in English as *Argonauts of the Western Pacific.* London: Routledge, 1922.

Malinowski, Bronislaw. 1954. *Magic, Science and Religion, and Other Essays.* Garden City, NY: Doubleday.

Mauss, Marcel. 1974a. *As técnicas corporais.* Sociologia e antropologia, vol. II. São Paulo: EPU. Published in English as 'Techniques of the Body'. *Economy and Society* 2(1) (1973): 70–87.

Mauss, Marcel. 1974b. *Ensaio sobre a dádiva: forma e razão da troca nas sociedades arcaicas.* Sociologia e antropologia, vol. II. São Paulo: EPU. Published in English as *The Gift: The Form and Reason for Exchange in Archaic Societies.* London: Routledge, 1990.

3

Santo Daime in the context of the new religious consciousness

Luiz Eduardo Soares[*]

Translated by Paulo Henriques Britto, revised by Matthew Meyer

Introduction

In the late 1980s, at the Institute for Studies on Religion (ISER), I coordinated an anthropologically oriented research project on what we decided to call the 'new religious consciousness'. Names, titles and labels should always be taken with a grain of salt, and this one is no exception. Indeed, as we suspected and the first results of our investigation have confirmed, the characteristics of the phenomenon are not always all that 'new'; the pitfalls contained in the idea of 'consciousness' are well known; in addition, although its religious dimension is important, the phenomenon in question cannot be described as 'religious' pure and simple. However, all these caveats and qualifications notwithstanding, there *is* a phenomenon, and it is a significant one, relevant from the sociological and anthropological viewpoints because it raises questions concerning the path taken by cultural development in modernity in general, and in Brazilian society in particular. I propose the following definition for the phenomenon we examined at ISER: individuals with an urban, middle-class background, generally with access to reasonably sophisticated cultural resources, whose personal careers are to a certain extent attuned to the typical modern ethical and political program – often including such episodes as being psychoanalyzed and actively participating in politics – and whose life experience is identified with what has come to be historically associated with the year 1968, individuals who are therefore 'liberated', 'libertarian', 'open' and critical about tradition, particularly the 'repressive burden' of religious traditions, who are exemplary representatives of the lay individualistic model, attuned to the 'up-to-the-

[*] Article translated from: Soares, L. E., 1994, O Rigor da Indisciplina. Ensaios de Antropologia Interpretativa. 213–22. Rio de Janeiro, Iser/Relume-Dumará. Used with permission of Luiz Eduardo Soares. Originally published in Sinais dos tempos: Diversidade religiosa no Brasil, edited by Leilah Landim, ISER, 1990.

minute' cosmopolitanism of the most 'advanced' metropolises, are increasingly showing interest in religious faith, the mysteries of mystic ecstasy, the rediscovery of communitarian communion, the challenges of esoteric forms of knowledge, the effectiveness of alternative therapies and 'natural' diets. Meditation, contemplation, the search for 'equilibrium with oneself, nature and the cosmos' are given unexpected emphasis and contrast with the decline of the sort of actively rebellious postures that were highly valued at an earlier period. To these individuals, the wanderers of the new century, as they would probably like to be called, a mystical-environmental 'holism' has taken the place of the outcry for social and sexual 'revolutions'. They are now interested in alternative rather than revolutionary lifestyles, and the ideal of cosmic unity has replaced their passionate projects restricted to the 'secular' life. Sex tends to be seen from the perspective of a wider category that relates it to the cosmological structure: energy; social equality gives way to communitarian fraternity; freedom turns into transcendent spiritual liberation. The very idea of conservation is once again valued, since predatory devastation is the enemy and environmental balance is the object, as Octavio Paz reminds us. The body and health are given pride of place in the context of this subculture now emerging and prospering in Brazil, with meanings that are, however, quite specific and different from those we have come to consider hegemonic in our recent tradition. The body is inextricably associated with the spiritualized psyche, and health presupposes qualities extrinsic to the autonomous functioning of the human machine, such as adhesion to values, patterns of attitudes, relationships with others and nature, as well as with spirituality itself and nutrition. Health is the index of 'cosmic integration' or 'equilibrium with the harmonic unity of the whole'. Virtue, beauty, truth and health are all interconnected. A certain classicism, reinterpreted in the light of a modern syncretism – which even includes some traits adapted from Eastern traditions, as well as characteristics that have always been primary elements in the jigsaw puzzle of Brazilian culture – seems to point to a modified return to the cultural or 'countercultural' hippie movement that characterized the late 1960s and that was eventually critiqued in the bonfire of co-optation and political radicalization. This occurs, not coincidentally, precisely at the moment when the economic crisis and the shrinking of the labor market have drastically reduced the Establishment's (if I can be excused for resorting to such an anachronistic term, for the sake of reinforcing the period atmosphere) ability to co-opt, narrowing the possibilities for yuppie-style social mobility, and when political disappointment has crushed other dreams. Even if all sociological hypotheses are set aside, the fact remains that what is involved here are themes, conceptions and behaviors that have to do with basic spheres of social life and existential experience: from the family to politics, from education to career choices, from identity to care of the body – often, in fact (contrary to certain appearances and some common-sense observations), closer to Spartan discipline than to a vague, pervasive 'hedonistic narcissism', more attuned to such projects of spiritual formation as *paideia*, *Bildung* and grandiose religious programs than to the sensual glamor of bodybuilders. It should also be said that, although in strictly quantitative terms the groups directly involved with alternative, religious, mystical and environmentalist cosmologies are not very significant, their hybrid position – integrated and marginal, mainstream and deviant, admired and stigmatized – and their visibility – determined by the status of some of its members or by their symbolically strategic interference in key points of the collective experience – invests them with a qualitatively significant social representativeness.

The strategic place of Santo Daime within the new religious consciousness

If one maps the universe of emerging and 'alternative' religions in Brazil and Rio de Janeiro in particular, one is bound to come across Santo Daime. To us, at first it seemed to be just another manifestation of the phenomenon we were interested in, the object we wanted to (re)constitute and interpret analytically. But closer involvement with the field of investigation and more intimate knowledge of the various aspects of the issues it raised had the effect of sharpening our interest in Santo Daime. We gradually came to the conclusion that this was a unique and particularly rich movement, which attracted a significant part of the attention directed at the rediscovery of mysticism and religion. Indeed, there was a natural convergence between our own interests and those identified in the field itself, empirically or ethnographically defined. Our curiosity was analogous to the wandering sensibility, the displacement, the spiritual migration toward Santo Daime, sometimes characterized by voyeurism, sometimes by the spiritual experimentalism commonly associated with the religious, mystic or symbolic nomadism that characterizes the 'alternative' world, and sometimes by the more intense and permanent commitment that may culminate in formal association: baptism, or *fardamento*

There are a number of reasons why the field tends to be polarized by Santo Daime; that is, why the movement not only attracts so many but also causes so much rejection. If today Santo Daime occupies a unique position, it is because it not only seduces, fascinates and recruits many but also raises concern, causes shock and gives rise to polemics and radical criticisms. Finally, the Santo Daime religious group is unique because it represents a limit-case and also establishes a point of inflection for the dynamics of the field to which it belongs and in which it asserts itself and develops: while wandering and experimentalism define the nature of relationships between 'alternative' individuals and religious perspectives, in our field of observation Santo Daime inverts expectations and invites a proto-institutionalizing or -routinizing pause, a suspension of mystic circulation – that is, of the ceaseless transit that preserves permanent availability to (prophetic) calling, to (charismatic) devotion, to (messianic) reconciliation *of, to* and *with* the 'sacred'.

Let us examine some of these reasons, which may help us to understand why Santo Daime occupies such a central position.

From darkest Brazil: an archeological journey of identity, or Delphos in Mapiá: a (subjective) journey to the (cosmic) center of the Earth

A brief summary of the history and the most visible characteristics of Santo Daime will be enough to give us a first glimpse of the reasons for its centrality, which today is evident just from reading the newspapers. This would not be the place to present conclusions and results; rather, my intention is to sketch out, in essay form, some general hypotheses and hints suggested by the research. Here is a short and superficial presentation of the justifications for what has been said so far.

Master Irineu was the founding prophet of the religion, according to standard histories. He is a popular figure in the imagination of the followers of the revelations of which he was the mediator. According to some, 'Dai-me Santa Maria' (literally, 'Give me Santa Maria') derives from a syncretic combination of the spiritualism of Tambor de Mina, which Irineu reportedly learned from his mother, and the ritual use, common among Amazonian tribal societies, of ayahuasca, a beverage made from caapi (*Banisteriopsis caapi*), a liana locally known as *jagube*, and the leaves of the *chacrona* shrub (*Psychotria viridis*). Particularly among rubber tappers, faith in the illuminating and curative powers of the holy beverage, soon given the name of 'Santo Daime', became widespread. In the beginning was the word: transformed into a noun, Daime blended the 'powerful plant' with the belief in the plant's power: flexible, loose, with little internal integration and open to any number of syncretisms or to relatively free creative reappropriations, visually translated or produced as a flux of images, revealed and mystically investigated *by* vision and *as* vision. The notion of cosmovision here finds its perfect expression: the alteration of consciousness caused by drinking the beverage affects the visual field above all, often giving rise to *mirações* (visions). These are, so to speak, the noblest instrument of spiritual work, with powerful didactic effects: for the doctrine, precisely on account of its flexibility and openness, is (re)constructed and attained (through divine grace) – and there is no paradox here – by the subject of each spiritual adventure or introspective journey. There is no paradox because the construction resulting from individual and subjective efforts, translated into images, concepts, narratives, teachings, moral conclusions and emotions – always firmly rooted in the experiences, sometimes harsh and painful, physically felt, that are associated with sensible movements of the imagination – coincides, according to shared convictions, with cosmic truth, made accessible as a divine gift, the revelations being precisely the awareness of this coincidence, the matrix of acknowledgment of the holy unity, which reconciles, with the supreme connection it brings about, matter and spirit, self and other, individual and collectivity, the human and the natural, the natural and the cosmic whole, the cosmic whole and the deity, and – through this association – the human and the divine. To the holy and holistic unity there corresponds the ceremonial practice, in which the singing of hymns in unison and the collective uniform dance (which establishes oppositions only between male and female, and between proto-priests or propitiating leaders and the congregation of the faithful), in a space ritually circumscribed, is counterposed to the fragmentary, solitary, individualizing and rigorously intrasubjective multiplicity of the meditations and *mirações*. The contrast suggests that unison is a preparation for the univocal, the choir anticipates the communion, and the uniform common movement announces the participation that is responsible for the passage to the polyphony of the senses, the passage from multivocality or polysemy to the harmonic, totalizing unity, the condition of the belief from which, paradoxically, it results. The subject is atomized and dissolved by fragmentation – so that the polyphony corresponds not only to interindividual but also to intraindividual differences – only to be reconstructed under the sign of harmonic integration, of the most intimate and profound unity, of the full superimposition of individualities and subjectivities, blended into a common essence, the sacred substratum of the cosmos, 'divine love': the multiple collectivity manifests, in the form of community participation, the underlying unity that is its essence. The price of this ritually figured harmony is the need to carry forward this unity, given the transcendent nature of the integrating essence. In other words, the community must be extended into secular existence, into routine (even if it means ritualizing, regulating or disciplining it according to a univocal and totalizing logic), leading individuals to acknowledge (and practice) the supremacy of all aggregations, disposed in increasingly wide layers, united by reference to the common omphalos, celebrated in the same *aditon*, subject to the mediation of the holy plant, the prophet and his offspring.

Who, given such complete unity, would hesitate to acknowledge in oneself, under the various forms of emotion and personal biography, the living, correcting presence of a common and transcendent agency, and of its authority – in the wide sense of the term, which includes authorship and origin? Of course, actual flesh-and-blood people, moved by inclinations, passions and doubts deriving from reason, often hesitate. But the model seems strong, attractive and seductive; it engages in a dialogue with other theological traditions, in spite of its avowed affiliation to Christianity, with the uncertainties of our time, the weaknesses and grand dreams of mankind; in addition, it operates on the register of sensibility, allowing an ecstatic experience of a very specific kind, significantly attuned to the well-known repertoire of experiences of the generations that dared to alter, by artificial means, the flow of consciousness, eagerly searching for, among other things, in many cases, what in the 1960s went by the name of 'self-knowledge'.

In the past, the 'trips' were different, but drugs were not always simply a hedonistic high, a regressive escape, a form of self-destruction. Hallucinogens were not just a factor of gregariousness in (playful) rituals of sociability and a differentiating index (triggering factor of crises? propitiator of punishment that required remote guilt?), but were often associated with 'the expansion of consciousness', 'self-exploration' and 'self-knowledge'. They were probably used as an instrument – whether or not they were adequate or efficient is beside the point – of a thirst for knowledge that, *aimed* at the unconscious, was ultimately concerned with its own origin and with the *principle* of identity. Is the intense desire for knowledge found among the Daime faithful any different? The answers offered by Daime seem compatible with the questioning, produced by this desire, about this radical curiosity, *reflectively* turned onto itself, its own root, its navel and origin; compatible with the levels of generality and uniformity on which questions about the subject are abstracted from subjects and their histories. The global meaning is derived from the reassembly of the *mirações* from the end to the beginning; that is, starting from the theological and doctrinal holistic conclusions that are their vanishing point. The mystery of mystic knowledge, which emerges *in* and *as* ecstatic difference, is precisely in the sensible (and therefore particular and contingent) production of the abstract generality of universal truth. Perhaps Santo Daime does not need, at least for the moment, any further rationalizing elaborations, with a greater conceptual, doctrinaire, systematic and theological precision, because it relies on an extraordinary resource of *mixing*, of fusion: induced and ritually regulated ecstasy, which endows the individual with a surprising power to experience – with visual imagination, emotion and the corresponding physiological echoes – the intelligibility of the absolute. Or yet: the surprising power of finding in memory, with the help of imagination, the future – which is the truth of the belief and its confirmation, in the form of fate. The transcending and essential unity is presented to the senses as images. That is why I am encouraged to suggest that the intelligible and the sensible are, under the effect of Daime, subject to the logic of 'native' categories: after all, images are contained in the narratives; it is possible to project the teleological design of the (tautological) meaning of the belief on the connections, networks and intertwinings of images, just as reason often does with dreams. The difference is that, in Daime, 'dreams' are valued as highly as the most noble and illuminating moments of waking life, and the keys to their interpretation are asserted collectively. In short, when the *mirador* (the one who experiences a *miração*) attributes meaning to his or her *mirações*, it is in the light of the cosmology that is implicit in Daime. In other words, the success of his or her enterprise in self-knowledge will imply the reassertion of the cosmology, the truth of the belief; alternatively, individual success actualizes collective glory, reinforcing the group, its identities and its values (although, as we know, there are so many differences, so many shades of opinion and conflicts, when we move on from the underlying plane of the ideal model proposed in religious practice to the plane of the actual reality of individual trajectories and concrete relationships, experienced and acted out by empirical actors). Whoever plays the language game proposed by Daime will end up enriching and reinforcing the religious language with which he or she investigates his or her own *mirações* and explores his or her spiritual adventures in the cosmos.

From a certain perspective, Daime stands for the opposite of the underlying motives of the experiences with hallucinogens in the 1960s and 1970s: back then the ideal that was assumed (whether or not it corresponded to reality is not in question here) had to do with 'liberation' – liberation from the repressive restrictions and culture, inoculated by education and introjected as guilt feelings and persecutory phantoms, restrictions to the flow of spontaneous and authentic passions, to desire, to the uninhibited movements of the body. The liberation promised by Daime involves freedom from sensual torments, the exorcism of the body's impulses, the neutralization of the desire that enslaves us to secular existence, its fetishes and illusions. From the viewpoint of Santo Daime, it is the spirit that thirsts for freedom, in order to be reconciled, at the end of its cosmic journey, with its lost origin, with the supreme unity that has been shattered, with its own alienated essence.

A dangerous misunderstanding must be avoided. There are several Santo Daime communities in Brazil. There are sharp differences among them, and sometimes disputes and conflicts as well. What has been sketched out above is based on a number of testimonies and interviews collected so far, in addition to direct observation, and an attempt has been made to preserve what seems to be possible to deduce from the beliefs common to all groups – but in any case this is an important issue. Another point of contact, which transcends divergences, is acknowledgment of the centrality of the Céu do Mapiá community in Acre, from which the highest teachings and the 'purest and strongest energies' are derived. 'Nothing' compares to drinking Daime in Mapiá.' There is also consensus about the veneration and hierarchical respect for Padrinho ('Godfather') Sebastião and, more recently, his son and successor.

This profound admiration, this intense enthusiasm for Céu do Mapiá amounts to one of the most important cultural dimensions of Santo Daime. To sum up an interpretation that would require a large amount of data and much analytical mediation, this is the hypothesis I would like to present here, even before it is borne out by further research: Santo Daime proposes, in its nomadic practice, with its periodical displacements, which are sanctified and ritualized in Acre, and also in the discourse of its followers, a reinvention of Brazil, of the Brazilian identity, articulating it with a quite wide-ranging and ambitious project of religious identity, as the presentation above must have suggested. The hegemonic cultural view emphasizes the growth and maturing of the Brazilian Southeast, which is metropolitan, cosmopolitan, developed and intelligent. The pockets of poverty to be found in this region are no more than residual in nature, or else they are representatives of the poverty-stricken regions, which are uncultured, savage, wild and primitive – regions that represent, on the plane of geography, the past. Behind this cultural map another one may be glimpsed, one that is derived from popular wisdom: Brazil is rational in the South and the Southeast; affectionate, cordial, hospitable and generous in the Northeast and the Center-West. But cordiality implies all that comes from the heart, and that includes anger as well as mercy; thus these cordial regions are also associated with the raw strength of hatred, which finds its bitterest expression in the phenomenon of *cangaço* and in duels motivated by honor. Amazonia, this huge forest, contains the deepest and most secret impulses, the most enigmatic and primitive, unexpected, ferocious, indomitable and wild; but they are also generous, and they generate abundant riches. Neither heart nor reason, what throbs in the dark and impenetrable jungle is something living and excessive, an inexhaustible source of life and permanent threat of annihilation and death, something that is irreducibly other, exterior, distant, but also sensual, intimate, close, present; in short, something that, in the symbolic topology of the nation, occupies the place of the unconscious, or, more precisely, perhaps, of the *id*, the 'it', in Freud's model of the human spirit.

In addition to elaborating and questioning so many other values (some of which I have mentioned), Santo Daime appropriates in a creative way a number of topoi from the repertoire of Brazilian culture (it should be stressed that each one of these statements and suppositions must be demonstrated; here they are presented as no more than analytical hypotheses, even if some of them are expressed in a conclusive tone). Taking the interior of Acre as their mecca, upon which they converge, in real or symbolic pilgrimages (though, of course, 'real' pilgrimages are also symbolic), the religious groups associated with Santo Daime, particularly those based in Rio de Janeiro State (three at the moment), suggest a significant inversion: the truth, the essence, the revealed secret of the origin (and the end) are in the most primitive and archaic part of Brazil, and will produce projects for the future that, being based on the vacuum of a minimally elaborated identity, will necessarily be artificial, until the day that an archaeology reconciles us with the phantom of our origin. Only archaeological reinvention can nourish and animate a vivifying teleology. Could this be a new way of conceiving the articulation between the modern Enlightenment program of emancipation and the collective imagination, in this case translated into a religious language? But is this language compatible with the liberating project of modernity? Alternatively, is it possible to think of utopias, teleologies and social identities without defining them politically? Whether or not this is done, can collective identities arise without relying on and even opposing authoritarian uniformization? And is it possible for the program of modernity somehow to overcome individualism in the strict sense – utilitarianism in its contemporary and conservative versions – without perverting the very principles from which its uniqueness and its historical strength derive? To what extent can the study of the collective imagination produced and spread by Santo Daime help us to decipher these famous and ancient enigmas? And, last, just what is the meaning of a form of self-knowledge that ideally dissolves us into a common essence but presents itself to sensibility in an experience that cannot be separated from collective participation and that eventually makes a markedly Brazilian cosmic topology depend on the individual fate of an unconscious challenge?

Clearly, research on Santo Daime will give us much food for thought, and not only in the field of what is conventionally thought of as the religious phenomenon.

Stigmata and prejudices have the effect of threatening, annihilating and establishing patterns of domination, which in turn almost always provoke equivalent reactions. In contrast, the interpretation of a phenomenon points to limits, differences and also unsuspected possibilities of communication among discourses, standpoints or orientations that seem to be mutually unintelligible at first sight. It is to be hoped that this essay will encourage a cultural dialogue that is clearly the single alternative to violence. In this precise sense, this is the way of reason, reason being above all – although virtually – a *reconnection*, an expression of belief in what is common to all men and women, the minimal condition for communication and sociability.

4

The Barquinha: symbolic space of a cosmology in the making[*]

Wladimyr Sena Araújo

Translated by Robin M. Wright, revised by Matthew Meyer

The aim of this text will be to present in a summary way the symbolic space of one of the religions of Western Amazonia called the Spiritist Center and Cult of Prayer 'House of Jesus – Source of Light',[1] more commonly called the Barquinha ('Little Boat') by its members. This Center was created in 1945 by Daniel Pereira de Mattos in the rural area of Rio Branco, capital city of the state of Acre. It has been studied very little and is basically restricted to the state of Acre. Based on fieldwork done between July and December of 1995, I determined that there is a strong influence in this Center of religious practices derived from popular Catholicism, indigenous shamanism, Afro religions and the philosophy of the Esoteric Circle for the Communion of Thought.[2]

It is necessary to emphasize that the essential, but not the only, component of Barquinha is Daime. Through it, practitioners acquire a differentiated perception of reality, entering an altered state of consciousness.

The Beginnings

Daniel Pereira de Mattos (1888–1958) the founder of the cult, was born in São Luís do Maranhão in northern Brazil, the son of slaves. When he was a child, he was put in a sailor training school, where he learned about the sea. However, his life story before arriving in Acre is still quite obscure. It is known that he arrived in Acre in the mid-twentieth

* First published in *Fieldwork in Religion* (2006) 2.3: 350–62. This translation is of an article in Labate and Araújo (2004), 541–55.

1. Centro Espírita e Culto de Oração 'Casa de Jesus – Fonte de Luz' [name has been corrected – ed.]

2. *O Círculo Esotérico da Comunhão do Pensamento* [an esoteric organization based in São Paulo – ed.]

century, where he settled in the capital city, Rio Branco, first in the district called 6th of August and later in the red-light district called Papôco, which is still situated on the banks of the Acre River.

He was a man of many skills and it is said that he was skillful in 12 different kinds of work: he was a boat-builder, cook, musician, barber, tailor, carpenter, woodcarver, artisan, poet, bricklayer, shoemaker, and baker.

Extremely sensitive, he was considered a great bohemian in the nightlife of Rio Branco. He composed songs that spoke of love, friendship, and the desired woman. In one of his bohemian wanderings, he slept under heavy rain very near the Acre River. Still drunk, he received a message in which two angels came down from heaven with a book that they delivered to him. Years later, he received the same message when he fell sick and was treated by Raimundo Irineu Serra, founder of the Center for Christian Illumination Universal Light (or Universal Light Christian Enlightenment Center) (CICLU),[3] one of the centers most responsible for the introduction of the tea [i.e. ayahuasca –ed.] into the urban area.

After his revelation, Daniel resolved to create his own doctrinal line, thus forming the 'Little Chapel', which in the beginning catered for hunters and their families passing through the area. This space was rustic, like the houses of the rubber tappers of the Amazon region. Little by little, the 'Little Chapel' or 'Little Chapel of Saint Francis' as it was called, grew in size and gathered more followers who came to accept the doctrine. Today *the Barquinha has approximately* 500 followers.

Founding symbols

One of the striking features of the Center created by Daniel is the fact that many of the symbols of the house are related to the sea. This man's life history reinforced these elements, which make references to aquatic beings and to a ship, affectionately called 'Barquinha' by the disciples. The boat has two meanings for its members: the first represents the mission left behind by Daniel, and the second expresses the journey each member must make. This boat is the journey of their lives, in short, a journey within the great journey.

Even so, members believe that the vessel of the church, the place where they assemble to hold sessions, is the boat itself. We must consider that the boat is compared to the typical kinds of vessels that pass along the rivers of this region. It is even said that the owner of the 'Barquinha' is God and it is piloted by Saint Francis of the Wounds, Martyr Saint Sebastian, Saint Joseph and Daniel Pereira de Mattos, whose mission is to guide the ship to its encounter with Jesus, trying, along with the faithful, to avoid great storms, that is, the profanities that occur in this world.

It is a boat that bears the name of 'Holy Cross boat', the nature of which is eschatological. Hence, the faithful constantly receive instructions from invisible planes to continue the voyage over the sea.

---

3. *Centro de Iluminação Cristã Luz Universal* (CICLU).

The journey is nothing more than a trial, in which the agitated water reflects the temptations of the mundane world. The water is agitated because human society has broken certain divine rules. The maritime waters express the uncontrolled sentiment of human beings and the displeasure of the Creator (Araújo Neto, 1995: 13).

In a wider sense, the boat is considered the mission that was left behind by Mestre Daniel and life in its fullest form. God is the owner of the boat, but it is the faithful who define the course it takes, through their views and attitudes.

The boat travels through three cosmological planes: the sky, the earth and the sea. Those who are part of the great boat are called sailors of the sacred sea and receive this title at the moment of their first dressing in uniform (*fardamento*).[4] Once they are uniformed members, they perform tasks in order to attain a higher degree of light at the time of each individual's de-incarnation (death). The faithful declare that if their preparation has been good, sailors will be called officers after death.

Certain entities are also called officers, as is the case of Dom Semião, who is chief over a part of the Works of Charity. When these officers come to 'work', they use certain instruments that derive from the armed forces, such as spears, swords, handcuffs, dogs, and so on. The use of these instruments is revealed in the psalms (*salmos*) sung by those present. These armed forces, consisting of entities of light, seek to combat the entities of evil. There is thus a duel between entities of light and entities of darkness; in this sense, the boat, together with the sailors and officers, becomes a receptacle for the conversion of evil and beneficent entities. This conversion occurs through battles on the high sea.

The sea over which these sailors constantly navigate is called the sacred sea, due to the fact that Daime is considered sacred water. Thus, they journey on the waves of Daime, on the swaying Holy Cross boat.

The sea also means light. The light is associated with knowledge; thus, those who partake of Daime are taking in Holy Light (*Santa Luz*) and acquiring new knowledge, seeing oneself, the other, and other worlds. Besides that, the sacred tea represents renewal, revitalization and cure. By 'navigating' with it, the person is born again and with that experience, s/he becomes whole again.

In two of Daniel's visions, we note the presence of water, because no doubt he found himself lying on the banks of a river or stream. The first vision occurred without the use of Daime, and the second under the effect of this entheogen. These visions recall a passage, a connection with primordial times, with God, and with the beginning of the mission.

Daime is considered a substance of power; however, this sacred water is not accessible at just any moment. A person will have to go through a series of trials, thus demonstrating that s/he is worthy of it.

The sacred drink is also considered a teacher that instructs the participants in the rituals in which it is utilized. These teachings have been present from the moment when Mestre Daniel decided to form the mission through his vision of the Blue Book. The Blue Book includes the teachings and is the source from which the faithful receive, in synthesized

---

4. The wearing of the uniform represents the loyalty of the participant to the group in which s/he is participating. In Paskoali's view, it is also a rebirth, seeing as how through it individuals obey certain rules of conduct so that they can be really recognized as followers of the doctrine (Paskoali, 1998).

form, the instructions which ultimately derive from the highest sacred planes. These instructions are passed on through beautiful melodies, rich in symbolism, called psalms.

Symbolic and ritual axes[5]

The symbolic repertoire of Barquinha, which is expressed in the architecture of the church, can be imagined as a patchwork quilt, in which the parts come together to form a whole. We designate the ritual experience in the places of the boat as the sewing, for it is in the ritual that we find the key to the expression of the logic and the felt experience. It is not my intention to discuss all of the symbolism of Barquinha, but rather to focus on several axes, in order to understand the rituals within the spatial structure, as they are presented/represented by the sailors and officers of the sacred sea.[6] From the extensive symbolic composition, I have selected three main architectural symbols: the table in the form of a cross, the outdoor Cross of the church, and the park.

1. The table in the form of a cross is at the center of a whole set of symbols. The experience of the sacred reveals the foundation of the world and Mestre Daniel, on making contact with the sacred, founded the mission and revealed the true reality, removing himself from the profane world of illusion. In this space is the main symbol, the table. The table is shaped in the form of a cross and becomes the crystalline spring for a garden of symbols.

Around it, there are six chairs on one side and six on the other, representing the 12 apostles of Christ. It should be noted that there is a hierarchy that must be followed in order to get to the table. Initially, instructions are given to Saint Francis of the Wounds, who then passes them on to the President of the space.

The table is the main piece of a great origami [the Japanese art of paper-folding – ed.] since rituals are opened and also closed from it. On it, there is an open blue book containing the Ten Commandments.

The Works of Charity form the main work of the house and the principal performance in which the table is used. It is important to note that the work emerges from the cross-shaped table, thus producing a spatial amplification, when the curtains are opened giving depth to the rest of the space.

This spatial amplification has its point of departure at the center of the church, which becomes the main channel for connection between the vertical and horizontal planes, that is, the sacred mythical planes and the sacred beings, and the other places of architectural space and religious human beings. Gradually, and in a subtle and harmonic way, the places around the table gain importance during the ritual process.

The first part of the ritual consists simply of the recitation of prayers and singing of psalms by those present. The second part is the opening of the Works of Charity, in which

---

5. [Plural of axis, in the sense of *axis mundi* – ed.]

6. Presentation and representation go hand-in-hand because the practitioner can represent the sacred during a ritual performance. On the other hand, spiritual entities can manifest themselves in the rituals, including by using the bodies of followers. The architecture, gestures and melodies represent other planes and other beings, but when felt, they assume a presence.

seven spirit entities are called to offer charity. These beings belong to the mysteries of the sky, earth and sea.

Behind the church, there is a room (*terreiro*) where mediums attend clients. There are seven cabinets or shrines (*congá*). Three mediums work at each, including the one who incorporates the spirit entity responsible for attending in this room. The entity that has overall responsibility for the room is an entity by the name of Dom Semião. This spirit was incorporated by Francisca Gabriel, one of the mediums who worked with Daniel Pereira de Mattos. Today, Francisca Gabriel is one of the leaders of a Center that she founded, called the Prince Espadarte [Swordfish] Spiritist Center, located near the first Barquinha church.[7]

The mediums perform the passing of hands (*passes*) on the clients who come to the church seeking treatment for illnesses, family problems and harmful spirits. Depending on the seriousness of the problem, the mediums advise individuals to return in order to undo the effects of sorcery (*Quimbanda*).[8] These services are done on Thursdays.

The services to undo the effects of sorcery were performed back in the decades of the 1940s and 1950s, in Mestre Daniel's Center. At that time, the Spiritist Center and Cult of Prayer 'House of Jesus – Source of Light' already had three mediums: Francisca Gabriel, Maria Baiana and Dona Inês. These were ladies who coordinated the Works of Charity for the mission of Daniel, as well as undoing evil, which they considered to be black magic.

For the Christian apostolic spiritists (sailors of the sacred sea/soldiers of Jesus' armies), when a patient who comes to be treated, s/he brings with her/him a spirit entity of *Quimbanda*, a spirit of darkness, which for various reasons tries to harm the material and spiritual life of the individual.

The services to undo evil sorcery end up engaging a struggle between good and evil, between spirit entities of light and those of darkness. The latter are considered arrogant and stubborn. These wayward and offensive beings, when converted through the entities of light, return to work in the Barquinha.

This ritual activity begins in the room for attendance and only the mediums who work in the cabinets (*congá*) are authorized to take Daime; however, they can perform their activities without the help of the substance.

Each cabinet is occupied by three mediums: one of them is responsible for the work to be done in that place and receives the spirit entity in charge of that *congá*. The other mediums receive entities in their bodies, that is, they incorporate entities which have not been baptized in the house and are not entities of light.

---

7. Besides the *Prince Espadarte Spiritist Center*, created in 1994, the *Spiritist Center Daniel Pereira de Mattos* was created by Antônio Geraldo, his family and supporters. There is also the *Spiritist Center Faith, Light, Love and Charity* (Maria Baiana's Center), located on the Amapá Road (rural area of Rio Branco). This center was created in 1962 by Juarez Xavier and his wife Maria Rosa. The *Spiritist Center Saint Ignatius of Loyola* was created in 1994, being one of the smallest of the centers and located in the district of Sobral. This Center is headed by Antônio Inácio da Conceição. Finally, the *Spiritist Center Our Lady Aparecida*, was established in 1998 in the municipality of Porto Acre. This Center is headed by the couple Sheila and José do Carmo, who used to belong to the *Spiritist Center and Cult of Prayer 'House of Jesus – Source of Light'*.

8. For the faithful, *Quimbanda* expresses the opposite pole of *Umbanda*. In this way, the *Quimbanda* entities are seen as pertaining to the side of black magic. The principal goal of the works to undo the services of *Quimbanda* is to take out *exus* from the matter, the body. The *exus* can be converted by entities of light.

Through incorporation, the lightless entity is taken to a small room where it is commanded by an entity of light to draw a *ponto riscado*[9] on the ground. Over this design are placed various materials, such as colored candles, herbs, and cloths, among other things. This done, the being of the depths is obliged to undo the 'work', in most cases originally performed at the behest of a third party. Undoing the work involves burning all the materials that the lightless entity requested during the Works of Charity, thereby freeing the victim of its malevolence. After that, the *Quimbanda* spirit is imprisoned in a place on the Astral plane called the 'concentration camp' and when it is ready, it returns as an entity of light, doing services in benefit of the Barquinha.

As well as for the Works of Charity, the table in the form of a cross is a part of the works of concentration held on Wednesdays. These sessions are done exclusively inside the church, thus there is no opening of curtains. The ritual performance lasts between an hour and an hour-and-a-half, and there are no restrictions regarding positioning of those who participate in the Works of Charity for these concentration sessions.

Several differences, however, can be noted between the Works of Charity sessions and the sessions practiced on Wednesdays. One of the distinctions is made explicit in the concentration itself, for in the minds of the practitioners, the 'Barquinha' is a school and Daime, the sacred sea, brings with it teacher entities. This notion is related to the use that the *caboclo* (mestizo) vegetalistas make of this substance (Luna, 1986).

This explains what the principal goal of the concentration session really is: the spiritual development of the mediums, which in turn seeks to prepare the member of the house to work in the Works of Charity and in sessions that undo the effects of *Quimbanda*. The spiritual development of mediums is one of the most difficult tasks the faithful undergo.

Another factor to consider is that during this ritual, the quantity of Daime served is greater than in the Works of Charity sessions. In this sense, followers mentioned that the quantity ingested in the Wednesday sessions is for the purpose of people's interior 'works' (in the sense of spiritual processing). It is a day of 'instruction', hence, of reflection.

2. The outdoor Cross is the pillar of the Holy Cross boat. On it, we can see a heart with 12 stars representing the mysteries of the passion and death of Christ. Beyond that, this place has four access entrances, representing the four cardinal points.

Together with the 12 columns it also represents a rosary, which can be seen on the days of sessions from inside the church through the positioning of the candles.[10]

In this place, the indoctrinations of souls are held on November 2 (Day of the Deceased). The main objective of these indoctrinations is to prepare souls within a certain Christian norm, which constitutes the major part of the concepts of the house.

The souls are shepherded by Friar José Joaquim, the Pastor of the Souls. It is he who takes them to be indoctrinated through Saint Francis. The souls are received during the sessions and are, in this way, summoned to be indoctrinated. The indoctrination, in turn, does not imply that the soul is saved but that it has been placed in a state of preparation

---

9. [Literally meaning 'scratched point', in this Barquinha church, as in mainstream Umbanda, they are graphic symbols that represent Umbanda spirit entities, similar to the *veves* found in Haitian *Vodun*. – ed.]

10. It is also the great mast that sustains the Barquinha on official festivities.

within the process of evolution, in which it will remain for a period of penitence to be relieved of its sins. With that, it will be preparing itself for the Final Judgment.

It is the practitioners who receive the souls and it is the President of the space who sends them to a hall of light. There they will undergo preparation for several days in order to receive the doctrine. Once indoctrinated, the Pastor of the Souls takes them again on the appropriate session days to fulfill the indoctrination.

Several faithful say they have visited the hall of light inhabited by the penitent souls. These journeys are marked by ample subjectivity, but it is important to highlight that as a symbol of the context of space, the hall of light has collective importance and the individual journeys reinforce its existence.

Inside the fence surrounding the outdoor Cross are those who participate, sitting at the table for services held inside the church. Surrounding them nearby are the other members and participants who sing psalms and recite the prayers.

Similar to the work of indoctrination is the baptism of the *eguns* without light, the *exus*, whom they consider to be 'entities of darkness'. For the President of the church, Manuel Hipólito de Araújo, there is a difference between indoctrination of souls and baptisms of *eguns* without light. A vast majority of souls have already been baptized. According to him, however, what they lack is a Christian preparation.

The *exus* are converted into spirits of light when they are taken to a mythical place in the Astral plane called the concentration camp. Like the souls, these *exus* will be submitted to a process of symbolic re-signification and will even have their names changed.

3. The third axis consists of the park (*parque*). It was created in 1959 by Antônio Geraldo da Silva. The place is intended to be for the 'playing' of the fraternity with the entities of the three mysteries. Architecturally, it takes two forms: the first as a boat and the second as a chalice. This chalice is an instrument of consecration, because on taking Daime, the individual communes and establishes a link with God.

The space of the park is composed of a series of symbols. There are 12 pillars that surround the dance hall. The 12 pillars always represent the apostles of Christ, but, during the festivities, banners are placed over these pillars symbolizing entities of the mysteries of the sky, earth and sea.

The bandstand, which is in the center of the dance hall, represents Jesus Christ or Oxalá during the celebrations. Above the bandstand there is a small replica of a boat much like the boats that navigate the rivers of Amazonia, and above this little boat one can see a yellow light. The light is Daime, the sacred sea, over which the sailors journey.

The dances held in the park are considered an extension of the works done in the church. There is spatial mobility, that is, space becomes movable through the dynamics of the dance.

The goal of the dance is to please the entities who participate in the Works of Charity on specific sacred dates. The beings that are called to play are allowed to satisfy their material pleasures – in this case, dancing – and utilize the 'apparatuses' [i.e. mediums] to dance 'points' (*pontos*)[11] that identify them. The entities also have the power to send 'points' through the apparatuses, which receive them and write them in sequence. These points praise the entities of the three mysteries.

---

11. [Like the *pontos riscados*, these are patterned melodies associated with the entities – ed.]

The 'playing' also serves as initiation to incorporation, because very rarely does this kind of practice occur within the church. By leaving people more at ease through the Daime, the 'points', and most of all, through movement, dancing helps people to develop their mediumship. Incorporation, it should be emphasized, can also occur without the use of the substance.

Thus, the dance has this purpose of attending the entities that are progressing toward rendering charity in that house and the individuals who work in the Center use the place to make merry and at the same time analyze their lives. The 'merrymaking' produces ways for thinking about the problems each one has through the instructions received. The dance also serves to cure, to herd together dark entities and to establish a gift, for people exchange with other people and also with divine beings.

The place of the park becomes dynamic because bodies are involved by it. It is a dance partner. In this way, those who participate in the dance perceive the place, the sacred circle, because through their perception of the place, it is perfectly possible to see other worlds and make them visible through gestures. There begin to circulate on the disk, on the edge of the sacred chalice or in the boat, symbols that relate the mythic to the architectural space. Those who dance together with the space become dancing sculptors because they give shape to the invisible reality.[12]

Internal elements, such as sentiments and thoughts, become connected to external elements (music, smells, lights, etc.) and produce movements that speak of other realities and other beings. Daime can establish a connection, a channel that connects to other dimensions of the three mysteries.

The dance, like the other ritual performances, serves as a means for making cosmology dynamic when symbols are transformed and/or modified. The works of Daniel try to say something: the various acts inscribed in the ritual performance constitute action, and thus, expression; they express not only ideas, but also sentiments. In this case, the mission Daniel left goes beyond the frontier that separates the sacred from the profane world. People come back to daily life inebriated by their apprenticeship of the sacred.

Cosmology in construction

The Barquinha fits in with the so-called religious eclecticism which, according to the anthropological literature, offers the individual an experience that takes place:

By an operation…through which elements derived from various traditions, native and imported, which the geographical mobility of people and cultural products today puts at their disposal, are eclectically brought together, superimposed and/ or refounded. New collective entities appear on the horizon of these operations, but they tend to be transconfessional, threatening from the beginning, in this sense, to reconfigure the map of the contemporary religious field on these central societies.

---

12. See Arruda (1988) for this concept concerning the relation between performer and space.

It seems possible to expect of the consequences of this phenomenon some effects of more radical transformations than those of the traditional 'Brazilian syncretism' (Sanchis, 1995).

In this sense, we think that the idea of religious eclecticism fits in very well with the formation of religious thought of the non-indigenous religions that make use of ayahuasca. But, we believe that, instead of this more fluid circulation of the individual through various religions, without being concerned in settling in one, thus respecting the religious differences, the followers of the Barquinha have a more regular doctrinal relation with one religion. It is the religious practices that circulate in this kind of Amazonian religion that are more fluid.

We suggest that what we have here is a *cosmology in construction*. By cosmology in construction, I mean a set of religious practices that tend to form a specific doctrine in which there is a great velocity of incorporating and removing elements from diverse religious practices. Beyond that, the hymnal is another source for such a notion, because the members of Barquinha do not speak of the book as something that is complete. Its words are passed on to them as instructions and when new psalms are received, it is a sign that new instructions have just arrived.

The symbolic composition of this doctrinal line is in part elaborated in Mestre Daniel's proposal, as well as by the worldview of these religious leaders who come from distinct places and diverse cultures. Thus, the Center becomes an agglutinator of cultures. But the term agglutinator does not suffice, because it is also puts cultural elements into an order, establishing something authentic, new and dynamic. And in this case, Barquinha is a ship of re-signification through its incredible flexibility of space – hence the metaphor cosmology in construction.

To better exemplify what we mean by cosmology in construction, we take as an example the building of a large boat. A boat being built will have various types of wood in various places. Thus, we find beams, boards, mast, rudder, and so on, all made of wood that is compatible with the boat. In the same way, we find the various elements which hold the boat together: screws, nails, and others. After the boat is built, the large boat, we can say that it is 'structured'.

But the purpose of the boat is to sail, journey into the sea, for days and nights, in the heat or cold. Its owner decides to make it different and begins to color and design geometric shapes on the cabin where he pilots the ship. These are small changes of great meaning that, little by little, will be shared by the boat's crew.

This boat travels to different places and comes up against great storms. Soon, the boat needs urgent repairs to continue the voyage. The journeys continue and the crew, especially the owner of the boat, comes to know different places and, consequently, distinct people. They go on to dialogue, they establish trade, give and receive, experience, learn, and come back changed. They decide to remember, make the memory dynamic, look for the threads of meaning and, with that, they trace new designs, motifs through which they remember the *other*.

But the boat changes over time. Despite the internal support structure of the ship, each day that passes the crew seeks to give it a new look. And so they continue beyond the horizon to navigate with present memories.

81

This re-signifying derives from the purpose of the journeys to other planes as envisioned by the guides, and, with that, the visions of these mythical places are manifest in the architecture. The journeys are the visions that they had for the symbolic construction of the place, because it was in these visions that these leaders saw the sacred and these revelations justify a collection of symbols that have been incorporated over the decades.

The religious person of Barquinha is immersed in symbols and is consciously or unconsciously marked by them. These places are lived, experienced individually or collectively during a long period of activities. One only needs to recall that Barquinha is the line of ayahuasca that holds the greatest number of ritual performances in Acre and the surrounding regions.

The works form the subject's action within the places of space. The action of the subject fits in with what we can call performatic space and, together with this performatic space, spatial amplification, in which the places are mixed together in the course of the rituals.

The rituals of Barquinha deeply mark the re-encounter of European, indigenous, and African traditions. The ritual functions as a manifestation of these cultures which are present through prayer, vision, and incorporation.

In the case of prayers, these represent an element of European Catholic religion reshaped in the Brazilian northeast. The vision is related to indigenous shamanism and incorporation to African cults. To better exemplify what we wish to say, we recall the indoctrination of the souls where the three aspects are related to performatic space. In short, the re-encounter of these cultural traditions marks the permanent construction of its cosmology.

Finally, it must be observed that, during the rituals, the participants of Barquinha make symbolic re-elaboration a dynamic process. It is when something new can be seen in the works of the mission of Daniel. The mobility of the boat caused by the subjects who are part of it produces this dynamic, for they come back changed, transformed. This is the sense of construction, not only of producing an effect on the architecture of the place, but also of touching the subjects, the sailors of the sacred sea.

References

Araújo Neto, Francisco Hipólito de. 1995. 'Com quantos paus se faz uma nau'. Unpublished manuscript, UFAC (Federal University of Acre).

Arruda, Solange. 1988. *A arte do movimento – as descobertas de Rudolf Laban na dança e ação humana*. São Paulo: PRN Gráficos e Editores associados Ltda.

Groisman, Alberto. 1991. 'Eu Venho da Floresta: Ecletismo e Práxis Xamânica no Céu do Mapiá'. Master's thesis, UFSC (Federal University of Santa Catarina).

Labate, Beatriz C. and Wladimyr Sena Araújo, eds. 2004. *O Uso Ritual da ayahuasca* (*The Ritual Use of Ayahuasca*). 2nd edn; Campinas, Mercado de Letras.

Luna, Luis Eduardo. 1986. *Vegetalismo: Shamanism among the Mestizo Population of the Peruvian Amazon*. Stockholm: Almqvist & Wiksell.

Monteiro da Silva, Clodomir. 1983. 'O Palácio de Juramidam. O Santo Daime: Um Ritual de Transcendência e Despoluição'. Master's thesis, UFPe (Federal University of Pernambuco).

Paskoali, Vanessa Paula. 1998. 'Navegar é preciso, morrer não é preciso'. Undergraduate thesis, UFAC (Federal University of Acre).

Sanchis, Pierre. 1995. 'As Tramas Sincréticas da História'. In *Revista Brasileira de Ciências Sociais*. 10(28).

Sena Araújo, Wladimyr. 1999. *Navegando nas Ondas do Daime: História, Cosmologia e Ritual na Barquinha*. Campinas: Editora da Unicamp.

5

Healing in the Barquinha religion[*]

Christian Frenopoulo

Introduction

In the city of Rio Branco, nestled in the state of Acre in the Brazilian Amazon, there thrives a religion called Barquinha ('Little Boat'), founded in 1945. Participants dressed in naval uniforms evangelize the rebellious pagan spirits of non-Christian Amazonia as well as unrepentant souls that died in sin. Healing is offered to the general public as part of the mission's commitment to charity, and is the main theme of this article.

Charity is a fundamental value and mission of the Barquinha religion. The kinds of charity that are offered spontaneously are many (for example, adopting children, organizing events for poor children, and hosting visiting anthropologists in their homes), but it is the healing service that is typically singled out as the mark of the mission. In the course of the standardization and development of Barquinha liturgies, this service came to be offered within a worship ceremony basically comprised of devotional singing and praying after the sacramental ingestion of Daime.

The healing service generally goes by the designation *Obras de Caridade* (Charity Works)[1] and is offered at least once a week, on Saturday evenings, in a very organized manner. Most healing in this service is offered through the work of healer-spirits, visibly incorporated into trained mediums. The healing service is offered freely, and no form of compensation is required or expected. Clients may be responsible for defraying the costs of materials involved in the therapy (e.g. candles), but they do not directly compensate the spirits, mediums or church for the healing.

---

[*] First published in *Fieldwork in Religion* (2006) 2.3: 363–92.

1. In this article I have accepted the editor's recommendation to quote relevant terms in the original language, with an approximate English translation offered when first mentioned. In addition, for the sake of consistency, in some cases I have continued the use of English translations that appear in antecedent literature.

83

Daime, or more properly Santo Daime, is a brew made from the decoction of the *Banisteriopsis caapi* vine and leaves of the *Psychotria viridis* bush, which are both native to this region (Western Amazonia). The brew has been used by indigenous and mestizo shamans for centuries, mostly for religious and healing purposes (Metzner, 1999; Dobkin de Rios, 1970a, 1970b). The Quechua name is 'ayahuasca', and will be used in this article to refer to the brew in a context-free sense.[2]

The name Daime is directly derived from the Santo Daime church that was founded by Raimundo Irineu Serra (known by followers as Mestre Irineu) in the early 1930s in Rio Branco. The Santo Daime church, like the Barquinha, is an Amazonian form of Christianity. Two important distinguishing particularities of these two religions are the central sacramental use of ayahuasca in an ecclesiastical organization, and the recognition of the brew as a Christian sacrament. The founder of the Barquinha, Daniel Pereira de Mattos (known by followers as Frei Daniel), had been an early friend of Mestre Irineu and had belonged to his church. After a period, Frei Daniel set up his own mission. The communities of both religions in Rio Branco continue to retain cordial and close relationships.

The *Obras de Caridade* ritual distinguishes the Barquinha from other ayahuasca religions, because it is primarily oriented to non-members and participation does not necessarily require the ingestion of Daime.[3] The Barquinha has a defined mission of social outreach that helps ease the general public's insertion in their own individual living conditions. This is partially achieved through the healing service, which contemplates promoting social harmony and cohesion among non-members leading their own lives, and not just those who actively participate in the religion.

Healing may also occur in other rituals of the Barquinha. For example, *Festas* (Parties) are dancing festivities, held in a special outdoor courtyard, during which the largest number of spirit-entities descends into mediums (mediumship is least regulated on these occasions, compared to other rituals and spaces). The spirits are permitted to offer healing and other forms of interaction with participants, even though the ritual is – officially speaking – primarily intended for the benefit of the spirits themselves (as explained to me by an important member of the church during my fieldwork; also see Sena Araújo, 1999: 222). Cleansings (*limpezas*) of several sorts may occur during these occasions. These also occur during a ritual specifically called Cleansing (*Trabalho de Limpeza*), during which all participants

---

2. Ayahuasca – meaning the brew – is notoriously embedded in generally well-defined cultural and social prescriptions and interpretations regarding its use, meaning, value, and so on, which usually evoke strong emotional attachments and draw reactions among users or sympathizers who, regardless of the cultural milieu of use, are typically convinced of the propriety and veracity of their own particular complex or understandings. Here, I adopt a strict Cartesian position of treating the brew as *res extensa* wholly unconnected to my ideations.

3. It is possible to participate in rituals of the Santo Daime churches in the Alto Santo neighborhood without drinking Daime, as Beatriz Labate (pers. comm., 2005) has reminded me. In fact, there are occasions in which non-members may not be allowed to drink Daime. In this event, they are usually also not allowed to fully participate in the ritual (e.g. sitting in the main hall) and must remain quietly sitting on the outside. This is different from the Barquinha, in which full participation in the ritual is always possible (including sitting inside the church), while the consumption of Daime is always voluntary. Active members are generally expected to drink Daime, but they may be excused given the circumstances (e.g. they recently drank Daime in a previous ritual, just before the start of a subsequent ritual that immediately followed). They are not held accountable for refraining from consuming Daime.

are required to be attended by a healer-spirit. This ritual is primarily intended for active members of the church, though anyone else may participate, too. There is also a healing component known as *operações espirituais* (spiritual surgeries) that are incorporated into a monthly ritual called *Prestação de Contas* (Rendering Report) (Mercante, 2004).

Though the structure of each of these rituals is varied, the interaction between healer-spirits (visibly incorporated into mediums) and clients follows a basic template and involves a restricted repertoire of actions. These are the same actions and forms of interaction that occur during *Obras de Caridade* healing encounters. This article will primarily focus on the *Obras de Caridade*.

Participants may also spontaneously receive cleansings, purgings, or other forms of healing, during any other ritual, that are directly effected by ayahuasca or by the interaction of ayahuasca with other elements (e.g. the suggestive lyrics of hymns, or invisible spirit-entities). The possibility of consumption of ayahuasca is offered in all Barquinha rituals.

Scope of the article

In this article, I summarily introduce three approaches that I discern in studies of healing in the Barquinha. Authors often readily weave them into one another, but here I wish to consider them separately, for analytical purposes.

First, many studies of healing in the several ayahuasca religions regularly place central attention on the therapeutic transformations effected from the consumption of ayahuasca in these settings (e.g. Groisman, 1999; Labigalini, 1998). Generally speaking, the intense subjective experience is credited with providing individuals with the means to alter and modify practices and affects that come to be understood as harmful for their health. Most often, researchers include self-narrated biographical accounts of healing and redemption offered by their informants, in which the revelations and cleansings mediated through the brew are given a central status. These analyses frequently rely on interpretive approaches, as they often dwell on transactions and transformations in the ideological and symbolic dimensions of an individual that precede changes in routines of practice. Not infrequently, informants are regular members of the church, whose loyalty and commitment to the religion has often been existentially intertwined with their healing process. Consequently, they often employ a theological scheme to comprehend their biography (e.g. claiming that their illness was caused or aggravated by immoral or sinful behavior).

In the case of the Barquinha, Paskoali (2002) has included this approach in her study of one of the churches, eventually drawing on the concept of 'symbolic efficacy' to explain identity readjustments and other existential modifications that her informants described for their healing processes. I will restate some of her findings further below.

Secondly, a different approach is involved in the concern with elements of the setting (Zinberg, 1984) and social context that may also contribute to therapeutic efficacy. In this case, the subjective experience associated with the consumption of ayahuasca is not being considered directly. In the broad Santo Daime context, for example, authors have been interested in matters such as ritual structuring (e.g. Couto, 2002), formal and informal social controls that regulate behavior (e.g. MacRae, this volume), or the disciplining of the participant's body through extended participation in the complex (e.g. Cemin, this volume). More specifically in regards to healing rituals of the Santo Daime, MacRae (1999) focuses attention on elements of the ritual settings, behavioral prescriptions and other features. He points to an increase in suggestibility during the ayahuasca experience and, therefore, a more intense impact of symbolic representations.

In the case of the Barquinha, the ingestion of Daime is not usually inherent to healing performances.[4] This enhances the relevance of considering dominant motifs that are enacted during healing performances and justifiably focusing analytical attention on the setting and, more specifically, on ritual actions. Descriptions of the performances are regularly included in studies of healing in the Barquinha (e.g. Mercante, 2004; Paskoali, 2002; Sena Araújo, 1999). In this article, I wish to provide a little more detail and commentary regarding these performances.

The performances often seem to involve gestures of extraction and removal of harmful elements. Unenlightened spirit-beings are regularly held accountable for the client's predicament. Sena Araújo explains, 'Illnesses that develop from strictly spiritual causes are usually those caused by "obsessor spirits" who obsessingly stalk some people's "light", sapping their "energies"' (Sena Araújo, 1999: 198, my translation). Given this, I will devote some special attention to the casting 'up' (because they are sent to Heaven) of these malevolent or misguided creatures. Exorcisms[5] illustratively condense many of the salient motifs of Barquinha understandings about healing, and are rites in which the subjective experience of those clients who voluntarily consume Daime may not be central to the episode. Sena Araújo similarly remarks, 'It is important to underscore that it is not the substance [i.e. Daime] *per se* that provides regeneration, but rather a series of elements related to healing through the spirits' (Sena Araújo, 1999: 237 n. 15, my translation).

Mercante draws a similar distinction between healing in the Santo Daime – in which the ingestion of Daime is integral to therapy – compared to the Barquinha. He notes that in the Santo Daime, greater emphasis is placed on self-knowledge and transcendence, and individuals are encouraged to look for their own healing. In contrast, in the Barquinha, more attention is given to external causes of sickness, such as wayward spirits (Mercante, 2003). In sum, healing that centrally involves the ingestion of Daime often involves an introspective edge. Barquinha rites do not assume the consumption of Daime and are easily characterized as aesthetically expressive (e.g. see Rose, 2005a) and 'extrospective' (in the sense of looking outside the individual for the cause of affliction and publicly 'acting out' spiritual manifestations).

Thirdly, related to the focus on setting, MacRae (1999) and other authors (e.g. Groisman, 1999: 58, 62) have also recognized the importance of the quality and nature of the

---

4. The exception to this are the spiritual surgeries, in which clients are recommended – though not obliged – to drink Daime. The surgeries are usually prescribed for members or sympathizers of the religion who are accustomed to drinking Daime and share local interpretations regarding its divine nature and therapeutic agency (see Mercante, 2004).

5. I am using the term 'exorcism' as an analytical category, to refer to the rite that obtains the liberation of a person from the strong degree of influence exerted upon her or him by an unenlightened spirit-entity, in order to situate this article within the body of literature that deals with such events. There is no native term for this procedure. Informants most often simply say 'remove the *exú*' (I will describe this category of spirit-entity further below).

social relationships that are fostered in the ayahuasca religions and the healing potential of participation in such social contexts.

With regards to the Barquinha, this is also mentioned by Paskoali (2002: 151), for example, who points to the atmosphere of hospitality that characterizes Barquinha churches and links this to the suggestibility of the ailing client. She says that people needing treatment, comfort and comprehension of their situation are in a fragile position. The solidarity and warmth with which they are received become fundamental parts of their healing process and assist their collaboration with the treatment.

Not quite along the same line, but somewhat related to this insight, in this article I wish to consider Barquinha healing encounters as special forms of social interaction in which certain roles, largely defined by the category of healer-spirit serving as interlocutor, are staged. Amongst other benefits, I suggest that they model for participants appropriate modes of interaction (and, in numerous cases, soothingly contrast with the conflictive or problematic ones about which clients may be consulting).

There are several classes of healer-spirits that attend in Barquinha churches. Which class of spirit is invoked in a case can vary, depending on the type of ailment (as each spirit individually, but also according to its class, is somewhat specialized or has expertise in certain matters), historical reasons (as there has been a flux in the classes of spirits that predominate in a church at a given time), or also other factors (e.g. circumstantial availability of the mediums). In the church of my fieldwork, since its inception, the *Pretos Velhos* (literally, 'elderly Blacks') – who are the spirits of deceased elderly Brazilian Black slaves – have been the most common class of spirit to aid in the healing service.

As inferred from informants' accounts, and also from the *Pretos Velhos* that I have talked with, they are a class of spirit that emblematically embodies spiritual triumph borne from unjust suffering and cruelty. During their interactions with clients, these healers frequently empathize with the suffering clients and counsel them to respond with acquiescence, patience and tolerance. As brought to my attention by Peter Gose (pers. comm., 2003), there appears to an ideological redemption of the *Pretos Velhos* as a class subjected to structural violence, which I suggest may have parallels with some of the suffering endured by clients and church members. This is in addition to the fact that many of the clients and church-members are themselves descended from the slaves and, thus, might also be redeeming their own subaltern histories.

The article has been organized to sequentially present each of these three broad approaches under subheadings which identify them as positions that focus on biographical narratives, on actions and motifs in healing performances, and on therapeutic subjectivity, respectively. Before their discussion, though, the sections that immediately follow provide background information regarding the ethnographic context and the general structuring of the healing rituals and interactions.

Ethnographic background

The Barquinha mission was founded in 1945 in Rio Branco, in the Amazonian state of Acre. The region had been undergoing permanent transformation as a result of the migrations

Figure 1. Frei Daniel (copyright João Guedes Filho).

of people brought from the northeastern states of Brazil to work as laborers and military reinforcements during the Rubber Era (c. 1850–1945) (e.g. see Goulart, 2002).

The founder of the Barquinha was Daniel Pereira de Mattos (Frei Daniel), who was born into a family of slaves in the northern coastal state of Maranhão in 1888, the year of the abolition of slavery in Brazil. He came to Acre as a sailor, aboard a ship that was transporting military aid into the region, and decided to settle in Rio Branco where, among other trades, he worked as a barber. One of his clients was Mestre Irineu – his friend since Maranhão, and also descended from slaves – who was conducting rituals with Daime and had an incipient community living in close proximity. Frei Daniel joined Mestre Irineu in his church for a period, until he received an angelic vision that ordered him to depart and fulfill a personal mission. Mestre Irineu encouraged him to pursue the vocation, and gave him some Daime (Maia Neto, 2003; Oliveira, 2002; Sena Araújo, 1999). Frei Daniel was a humble and pious man who thenceforth lived very poorly. People spontaneously came to him seeking healing, and he also organized worship services. His work was gradually standardized – a process that continues – and became known as the 'Barquinha doctrine'.

There are now several Barquinha churches in Rio Branco. There are some differences in the way that the healing service is instrumented in each, but all seem to follow a general template. Most of my fieldwork has been carried out in the church that I shall call 'Casa Santa' (a pseudonym),[6] which is led by a prestigious and highly respected disciple of Frei

6. In appreciation for my informants' sensitivity, I have withheld the use of names, other identifying traits, and references to elements of the religious corpus that are not at public disposal (e.g. lyrics of hymns). I have also refrained from including anecdotes and other types of ethnographic detail that informants also consider inappropriate to divulge. The reader should especially note that an advanced draft of this paper, translated into Portuguese, was presented to an important member of the Casa Santa for his review and comments on its acceptability and representativity. He had a few suggestions to make, which I have included in this final

Daniel, though I have also participated sporadically in other Barquinha churches. Consequently, I will describe most events as they occur in the Casa Santa.

Nowadays, the healers that attend clients are almost always spirits. Originally, Frei Daniel himself prayed over the sick.[7] However, he also encouraged and authorized some disciples to develop mediumship.[8] Historically, the first healer spirits to descend in the Barquinha were *missionários* (missionaries), who are spirits of high ecclesiastical authorities, such as Catholic bishops, from Heaven (or the Sky realm).[9] They usually have dual identity as *Encantos* ('Enchanted beings'), depending on the moment of their biography that is being evoked. The *Encantos* are significant entities in the cosmology of Amazonian riverine peoples, and are often implied in accounts of illness, death by drowning or other unfortunate events, as well as being summoned to help shamans during curing rites. They are an array of beings basically associated with geographical or topographical elements of the environment, such as alligators, snakes and mermaids (Prandi, 2001; Ferretti, 2000; Harris, 2000; Reeve, 2000; Slater, 1994).

In the Casa Santa, however, most of the healer spirits are *Pretos Velhos*. They behave with gentle, humble and acquiescent manners. This category of spirit is derived from the

---

version. Also, even though he spontaneously told me that I could mention the church by its name and did not need to resort to a pseudonym, I have decided to keep to this convention in order to preserve the confidentiality of the number of informants, friends, clients and spirits whose authorization I did not explicitly and individually seek concerning this paper, and who, covertly or overtly, inform my writing. Also, the reader should note that I sought and obtained, in person, the permission of the president of the Casa Santa to publish this article.

7. Among riverine mestizo Amazonian peoples and rubber tappers, this category of healer is called *rezador*, that is, 'one who prays' (e.g. see Reeve, 2000). Other elderly members of the Barquinha are also *rezadores*.

8. In this article, the terms 'spirit possession' and 'incorporation' are used analytically, in order to situate the presentation within the broad literature on spirit-entity influence that alters an individual's own behavioral and attitudinal dispositions and enactments. Barquinha folk regularly inform that their liturgical form of spirit-possession is *irradiação* (irradiation), which means that the spirit does not fully occupy and take control of the medium's body, thoughts, and so on. Instead, the medium *consciously* acts out the spirit's 'irradiations'. Or, in Paskoali's words, 'The mediums claim that they are the interpreters of the spirits' (2002: 120, my translation). A negative overtone is sometimes implicated in forms of spirit-possession in which the medium might be somewhat overpowered by the spirit and, therefore, not exercising free will and free conscience. Examples are *incorporação* (incorporation) or, further, *possessão* (possession). For example, Sena Araújo describes that during dancing rituals, 'incorporation sometimes occurs, even though generally there is a predominance of irradiations infusing the participants, since most of the indoctrinated entities develop a *different kind of relationship* with the host' (1999: 230, my translation, my emphasis). However, Paskoali (2002: 118 n. 22) points out that this theoretical terminological distinction is not sustained across all churches. My fieldwork in the Casa Santa suggests that the use of the varied terms may depend on the sociolinguistic context, including the tenor of the conversation. For instance, I noticed that events which during the ritual and within formal ritual speech were labeled *irradiação*, in later informal colloquial conversations among friends were spoken of as *incorporação*.

9. Barquinha cosmography is quite elaborate and recognizes three major cosmological domains: *Céu* (Sky or Heaven), *Terra* (Land) or *Floresta* (Forest), and *Mar* (the Sea or Aquatic realm). Each domain consists of several regions and kingdoms, which are described mostly through European romantic imagery (e.g. castles, princesses, monasteries, etc.). Broadly speaking, these descriptions coincide with those held by mixed-race riverine Amazonian peoples and rubber tappers, the immediate precedent socioeconomic milieu of numerous members (see Prandi, 2001; Harris, 2000; Slater, 1994).

Umbanda[10] pantheon. Other spirits from the Umbanda pantheon may also be involved in healing, notably the *Caboclos* (proudly independent Indians who resisted Western domination) and the *Erês* or *Crianças* (the playful spirits of infants and small children). *Encantos* may also be involved in healing.[11] In the Casa Santa, the *missionários* are mostly occupied with sacraments and sermons, though they may assist with healing on occasions.

The charity works

The *Obras de Caridade* (charity works) are the flagship of the Barquinha mission. Generally speaking, the service is offered at least every Saturday evening. Basically, members of the general public (called 'clients'), who seek some form of treatment or assistance, meet briefly with a healer spirit who offers them advice, spiritual cleansing or some other kind of aid. The details of the way that the service is organized differ slightly among churches. Descriptions of the healing service in other Barquinha churches can be found in Sena Araújo (this volume; also 1999: 166–74) and in Paskoali (2002: 115–21). The following is an outline of events in the Casa Santa.

Clients come to the church around seven o'clock in the evening, before the *Obras de Caridade* ritual begins. They approach a person sitting in the courtyard with a notebook, which is a registry of consultations. The client is assigned a number to see a healer spirit. A proportion of consulting patients in the Casa Santa are the uniformed members[12] and their families and acquaintances. However, the service has sustained uninterrupted continuity with Frei Daniel's charity work for the general public, who are its proclaimed *raison-d'être*. If the client is already engaged in long-term treatment or has a special preference, she or he will ask to see a specific healer. Otherwise, the person with the notebook will assess

---

10. Umbanda is a national religion of Brazil that began in the coastal metropoli in the 1930s, such as in Rio de Janeiro (e.g. see Brown, 1994; Giobellina and Gonzales, 1989). Briefly, in regards to this paper, Umbanda restitutes Brazilian history by summoning the spirits of colonial social classes and employing their inherent agencies for the benefit of the living. Often, Umbanda rites summon spirits to perform errands, to provide information, or to provide healing. There is no authoritative sacred text intrinsic to the religion or a centralized ecclesiastical organization. Rather, Umbanda temples are independent and based on the charismatic authority and prestige of the leader, who is always a spirit-medium. The Umbanda pantheon is open and syncretic. In practice, the spirits that are summoned down into mediums are usually deceased humans from social classes or ethnic categories that are understood to have access to specialized knowledge or capacities (such as gypsies, slaves, or unacculturated Indians). Usually, but not always, spirits may demand some form of fee or payment (such as an offering or often an item of addictive or luxurious consumption, such as tobacco, sweets or perfume). In this way, the spirits appear to desire to sustain some form of connection to modernity and capitalism and to mediate their relationship with clients along those terms, even though they ideologically embody anti-modern or pre-modern knowledge, traditions and agencies.

11. The presence of *Encantos* as healers is more common in the older Barquinhas, where, in fact, there is less predominance of a certain class of spirit (e.g. see Sena Araújo, 1999). In the newer Barquinhas, spirits from the Umbanda pantheon tend to predominate in the healing service. This is especially the case of the Barquinha churches opened in recent years by former members of the Casa Santa.

12. The majority of the Brazilian ayahuasca religions have a uniform or some defined form of clothing that is the required dress for committed members during rituals. In the Barquinha, the design of the ritual clothing is based on a sailor's uniform.

the case and assign a healer. Healers are roughly specialized. For example, one of them is particularly knowledgeable about medicinal plants and thus attends cases that require this kind of prescription. Others are known for their wisdom for counseling, and so on.

The actual ritual usually begins just after 7.30 pm, with the toll of a bell that announces that Daime is being served. The ingestion of Daime is inherent to the worship component of the ritual, but not to the healing encounters between client and spirit. Some clients drink Daime, but they are not intrinsically required or expected to drink Daime. In Barquinha churches, the ingestion of Daime is voluntary for non-members. After drinking, participants take up a seat inside the temple. Most are uniformed members. Clients usually await their turn in an adjacent vestibule. However, sometimes they sit inside the church and participate in the worship component.

The liturgy begins with the recitation of basic Roman Catholic prayers, such as Our Father, Hail Mary and the Apostles' Creed. Then, a predetermined set of hymns – also called *salmos* (psalms) in this liturgical context – is sung to open the session. After this, the ceremonial leader, called the *Comandante* (Commander), begins to summon the healer-spirits. One by one, the spirits are called to 'fulfill their commitment in the Charity Works'. As each spirit is summoned, the medium frequently exhales a loud whooshing sound, stands up and assumes a posture that indicates the presence of the spirit (such as a rigid arm or semi-closed eyelids). The spirit exchanges some predetermined set of greetings with the congregation and remains waiting for the rest to descend. Once all spirits have been summoned, the mediums then move out of the temple into a special room in the back used for healing called the *Salão das Obras de Caridade* (Charity Works Room) where they begin to attend the clients.[13]

After the mediums have left the temple, the ceremony continues with the worship component, in which the remaining participants continue to sing hymns and to recite prayers for several more hours until the ritual is finalized, usually after midnight. Many of these participants often drink a second dose of Daime, just after the spirits have begun to see the clients.

Simultaneous to the worship component in the temple, there are roughly seven to twelve healers attending clients within the healing room. Each healer has an assistant who performs several supporting duties, such as running errands (e.g. to fetch medicinal leaves) and writing instructions for the client (e.g. a certain prayer requirement). The assistant also has an important role during exorcisms. Although clients often come to the church accompanied by family or friends, they consult with the healer on their own. Thus, healing episodes are typically formed by a compact triad of spirit, assistant and client.

Two dominant motifs in Barquinha healing episodes are empathy and intimacy. Although there is a gradation concerning the degree of privacy during healing episodes (which is reflected in the treatment genre), by and large, public participation in the therapy is infrequent. Generally speaking, when it occurs, the participation of third parties is supportive. For example, in the event of a particularly rowdy possession by an unenlightened entity, additional healer-spirits often intervene in the exorcism rite and more helpers may

---

13. Spatial distribution of liturgies and spirit-possession episodes is a salient characteristic of Barquinha temple compounds. See, for example, Sena Araújo (this volume, also 1999) for a presentation of some relevant spaces and symbolic referents.

spontaneously remain alert and on call. This is different from therapeutic performances elsewhere, such as spirit-medium séances among the Kaluli, in which the public's approval of the spirit/medium can be decisive in the determination of authenticity of the event (Schieffelen, 1996).

Clients rarely linger after they have seen a healer. Although the worship component continues in the main temple, the grounds gradually vacate as the evening transpires. By the end of the night, only the more committed members remain in the temple grounds once the ritual has finished, where they socialize with one another for about an hour or so afterwards.

Healing performance genres

Healer spirits address a variety of problems using a somewhat restricted battery of techniques. I distinguish healing performance genres on the basis of the concentration of techniques applied.

The most common and frequent genre is counseling. Clients spontaneously seek healers to talk about their problems, but healers themselves spend a while asking questions to assess the client's situation. Generally speaking, the healers provide comforting advice, pastoral support, and instill hope and positive emotions in the client, as well as recommending them to respond to the predicament with an attitude of patience, tolerance and serenity.

After this conversation (perhaps roughly 15 minutes), healers usually proceed with the performance of a set of dramatic cleansing gestures over the client's body. These are generically called *passes* (passing over). After the *passe,* the healer often chalks therapeutic drawings on the ground, called *pontos riscados* (engraved marks or scratched points), and lights candles over them. Counseling, *passes* and the drawing of a *ponto riscado* most often go together, but not necessarily.

Another very frequent genre is exorcism. People are often involuntary victims of attachment by unenlightened spirits, generically called *exús*.[14] These negatively affect a person's emotions, thoughts and attitudes. The exorcism rite requires transferring the *exú* to a trained medium. After this, it is interrogated and made to confess its name and misdeeds, including whether someone sent it.

Severe or lasting conditions may receive special treatment on a different day. These treatments usually ensue from the standard therapeutic interventions, upon the recommendation of the healer. Some of the more grave consultations are treated with a performance called *descarrego* (discharge). This occurs in a secluded area, such as the forest. The

---

14. All spirits are gendered. The term *exú* refers to male unenlightened entities of this class, but is also the generic term. Female entities of this class are called *pomba-gira*. *Exús* (males) are described as being like 'those rascal boys on the streets' or 'a drunk that's always outside your house'. *Pomba-giras* are described as being like 'those girl-prostitutes on the corners'. Thus, unlike the healer spirits from Umbanda which are basically identified with colonial non-urban social groups, the unenlightened spirit-entities are conceived through the imagery of contemporary urban class dynamics, and represent the epitome of contemporary urban immorality.

client is surrounded with candles and explosives are detonated, enveloping the client in pungent smoke (cf. Sena Araújo, 1999: 183). Spiritual surgeries are another genre, scheduled for the 27th of each month. The surgeries always take place behind closed doors, in the healing room.[15] Surgery patients are usually members or sympathizers who are acquainted and familiar with the religion. They typically drink Daime, and they remain lying on mats. According to second-hand reports, healers perform approximately the same kind of gestures as in other interventions. The surgeries take place simultaneous to a seated ritual in the main temple called *Prestação de Contas* (Rendering Report) that is roughly similar to the *Obras de Caridade* ritual (Mercante, 2004; cf. Sena Araújo, 1999: 195–96).

Having concluded the presentation of the *Obras de Caridade* ritual and healing genres, the following sections delve into three major analytical approaches to healing in the Barquinha.

Biographical narratives

Anthropological scholarship on healing in the ayahuasca religions has regularly considered the matter from interpretive and symbolic approaches (e.g. Rose, 2005b; Pelaez, 2002). Authors are frequently interested in analyzing narratives and biographies provided by informants, uncovering recurrent emblematic motifs. In most accounts of healing in the ayahuasca religions, the soteriological discourse of informants awards a central status to ayahuasca. The existential readjustments and lifestyle changes emergent from the ayahuasca experience are usually given major significance. Becoming existentially implicated in the religion, such as becoming a uniformed member, is not infrequent (e.g. Pelaez, 2002; Groisman, 1999).

Two positions emerge in studies of the Barquinha regarding the use of Daime and therapeutic efficacy. On the one hand, Paskoali (2002), who relies fundamentally on symbolic analytical viewpoints and interpretive medical anthropological insights, makes use of the notion of symbolic efficacy as she analyzes informants' narratives. Mercante (2004) offers another position. A researcher concerned with the consciousness-body interface, he draws attention to psychointegrative[16] processes.

Paskoali (2002) mostly interviewed committed members of a church, who claimed healing as an integral part of their conversion and commitment to the religion. She focuses on recurrent themes that appear in narratives, such as the notion of sin as the cause of illness, and the soteriological potential of suffering. Mostly, her informants claim that Daime is implicated in their healing by providing knowledge (such as revelations, visions, instructions), by purging (cleansing, purifying), or by facilitating contact and communication with healer-entities.

---

15. Or another special room in other Barquinha churches (e.g. Sena Araújo, 1999: 196).

16. Winkelman favors the term 'psychointegrators' to refer to substances such as ayahuasca, which 'stimulate the integration of behavior, protomentation, and socioemotional dynamics with language-based ratiomentation, egoic representations, and personal identity' (Winkelman, 2000: 210).

Mercante (2004) concentrates attention on a specific Barquinha healing rite, the spiritual surgery or operation that is offered on the 27th of each month during the *Prestação de Contas* (Rendering Report) ritual. Spiritual surgeries are not carried out very frequently and are not usually prescribed as primary treatments. This healing rite is also unique because the patients usually drink Daime as part of the therapy. They are often members of the church or close acquaintances who are accustomed to drinking Daime and, at the time of treatment, share much of the basic theological scheme.

Mercante centrally considers therapeutic efficacy in association with the involuntary mental imagery that surfaces during the Daime experience – his working definition of the native term *miração* (Mercante, 2003). Having performed a longitudinal study of several months, he contemplates psychointegrative processes. He explains that the *miração* mediates and makes conscious as a 'coherent and workable whole', 'the ritual, the Daime, the processes of self-transformation/knowledge/exploration, elements of the individual's consciousness and physiological condition' (Mercante, 2006: iii).

Symbolic efficacy

Paskoali works with the notion of 'symbolic efficacy'. She states that that the 'efficiency of healing should be sought in the symbolic system' (Paskoali, 2002: 167, my translation). Essentially, she proposes that increasing participation in the context leads to a resignification of concepts of health and illness which, in turn, leads to a modification of daily habits and, eventually, aggregation into the religion (Paskoali, 2002: 167).

She notes that the healing service primarily draws people with low incomes and considers that they use the religion's symbolic system as a language with which to understand their symptoms (Paskoali, 2002: 150). She explains that most people who come to the church for healing were referred to the church by someone else who had already been attended there, is a participant of the church, or lives in the neighborhood (Paskoali, 2002: 150). For example, Paskoali describes the case of a person who came to the church after a series of unsuccessful attempts at numerous other treatments. The author notes that the person in suffering is desperately searching for 'a language' that will provide an explanation with which she can understand what is happening with herself (Paskoali, 2002: 175).

Paskoali quotes the president of the church explaining that the root of all illness and problems is our own sin, and the purpose of illness and suffering is for us to become more humble and fraternal (2002: 152). Illness is the result of a lifestyle that is conflictive and disharmonic. She says that the Barquinha community stimulates, in the suffering individual, awareness of the urgency of reformulating her or his *modus vivendi*.

The transformative potential of Daime is brought to bear in the internally confronted individual, effecting purification and cleansing, in order to achieve a personal state of balance and a socially harmonious lifestyle (Paskoali, 2002: 153). According to Paskoali, Daime amplifies consciousness and therefore facilitates spiritual revelations that allow a new vision of the world and, principally, of one's own personal situation. Such learning specifically occurs during the *miração* (Paskoali, 2002: 169).

Paskoali (2002: 169) recalls that Monteiro da Silva (1983) had already described the *miração* as a process of transcendence (*transcendência*) and cleansing (*despoluição*). This suggests that the symbolic efficacy of the *miração* lies in the cognitive adjustments that result from the experience, and in any purging that may occur. For her informants, Daime offers a diagnosis and indication of treatment. The Daime also intrinsically participates in the re-establishment of harmony and health, for example through vomiting, which is considered to provide purification.

Actions and motifs in healing performances

In addition to narratives of the self, analyses of healing in the Barquinha regularly mention some of the standard actions that pervade therapeutic performances (e.g. Mercante, 2004; Paskoali, 2002; Sena Araújo, 1999). Here, I wish to provide more detail regarding the actions and motifs involved in these performances. I am especially interested in drawing attention to rites because, for informants, ritual actions are intrinsically efficacious. For example, consider the case recounted by Paskoali of a mother who felt remorse for having buried an infant unbaptized and without a religious service. The mother explains that the Daime showed her that she had done wrong and had persistently ordered her to 'simulate a funeral' for the child's post-mortem benefit (Paskoali, 2002: 154).

As inferred from conversations with informants, two major clusters of metaphors are involved in their understandings of spirit activity. On the one hand, there is ample use of a language of luminosity and darkness that is indicative of the morality of spiritual circumstances. For example, a sign that used to be under the tall Cross just outside of the main temple doors advised, 'He who loves his brother is in the Light'. Also, the Daime is frequently called *Santa Luz* (Holy Light). On the other hand, the physics of spiritual events is often spoken of through a language of electromagnetism. For example, the event of spirit-possession is talked of as a spirit's 'irradiation' (*irradiação*) that activates the medium's body – itself called 'apparatus' (*aparelho*). Therapeutic performances enact these metaphors coherently. Removal of noxious energies is usually achieved through extractive gestures. Luminosity is usually assured through the pervasive presence of candles.

Extraction and symmetrical restoration

During the typical healing encounter in the Casa Santa's healing room, counseling is usually followed by a series of performative gestures, called *passes,* which the healer executes over the body of the client. The movements mostly suggest to me the extraction and removal of invisible elements. Sena Araújo describes the *passes* as 'a series of expressive symbolic gestures that intend to act upon diverse parts of the body, such as the chest, head or limbs, attempting to extract negative influences and to re-establish the individual's health' (Sena Araújo, 1999: 172, my translation). Paskoali shows that participants experience *passes* in the same way. One of her informants explains, 'when you are receiving the *passe* here [points to abdomen] you feel something being pulled out, you feel and see that thing coming out, like a ray of smoke, and you feel that it's something negative, eh? Leaving your body in peace' (Paskoali, 2002: 156, my translation).

The extractive gestures of the *passe* can be performed with the bare hands, for example by executing scraping movements. Healers also make extensive use of the *Espada* (Sword), which is a wide scarf-like cloth. *Espadas* are usually white, but they can also be colored. Symbolic designs are sometimes painted onto them. The drawings manifest certain attributes of the spirit (for example, its cosmological domain), as I learned from an informant who once explained to me each of the designs painted on the *Espada* that belonged to her *Preta Velha*. Most of the time the spirit carries the *Espada* draped around her or his neck – which, incidentally, serves as a clear indicator to the general public that the medium is 'with' a spirit. When used in a *passe*, the *Espada* appears to function through contact. The *Espada* is briefly placed into contact with the body of the client, for example by draping it around the head, laying it across the client's back, or brushing a part of the body. The spirit then flicks away the cloth, as if shaking off some negative element that has been extracted from the client.

Passes are usually a symmetrically patterned set of movements. For example, the *Espada* may be placed across the client's back stretching from right shoulder to left waist and then flicked away. Immediately the spirit then places the cloth stretched from left shoulder to right waist, and again flicks it clean. Similarly, the *Preto Velho* with whom I often consulted would run his fingers across my crown in one direction and then run them around in the opposite direction of circulation, flicking away his fingers after each movement. A *schacapa*-type of leafy brush is also used by some healers. They brush it around the client in one direction and then in the opposite direction.

A *passe* may also include explosive noises, such as the clicking of fingers around the client's body or isolated claps. Additionally, as in Amazonian shamanry, the healer makes use of air currents (e.g. Luna and Amaringo, 1999: 26). These include blowing strongly over the client (e.g. on the crown or into the ears), whistling, emitting whooshing sounds and blowing tobacco smoke over the client.[17]

I assume that the restitution of a balanced symmetrical harmony of some invisible element seems to be integral to the *passe*. This resonates with many healing systems, including Amazonian ayahuasca shamanry (e.g. Gebhart-Sayer, 1986). Ayahuasca shamanry is also frequently oriented to removing invisible intrusive noxious elements from the patient's pristinely healthy body (e.g. Harner, 1972: 160–61).

Illumination and affirmation

In the Barquinha, candles performatively provide illumination and other spiritual benefits, collapsing the distinction between spiritual and empirical luminosity. For example,

---

17. With the exception of tobacco, it is not especially common for healers in the Casa Santa to make use of smells and smoke. Smudging with incense is performed only rarely. This is a striking contrast with Umbanda rituals elsewhere, generally speaking, which regularly include extensive use of incense and burning pungent leaves. Perfumed water, so common in mestizo shamanry (e.g. Luna, 1986) is sometimes sprinkled over clients, but this is exceptional in the Casa Santa. In fact, regular members sometimes seem to be very sensitive to odors and appear to find the smell of incense invasive, nauseous and disturbing. The use of incense is absent in other types of Barquinha rituals, too.

during fieldwork, I noted that committed members of the Casa Santa never pray without simultaneously lighting a candle. Furthermore, a Barquinha friend of mine once scolded a Catholic friend for praying in her room in the dark.

Generally speaking, it appears to me that candles indicate moralized spiritual presence or agency.[18] Amongst other things, candles can provide protection. They are necessary elements in all types of Barquinha rituals. White candles are placed at entrances, paths and doorways during all rituals. They are also placed in the hands of a healer-spirit when she or he descends into a medium – parenthetically indicating to others that the spirit is present. White candles are also lit beside the Daime during all ceremonies and also near the drums during dancing rituals.

Within therapeutic performances, *passes* may include the use of candles. These are lit and used for making the sign-of-the-cross over clients, for example in front of their face or on certain points of the body, such as the palms. Candles are also important for devotional practices that the healer may prescribe for the client.

Candles additionally play an important role in the execution of the chalk drawings called *pontos riscados*, which have an affirmative efficacy. Candles are typically lit over the drawing in strategic positions and left to burn out. These drawings are common in the Afro-Brazilian and Afro-Caribbean religions, in which they represent the spirit. A unique combination of abstract symbols (e.g. arrows, stars, etc.) is drawn, which provides information that identifies, and is particular to, the spirit (e.g. Krippner and Villoldo, 1976: 114). Sena Araújo reports that is also the case in the Barquinha church of his fieldwork (1999: 182; also this volume). However, this is not how these drawings are used in the Casa Santa. Instead, it appears to me that the *pontos riscados* represent the client.

For instance, the colors of the candles represent aspects of the client that require fortification. Also, the symbols that are drawn do not refer to facets of the spirit,[19] but of the client (or surrogate beneficiary). As explained to me by an informant, they represent characteristics of the client that require reinforcement or strengthening, such as certain values or attributes. Further, in the Casa Santa, the beneficiary's name is usually written on paper and placed in the middle of the drawing, with a candle left to burn covering it. Once the drawing is completed, the healer then begins to execute some performative gestures over the drawing. Many of these are the same kind of movements that were also performed over the client during the *passe*, such as blowing tobacco smoke, making signs-of-the-cross, and snapping fingers.

Informants also express that the *ponto riscado* strengthens the relationship of the client with her or his guardian angel or other protector spirits. In this sense, analytically speaking, it is structurally the opposite of exorcism.

---

18. In Umbanda lore, the color of a candle indicates the kind of spiritual agency that is being summoned. For example, informants report that black magic rites (called 'Quimbanda') make use of black, red, or black-and-red candles.

19. In the Casa Santa, symbols that identify the spirit are, instead, painted onto the *Espadas*.

Exorcisms

Exorcisms are a paradigmatic type of healing episode for the Barquinha mission. The rite neatly condenses familiar intervention techniques and metaphors. Barquinha folk routinely attribute spiritual manifestations, events and symptoms to the actions of spirits. Preying unenlightened spirit-entities are often held accountable for illness and misfortune episodes, while clients are often treated as innocent victims. Exorcisms clearly reveal this understanding, providing 'a language' (Paskoali, 2002) – verbal and enacted – for the client's distress. In all of the numerous cases that I have observed, the exorcism rite has always been successful.

The performance of exorcisms is frequent in the Casa Santa (and also in other Barquinha churches, e.g., Sena Araújo, 1999). Clients are regularly relieved of the involuntary attachment or parasitical proximity of unenlightened spirits, generically known as *exús*. These entities are a burden on the client, as they negatively affect thoughts and emotions.

The diagnosis of *exú* proximity is revealed during the therapeutic encounter, and is given by the healer. Typically, the client is unaware of the preying of the *exú* and simply feels unusually distressed or anxious, for example. Thus, the most frequent kind of exorcism is performed when healer and assistant spontaneously begin to execute the exorcism rite in the presence of the client who is fully conscious and not necessarily behaving aberrantly.

The exorcism rite includes praying some Catholic prayers and then transferring the *exú* from the client to a trained medium. The *exú* is passed through contact of the bodies. In the case of the Casa Santa, the forehead of the medium is gingerly placed into contact with the forehead of the client. In a snap, the medium then begins to shake or in some way manifests that the *exú* has been imprisoned in the medium's body and removed from the client (though the client may not have been acting in any remarkable way). The exorcism rite reinforces the pervasive metaphor of extraction that is recurrent in Barquinha healing, and the understanding that spiritual events obey electromagnetic principles – including when the source of affliction is a spirit-entity.[20]

Once trapped, the *exú* is then submitted to interrogation by the assistant. The interrogation seeks to identify the spirit-entity and its motivations for afflicting the client. This includes asking if it was sent by someone to stalk the client. The client witnesses the interrogation of the *exú* who, through the trained medium, confesses its purpose for attaching to the victim, whether it was hired to do black magic, and so on. Incorporated in the trained medium, the *exú* acts, responds and speaks in a manner and type of voice that is expected for this class of spirit and is recognizable to participants. The interrogation provides a verbalized response for the nature of the client's discomfort.

In terms of the interaction, the interrogation basically takes for granted that the client is the innocent victim of an external source of malice, who may even be another person who transacted with the *exú* to pester the victim. I think that exorcism in the Barquinha

---

20. Cf. the performance of this rite in the church studied by Sena Araújo (1999: 181), in which the entity is transferred instead into a second spirit-medium. I would like to note that, in that church, the main healer-spirit stands between the client and the second medium and gingerly rests a hand on each of their heads, as if mediating the transference of the entity.

is, in the least, oriented toward providing relief for the client (and, of course, the salvation of the *exú*). Possession by *exús* is a common diagnosis, and does not assume that the client has been engaging in aberrant or anti-social behavior. It is not a social diagnosis (e.g. suggested by the family), but offered by the healer during consultation and can catch the client unaware. It can be a primary diagnosis. Not being a social diagnosis, exorcism in the Barquinha is a quick and straightforward affair. By contrast, as an example, exorcism among the Sinhalese is a last resort treatment for dealing with a person that has been displaying deviant behavior. The family of the victim hires the exorcist. Kapferer suggests that the Sinhalese exorcism rite attempts to reconstruct the social self of the victim (Kapferer, 1979).

In the Barquinha, however, exorcisms are frequent events during which the clients are typically in full use of mental faculties and consciously witness the episode. Rather than a reconstruction of the social self, for instance, Barquinha exorcism seems to engage with the individual's emotional, intellectual and moral grounding by asserting innocence. The same theme appears in other therapeutic interactions. For example, I once consulted with a *Caboclo* in another Barquinha church. Without much oral exchange of information, he quickly began to perform an intensely vigorous *passe* upon me, that had me swaying and losing my balance. Throughout the *passe,* he was fervently praying to Jesus that I be released from the enervating bonds caused by some unidentified perpetrator's malice.

After interrogation, the *exú* is then commanded to go to Heaven, to a special enclosure where it will remain resting and being converted.[21] In this enclosure it is subjected to evangelization and spends its time singing hymns of praise. After a period, the entity will seek a Christian baptism and thenceforth perform charity and work for Good (Balzer, 2003; Sena Araújo, 1999).

Unenlightened spirits are not punished nor simply cast away. Instead, they are treated kindly and sent to Heaven. The intention is to transform not-good into good, disturbance into harmony, and spirits that prey into those that provide charity. This is fundamentally coherent with the general redemptive mission of the Barquinha.

Therapeutic subjectivity

Unlike biomedical or psychoanalytical treatments in which the healer is largely expected to maintain distance from the client (spatially, linguistically, interpretively, and even through clothing and the use of sterile medical instruments that avoid direct contact with the client), Barquinha healing is decisively empathetic. Barquinha counseling is based on an enhancement of subjectivity and the collapsing of therapeutic objectivity.

---

21. The enclosure is known by several names, including 'concentration camp' (*campo de concentração*). My informants were emphatic to make clear that it is a place of repose and peace. On the basis of their conversations, I have felt discouraged to name it 'concentration camp', which Sena Araújo (1999) reports as the term used in the church that he studied – although one of his informants calls it 'concentration hall' (*salão de concentração*) (Sena Araújo, 1999: 216). Instead, my informants spontaneously described this enclosure as a convalescent hospital or nursing home (*casa de repouso*), and other similar imagery.

Intimacy is integral to the actions and behavior of healers. In the Casa Santa's healing room, healing encounters occur with the client, healer and assistant sitting on low stools that oblige them to adopt stooped positions and interlocking legs. Clients and healers form small, intimate cliques in which they talk over problems and concerns in a low and hushed voice. Healers additionally engage in comforting body contact with clients, such as holding their hands or resting a hand on their heads while speaking to them.

Intimacy is also expressed linguistically. For example, healers and clients typically speak to each other using consanguineal kinship terms. Most healers in the Casa Santa are *Pretos Velhos*. The *Pretos Velhos* are elderly, soothing, wise spirits, who interact warmly with clients. People address them as 'grandfather' or 'grandmother' (or other terms). Reciprocally, the healers speak to clients calling them 'my daughter' or 'my son'. Also, clients typically solicit a blessing from the healer, as is customary for intimate kinship or kin-like relationships in Brazil.[22]

It seems to me that the basis of the therapeutic moral authority of the *Pretos Velhos* is also the justification for their intimacy with clients: a shared experience of suffering (see Hale, 1997: 404). The *Pretos Velhos* embody a history of successful endurance of unjust cruelty and suffering. They empathize with the client and offer counseling that reinforces compassion, understanding and patience. For example, I consulted several times with a certain *Preto Velho*, who frequently assented to what I was saying by interjecting 'I know, yes, I know how it is'.

I think that the efficacy of Barquinha healing and consultations includes the attainment of emotional, moral and intellectual reassurance of patients. Therapeutic performances and interactions provide clients with a sense of relief and may inspire hope regarding their condition and prognosis. For instance, the same *Preto Velho* also often reassured me, saying 'My son, be patient. Be sure that all will come out fine', and similar sorts of encouragements.

Ordered spontaneity

Though also characterized by intimacy and empathy, Taussig (1987) has used the apparently unstructured nature of ayahuasca shamanic healing in the Colombian Putumayo region to contest Lévi-Strauss's suggestion that shamanic healing intends to restore or construct order in the patient's and community's ideological environment. Impressed, instead, by its apparent disorderliness, Taussig suggests that amid stories, jokes, interjections and humming, patient and healer orchestrate the volatile moral and emotional ambiguities of social relations (Taussig, 1987: 460–63).

Barquinha healing routinely puts into action recurrent themes and motifs. In contrast to Taussig's observations for Putumayo therapeutic interactions, it seems to me that, in the Barquinha, patients, healers, and other participants, orchestrate the resolution of the predicament largely along structured idioms. Although Barquinha healing performances also include stories, humming, whistling, singing and, at times, even jokes (or rather, *Pretos Velhos* display a light-hearted attitude and often warmly cackle at a patient's

---

22. In contrast, the blessing is not solicited from other classes of spirits, such as the *Bispos* (Bishops).

remarks, dissolving their gloomy graveness), the interactions still seem to follow a basic template that pre-determines actor-positions, the therapists' modes of response, and sequences of acts (e.g. counseling precedes a *passe,* and a *ponto riscado* – if included – is sketched last). Order is also evident in therapeutic actions during the *passe,* which follows a symmetrical route over the client's body. Similarly, the symbols and colors used in a *ponto riscado* are coded.

The overall public visibility of spirits' behaviors in the Barquinha characterize the religion and its rituals as aesthetically expressive and 'extrospective'. Sena Araújo (1999: 236) has suggested that the ritual actions executed during Barquinha dancing festivities express emblematic ideas and feelings, while the performances render the cosmology dynamic. I think that a similar remark can be made for healing interactions. The actions and performances dynamize the cosmology and value-system, implementing and real-izing it in real time. Therefore, it is not that 'rituals' are some form of idealized artificial caricature of interpersonal interaction, nor is there an absence of ideological ordering amidst the hummings, stories and whistling. Rather, the actual informal interaction that occurs between parties is structured along resolute criteria.

And so, Lévi-Strauss's suggestion seems to be applicable in this sense. However, while other authors, such as Paskoali and Mercante, closely follow his approach by focusing their attention on the achievement of order and coherence in the ideological, symbolic, emotional and interpretive systems of the individual patient, I wish to draw attention to the social interactions staged and rehearsed during healing encounters. Paskoali (2002) confidently uses Lévi-Strauss's notion of 'symbolic efficacy', while Mercante (2006), instead, appeals to the notion of 'psychointegrative' processes. Here, I wish to enhance the discussion by supplementing their reflections on intrapsychological dynamics with the suggestion that Barquinha folk dissolve the boundaries between 'ritual' (understood as formal) interaction and spontaneous sociality.

I suspect that Barquinha healing encounters model socially appropriate types of inter-action. The therapeutic relationship models morally proper forms of social interaction, emphasizing intimacy, privacy and enhanced subjectivity. This type of social interac-tion between healer and client seems to agree with the kind of informal sociality widely reported for forest-dwelling populations in Amazonia (e.g. see Overing and Passes, 2000), and may be adaptively appropriate in a social milieu characterized by impermanence, migration and 'making kin out of others' (Vilaça, 2002) as the *Pretos Velhos* regularly do.

I see Barquinha *Pretos Velhos* as representatives of desirable moral character. The inter-actions with them possibly contrast with the damaged relationships that sometimes moti-vate the upset client to seek a comforting and understanding *Preto Velho.* The Barquinha has been developing in a sociohistorical milieu that does not conform to notions or aspi-rations of a bounded and stable community. In this sense, I would agree with Taussig that the healing interactions intend to address the instability of the social context. However, this is not achieved through pragmatic orchestrations, but through a series of defined techniques and displays. In addition, the healers who are called upon to address these matters are, primarily, the ancestors of the religion's founders, a people who had them-selves been subjected to cruel structural violences.

The actions portrayed in therapeutic interactions mostly suggest the extraction of noxious and disruptive alien intrusions, which must reflect back on the very history of these people as recent migrants deceptively lured or conscripted into Amazonia during the Rubber Era, themselves descended from the African populations forced to migrate to Brazil. Therapeutic performances purge the client of intrusions, restoring the pristine health of the innocent, but also proceed to strengthen and buttress the boundaries of the individual to avoid further infringement.

Healing history

Barquinha mediums incorporate spirits and souls from a diversity of origins. For example, some *Encantos* are members of the royal ranks of certain Enchanted kingdoms. Mediums also incorporate spirits that have some relevance to their immediate lived-history. This is the case, for instance, of the souls of deceased people known to the participants. These souls receive post-mortem redemption through the efforts of the living (e.g. through the *Doutrinação de almas* – Indoctrination of souls – rite; see Sena Araújo, 1999: 212 for a description).

Informants consistently explain Barquinha spirit-possession as an act of charity. The beneficiaries of this charity are unsaved spirit-beings and souls of the dead, which are the only kind of spirit-entity that Barquinha mediums incorporate. The highest of spirit-beings, such as the Catholic saints, do not descend into mediums. Neither do the mighty *orixás* (Yoruba deities invoked in Umbanda, Candomblé, and other Afro-Brazilian religions). The possession of mediums by ancestors and other deceased persons relevant to the participants' histories, as well as other unsaved beings, puts into action the redemptive ethos of the mission, continuously redeeming the group's own history and significant world.

Spirits have social identities and qualities that mirror the human social world. These qualities define agencies that are considered inherent to each class and that are harnessed by the spirit-mediums and implemented in the variety of rites and practices. Barquinha redemption of the stereotypes of Brazilian formative colonial social classes (e.g. the Black slaves, the Indians) does not overtly contest the basis of the classification system (e.g. race), nor does it straightforwardly deny its validity. Instead, while accepting the hegemonic classification *ipso facto*, its soteriological implications are redefined. Healers are mostly recruited from these ranks. Submerged knowledges associated with certain social classes are recognized as legitimate, though they are restrictively assigned to special locations and circumstances.

Barquinha cosmology reveals an ethnosociology that sees the universe as a unitary, but complex, social system. Spirits are at once individuals with unique personalities striving for their individual salvation, as well as members of corporate social classes that are relevant to the historical experience of the people who established this religion (for example, many are genealogically descended from the enslaved populations). Through the ongoing practices, redemption is offered for individual spirits, with their conversion to Christianity and performance of charity. However, redemption simultaneously occurs for the historical social classes that they belong to *qua* classes, as the latter are stripped of negative stereotypes that were (perhaps still are) imposed by hegemonic groups (such as the association between the clandestine African religiosity of the slaves, and the White masters' demonization of it and suspicion of vengeful black magic) and revalued within the Barquinha context as unique skills and abilities that should be harnessed into positive contributions (thus, the slaves are understood to have expert knowledge for countering the effects of black magic). Participants and spirits empathize with each other's suffering.[23] Ideological redemption of submerged classes is actively implemented during healing interactions, and this may be influential in patient compliance, if not also itself a veiled therapeutic target.

In addition, though, Barquinha cosmology is not a caste system. Spirits pass from one category to another in the course of their biography. As mentioned earlier, the exorcism rite redeems spirit-entities by moving them up the soteriological-cosmological ladder, the ascension of which is expressed in social class imagery. Consider, for example, one evening when Rita (pseudonym) casually asked me, 'did you know that *exús* become handsome young men when they convert?' and proceeded to tell me about a former-*exú* that appeared to her in a dream, now handsome and smartly dressed.

High ecclesiastical status appears to be the highest rank achievable for yet-unsaved spirits. For example, several notable *missionários* (missionaries) had been *Encantos* in the lower realms before becoming *missionários* in Heaven. Healer-spirits may also move up cosmological regions and change spirit categories. For instance, there are some known *Pretas Velhas* who are now nuns (and therefore, *missionárias*) in a monastery in Heaven. This form of redemption as redefining cosmological positioning as a form of social status re-positioning also reaches deceased members of the religion who, in several cases, have been recognized as *missionários*. Fundamentally, members of submerged social classes can aspire to achieving heavenly and ecclesiastical status by following Barquinha moral prescriptions.

The expressive execution of discourse through spirit-possession and the themes that are enacted in the healing encounters evoke the shifting living conditions and hybrid histories that are compiled in the biographies of the religion's participants and clientele. The ongoing redirection of spirits to appropriate and improving locations, accompanied by changes in agency, mission, and status, may have parallels with these people's own histories and aspirations as migrants in consolidating Acre.

Conclusion

Most healing in the Barquinha is generically referred to as 'charity works' and there is a ceremony by the same name conducted on Saturday evenings, in which the healing service is structured into the liturgy and, in a sense, emanates from the worship component (e.g. see Sena Araújo, 1999: 174). The ingestion of Daime is inherent to the worship component of the ritual, but not to the healing encounters themselves. Consulting clients are not required to drink Daime, nor to participate in the worship service. For many clients, the healing encounter is a circumscribed episodic experience, and they might not have further participation in the church.

---

23. Participants show an interest in exploring the biographies of the spirits.

Healing reports which implicate the Daime as a therapeutic agent, often support analyses that favor biographical self-narratives provided by informants. They regularly claim personality, lifestyle and moral transformations. This has been successively reiterated for the Santo Daime (e.g. Pelaez, 2002). In studies of healing in the Barquinha that take this approach, informants are often committed members or sympathizers who have some degree of long-term attachment to the religion. Paskoali (2002), for example, relies on interpretive insights and makes use of the concept of 'symbolic efficacy', highlighting the importance of adjustments in the individual's symbolic dimensions.

However, because the ingestion of Daime is not intrinsic to many healing encounters, it is important to consider the therapeutic potential of other aspects of these episodes. Here, I have described in some detail the enacted motifs implied in healing performances. These regularly suggest the extraction of intrusive noxious elements and symmetrical restoration. In addition, affirmative rites buttress the boundaries of the individual. Exorcisms dramatically enact these metaphors, withdrawing disturbing personalized alien influences from the victim.

Spirit-possession is a key feature of many Barquinha liturgies, and local understandings weave therapeutic discourse into their ideological comprehensions. Spirit-possession can be thought of as enacted discourse about relationships with alterities (Boddy, 1994). Barquinha folk moralize the degree of influence that alters should have upon an individual, largely rejecting being overpowered or domineered by such agents. Notably, they ideologically distinguish between their liturgical form of spirit-possession – *irradiação* (irradiation) – in which the medium is *consciously* and *willfully* acting out the spirit's influence, and those other forms – *incorporação* (incorporation) and *possessão* (possession) – that imply a reduction in the medium's threshold of consciousness and control.

Therefore, in accounts that include personality transformations ensuing from the ingestion of Daime, it is not uncommon for individuals to develop the notion that health and illness originates in their inner recesses, which the Daime reveals to them, assisting their cleansing and growth. Whereas, therapeutic performances in the Barquinha may often locate the client in a position of presumed innocence and seek the source of affliction in external agents. In this case, the therapeutic episode develops from a specific kind of social interaction established with a healer spirit, and may explicitly stage (as in exorcisms) the moral dimension of social interaction and interpersonal influence. It is possible, then, that a therapeutic target of these encounters is the quality and nature of social relationships – as compared to a therapeutic reorganization of the individual's inner self mediated through Daime.

In this sense, healer-client interactions might serve to model appropriate social relationships. The healers of the Barquinha often emblematically embody ideological stereotypes that speak to themes of racism, foreigner status, submerged knowledges, class solidarity, resistance and accommodation. Redeemed through the Barquinha, they enact the moral order and may provide templates for participants and clients to review their own modes of social insertion. The relatively structured idioms of Barquinha therapeutic performances seem to suggest that they respond to a distinct ideological framework, and are not volatile pragmatic orchestrations of the ambiguities of social life, as Taussig (1987) suggests for Putumayo ayahuasca healing. However, Taussig's insights may be suitable in the sense that Acrean social development has not conformed to notions of bounded communities and cultures, and perhaps this is one aspect that Barquinha healing encounters recurrently try to address. Unlike healing effected through Daime, which implies lasting personality adjustments, healer-client encounters are distinctly episodic.

As a religion of migrants developing in a variegated social milieu, it is probably very suggestive that their liturgies frequently enact a concern with reorganizing space and the positioning and influence of agents interacting within it. For this article, the notion that healing is achieved by extracting intrusive elements may be their strongest claim to historical innocence, as they come to terms with the structural forces that have been consistently pushing them into new lands and domineered societal relations. In their hearts, it is not that they are guilty of intrusion. Rather, it is the legacy of Brazilian history that needs to be cleansed out of them.

References

Balzer, Carsten. 2003. *Wege zum Heil: Die Barquinha*. Mettingen: Brasilienkunde-Verlag.

Boddy, Janice. 1994. 'Spirit Possession Revisited: Beyond Instrumentality'. *Annual Review of Anthropology* 23 (1994): 407–34.

Brown, Diana DeG. 1994. *Umbanda: Religion and Politics in Urban Brazil*. New York: Columbia University Press.

Couto, Fernando. 2002. 'Santo Daime: rito da ordem'. In Labate and Sena Araújo, 2002: 339–65.

Dobkin de Rios, Marlene. 1970a. 'A Note on the Use of Ayahuasca among Urban Healing Mestizo Populations in the Peruvian Amazon'. *American Anthropologist* NS 72(6): 1419–22.

Dobkin de Rios, Marlene. 1970b. 'Banisteriopsis in Witchcraft and Healing Activities in Iquitos, Peru'. *Economic Botany* 24(3): 296–300.

Ferretti, Mundicarmo. 2000. *Maranhão Encantado: Encantaria maranhense e outras histórias*. São Luís: UEMA Editora.

Gebhart-Sayer, Angelika. 1986. 'Una terapia estética: Los diseños visionarios del Ayahuasca entre los Shipibo-Conibo'. *América Indígena* 46(1): 189–218.

Giobellina, Fernando and Elda Gonzales. 1989. *Spirits from the Margin. Umbanda in São Paulo. A Study in Popular Religion and Social Experience*. Stockholm: Almqvist & Wiksell.

Goulart, Sandra. 2002. 'O contexto do surgimento do culto do Santo Daime: formação da comunidade e do calendário ritual'. In Labate and Sena Araújo (2002), 313–37.

Groisman, Alberto. 1999. *Eu Venho da Floresta: Um estudo sobre o contexto simbólico do uso do Santo Daime*. Florianópolis: Editora da UFSC.

Hale, Lindsay. 1997. 'Preto Velho: Resistance, Redemption, and Engendered Representations of Slavery in a Brazilian Possession-Trance Religion'. *American Ethnologist* 24(2): 392–414.

Harner, Michael, 1972, *The Jívaro: People of the Sacred Waterfalls*. Berkeley, CA: University of California Press.

Harris, Mark. 2000. *Life on the Amazon: The Anthropology of a Brazilian Peasant Village*. Oxford: Oxford University Press.

Kapferer, Bruce. 1979. 'Mind, Self, and Other in Demonic Illness: The Negation and Reconstruction of Self'. *American Ethnologist* 6(1) (February 1979): 110–33.

Krippner, Stanley and Alberto Villoldo. 1976. *The Realms of Healing*. Millbrae, CA: Celestial Arts.

Labate, Beatriz C. and Wladimyr Sena Araújo, eds. 2002. *O Uso Ritual da Ayahuasca*. Campinas: Mercado de Letras.

Labigalini, Eliseu. 1998. 'The Use of Ayahuasca in a Religious Context for Former Alcohol-dependents'. Master's thesis, Escola Paulista de Medicina, UNIFESP (São Paulo).

Luna, Luis Eduardo. 1986. *Vegetalismo: Shamanism among the Mestizo Population of the Peruvian Amazon*. Stockholm: Almqvist & Wiksell.

Luna, Luis Eduardo and Pablo Amaringo. 1999 [1991]. *Ayahuasca Visions: The Religious Iconography of a Peruvian Shaman*. Berkeley, CA: North Atlantic Books.

MacRae, Edward. 1999. 'The Use of Ayahuasca in the Santo Daime Healing Rituals'. Work in progress paper for paper presented at the X International Conference on the Reduction of Drug Related Harm, Geneva. March 21–25.

Maia Neto, Florestan J. 2003. *Contos da Lua Branca: Histórias do Mestre Raimundo Irineu Serra e de Sua Obra Espiritual Contadas por Seus Contemporâneos*. Volume 1 (132 Flores). Rio Branco: Fundação Elias Mansour.

Mercante, Marcelo S. 2003. 'Images of Healing: Investigating the Possible Connections between Spontaneous Mental Imagery and the Processes of Sickness and Healing in a Brazilian Ayahuasca Religion'. PhD research proposal, Saybrook Graduate School and Research Center.

Mercante, Marcelo S. 2004. 'Miração and Healing: A study Concerning Involuntary Mental Imagery and Healing Process'. Paper presented at the Toward a Science of Consciousness 2004 Conference. Center for Consciousness Studies, University of Arizona.

Mercante, Marcelo S. 2006. 'Images of Healing: Spontaneous Mental Imagery and Healing Process in the Barquinha, a Brazilian Ayahuasca Religious System'. PhD dissertation, Saybrook Graduate School and Research Center.

Metzner, Ralph. 1999. 'Introduction: Amazonian Vine of Visions'. In Metzner (ed.), *Ayahuasca: Human Consciousness and the Spirits of Nature*, 1–45. New York: Thunder's Mouth Press.

Monteiro da Silva, Clodomir. 1983. 'O Palácio de Juramidam – Santo Daime: um ritual de transcendência e despoluição'. Master's thesis, UFPe (Recife).

Oliveira, Rosana Martins de. 2002. 'De Folha e Cipó é a Capelinha de São Francisco: A Religiosidade Popular na Cidade de Rio Branco – Acre (1945–1958)'. Master's thesis, UFPe (Recife).

Overing, Joanna, and Alan Passes. 2000. 'Introduction: Conviviality and the Opening Up of Amazonian Anthropology'. In Overing and Passes, eds, *The Anthropology of Love and Anger: The Aesthetics of Conviviality in Native Amazonia*, 1–30. London: Routledge.

Paskoali, Vanessa. 2002. 'A Cura Enquanto Processo Identitário na Barquinha: o sagrado no cotidiano'. Master's thesis, PUC/SP (São Paulo).

Pelaez, Maria Cristina. 2002. 'Santo Daime, trascendência e cura: Interpretações sobre as possibilidades terapêuticas da bebida ritual'. In Labate and Sena Araújo (2002), 427–45.

Prandi, Reginaldo, ed. 2001. *Encantaria Brasileira: O Livro dos Mestres, Caboclos e Encantados*. Rio de Janeiro: Pallas.

Reeve, Mary-Elizabeth. 2000. 'Concepts of Illness and Treatment Practice in a Caboclo Community of the Lower Amazon'. *Medical Anthropology Quarterly* 14(1): 96–108.

Rose, Isabel Santana de. 2005a. 'A expressão da experiência na Barquinha: Um estudo sobre cura e mediunidade'. PhD research proposal, UFSC (Florianópolis).

Rose, Isabel Santana de. 2005b. 'Espiritualidade, terapia e cura: um estudo sobre a expressão da experiência no Santo Daime'. Master's thesis, UFSC (Florianópolis).

Schieffelin, Edward. 1996. 'On Failure and Performance: Throwing the Medium out of the Seance'. In Carol Laderman and Marina Roseman, eds, *The Performance of Healing*, 59–89. New York: Routledge.

Sena Araújo, Wladimyr. 1999. *Navegando sobre as ondas do Daime: História, cosmologia e ritual da Barquinha*. Campinas: Editora da Unicamp.

Slater, Candace. 1994. *Dance of the Dolphin: Transformation and Disenchantment in the Amazonian Imagination*. Chicago: The University of Chicago Press.

Taussig, Michael. 1987. *Shamanism, Colonialism, and the Wild Man: A Study in Terror and Healing*. Chicago, IL: The University of Chicago Press.

Vilaça, Aparecida. 2002. 'Making Kin out of Others in Amazonia'. *Journal of the Royal Anthropological Institute* NS 8: 347–65.

Winkelman, Michael. 2000. *Shamanism: The Neural Ecology of Consciousness and Healing*. Westport, CT: Bergin & Garvey.

Zinberg, Norman. 1984. *Drug, Set, and Setting: The Basis for Controlled Intoxicant Use*. New Haven, CT: Yale University Press.

6

Religious matrices of the União do Vegetal[*]

Sandra Lucia Goulart

Translated by Christian Frenopoulo, revised by Matthew Meyer

Introduction

Chronologically, the União do Vegetal (Union of the Vegetal) – or UDV, as it is also known – is the third ayahuasca religion to appear in Brazil. The term 'Vegetal', analogous to the case of 'Daime', is used to designate both the decoction that results from the combination of the *Banisteriopsis caapi* vine with leaves from the *Psychotria viridis* bush, as well as for the church itself. The UDV began in the early 1960s in a region near to what is now the state of Rondônia. It was created by José Gabriel da Costa. According to participants, the exact date of the creation of the União do Vegetal was July 2, 1961. The site was the rubber camp[1] Sunta, located on the border between Brazil and Bolivia. It was in that place where the UDV began to be organized. It was only in 1965 that Mestre Gabriel definitively moved to the city of Porto Velho, developing and more systematically structuring his ayahuasca religion in an urban setting. Initially, the name of the religious group founded by Mestre Gabriel was *Associação Beneficente União do Vegetal* (União do Vegetal Beneficient Association). In 1970, however, one year before his passing away, he changed the name to *Centro Espírita Beneficente União do Vegetal* (CEBUDV) (União do Vegetal Beneficient Spiritist Center), as it is still called to this day.

It is worth pointing out that historical events such as these possess a special significance for this religion. Similarly, other kinds of events considered important for the faithful –

---

* First published in *Fieldwork in Religion* (2006) 2.3: 286–318.

1. Rubber camps (*seringal* in Portuguese) are called so due to the rubber tree (*Hevea brasiliensis*), from which latex for producing natural rubber is extracted. The Portuguese term refers to an orchard of rubber trees, and also to the land (property, plot of land in a settlement, or municipality, forest, etc.) where the trees are concentrated and where those who work directly in the extraction of latex reside (that is, the rubber-tappers, as well as their bosses, who control and appropriate the labor of the former, concentrating their gains).

episodes involving the founder or leaders – have given rise to a number of special dates that make up the UDV calendar.[2] It is also important to underscore that, in the perspective of the followers of this religion, when we speak of the beginning or foundation of the UDV, we are not referring to its creation, but to its 're-creation'. This is in accordance with their belief that their Master, José Gabriel da Costa, was only remembering his previous incarnations and reactualizing his sacred 'mission'; specifically by restoring the União do Vegetal on Earth, re-creating it.[3]

José Gabriel da Costa or Mestre Gabriel, as he is called by followers, was born in Coração de Maria, in the state of Bahia, in 1922. According to my research,[4] he left his birthplace around 1942, to go and live in Salvador, the capital of Bahia. His stay in the Bahian capital, though, was short. Mestre Gabriel joined the 'Rubber Army'[5] in the following year, 1943. He transferred to the Amazon and became a part of the mass of Northeastern laborers who were migrating into the region to join the rubber industry at that time.

Roots of the União do Vegetal

Not a lot is known about the life of Mestre Gabriel in Bahia. Regarding his religious background, as is the case of the other founders of the ayahuasca religions, Mestre Gabriel grew up in a context strongly marked by the typical manifestations of Brazilian popular Catholicism. His family frequently participated in the regional festivities of the Catholic calendar, as well as the monthly mass, or in commemorations that occurred with less frequency, such as the feast of a saint. In the Brazilian rural context, principally up until the middle of the past century, feasts of Catholic saints were a widespread event. These feasts assembled numerous residents of a locality, or even a whole region, who ordinarily lived in a relative isolation or with little contact, due to the pattern of population dispersal. The feasts of the saints interrupted this configuration, and involved pilgrimages, *novenas*, *folias*, and processions. In these celebrations, which often lasted for several days, and sometimes even months, a group of faithful traveled a considerable distance (by boat or by land), transporting the images of the venerated saints to the homes of the inhabitants.

Hence, since his childhood, Mestre Gabriel had participated in this religious context, accompanying his parents and older siblings in the feasts of the saints carried out in the

---

2. Some of the dates, such as the Re-creation of the União do Vegetal or the Confirmation of the UDV in the Astral are listed in the 'Timeline: Mestre Gabriel and UDV' section appended at the end of this article.

3. These prior incarnations of Mestre Gabriel are narrated in the *History of Hoasca*, the central myth of the UDV, recounted in some ritual sessions of Vegetal, such as on the birthday of Mestre Gabriel, February 10.

4. I conducted fieldwork for my doctoral disseration (Goulart, 2004a) from 2001 to 2002 in the city of Rio Branco, Acre state, among different nuclei of the União do Vegetal.

5. The term 'Army' and 'rubber soldier' refer to the workers recruited from the northeast by the Brazilian government to work in the Amazonian rubber camps tapping latex from the rubber tree (*Hevea brasiliensis*) to produce rubber during World War II. In Brazil, the 'rubber economy' was concentrated in the Amazon region, basically in two periods. The first, the apogee, was from 1879 to 1912; the second, shorter, from 1942 to 1945, when, due to the difficulty of access to the rubber camps in Malaysia during World War II, the extraction of Brazilian rubber was reactivated (Almeida, 1992).

town close to the farm where they lived. Additionally, during the periods when there were no communal festivities and little contact among regional families, Mestre Gabriel's family (especially his mother) would engage in other Catholic practices, such as litanies, novenas, short homages to a saint, and so on, also in concurrence with the milieu. As numerous authors have explained, the existence of these kinds of Catholic practices – to some degree independent from official Church agents – was very common in the Brazilian rural context of the time. In those far away and relatively isolated regions, priests were substituted by women who knew prayers, or by the so-called *beatos* (lit. 'blessed') and *penitentes* (penitents) (Pereira de Queiroz, 1973 and 1978; Galvão, 1955). According to some accounts and sources, it seems that Mestre Gabriel's mother fulfilled, at least in part, this type of function. In Edson Lodi's book (2004), which provides an account and biography of the youngest brother of Mestre Gabriel, this childhood context of the founder of the UDV is narrated in more detail. For instance, Antonio Gabriel (Mestre Gabriel's brother) recounts how Prima Feliciana (Mestre Gabriel's mother) was devoted to the saints Cosmas and Damian. As a result, she assembled her neighbors in her house on the day dedicated to these saints and, in front of a shrine (a small box, where the images of saints are kept), she led the praying of the rosary, other Catholic prayers, and the *benditos*, which are prayers that are sung in which the main verses praise the saint that is being homaged with the expression 'bendito' ('blessed'). The book explains that Mestre Gabriel was the son who most accompanied his mother's devotions, helping her, and displaying a special vocation for singing the *benditos* and for leading prayers.

This tradition relating to the saints Cosmas and Damian that Mestre Gabriel carried from his childhood in Bahia is absorbed into the ritual and mythical complex of the new ayahuasca religion that he created in Porto Velho. In the União do Vegetal, the *bendito* of saints Cosmas and Damian was transformed into a *chamada* – a term from this religion which designates melodies that are sung, solely modulated by the performer's voice. *Chamadas* are fundamental elements in all UDV ritual ceremonies. Together with other elements, such as the questions put by participants to the group leaders, the reading of internal documents, explanations and speeches on doctrinal principles – all accompanied by the consumption of Vegetal – these constitute its basic structure.[6] Mestre Gabriel's brother (whose biography is also recounted in Edson Lodi's book) was separated from him when he left Bahia to work in the Amazonian rubber camps and only met up with him again almost 30 years later, in 1971, when Mestre Gabriel decided to return to Bahia to attempt to reestablish contact with his family. At that time, he already led a relatively structured União do Vegetal group in Porto Velho. The interest of his youngest brother, Antonio Gabriel, in the UDV resulted from this trip back to his birthplace where he regained contact with his family. With time, he converted to the religion founded by his brother. Antonio Gabriel recounts how, during his first experiences with Vegetal in Porto Velho, he recognized the old *bendito* that his brother used to sing in his childhood in Bahia when he heard the *chamada* of saints Cosmas and Damian. According to him, there are only slight differences between the *chamada* and the *bendito*, such as a few substituted words (Lodi, 2004: 42).

---

6. There are around 170 *chamadas*. Many of them were authored by Mestre Gabriel. However, we must qualify the notion of authorship since, in UDV belief, all *chamadas* are ultimately 'brought' by a spiritual being. As mentioned, in all UDV rituals, called 'sessions', *chamadas* are sung, but they vary, since there are *chamadas* that are specific for certain types of 'sessions' (somewhat reserved).

Figure 1. A UDV ritual (copyright Bento Viana).

The case of the devotion to the saints Cosmas and Damian is not an isolated incident, since the UDV ritual calendar adopts various other devotions and dates from Catholicism, such as the dates dedicated to the Three Kings, Christmas, the Resurrection of Christ, and others. Also, many Christian figures (such as Jesus and the Virgin Mary) are frequently mentioned in the *chamadas* and *histories*[7] of the UDV. It is also important to note that the UDV is always represented as a religion or doctrine of Christian principles in its documents, registers, and public positioning. It is reported that in the beginnings of the UDV, Mestre Gabriel even prayed an Our Father and Hail Mary before opening the ritual sessions with Vegetal.

It is true that this practice seemingly possessed, at least partially, a strategic character, seeking to lessen the alienation or stigma of a religion that made use of a brew of indigenous origin, linked to non-Christian traditions. I obtained information that the performance of these prayers was abandoned after the União do Vegetal became more 'accepted' in Porto Velho. Even so, this does not deny the factual incorporation of Christian beliefs or elements of Catholicism in the UDV religion, though it does indicate that these elements were reinterpreted according to a new set of principles and the distinct logic of this ayahuasca religion.

Thus, for example, followers of the UDV associate Mestre Gabriel with Jesus Christ or 'his teachings'. In the understanding of many UDV followers, both of them opted for the

---

7. The transmission of mythical and doctrinal aspects of the União do Vegetal occurs through a series of stories, which constitute diverse types of narratives. They may have an informal character, even appearing humorous, similar to other narratives typical of Brazilian popular culture. There are also histories that have a more formal character, functioning as myths and that are told or mentioned under more restrictions. Some of them, in fact, are only recounted during sessions in which members with high hierarchical degrees participate.

'poor', 'simple' and 'excluded'. As Andrade recounts in his master's thesis on the União do Vegetal, in the same way that Christ chose humble fishermen to be his apostles, Mestre Gabriel chose disciples from among 'caboclos' (1995: 181–82). In fact, references to Jesus, and associations between him and Mestre Gabriel or his religious doctrine, are highlighted in the cosmology of the UDV. They even appear in the principal myth, the History of Hoasca. This history, narrated by Mestre Gabriel himself (in a recording made shortly before his passing away), is an account of the origin of Vegetal, or rather, of the two plants that compose it, the *Banisteriopsis caapi* vine and the leaves of the *Psychotria viridis* bush, respectively called *mariri* and *chacrona* in the UDV. It is a long narration, with several episodes, covering different historical periods. In one of the passages situated in the time of King Solomon (of the Hebrew tradition), Mestre Gabriel talks of the birth of Jesus, also mentioning the Virgin Mary, revealing a typical process of mythical logic, in which time is reversible and events and different characters may mix, as they are not conditioned to a progressive succession that would inevitably separate them.

It is also common among UDV followers to draw parallels between the birth of Jesus and that of Mestre Gabriel. The founder of the UDV was reportedly born at noon, and this fact is swathed in symbolic significance, originating a series of ritual and mythic interpretations in this religious group. One of these exegetic developments is, precisely, the idea that there is an important relationship between the time of Jesus' birth and that of Mestre Gabriel's. Thus, in informal conversations with followers who belong to the highest hierarchical ranks of the UDV, it was explained to me that, while Jesus was born at the moment in which the day was starting (midnight), Mestre Gabriel was born at its peak (noon), that is, when the sun is at its zenith. As a follower once told me, 'Mestre Gabriel was born on the peak of noon, that is, when the sun is at its peak and there is the most light'. In this sense, we can say that the birth of Jesus and Mestre Gabriel are equally important in the views of UDV followers, as they mark crucial moments in time, determining the principal moments of the day.[8]

In addition to popular Catholicism, another significant source for the formation of the União do Vegetal religion is the Spiritism of Allan Kardec. As it is well known, Kardec (a French pedagogue) was responsible in the mid-nineteenth century for the structuring of a doctrine called Spiritism (due to the belief in the intervention of the spirits of the dead in earthly phenomena, the world of the living), which he simultaneously considered to be religion, philosophy and science. Kardec's Spiritism included a series of spiritualist and esoteric beliefs that circulated through Europe and the USA, largely beginning in the end of the eighteenth century, such as the theories of magnetism or psychism. Kardec's doctrine, also known as Kardecism, spread through Brazil toward the end of the nineteenth century, initially among urban high and middle classes. Later, it extended widely into different regions of the country and various segments of the population.

Several authors have shown that the expansion of Kardecism in Brazil involved a particular development that involved a mediation between the beliefs of the popular segments

---

8. We recall here that the association with Jesus or with his Christian teachings is also common in other ayahuasca religions. Thus, the founder of the Santo Daime, Raimundo Irineu Serra (Mestre Irineu) is constantly associated by followers with Christ, and his doctrine expressed in an assemblage of hymns is often understood as a kind of 'Third Testament', which carries on the principles of the Christian New Testament.

of the population and those of the urban elites that emerged toward the end of the nineteenth and the beginning of the twentieth centuries. Thus, Ortiz (1978) highlighted the importance of Kardecist beliefs in the process of adaption of African traditions to the new lifestyle that was consolidating in the nation during the period of industrialization of the first decades of the twentieth century. Ortiz was seeking to demonstrate how this process developed into the formation of Umbanda, an Afro-Brazilian religion in which, according to him, some Kardecist notions rendered beliefs of African origin more palatable to the standards of rationality of the emerging Brazilian society – more urbanized, modern, and white. For Ortiz, this movement of integration of Umbanda into the new Brazilian social context through the adoption of Kardecist notions was framed by social class conflict. The first *terreiros* or Spiritist centers revealed these conflicts through the greater or lesser acceptance of beliefs of African origin or, instead, of Kardecist notions. Some Kardecist notions, such as 'evolution', fulfilled a special role in indicating a *terreiro*'s or center's closer or more distant relationship to the values of a society that presented itself as 'white', 'rational' and 'modern'. Thus, levels of 'spiritual evolution' corresponded to levels of 'social evolution'.

Other authors have also emphasized the presence of class, cultural and racial conflicts in the process of expansion of Kardecist Spiritism in Brazil, and in its fusion with other beliefs and traditions. Trindade (1991), for instance, analyzes how Bezerra de Menezes,[9] a nineteenth-century physician from Ceará, played an important role in the process of adaption of Kardecist ideas (such as the existence of magnetic fluids) to old magico-therapeutic beliefs held by different popular segments (such as the belief in the healing powers of spirits). With time, Brazilian Kardecism acquired a distinctly therapeutic character, though emphasizing that the spirits of the dead (rather than magnetic fluids) were the true healing agents. In this way, according to Trindade, the adherence to Kardecism allowed the emerging Brazilian elite to resolve the contradiction between their aspirations for progress, rationality and modernity, on the one hand, and their link to a mentality with superstitious or magical tendencies, on the other. The theories of magnetism and psychism present in Kardecism seemed germane to aspirations for 'modernity', while the belief in the therapeutic action of spirits linked to the old mentality. Even so, according to Trindade and also other scholars (Ortiz, 1978), although the process of expansion of Kardecism in Brazil implied the blending of beliefs originally belonging to different social classes, this process was not without conflict. Different authors (Trindade, 1991; Maggie, 1992; Negrão, 1996) have shown that *terreiros* or Spiritist centers of the first decades of

---

9. After his passing away, Bezerra de Menezes, became a 'spirit-guide', that is, a spiritual entity who returns to Earth to guide humanity. The 'guide' communicates through 'mediums', who are people that possess the ability to communicate with the spirits of the dead. This capacity is called 'mediumship' –a gift that can be manifest in several manners, such as through hearing, visions, dreams, intuitions of the presence of a spirit, or even the incorporation of the spirit. In Kardecism, the most typical form of manifestation of the spirits of the dead is through their words. The notions of mediumship and spirit-medium come from Kardecist Spiritism, but were amply adopted in the Umbanda milieu. The term 'spirit-guide', though, is used in Afro-Brazilian religions. The meaning intended here is that of Umbanda, since in Candomblé it has a different meaning (Calvacanti, 1983; Cacciatore, 1988). In some testimonies provided by early members of the UDV who knew Mestre Gabriel personally, I was told that he incorporated the spirit-guide Bezerra de Menezes during the period in which he participated in Afro-Brazilian religions, before the founding of the UDV.

the nineteenth century were plagued with disputes. Manifestly expressed in different symbolic choices (types of trance,[10] types of spiritual entities that descend, moderately ritualized actions, rituals that include or not the use of alcoholic beverages or animal blood, practices with more or lesser therapeutic content, etc.), they additionally revealed racial, cultural and class conflicts. Many of these analyses (Maggie, 1992; Negrão, 1996) even assert that the drawing of boundaries (and of practices, beliefs and identities) among the different centers defined as more or less Kardecist or Umbandist, was marked by this type of conflict.

The expansion of Kardecism also occurred in the Brazilian Amazon region. There, it also involved a transformation of its notions when they entered into contact with beliefs from other traditions. In the ayahuasca religion created by Mestre Gabriel in the state of Rondônia, Kardecist notions such as reincarnation were blended with Judeo-Christian elements, as well as beliefs from local populations, such as indigenous or other groups that interacted with them. In this manner, in the principal myth of the UDV (the History of Hoasca, previously mentioned) it is asserted that Mestre Gabriel is the reincarnation of the first person on Earth to drink Vegetal. This event, according to the story, occurred during the times of the Israelite King Solomon. One of the most famous characters of the Old Testament is also one of main protagonists of the mythical narrative. In the latter, he is mentioned alongside tales of men and women who are transformed into plants (specifically those that compose the Vegetal), in accordance with the typical logic of mythical thought among Amazonian peoples, especially groups that use ayahuasca. The myth recounts that the first man to drink Vegetal (also called Hoasca – hence the name of the story) was a vassal of King Solomon called Caiano. Caiano, 'the first hoasqueiro', reincarnated several times, and in his last reincarnation returned as Mestre Gabriel. This is the reason why, according to followers of the UDV, Mestre Gabriel did not create but rather re-created (reinstalled) the União do Vegetal, because when he was incarnate as Caiano, he already had the knowledge of Hoasca and the mysteries of the union of its plants. Incarnate as Mestre Gabriel, he merely remembered his mission, understood by followers as the task of 'restoring the União do Vegetal on Earth'.

This concept of remembering previous incarnations is quite common among UDV followers. I observed that recurring to memories of prior 'other lives' was common, especially when there was an intention to affirm a position of spiritual distinction or superiority. These generally coincided with the periods of other incarnations of the founder of the UDV. In this sense, the process of spiritual development in this religion involves a kind of awakening of the 'memory' of spirits closely linked with the history of Hoasca and the União do Vegetal. Regarding the belief in reincarnation, it is worth highlighting, additionally, that followers of the UDV frequently assert that it was a part of the original Judeo-Christian tradition. To support this notion, they even cite biblical verses that reveal a belief in the principle of reincarnation.[11]

---

10. In this article, the term 'trance' is used primarily in the sense defined by Lewis, that is, as a state of complete or partial mental dissociation, which is often accompanied by extraordinary visions, related with aspects of mediumship (Lewis, 1977: 41).

11. This type of association between the Judeo-Christian Biblical tradition and the belief in the reincarnation of spirits is also common in other ayahuasca religions, such as the Santo Daime, in which the leaders of some

Also, we should not overlook that, in fact, the relation between the UDV and Kardecist Spiritism is found in the official name of the religious group: Beneficient Spiritist Center União do Vegetal (*Centro Espírita Beneficente União do Vegetal* – CEBUDV). As I mentioned earlier, the original name of the group founded by Mestre Gabriel was Beneficient Association União do Vegetal (*Associação Beneficente União do Vegetal*). The words 'Spiritist center' were included only in 1970. Based on the testimonies of followers who accompanied this period of UDV history, we observe that the name change ocurred, in part, due to persecutions and stigmatizations endured by Mestre Gabriel's group in Porto Velho. It is said that the designation 'Spiritist center' was adopted after a series of conflicts with the police and other local authorities. These included, amongst other episodes, the detention of Mestre Gabriel in 1967, and a moratorium on the admission of new members for some months during 1970. According to accounts collected during my research (Goulart, 2004a) as well as other sources (Brissac, 1999), it was during these conflicts that followers and others suggested the designation 'Spiritist center' to Mestre Gabriel, as a way to assuage the prejudices endured by the new religion. In his Master's thesis, Brissac cites reports stating that the term 'Spiritist' was adopted because there were many people in Porto Velho who 'wanted to close down the União do Vegetal' (1999: 76) at the time.

This episode of the adoption of the designation 'Spiritist center' brings the history of the UDV close to that of Afro-Brazilian religions, such as Umbanda. In fact, as several studies of the process of formation of Afro-Brazilian religions show (Maggie, 1992; Negrão, 1996), recurrence to the label 'Spiritist center' was very common among Afro-Brazilian religious groups, especially during the period of their emergence and consolidation. In the case of Umbanda in São Paulo, according to Negrão (1996), most of the Umbanda *terreiros* during the decades from 1920 to 1940 were registered as 'Spiritist centers', masking their African origins, as a way to moderate prejudices and persecution against their religious practices, since Kardecist Spiritism had more acceptance among the middle and higher classes. In addition to the UDV, other ayahuasca religions have also recurred to the designation 'Spiritist' or 'Spiritist center'. This is the case of the religion known as Barquinha, which began in Rio Branco, in the state of Acre, around 1945, and spread into a series of independent groups, but which all include the designation 'Spiritist center' in their respective institutional names (that is, in the names under which they are registered). At the same time, as mentioned before, scholars (Ortiz, 1977 and 1978; Procópio, 1961) have claimed that notions and beliefs from Kardecist Spiritism even became current within Umbanda as a strategy of legitimation in the context of the evolving Brazilian society of the decades of the 1920s and 1930s. The adherence to scientific discourses or to those that value the idea of science, and the defense of a 'more conscious' type of mediumship less linked to materialistic and magic forms of the religion (exemplified by the use of artifacts, alcoholic beverages, or tobacco by incorporated spirits) would be examples of these shifts (Procópio, 1961; Ortiz, 1977: 48).

The case of the ayahuasca religions has, of course, its own specificity, and in various aspects differs from the process of formation of Umbanda. While the latter began in an

---

groups are sometimes seen as the reincarnation of Christian saints or Biblical characters (from the Old and New Testament). Indeed, the association between these beliefs and traditions (Judeo-Christian and Spiritism) occurs, more widely, in Brazilian popular Catholicism.

economically more developed and urbanized region in the southeast of the country, the former originated in the Brazilian Amazon in a later period, after the emergence of Umbanda. The cultural contexts in which Umbanda formed, on the one hand, and the ayahuasca religions, on the other, also diverge. The marked influence of indigenous traditions and the confluence of these with other traditions characteristic of the populations that migrated into Amazonia and occupied it during diverse historical moments (such as the 'nordestino' workers, i.e., migrants from the northeast of the country) led to the constitution of very singular religious phenomena in the region. Thus, elements of popular Catholicism, Masonry and the Rosicrucian doctrinal order, the diffusion of Kardecist Spiritism or esoteric groups such as the Esoteric Circle of the Communion of Thought (*Círculo Esotérico da Comunhão do Pensamento*), as well as the influence of beliefs from Afro-Brazilian religions, can be identified in diverse Amazonian religious movements, such as the ayahuasca religions. As in the history of Umbanda in São Paulo, we can perceive typical notions of Kardecist Spiritism (such as 'conscious mediumship' or the idea of a religious doctrine that is also scientific) in the União do Vegetal that were important in the process of affirmation of this ayahuasca religion, first in its place of origin and later within the wider Brazilian society.

In fact, the concept of 'science' possesses a central place in UDV cosmology, appearing in rituals, in the doctrine, in mystical elements and, generally speaking, in the speech and behavior of members. In a certain way, members understand the assemblage of doctrinal contents, the principles of the religion, and so on, as composing a kind of 'science' that constitutes the 'true knowledge' revealed by Mestre Gabriel and by Hoasca (Vegetal). In the History of Hoasca, this notion of science can be perceived in several instances. As described before, one of the central characters of the myth is Solomon who, in the Hebrew biblical tradition and the folklore of popular Catholicism, and also in esoterism, is associated with wisdom and science. In the behavior and speech of followers, this valorization of scientific knowledge or positions is expressed in other ways. As a result, of the three major ayahuasca religions, it is the UDV which has really shown a strong interest in establishing a dialogue between its oficial institutions and science. In this sense, their process of institutionalization has included the constant creation of organs self-designated as scientific and which have the primary objective of establishing communication with the academic sphere. This is the case of DEMEC – Medical Scientific Department of the UDV (*Departamento Médico Científico da UDV*), created in 1986. It is mostly composed of health professionals linked to the UDV and dedicated to research on the effects of ayahuasca, especially clinical analyses. In addition to DEMEC, the Department of Memory and Documentation (*Departamento de Memória e Documentação*) is concerned with registering information about the history of the União do Vegetal and its founder. Other organs have been created more recently, including some that appear to have the mandate of debating and evaluating academic investigations on the religion (whether carried out by researchers linked to the UDV or not).

This adherence to scientific discourse and logic in the UDV occurs simultaneously with a rejection of folk healing practices referred to by the umbrella term 'curandeirismo'. This is evident in the ritual forms of the religion, as well as in attitudes and statements given by members. It is also revealed in statements and texts intended for the broader public, or also in UDV documents, such as the book *Hoasca – Fundamentos e Objetivos* (*Hoasca: Fundamentals and Objectives*; CEBUDV, 1989), which is the first publication of

115

the group. One document in this publication explains the purposes for the use of aya-huasca in the UDV, establishing a clear distinction between healing of the body and spiri-tual healing. The text explains that the UDV religion is characterized by the use of Vegetal for spiritual healing, in accordance with the orientations of its founder, and not material, that is, of the 'body'. It very explicitly declares at one point that the União do Vegetal does not preach any 'healing properties of the brew' and 'does not practice or advocate acts of folk healing (ações curandeiristas)' (CEBUDV, 1989: 34).

Here, we can also draw a parallel with the case of Umbanda. Some authors indicate that the process of the constitution of Umbanda implied a distancing from a series of therapeutic practices based on phytotherapy and an empirical knowledge of sicknesses that were current in popular Brazilian religiosity since the early centuries of colonial-ism until the eighteenth century (Montero, 1985). The old religiosity changed with the new sociocultural panorama that had emerged since the nineteenth century with the arrival of the Portuguese royal family. This led to the gradual expansion of universities and academic institutions – especially medical schools – and also the intensification of the process of urbanization. The abandonment of more empirical therapeutic practices is a salient feature of these changes. Other religious manifestations, more adapted to the new reality, emerged in this panorama. According to Montero (1985), this is the case of Umbanda. According to this author, empirical knowledge of sicknesses is not emphasized in this religion. Through their 'spirit-guides', Umbanda 'spirit-mediums' do not focus on specific organic symptoms when treating the hardships of patients. Instead, they focus on the general clinical condition of the sick person, seeking to eliminate the 'bad fluids' that caused the misfortune. In a general manner, Umbanda therapeutic practices thus tend to operate in the symbolic domain. Plants and herbs are used more for their mystical power functions than for their particular phytochemical properties (Montero, 1985: 55). The constitution of scientific medicine was a major conditioning factor of this transformation of popular Brazilian religiosity which, as we have said, implied an empirical therapeutic knowledge. In this sense, it constituted an obstacle to the legitimacy of the new medical knowledge seeking hegemony (Machado, 1978; Montero, 1985).

It is important to highlight that the expansion of the legitimacy of scientific medi-cine simultaneously included the establishment of a definition of 'quackery' for a set of practices. In fact, this was an official process orchestrated by the State when a new Penal Code was established in Brazil in 1890. Through articles 156, 157 and 158, it explicitly prohibited the practice of medicine by non-medical agents, as well as prohibiting magic and Spiritism if they stimulated feelings related with the healing of discomforts (whether curable or not), institutionalizing the repression of these practices, generally classifying them as quackery (Maggie, 1992: 43). From that moment on, popular therapeutic beliefs – even derived from the old religiosity – were no longer just seen as 'inferior' or 'back-ward', but actually became a crime.

Regardless of these actions, we think that the distancing from therapeutic practices based on empirical medical knowledge or a direct knowledge of plants is not, in any way, total in the Umbanda milieu, nor in that of the ayahuasca religions. In the case of the aya-huasca religions – and especially the UDV – I attempted to demonstrate in my dissertation (Goulart, 2004a) that there is a simultaneous movement of approximation and distanc-ing from an empirico-phytotherapeutic mentality that is linked to the old Amazonian traditions of ayahuasca use. Not always, yet in some cases, this movement of taking distance is explained by an apprehension regarding persecution or stigmatization. The emphasis on the use of Vegetal for spiritual healing and not for healing the body, the attachment to a scientistic discourse, as well as the recourse to Kardecist beliefs that are more appealing to a 'progressive' mentality – as well as the designation 'Spiritist center' or the option for a type of mediumship considered to be more conscious – can be understood as indicators of this type of cautiousness, rather than a total rejection of the old traditions and practices which, as we will see, in fact continue.

It is also worth pointing out that, in many cases, it is difficult to identify the original source of some notions, principles or practices found in the UDV religion. Such is the case of the notion of 'science' or the recurrent references to Solomon. The former, as explained, may be linked to Kardecist doctrine, but equally to other sets of beliefs, such as the positivist mentality that gained importance for the nineteenth-century Brazilian society or, even, Masonry. As is known, the notion of science is quite important for the latter philosophical-esoteric organization, which has its origins in the Middle Ages (Beck, 2005). Identified with wisdom or true knowledge, science has utmost value in this organization. Similarly, and allied to this idea of science, Solomon is a central figure in the masonic universe – is, in fact, a personification of true science. Another ostensible parallel between the UDV and Masonry is the existence, in both organizations, of initiated degrees and doctrinal learning. Thus, teachings are transmitted according to 'degrees' in Masonry, which rank from 'apprentice' to 'venerable master'. For each initiated degree there are corresponding terms of reference and speech which are kept secret from lower 'degrees' (Beck, 2005; Figueiredo, 1998).

This hierarchy based on secret word knowledge is also evident in the UDV, in which adepts are distributed and organized into four segments of disciples, according to their 'degrees' of doctrinal initiation. In increasing order of 'evolution' in initiated 'degree', these are: membership body (*quadro de sócios*), instructive body (*corpo instrutivo*), council body (*corpo do conselho*) and body of mestres (*quadro de mestres*). A disciple initially joins the membership body when entering the UDV. As the disciples in higher degrees gradually recognize the new member's evolution, he or she can move into the other segments. Each level has corresponding specific functions. The knowledge of the doctrinal secrets, of the rites, and so on, is transmitted to few, and for this there are special Vegetal 'sessions' for each segment of disciples (members, instructive body, council body, body of mestres). Although the ritual form is practically identical in all these cases,[12] the exposure

---

12. Ritual sessions of the União do Vegetal are characterized, in a general manner, by the reading of documents (such as statutes and texts authored by Mestre Gabriel), the execution of vocal chants called 'chamadas', recorded music (usually derived from popular Brazilian repertories), and asking questions on doctrinal issues (which can be posed by any participant to the *mestres* of the religion). The sessions are always initiated with the distribution of Vegetal, which is given out in a line, according to the hierarchical degree of followers. Vegetal is distributed last to visitors. All those who have received their glass with Vegetal have to wait for the distribution to be completed among all participants, since all have to drink the Vegetal at the same time, upon a signal from the *mestre* leading the session. During the ritual, all participants remain seated. There is also a considerable amount of formality during the sessions, for instance, all participants must refer to one another as 'senhor' ('sir') or 'senhora' ('madam'), or having to request permission to speak or to leave the room. Normally, a Vegetal session lasts about four hours.

to a certain set of topics, stories, explanations and principles is different according to the type of session. Evidently, more elementary 'mysteries' are revealed – less doctrinally secret – in the sessions for lower ranks, while deeper mysteries are transmitted in sessions for higher ranks. The transmission of these mysteries involves an emphasis on the word, in which certain terms or expressions acquire a new meaning according to a reading inspired by the revelation provided by initiation into a higher hierarchical rank. Additionally, during a Vegetal session, certain words cannot be spoken and must be substituted with a synonym.[13] It can be said that the word has ritual, magical, doctrinal power in the UDV. It is important to highlight that the language spoken in UDV rituals must always be Portuguese. Even when the ritual is being carried out in countries that speak other languages, the secret stories and the *chamadas* must be performed in Portuguese.

Still more about King Solomon. He is simultaneously one of the central figures of an important legend of Masonry and, as seen, of a principal myth of the UDV. The history of Masonry recounts that when Solomon designated Hiram as the architect to build a great temple, Hiram divided the temple builders into different categories (apprentices, companions and masters), giving each category specific signs and passwords. According to the story, some companions, desiring to usurp the signs that gave access to the master's post, rebelled against Hiram, murdering him with an axe. The story continues that an acacia bush grew above the tomb where Hiram was buried. Seeing this plant above the tomb allowed Solomon to discover the culprits (Figueiredo, 1998; Hall, 2006). Performing immediate analysis, we can discern several relations between this story and the History of Hoasca. Accordingly, in the first part of the History of Hoasca, another king – the 'Inca king'[14] – had servants who carried out important duties (counselor Hoasca and marshal Tiuaco) who died and whose tombs bore plants. In the second part of the History, King Solomon is mentioned. According to the story, as said before, he had a vassal called Caiano – 'the first hoasqueiro' and the same spirit who would later reincarnate as Mestre Gabriel. Caiano is the first person to drink Vegetal, but it is Solomon who discovers and reveals the mysteries of the brew and the plants that compose it (the *mariri* vine and *chacrona* leaf), explaining to Caiano that the bush with leaves that emerged from the tomb of counselor Hoasca *is* counselor Hoasca, and that the vine growing from the tomb of marshal Tiuaco *is* Tiuaco. The story continues saying that Solomon, the 'king of science', made the 'Union of the Vegetal' with a piece of vine (*mariri*) and with the leaves of *chacrona*.

There is another part in the History of Hoasca that recalls the masonic legend of Solomon and his architect Hiram. This is the part that mentions Mestre I-Agora. It is told that Caiano, in another of his incarnations, returned to Earth as a Mestre I-Agora, in Peru, after Christ. Mestre I-Agora had several disciples to whom he distributed Vegetal, telling them the story of the Inca king, Solomon and Caiano. At a certain moment, the

---

13. This is the case, for instance, of saying 'thank you', which in Portuguese is *'obrigado'* (literally, 'obliged') and must be substituted by *'grato'* or *'grata'* (literally, 'grateful'), since, according to followers, the term *'obrigado'* for 'thank you' implies an idea of 'obligation' or 'duty' and nobody is being 'obliged' or, rather, 'forced' to anything, but is, however, expressing 'gratitude' for a certain event.

14. In UDV perspective, this Inca king is not related with the historically known Peruvian Inka Empire. Instead, it existed further in the past, in a period considered 'before the Biblical Flood'. On other hand, some facts linked with the history of the Peruvian Inka Empire are embedded in another passage of the History of Hoasca, related with the character I-Agora.

disciples of Mestre I-Agora begin to envy him, then revolt and murder him, slashing his throat. This is the event that originates the people known in the UDV as 'mestres da curiosidade' (masters of curiosity), who use Vegetal 'without any knowledge of any kind'. This explains the contemporary existence of other uses of Vegetal different from the use made in the UDV.

Although we don't have records of any relationship of Mestre Gabriel with Masonry, it is known that many of the first followers of the UDV were Masons. We also have data that several of them continued their link with Masonry even after joining the UDV, not suffering antagonistic pressure from Mestre Gabriel. Masonic issues have been important in the fissions of this religion. Thus, although we cannot prove a direct link between Mestre Gabriel and Masonry, there are strong indications of the influence of this tradition in the UDV.

Alongside the relationship between the União do Vegetal and traditions such as Masonry and the Judeo-Christianity,[15] it is difficult to find more evident and direct influences between this ayahuasca religion and the traditions linked to its immediate context of emergence. These are, on the one hand, the Afro-Brazilian tradition, given the UDV founder's proven participation in one of those religions; and, on the other hand, Amazonian traditions linked to the use of ayahuasca. We will confine ourselves to these topics next.

The Afro-Brazilian influence

Data about Mestre Gabriel's religious life before founding the União do Vegetal are more plentiful and precise for the period when he was already in Amazonia. Mostly, the data points to the involvement of the founder of the UDV with Afro-Brazilian religions. In my doctoral dissertation (Goulart, 2004a), I worked with information provided by people who knew Mestre Gabriel from 'terreiros', 'batuques', 'macumbas' or 'tambores',[16] situated in the current state of Rondônia. In many cases, it was the *terreiro* in Porto Velho called 'São

---

15. We recall that Masonry is itself a fusion of diverse traditions, which stretch from Judaism to Christian hermetism, passing through the Protestant Reform, and even alchemy, amongst others.

16. These terms can acquire different meanings depending on the situation, but all refer to the context of Afro-Brazilian religions, though the latter may also vary (e.g. Candomblé, Umbanda, or religions that developed in specific regions of the Brazilian northeast, such as Xangô in Pernambuco or the Casa das Minas in the city of São Luís in Maranhão). The term 'terreiro' is used in all these religions to refer to the physical location where ceremonies are carried out (which may be a house, room, or open space, with a floor made of earth or other material) and, sometimes is used as the name of the group (e.g. 'terreiro of Mãe Menininha', 'terreiro of São Benedito', etc.). 'Batuques' and 'Tambores', generally speaking, and specifically for the cases mentioned of this article, usually refer to the context of Afro-Brazilian religions from the state of Maranhão, such as the Casa das Minas, designating the ceremonies carried out there as well as the religion itself. Both terms highlight the importance of percussion instruments ('*tambores*' means drums, and '*batuque*' is the act of drumming) to provoke trance and the manifestation of spirit entities through dancing. The term 'macumba', now, has a wider array of meanings, and can be used as a generic reference to the different types of Afro-Brazilian religions or those formed in the southeastern region (such as Umbanda) and, can even be used with derogatory or discriminatory meanings in relation to these religions (implying the idea of 'black magic', 'sorcery', 'black line of Umbanda', etc.) (Cacciatore, 1988; Ferreti, 1995).

Benedito' or 'of Chica Macaxeira' (the name of the *mãe-de-santo*[17] who commanded it). The *terreiro* functioned for several decades and became an exemplar of the Afro-Brazilian religious tradition in Amazonia. The scholar Nunes Pereira (1979) visited the place in the early 1970s, identifying the influence of the Casa das Minas tradition (which was a *terreiro* inaugurated in the late-eighteenth century in São Luís, capital of the state of Maranhão).

The Casa das Minas has African origins and was founded by members of the royal family of Dahomey, from the Guinea Coast region, brought to Brazil as slaves. The Dahomean tradition is also known as 'jeje'. 'Minas' or 'mina' was a generic term for slaves brought from Guinea, thus the term 'mina-jeje'. The spiritual entities worshipped in the Casa das Minas are the 'vodunsi', who only incorporate into female participants during a dance characterized by twirling. Trance is stimulated by drums and the religion is sometimes called 'tambor de mina' (drum of mina) (Cacciatore, 1988) – though the expression 'tambor de mina' includes a broad variety of Afro-Brazilian variants. In any case, the tradition that began in Casa das Minas in São Luís, Maranhão, influenced various other *terreiros* and Afro-Brazilian temples in the Northeast and, given the proximity of Maranhão to Amazonia, was also important in the diffusion of Afro-Brazilian practices in that part of the country.

The intense and intimate relationship between Mestre Gabriel and Afro-Brazilian religions was frequently asserted in the testimonies that I gathered, surviving beyond the creation of the UDV. According to the sources, José Gabriel da Costa had participated in different types of *terreiros*, and was 'pai de terreiro' (the male who has the function of commanding alongside the *mãe-de-santo* the 'work' of the *terreiro*) in that of Chica Macaxeira. I will attempt to record here some data about the religious biography of Mestre Gabriel and how these are understood by União do Vegetal members.

I noticed that current members of the UDV generically call the Afro-Brazilian groups in which Mestre Gabriel participated 'macumba', 'umbanda', 'batuque', 'tambores' or simply 'terreiros'. It would seem that the *terreiro* of São Benedito – influenced by the tradition of Casa das Minas and led by the *mãe-de-santo* Chica Macaxeira – was not only where he most participated, but also the one that exerted more influence in the subsequent organization of the rituals of the União do Vegetal. It is said that, in this period of his life, Mestre Gabriel would throw 'búzio'[18] cowry shells and receive 'spirit-guides'. Of these, 'Sultão das Matas' (Sultan of the Forest) was important. He is described as a 'Caboclo', that is, the spirit of an Indian, knower of medicines and secrets of the forest.[19]

---

17. Designation of the leader of Afro-Brazilian religions. The *mãe-de-santo* (literally, 'mother-of-the-saint') directs the ceremonies, and is responsible for the orientation of followers (her 'sons' and 'daughters-of-the-saint') and is the 'owner' of the *terreiro*, house or center. There are also men, called 'pai-de-santo' ('father-of-the-saint').

18. Small shells used in religions in Africa, and also in the Afro-Brazilian religions, as ritual elements, offerings, and principally for divining, as an oracular medium. In this latter sense, 'throwing *búzios*' (*jogo de búzios*) involves the *mãe-* or *pai-de-santo* casting the small shells to foresee, divine or explain the determinations of the deities (which in Candomblé are the *Orixás*) to consulting clients.

19. The spirit entities called 'Caboclos' represent the spirits of Brazilian Indians. There are several 'caboclos', with different personalities and names (e.g. 'caboclo Arranca-Toco', 'caboclo Arruda', 'da Pena Branca', 'Cobra-coral', etc.). According to Nunes Pereira, Sultão das Matas was a popular *Caboclo* in the *terreiros* of the Northern region of Brazil, sometimes identified with sacralized folkloric characters (Pereira, 1979: 224). It is important to note that the *Caboclos* are a part of the Umbanda pantheon but are also found in other Afro-

Nunes Pereira (1979) refers to this spiritual entity in one of his works, observing him in some *terreiros* in the north of the country, concluding that he represents a marked syncretism between the indigenous and African traditions.

The accounts of the 'guide', 'force' or 'Caboclo' Sultão das Matas are a crucial point in the process of legitimation of the spiritual power of Mestre Gabriel and the consolidation of the new ayahuasca religion that he founded. In this sense, there are accounts that associate the process of formation of the UDV to an event in which Mestre Gabriel summoned his disciples to explain that, in fact, he himself was the Sultão das Matas. 'I am the Sultão das Matas', Mestre Gabriel emphatically declared. It is said that from that moment on, Mestre Gabriel abandoned Afro-Brazilian practices and dedicated himself exclusively to working with Vegetal, structuring a new religion around the brew. Some authors interpret this episode as a symbolic marker for the creation of the União do Vegetal and its ritual context, characterized by a rejection of the typical Afro-Brazilian possession trance (Andrade, 1995; Brissac, 1999). As a result, while trance in religions such as Umbanda and Candomblé involves a loss of consciousness, trance in the UDV is marked by an experience of 'enlightenment' of consciousness, for which the consumption of Vegetal is essential (Brissac, 1999).

However, I think that this issue deserves further analysis. Firstly, it is important to highlight that even in the milieu of Afro-Brazilian religions there is a series of degrees and stages which lead to intermediate levels of conscious or unconscious trance, which contradicts radical dualistic theoretical classifications. Secondly, the idea that the UDV ritual completely breaks with the practices of Afro-Brazilian religions is, above all, one of the arguments of the UDV's discourse in its attempt to legitimize itself and define its boundaries with respect to other religious groups. The assertion of a complete rupture between the new religion founded by Mestre Gabriel and the Afro-Brazilian milieu is, in practice, difficult to sustain. How could such a total distance be sustained between religions that, in the past, even Mestre Gabriel had actively and intensely participated in? I found in my research that, in addition to Mestre Gabriel, a large part of the initial members of the União do Vegetal had also had previous involvement in 'terreiros', 'macumbas' or 'batuques'. Their relationships seem to have been more intense, in fact, with the *batuque* of São Benedito, of Chica Macaxeira. As Mestre Gabriel occupied a high position in that *terreiro*, this led him to seek the first members of the União do Vegetal there.

In this sense, according to testimonies gathered during my research, Mestre Gabriel and the first members of the UDV sustained frequent contacts with the *terreiro* of São Benedito. It is claimed that even the *mãe-de-santo* of this *terreiro* drank Vegetal with Mestre Gabriel on several occasions, in the context of the first sessions of the UDV. The following is a quote from one of these interviews,

> This was right at the beginning, before he declared the Re-creation the União do Vegetal... I think it was back in '59 or '60... Mestre Gabriel had just come back from spending time in the rubber camp and when he got to Porto Velho, he said that he was going to invite all the *macumba* people to drink some tea, a special one, it was

---

Brazilian religions, especially those more influenced by indigenous traditions (Cacciatore, 1988). As we will see, the word 'Caboclo' also has other meanings in Portuguese.

Vegetal... A group from the macumba that we used to go to came...old Chica, Luís Lopes... Mestre Gabriel invited the *macumba* people because they were the ones who were close him at the time.

As we said earlier, the 'Re-creation of the União do Vegetal' (July 22, 1961) was one of the main dates of the calendar of this religion; but before this date, we know that in 1959, after drinking ayahuasca for the first time, Mestre Gabriel had been organizing some experiences with the brew that he called Vegetal.[20] Thus, he began to organize and direct a stable group around ayahuasca, holding regular sessions in Porto Velho, which, in a general way, had a similar basic structure to current UDV sessions. This new religious group formed by Mestre Gabriel needed legitimacy and to defend itself in the local religious field. The *batuque* of Chica Macaxeira, given its prestige, was an important opponent to this process of legitimation. In fact, I heard several accounts about episodes in which Mestre Gabriel, after having started to work with Vegetal, continued to visit his old *batuque*, even defying the *mãe-de-santo*. Consider, for example, the following account,

> Somedays, on a celebration date, we would go there to Chica's *batuque*. Mestre Gabriel would gather a group and go and visit them, participate in the celebration; he always liked it... He was also co-godparent with Chica. They were friends... Once, after a Vegetal session, we went and he said, 'let's go to my co-godmother Chica's, because I want to show her the power that the Vegetal has'... When we got there, they were in activity, and old Chica was like fire! In those days she had a spanking paddle and would slap the hands of the *filhos-de-santos*... Mestre Gabriel arrived with all of us and first stood watching... Then, he went up to old Chica and, by the time we realized, he had taken her spanking paddle! Then he began to mock her! He slapped on her hands with her spanking paddle saying, 'Come here, now I am the one going to put you right'...and everybody laughing. They knew Mestre Gabriel's power, because he had worked there.

This dispute among two groups from the same local religious field – on the one side, the *batuque* of Chica Macaxeira and, on the other, the religion of the Vegetal founded by Mestre Gabriel – did not obstruct the occurrence of exchanges and mutual influences between them. The excerpts cited above show that there was an affective and historical link between the two religious groups. Mestre Gabriel and several of the first UDV members were former participants of the *batuque*. Mestre Gabriel and the *mãe-de-santo* were friends and co-godparents. They visited each other and, on occasions, participated in each other's rituals. These mutual visits persisted for some time, even after the União do Vegetal group was more established in Porto Velho. In this sense, I consider that here there was a simultaneous proximity and rupture between the Afro-Brazilian religious universe and the UDV. The proximity can be seen in the similarity between some ritual

---

20. We know that the brew has many names according to the region where it is consumed or the population who consume it. Thus, among the *caboclo* population in Brazil, we find names such as 'cipó', 'uasca' or 'oasca', among others. In Colombia, one of the most common names is 'yagé'. In Peru and some parts of Bolivia, the name is 'ayahuasca', of Quichua origin, which can be translated as 'rope of the spirits or souls' (Luna, 1986b). Among mestizo healers that use the brew in Peru, the name Vegetal is common (Luna, 1986b), the same name used in the UDV.

aspects of the UDV and those proper to Afro-Brazilian religions. For example, I noted that some of the *chamadas* sung during UDV sessions are similar to Umbanda songs, as well as frequently mentioning spiritual entities from that type of religion, such as Saint Barbara, Princess Janaína or Mariana, among others. I also obtained data that some of the elements used by participants during Vegetal sessions, such as the shirt worn by the leading Mestre, are derived from Umbanda, where a blue shirt of lamé fabric[21] is used. An early member of the UDV, a contemporary of Mestre Gabriel and currently leader of a dissident group of the religion, Augusto Jerônimo da Silva or Mestre Augusto, mentioned some of these topics in an interview with me. Augusto talked about one of the first Vegetal sessions in which he participated. He was surprised when he felt the impression of having heard before many of the *chamadas* sung by Mestre Gabriel during the session.

> After we drank Vegetal, Mestre Gabriel began to sing the *chamadas*... When he sang one, I thought, 'I've heard this before', it was 'Senhora Santana'... Then, he sang another one and I also knew it... At the end, when he was concluding the work with the *chamada* for divine protection, I remembered that I had heard that song in Umbanda. It was all Umbanda.

The explanation given by my informant at another point in his account about the reason for the similarities between songs[22] of Umbanda which evoke the spiritual entities of the religion and the UDV *chamadas* is even more interesting. According to Mestre Augusto, Mestre Gabriel had explained to him that this occurred because the people in Umbanda had been in the União do Vegetal in other incarnations. 'Mestre Gabriel explained to me that *macumbeiros*[23] had drunk Vegetal in other lives, but then got lost and taken the wrong way. This is why, to this day, Umbanda knows many stories and songs which are similar to those of the União', says Mestre Augusto.

Despite the uniqueness of this testimony, I observed that, in other cases, followers of the UDV used similar reasoning, explaining the relation between their religion and other religous traditions using the same interpretative frame. Thus, as I will attempt to demonstrate in the following section, this same type of logic seems to be used in relation to old Amazonian traditions of ayahuasca use, which are the other major reference in the organization of the ritual, mythical and doctrinal complex of the União do Vegetal.

The Amazonian tradition: Masters of Curiosity and re-creation of the UDV

Above all, it was in the Amazonian rubber camps where Mestre Gabriel had the deepest contact with the complex of practices relating to ayahuasca. This began in the 1950s,

---

21. A fabric similar to satin.
22. In the context of Umbanda from the southeastern part of Brazil, these songs are sung in Portuguese. In the tradition of the Afro-Brazilian religion Candomblé, from Bahia, the language is usually Yoruba. Called 'pontos' (literally, 'points'), the term can also refer to symbols or designs drawn on the floor of the *terreiro*, as well as songs. In both cases (whether songs or drawings), they function to summon the presence of the deities or spirit entities (or 'saints' in Umbanda and 'Orixás' in Candomblé) (Cacciatore, 1988).
23. The term is related with *macumba*, that is, it refers to those that practice *macumba*.

when the future founder of the UDV began to travel between the city of Porto Velho and a series of regional rubber camps located in the rural areas. His first experience with the brew was in 1959, in the Guarapari rubber camp, on the border between Brazil and Bolivia. There is some evidence, though, that Mestre Gabriel had some contact with the ayahuasca traditions before that. It is said, for instance, that in the early 1950s he knew a man in the Porto Luís rubber camp, locally known as Mestre Bahia, who conducted 'trabalhos' with Vegetal – in this case called ayahuasca, cipó, or other names.

I believe that, in the case of Mestre Gabriel and the UDV, the contact and influence of *caboclo* or mestizo[24] culture was greater than that of the indigenous. Several studies, in fact, state that the formation of a new set of practices and beliefs surrounding the use of ayahuasca, especially those linked to therapeutic uses, occurred through a process of intense relations and exchanges between indigenous Amazonian groups or mestizo populations already influenced by Christian missionization on the one hand, and non-indigenous populations who migrated into the region mostly to work in rubber extraction on the other (Luna, 1986a; Dobkin de Rios, 1971 and 1972). Scholars disagree on the moment in which the formation of this new (i.e. not exclusively indigenous) complex of beliefs regarding ayahuasca began. Some authors speculate that it occurred some 200 or 300 years ago (Gow, 1996). On the other hand, Luna (1986b, 2004), who studied the phenomenon in the Peruvian rainforest, maintains that the period of regional rubber exploitation – from 1840 to 1914 – created the conditions for an intensification of contacts between indigenous groups and the white and black populations, especially rubber workers. The use of ayahuasca for therapeutic objectives would be one of the main elements in these exchanges. Thus, populations little accustomed to the Amazonian rainforest who began to live there, somewhat isolated and in generally precarious health conditions, chose some aspects of neighboring traditional cultures that were more appropriate for their new situation. This was the case of the use of ayahuasca for healing, noting that, even though the brew was used by several indigenous Amazonian groups, numerous authors claim that the therapeutic use of the brew was likely secondary in those original indigenous contexts (Bianchi, 2005). In this sense, Luna (1986a: 35) quotes commentaries from the Peruvian *ayahuasqueiro* healers that he researched claiming that it was the 'caucheiros'[25] who discovered ayahuasca, in their attempt to treat the ills that afflicted them. Other analyses relate the origin of the Brazilian ayahuasca religions with the *caboclo* (or mestizo) and rubber tapper culture (Luna, 2004; Goulart, 1996, 2004a; Araújo, 1998; Franco and Conceição, 2004; Labate, 2004).

---

24. Luis Eduardo Luna (1986a) uses the Spanish term *mestizo* to refer to the Peruvian ayahuasca healers, principally in the region of Pucallpa and Iquitos. *Mestizo* has a similar connotation to the Portuguese term 'caboclo', used to refer to the cultural and physical types that developed in Brazil through processes of acculturation, exchange and syncretism between indigenous populations and whites who were in contact with them. Although the term is sometimes used to refer to physical traits (e.g. skin color), the term is more correctly a cultural evaluation. The expression 'caboclo' (or 'cabocla') is frequently used to designate the Amazonian population and their culture, also in view of the major influence of indigenous groups in the region. In this article we use the term 'caboclo culture' mostly with this meaning, intending to stress the practices and beliefs that were shaped in the relationships between indigenous and non-indigenous (white, black, or mestizo) groups in contact with them after migrating into the Amazon region.

25. This term, in Spanish, means the same as 'seringueiro' in Portuguese (i.e. rubber-tapper). *Caucho* is translated into Portuguese as 'borracha' (rubber); and *caucheiro* is the person who works with rubber.

In the União do Vegetal the influence of this cultural background appears evident and pronounced. We find analogies, for example, between terms used by members of the UDV and by Peruvian ayahuasqueiro healers, such as *mariri* and *chacrona* (Quechua terms that in the religion of Mestre Gabriel refer to the *Banisteriopsis caapi* vine and the leaves of the *Psychotria viridis*, used to make the Vegetal brew). In the Peruvian *ayahuasqueiro* context studied by Luna (1986a), *mariri* is a type of phlegm located in the chest of shamans or healers that works like a magical magnet and which serves to extract the 'evil' from the bodies of the sick. Another analogy occurs with the term 'maestro'. In Peruvian shaman-ism, *maestro* or *maestras* indicate the spirits of certain plants, such as ayahuasca. Some-times the term is also used for the healer or shaman. In the UDV, the term 'mestre' indicates a member category that refers to the highest achievable hierarchical rank.[26] Finally, the name Vegetal itself suggests a parallel with the Peruvian folk healing tradition and the UDV. Several healers studied by Luna are known as 'vegetalistas', given that their knowl-edge is attributed, in a large part, to the teachings of some plants, themselves called 'plant teachers' (*plantas maestras* or *plantas professoras*). Some of these healers also use the term Vegetal to refer to ayahuasca, as well as other plant teachers (Luna, 1986a: 60).

As an example of the relationships between the Brazilian Amazonian context and the UDV, we can mention the case of the notion of 'enchanted beings' (*encantos*), 'enchanted regions' (*encantes*) or 'enchanted nature' (*natureza encantada*). These are fundamental notions in the cosmology of the UDV, through which they explain the spiritualization of the beings in their pantheon and communication with them. Thus, in the UDV, nature is considered divine and crowded with enchanted beings. In their work on the culture of Brazilian *caboclo* peoples, authors such as Galvão (1955), Maués (1995) and Wagley (1977) have described enchanted beings – often characterized by an ambiguity or intermedia-tion between the human and animal states. These creatures inhabit the depths of rivers, 'companions from the deep' (Galvão, 1955), who can transform into animals, plants and stones, or appear and disappear suddenly. They can cause illnesses, bad luck in hunting, and family problems, amongst other things. It is also possible to negotiate with these beings, establishing pacts or alliances between them and humans. Some recent studies have analyzed how these beliefs are integrated with the use of ayahuasca among Brazilian rubber tappers. For example, in an ethnography of the religious universe of the rubber tappers and farmers of the Extractivist Reserve of the Upper Juruá, in Acre state, orga-nized in the late 1980s, Araújo showed how the notion of enchanted regions was closely linked to some practices of ayahuasca consumption in that context. Many of the rubber tappers researched by Araújo associated 'cipó' – one of the names for ayahuasca in this milieu – with enchanted regions and beings, typical of the collection of Amazonian beliefs, while others declared that the brew contained 'all the enchanted regions' (Araújo, 1998: 70). Therefore, it is necessary to locate Mestre Gabriel's early experiences with ayahuasca within the broader Amazonian cultural context.

---

26. Nevertheless, we stress that the term *mestre* is amply used in the context of Brazilian popular culture. To provide but one example, there are *mestres* of Capoeira, a type of martial art that combines dance, acrobatics, combat, sport, and so on, which emerged in Brazil among the black slave population. We know, as well, that Mestre Gabriel practiced Capoeira when he lived in Bahia.

In this sense, we recall that one of the principal characteristics of the tradition represented by the *ayahuasqueiro* healers studied by Luna is the use of a wide variety of plants, in addition to ayahuasca itself. The practice of these people is, therefore, based on an extremely vast empirical phytotherapeutic knowledge (Luna, 1986a). In the same way, ambiguously however, we can perceive in the União do Vegetal, as we will see, a valorization of knowledge about the forest, about plants and herbs that is typical of an old Amazonian culture in which other uses of ayahuasca are found. Thus, for example, the accounts of the early experiences of Mestre Gabriel with Vegetal, even before he founded (or 're-created') the UDV, stress an episode in which he declared himself 'mestre' (i.e. teacher or master) after bringing back with him from a trip to Acre a large quantity of *mariri* and *chacrona*, stating that he was capable of recognizing these plants and of preparing a tea with them. Here, therefore, what testifies to his condition of 'mestre' and 'leader' of a new religion based on ayahuasca is his familiarity with an empirical phytotherapeutic knowledge.

We also underscore that, in addition to ayahuasca, another nine plants are highlighted in the ritual and mythical assemblage of the UDV. The vernacular names of these nine plants are: *maçaranduba, cumarú-de-cheiro* (also called *imburama* or *cerejeira*), *carapanaúba, apuí, pau d'arco, castanheira, mulateira, breuzinho* and *samaúma*.[27] Although we are not aware of possible psychoactive alterations produced by these plants, there is a tradition in the União do Vegetal that classifies them as healing plants. The infusion of all of them can be mixed with Vegetal under some circumstances, such as during a session in which there are sick people. Vegetal with these nine plants is offered to them especially.[28] In addition, there is a *chamada* of the nine plants, in which they are named one by one, and associated with some notions, persons, symbols, and so on, of the UDV cosmology, such as 'force', 'princess', 'prince'. Thus, the presence of a body of practices and beliefs relating to these nine plants in the UDV again points to a link between the religion and the indigenous and mestizo *ayahuasqueiro* traditions marked by an ample use of plants, which may or may not function as additives of ayahuasca.

It is said that Mestre Gabriel drank Vegetal for the first time with a rubber tapper called Chico Lourenço. Invariably, however, the practices carried out by Chico Lourenço with ayahuasca and the rubber tapper context related to them, appear as something erroneous, incomplete or even negative and inferior in the immediate discourse of UDV followers. One notion that is present in the doctrinal corpus of the União do Vegetal and which expresses this type of perception is that of 'curiosity'. The notion of curiosity is crucial

---

27. The *samaúma*, the largest tree in the Amazonian forest, is associated with ayahuasca among some indigenous populations that use the brew and is considered sacred.

28. For some years, the leadership of the *Centro Espírita Beneficente União do Vegetal* (Beneficient Spiritist Center União do Vegetal) has been publicly denying the use of Vegetal mixed with the nine plants, attempting to eliminate this practice from their ritual assemblage. The motives for this action range from an apprehension of persecution or discrimination for practicing acts of 'quackery' or 'curandeirismo' to agreements established with other Brazilian ayahuasca groups which intend to conquer and maintain the juridical legality of the use of ayahuasca.

in the UDV and is linked to an collection of myths in which the 'Masters of Curiosity' emerge as important persons who affirmed the spiritual leadership of Mestre Gabriel and the new religion that he founded.

In the perspective of UDV followers, the tradition of the Masters of Curiosity seems to represent, precisely, the various types of use of ayahuasca linked to the rubber tapper milieu and associated with the Amazonian indigenous and *caboclo* contexts. It is said that about two years before declaring the 'Confirmation in the Astral of the União do Vegetal', Mestre Gabriel met with 12 Masters of Curiosity in Vila Plácido, in Acre, to drink ayahuasca. In the meeting, the Masters of Curiosity themselves acclaimed him as the superior Mestre over the others. I include below an extract of a report about this story, which also includes comments about Chico Lourenço and the broader tradition of the Masters of Curiosity.

> Chico Lourenço and the Masters of Curiosity worked with fantasy... They often used Vegetal to do evil on someone, to ensorcell... It was a black magic affair... When Mestre Gabriel met with the twelve Masters of Curiosity to drink Vegetal, in the force of the Vegetal, in its light, the Masters of Curiosity themselves recognized that Mestre Gabriel was a superior Master... Because they recognized Mestre Gabriel's knowledge... Only Mestre Gabriel had the answers to the questions. He was able to explain many things...
>
> The Masters of Curiosity, and Chico Lourenço too, already knew some of the stories and some *chamadas*, but not like Mestre Gabriel did, because only he had complete knowledge.

This type of argumentation suggests the idea, widespread among UDV followers, that Mestre Gabriel was a superior spiritual leader due to the fact that he possessed knowledge that was more complete than that of the old Masters of Curiosity. The stories and *chamadas* mentioned in the extract express the doctrinal and mythical corpus of the União do Vegetal. Generally speaking, the Masters of Curiosity are considered to have fragments of this knowledge. It is also even asserted that some parts of the History of Hoasca, the principal myth of the UDV, were already known by the Masters of Curiosity. The idea is that Mestre Gabriel was elected 'superior master' precisely because he was able to explain and complete many of the elements that were a part of the old tradition of 'curiosity'.

The notion of curiosity allows, therefore, to distinguish the use of ayahuasca in the context of the UDV from its other uses, especially those from the rubber tapper and *caboclo* context, which are understood as 'incomplete', 'false', 'illusory' knowledge, opposed to the 'true' knowledge of the brew practiced by Mestre Gabriel with the União do Vegetal. The same pattern is repeated here as in the previously commented relations of the UDV with the Afro-Brazilian religions. In both cases, we can observe an attempt, realized in the myths and exegetic discourses, to resolve the contradiction of the historical and ritual proximity of both universes and the assertion, on the other hand, of the radical autonomy of the new religion. With regards to the old tradition of the consumption of the brew, this perspective is accentuated, as it refers, precisely, to the fundamental core of the UDV: the ritual use of Hoasca or Vegetal and its symbolic implications.

The ambiguity is that, on the one hand, the old Amazonian traditions of ayahuasca are described by UDV followers as 'incomplete', 'inferior' or 'illusory', and on the other hand, the narratives rely on the religious context of *caboclos* and rubber tapper populations to assert the legitimacy of the new religion founded by Mestre Gabriel. We note, moreover, that the actual spiritual 'confirmation' of the União do Vegetal was only realized after the meeting between Mestre Gabriel and the Masters of Curiosity. Thus, according to the UDV myths themselves, it is the old Masters of Curiosity who publicly confer upon José Gabriel da Costa the status of superior Master, and only after this recognition is the União do Vegetal spiritually proven. The Masters of Curiosity, expressing the old Amazonian tradition of ayahuasca are, in this way, inserted into the History of Hoasca, just as some elements of the Afro-Brazilian religions (in which Mestre Gabriel and some of the first followers of the UDV had participated) are integrated into the doctrinal and ritual assemblage of the UDV.

Concluding considerations

On the basis of the analysis presented here regarding the cultural and religious matrices of the União do Vegetal, we can discern a noticeable articulation between the tradition of indigenous and mestizo populations of Amazonia, especially those that use ayahuasca, and another assemblage of traditions, such as the Judeo-Christian, Masonry, and even Kardecist Spiritism and beliefs from Afro-Brazilian religions. Thus, if on the one hand the influence of traditions such as Masonry or the biblical Judeo-Christian is visible in the UDV, this occurs simultaneously to the strong presence of elements from Amazonian cultures and populations. Even the notion of 'science' (which, as seen, is highly valued in the cosmology of the UDV) indicates a parallel with Masonry and Kardecism, but also remits to another different set of beliefs linked to the context of Amazonian populations. In this sense, some scholars speak of the existence of a 'science of the rubber tappers' (*'ciência dos seringueiros'*), which is constituted by a body of knowledge and techniques involving the environment and implies logics and principles that are different from modern Western science, such as explanations about illnesses derived from the metamorphoses of certain animals and insects (Araújo, 1998; Franco and Conceição, 2004; Almeida and Carneiro da Cunha, 2002). For Araújo, for instance, in the rubber tapper context, the knowledge about ayahuasca and its preparation expresses, in many aspects, the broader logic of this cultural universe, remitting to principles of its science (Araújo, 1998: 70).

In the histories, mythology, *chamadas*, and morals of the UDV, we can perceive the typical mentality of the Brazilian *caboclo* context, which seems similar to Lévi-Strauss' (1989a) 'concrete' thinking found in traditional societies, characterized by classifications and associations based on sensorial aspects related to the physical environment. The meaning of cosmological elements and of words and expressions in the UDV occurs along a similar logic. In the History of Hoasca, for example, the plant called 'chacrona' in the UDV (that is, the species *Psychotria viridis*) is associated with the brew that is made from it (i.e. Hoasca). Thus, when narrating the story, Mestre Gabriel stresses the syllable 'cha' in the word 'chacrona', linking it to 'tea' ('chá' in Portuguese) which is how ayahuasca is referred to in the UDV. In this way, the plant species 'chacrona' is immediately related to the Vegetal tea. In the same way, there is a *chamada* in which Mestre Gabriel mentions the 'burracheira'[29] (the name given in the UDV to the effects of the brew), associating through the melody and modulation of the voice the expressions 'todos pede burracheira' ('all ask for burracheira') and 'todos os pés de burracheira' ('all the plants of burracheira'). In the *chamada*, Mestre Gabriel clarifies that he is singing 'pede' ('asks') in the singular precisely to stress this association, or better, so that the participants hearing the *chamada* under the effects of Vegetal with think about stems of the vine.[30] Many other *chamadas* and stories of the União do Vegetal use similar mechanisms. Therefore, it seems that the religious logic of the UDV operates by combining elements from the Amazonian universe of popular beliefs, related to oral tradition, with principles, symbols and practices from other more erudite cultural and religious matrices, such as the Judeo-Christian, Masonry or Kardecist Spiritism.

An anecdote about the founder of the UDV exemplifies our hypothesis. Told by Mestre Braga, it involves a recommendation left by Mestre Gabriel about the growth of his doctrine. According to the testimony, found in Brissac (1999), Mestre Gabriel warned his disciples about the possibility of the União do Vegetal becoming tampered with as it reached large cities, as 'learned and scholared' people would try to alter many things, such as the meaning or words of the *chamadas*. For this reason, Mestre Gabriel recommended his disciples always to speak 'the language of the *caboclo*', a language all would understand, both 'the more and the less learned'. His advice was not to take the UDV to the people, but to let the people come to the UDV. In this way, the doctrine would be preserved (Brissac, 1999: 72–73). We can see, therefore, that Mestre Gabriel intended 'learned' folk to adapt and adjust to the 'caboclo' mentality.

The relation of the UDV with Afro-Brazilian religions, also a popular tradition, like the complex of Amazonian beliefs corresponding to the use of the brew, is fundamental for the affirmation of this ayahuasca religion. Thus, in official discourses of its representatives, there is an emphasis on distancing themselves from elements derived from Afro-Brazilian religions. However, regardless of this legitimation practice, we can verify that, from a historical point of view, there are factual continuities between the Afro-Brazilian religious universe and the União do Vegetal. These continuities result, even, from the prior participation of Mestre Gabriel and some of the early members of the UDV in these types of religions. The self-representational myths and discourses of the União do Vegetal, however, endeavor to deny the existence of the influence of Afro-Brazilian religions upon

---

29. 'Burracheira' is a term that appears to be derived from Spanish. In that language, 'borracho' means drunk from alcohol. We recall that, in this sense, the use of Spanish expressions is common in the region near the border with Bolivia where Mestre Gabriel came into contact with ayahuasca. Therefore, in this case we can also probably discern the influence of old Amazonian traditions regarding the use of the brew. This type of relationship is equally frequent in other ayahuasca religions, such as the Santo Daime of Mestre Irineu, in which expressions such as *miração* (also used to designate the psychoactive effects, especially visual, provided by the brew) reveal the influence of Spanish. Thus, 'mirar' in Spanish means 'to see' or 'to look'. Also, in several of these religions, relatively conscious parallels are established between states of drunkenness or unconsciousness produced by alcohol and mystical ecstasy expressed in visionary experiences produced by ayahuasca.

30. This association relies on a slip between the word *pede*, from the verb *pedir* (to ask), and *pé* or *pés* which is a generic term to designate an individual plant, tree or bush (in this case, the *mariri* vine which is used to prepare Vegetal). Thus, in Portuguese one says, 'um pé de' *jacarandá, de salgueiro, de abacateiro*, and so on ('one Jacaranda tree', 'one *Salgueiro* tree', 'one Avocado tree').

the UDV, asserting, on the contrary, the novel character of the UDV cosmology and its superiority compared with other religions. Many of the ritual elements of the UDV (such as the type of trance) are consolidated in opposition to the 'Afro' religious universe, even though, in practice, components of the latter are put in action during the elaboration of UDV ceremonies and symbology. Such is the case of some of the *chamadas* and histories evoked during Vegetal sessions, in addition to terms and embellishments that appear within them.

Meanwhile, in relation to the traditions that are historically closer to the process of constitution of the União do Vegetal, those whose influences are easier to detect are precisely where we observe an ambiguous development on behalf the representatives of this ayahuasca religion, expressed in their discourses, attitudes, beliefs and practices. Thus, myths, speeches, pronouncements and behavior of UDV followers repeatedly assert a discontinuity with 'curandeirismo' (folk healing) and the healing properties of ayahuasca, or with the 'curiosity' of the old complex of beliefs associated with the brew, as well as with practices associated with Afro-Brazilian religions. However, the actual myths and rituals of the União do Vegetal, in fact, reveal this link; that is, continuity with the traditions from which they attempt to distance themselves. Indeed, this is a basic mechanism that is equally present in the emergence of new religions, when they attempt to assert their differences in order to guarantee their legitimacies. Mythical logic especially follows this pattern, since, as Lévi-Strauss (1989b: 237–65) demonstrated, myths always oscillate between continuous and discontinuous structures, historical and synchronic, which belong to different domains and maintain their ambiguous character.

Timeline: Mestre Gabriel and UDV

1922   Birth of Mestre Gabriel, in Coração de Maria, in the state of Bahia.

1943   Arrival of Mestre Gabriel to Rondônia (Alto Guaporé region). Works in rubber camps.

1945–46 Mestre Gabriel begins to work as a nurse in the São José hospital in Porto Velho; Mestre Gabriel attends the *batuque* São Benedito, of Chica Macaxeira.

1947   Mestre Gabriel marries Raimunda Ferreira (Mestre Pequenina) in Porto Velho.

1947–50 Residence of Mestre Gabriel's family in Porto Velho.
Mestre Gabriel continues to attend the *batuque* of Chica Macaxeira and also provides consultations with cowry shells in his house. He receives the 'Sultão das Matas'.
Mestre Gabriel is a nurse in the São José hospital.

1950   Return to the rubber camps.

1950–65 Frequent movements between the city of Porto Velho and the regional rubber camps;
Porto Luís rubber camp – Mestre Gabriel hears about Mestre Bahia, who works with Vegetal.
Orion rubber camp – Mestre Gabriel opens a *terreiro* in which he receives the *Caboclo* spirit Sultão das Matas.

1959	Guarapari rubber camp (on the border with Bolívia) – Mestre Gabriel drinks Vegetal for the first time with Chico Lourenço; first trip to Vila Plácido, in Acre.
1961	July 22 – Sunta rubber camp – Re-creation of the União do Vegetal.
1962	January 6 – Vila Plácido (Acre) – Mestre Gabriel meets with the 12 'Masters of Curiosity' and is declared 'Superior Mestre'.
1964	November 1 – Sunta rubber camp – Confirmation of the União do Vegetal in the Higher Astral.
1965	Mestre Gabriel and his family move to Porto Velho.
1967	Imprisonment of Mestre Gabriel in Porto Velho and publication of the article 'The Conviction of the Master' in the Alto Madeira newspaper; elaboration of the UDV statutes.
1970	Name change: from Beneficent Association União do Vegetal (*Associação Beneficente União do Vegetal*) to Beneficient Spiritist Center União do Vegetal (*Centro Espírita Beneficente União do Vegetal*) (CEBUDV).
1971	Passing away of Mestre Gabriel.

References

Almeida, Mauro W. Barbosa. 1992. 'Rubber Tappers of the Upper Juruá River, Brazil: The Making of a Forest Peasant Economy'. PhD dissertation, University of Cambridge.

Almeida, Mauro W. Barbosa. 2004. 'A ayahuasca e seus usos'. In Labate and Araújo (2004), 15–19.

Almeida, Mauro W. Barbosa, and Maria Manuela Carneiro da Cunha, eds. 2002. *Enciclopédia da Floresta: o Alto Juruá: práticas e conhecimentos das populações*. São Paulo: Cia. das Letras.

Andrade, Afrânio P. de. 1995. 'O fenômeno do Chá e a Religiosidade Cabocla: um estudo centrado na União do Vegetal'. Master's thesis in Religious Sciences, Instituto Metodista de Ensino Superior.

Araújo, Gabriela Jahnel. 1998. 'Entre almas, encantes e cipó'. Master's thesis in Social Anthropology, Unicamp.

Beck, Ralph T. 2005. *A maçonaria e outras sociedades secretas*. São Paulo: Editora Planeta do Brasil.

Bianchi, Antonio. 2005. 'Ayahuasca e xamanismo indígena na selva peruana: o lento caminho da conquista'. In Beatriz C. Labate and Sandra Lucía Goulart, eds, *O uso ritual das plantas de poder*, 319–29. Campinas: Mercado de Letras, 2005.

Brissac, Sérgio. 1999. 'A Estrela do Norte Iluminado até o Sul: uma etnografia da Uniaõ do Vegetal em um contexto urbano'. Master's thesis in Social Anthropology, Museu Nacional/UFRJ.

Cacciatore, Olga Gudolle. 1988. *Dicionário de Cultos Afro-Brasileiros*. Rio de Janeiro: Forense Universitária, 3rd edn.

Cavalcanti, Maria Laura Viveiros de Castro. 1983. *O mundo invisível: cosmologia, sistema ritual e noção de pessoa no Espiritismo*. Rio de Janeiro: Zahar.

Centro Espírita Beneficente União do Vegetal (CEBUDV). 1989. *Hoasca. Fundamentos e objetivos*. Brasília: Sede Geral.

Dobkin de Rios, Marlene. 1971. Curanderismo com la soga alucinógena (ayahuasca) en la selva peruana. *América Indígena* 31(3): 575–92.

Dobkin de Rios, Marlene. 1972. *Visionary Vine: Hallucinogenic Healing in the Peruvian Amazon*. San Francisco: Waveland.

Ferretti, Sérgio Figueiredo. 1995. *Repensando o Sincretismo*. São Paulo: EDUSP/FAPEMA.

Figueiredo, José Gervásio. 1998. *Dicionário de Maçonaria: seus mistérios, seus ritos, sua filosofia, sua história.* São Paulo: Editora Pensamento.

Franco, Mariana C. Pantoja, and Osmildo Silva da Conceição. 2004. 'Breves revelações sobre a ayahuasca: O uso do chá entre os seringueiros do Alto Juruá'. In Labate and Araújo (2004), 201–25.

Galvão, Eduardo. 1955. *Santos e Xamãs.* São Paulo: Cia Editora Nacional.

Goulart, Sandra Lucia. 1996. 'As Raízes culturais do Santo Daime'. Master's thesis in Social Anthropology, University of São Paulo.

Goulart, Sandra Lucia. 2004a. 'Contrastes e Continuidades em uma tradição amazônica: as religiões da ayahuasca'. Doctoral dissertation in Social Sciences, Unicamp.

Goulart, Sandra Lucia. 2004b. 'O Contexto de surgimento do culto do Santo Daime: formação da comunidade e do calendário ritual'. In Labate and Araújo (2004), 277–301.

Gow, Peter. 1996. 'River People: Shamanism and History in Western Amazonia'. In Nicholas Thomas and Caroline Humphrey, eds, *Shamanism, History and the State,* 90–113. Ann Arbor, MI: University of Michigan Press, 1996.

Hall, Manly P. 2006. *As chaves perdidas da maçonaria: o segredo de Hiram Abiff.* São Paulo: Madras.

Labate, Beatriz C. 2004. *A Reinvenção do uso da ayahuasca nos centros urbanos.* Campinas: Mercado de Letras.

Labate, Beatriz C. and Wladimyr Sena Araújo, eds. 2004. *O uso ritual da ayahuasca.* 2nd edn; Campinas: Mercado de Letras.

Lewis, Ioan M. 1977. *Êxtase religioso: um estudo antropológico da possessão por espírito e do xamanismo.* São Paulo: Perspectiva.

Lévi-Strauss, Claude. 1989a. *O Pensamento Selvagem.* Campinas: Papirus.

Lévi-Strauss, Claude. 1989b. *Antropologia Estrutural.* Rio de Janeiro: Tempo Brasileiro.

Lodi, Edison. 2004. *Estrela da minha vida: histórias do sertão caboclo.* Brasília: Edições Entre Folhas.

Luna, Luis Eduardo. 1986a. *Vegetalismo: Shamanism among the Mestizo Population of the Peruvian Amazon.* Stockholm: Almqvist & Wiksell International.

Luna, Luis Eduardo. 1986b. 'Bibliografia sobre el ayahuasca'. *América Indígena* 46 (Jan–Mar).

Luna, Luis Eduardo. 2004., 'Xamanismo amazônico, ayahuasca, antropomorfismo e mundo natural'. In Labate and Araújo (2004), 181–200.

Luna, Luis E., and Pablo Amaringo. 1993. *Ayahuasca Visions: The Religious Iconography of a Peruvian Shaman.* Berkley, CA: North Atlantic Books.

Luna, Luis E. and Steven White, eds. 2000. *Ayahuasca Reader: Encounters with the Amazon's Sacred Vine.* Santa Fe, NM: Synergetic Press.

Machado, Roberto, *et al.*, eds. 1978. *Danação da norma.* Rio de Janeiro: Graal.

MacRae, Edward. 1992. *Guiado pela Lua: xamanismo e uso ritual da ayahuasca no culto do Santo Daime.* São Paulo: Brasiliense.

Maggie, Yvonne. 1992. *O Medo do Feitiço: relações entre magia e poder no Brasil.* Rio de Janeiro: Arquivo Nacional.

Maués, R. Heraldo. 1995. *Padres, pajés, santos e festas: catolicismo popular e controle eclesiástico – um estudo antropológico numa área do interior da Amazônia.* Belém: CEJUP.

Montero, Paula. 1985. *Da doença à desordem: a magia na umbanda.* Rio de Janeiro: Graal.

Negrão, Lísias Nogueira. 1996. *Entre a cruz e a encruzilhada: formação do campo umbandista em São Paulo.* São Paulo: EDUSP.

Oritz, Renato. 1977. 'A Morte Branca do Feiticeiro Negro'. *Religião e Sociedade* 1 (May).

Oritz, Renato. 1978, *A morte branca do feiticeiro negro: umbanda, integração de uma religião numa sociedade de classes.* Petrópolis: Vozes.

Pereira, Nunes. 1979 [1947]. *A Casa das Minas: contribuição ao estudo das sobrevivências do culto dos voduns do panteão daomeano, no estado do Maranhão.* Petrópolis: Vozes, 2nd edn.

Pereira de Queiroz, Maria Isaura. 1973. *O Campesinato brasileiro: ensaios sobre civilização e grupos rústicos no Brasil.* Petrópolis: Vozes/São Paulo: EDUSP.

Pereira de Queiroz, Maria Isaura. 1978. *Cultura, sociedade rural, sociedade urbana no Brasil.* São Paulo: EDUSP.

Procópio, Cândido Ferreira. 1961. *Kardecismo e Umbanda.* São Paulo: Pioneira de Ciências Sociais.

Stafford, P. 1992. *Psychedelic Encyclopedia.* 3rd edn; Berkley, CA: Ronin Publishing.

Trindade, Liana. 1991. 'Construções míticas e história: estudo sobre as representações simbólicas e relações raciais em São Paulo do século XVIII à atualidade'. Professorship thesis, University of São Paulo.

Wagley, Charles. 1977. *Uma comunidade amazônica – um estudo do homem nos trópicos.* São Paulo: Brasiliana.

7

In the light of Hoasca: an approach to the religious experience of participants of the União do Vegetal[*]

Sérgio Brissac

Translated by Lyzette Góes Telles Brissac[†]

On July 22, 1961, on a rubber plantation in the Amazon Forest, near the Brazil-Bolivia border, a 39-year-old rubber tapper named José Gabriel da Costa declared, before a small group of people with whom he drank ayahuasca, that on that day he was founding the União do Vegetal. His disciples started to call him Mestre[1] Gabriel. Later, the União do Vegetal (UDV) was structured as a religious institution, present in all the major cities of Brazil. At present, there are also participants of the UDV in the United States, in the states of New Mexico, California, Colorado and Washington. Since 1999, the United States government attempted to ban the UDV members in the US from performing their religious ritual, in which they drink ayahuasca.[2] In 2006, the Supreme Court decided unanimously to affirm religious liberty, restoring the UDV members' right to use ayahuasca in their rituals.

Hoasca is the name given by the participants of UDV to ayahuasca, also simply named 'the Vegetal', a tea with psychoactive properties made from the concoction of the leaves of *Psychotria viridis*, which they call *chacrona*, with the vine *Banisteriopsis caapi*, known as *mariri*. Although in Quechua *huasca* means 'vine', for the UDV members Hoasca is the name for the *chacrona* as well as for the tea. However, in a higher significance, to the members of the UDV Hoasca[3] is a spiritual being whose main attribute is the Light. So,

---

* First published in *Fieldwork in Religion* (2006) 2.3: 319–49.

† I wish to express my gratitude to Lyzette Góes Telles Brissac, my mother, who kindly did the translation of this article. This was her last work as an English teacher, before she passed away in 2006. I thank her not only for this accurate translation, but especially for her enthusiastic support, essential to my formation as an anthropologist.

1. *Mestre* means Master. Often in this article I maintain the word in Portuguese, as the participants of UDV in the United States used to.
2. See the article by Matthew Meyer, this volume.
3. When writing about that 'higher significance' I capitalize 'Hoasca'.

the ingestion of this tea is to them an experience in the light of the Hoasca. The aim of this article is to enquire into the fundamental axis of such an experience and to analyze, under a hermeneutic focus, the principal categories present in the speech of the UDV participants. Having presented such native categories, an interpretative hypothesis will be sought for the articulation of the different elements of the participants' life with aspects of UDV's world-view. It will be argued that the concept of syncretism is not adequate to consider such a relation and the idea of an 'encompassment in the force of the *burracheira*' will be proposed.

This text is based on the anthropological observation of UDV, which I started 15 years ago and continue up to the present, as well as on field research that I carried out in 1998 in the UDV unit called Nucleus *Alto das Cordilheiras*,[4] in Campinas, which was the basis of my Master's thesis in social anthropology. The city of Campinas is situated in the State of São Paulo, southeast of Brazil, in one of the country's most economically developed and industrialized regions. By this approach I seek to reach an interpretation of the symbolic experience of the urban Brazilian participants of the União do Vegetal.

UDV organization

Before analyzing the categories of speech of UDV members, a brief resumé of its orga-nizational structure will be helpful. At the local level, UDV is organized in 'nuclei'. The nucleus is the place where the participants are gathered, where members or disciples, so designated, drink hoasca tea in a ritual called 'session'. When a local unit is started, it is first called an 'authorized distribution', after that a 'pre-nucleus', and only later on, when it acquires a more solid material structure and a greater number of participants, does it reach the status of nucleus. It is common for a nucleus, when reaching a level around 150 members, to start a process of segmentation by which some people leave the nucleus and begin a new unit at another site in the same city.

The nucleus is directed by a *Representative Mestre*. This function is thus named because the one occupying it represents Mestre Gabriel, the founder of UDV. The *Representative* heads the nucleus's *Body of Mestres*, the entirety of those who have the function of com-municating the UDV doctrine, designated with the name of greatest symbolic power in the UDV, that is, *Mestre*.[5] Next to the *Body of Mestres* in the hierarchy is the *Council Body*, formed by men and women *Counsellors*, who are auxiliaries to the *Mestres* and, with them, form the *Administration* of the nucleus. Then, there is the *Instructive Body*, formed by those disciples who have been participating in the UDV for a certain period of time and have a commitment to greater involvement in its activities, summoned by the *Representa-tive Mestre* to attend the 'instructive sessions'. These are restricted sessions that take place

---

4. High of the Cordilleras. *Nucleus* is the name of each local center of UDV.
5. Only men can reach the position of Mestre. The sole exception is Mestre Pequenina, Mestre Gabriel's wife, who was personally appointed by him. Some people question the exclusion of women from the *Body of Mestres*, arguing, for example, that when Mestre Gabriel made a selection for Mestres of the UDV, some women participated in the process. Although those women were not selected to be Mestres, this would not mean that *no woman* could be Mestre. On the other hand, the official vision of the UDV emphasizes that, for spiritual reasons, the best place for a woman is as Counsellor, which would be as important as a Mestre.

approximately every two months, in which esoteric teachings of the União do Vegetal are transmitted. Finally, at the base of the hierarchy is the *Membership Body,* formed by the other disciples who are only associated to the UDV.

Burracheira

The altered state of consciousness catalyzed by the ingestion of hoasca is called *burracheira*. Although the Spanish term 'borrachera' indicates the intoxication motivated by an alcoholic drink,[6] the meaning of the word *burracheira* for disciples of UDV is 'strange force', according to Mestre Gabriel. The effect of hoasca tea is difficult to characterize due to the plurality of possible experiences brought about by its use. In general, one can mention an intense alteration of sensations, feelings and perceptions during the period of the effect of hoasca which usually lasts about four hours, the duration of a UDV session. The experience of modified visual perceptions, called *mirações,* is quite frequent.

Roberto,[7] university student, a young man in his twenties, answered the question I asked about the *burracheira* as follows;

> For me, the *burracheira* is a state of consciousness that we encounter, a condition of the spirit. I see it as nurturing my spirit. The *burracheira* shows the new senses of reality. The little plant which is over there…you look at in a different way from before, you are able to see the reality in a much deeper way. You also happen to see new styles of thinking, you think about certain things which are only possible to think when in the state of *burracheira*.[8]

In addition to thoughts, he also mentions the feeling he has most experienced during the *burracheira*, gratitude:

> Ah, that feeling of gratitude, really! Gratitude for being a guy. I am alive, this is a reality. There are other things of post-mortem life in which I believe, but there are those other guys who are skeptical, so there is no way of proving it. But there is one thing that can be proved, which is: I am alive here, thinking, with my consciousness, the whole world, a lot of little heads thinking…but I know that I am here, and all of a sudden I am *Roberto,* I have my life, my friends, the things that happen, so, I play the guitar, I can do such things… Then, when I am there like this, something that always remains present, for me, is gratitude. I think the most remarkable feeling is gratitude.[9]

The book that institutionally presents the Centro Espírita Beneficente União do Vegetal[10] (CEBUDV), the official name of UDV, states that 'the effect of the tea can be compared to religious ecstasy…a state of contemplative lucidity that places the person in direct contact

---

6. In some Spanish-speaking Amazon communities, e.g., in Colombia, the term 'borrachera' is also used to designate the effect of the ayahuasca.

7. Pseudonym. I have adopted the practice of changing the participants' names in order to protect their privacy. The pseudonym will be shown in italics.

8. Interview with *Roberto* on October 26th, 1998, in Campinas.

9. Interview with *Roberto* on October 26th, 1998, in Campinas.

10. The translation of the center's name could be something like 'Beneficent Spiritist Center Union of the Plants'.

Figure 1. Mestre José Gabriel da Costa (copyright Cícero Alexandre Lopes, Department of Memory and Documentation of the Centro Espírita Beneficente União do Vegetal)

with the spiritual plane' (CEBUDV, 1989: 30). The *burracheira* is conceived of in UDV as a *force*, something that has its origin in the very 'Superior Force' – an expression frequently utilized to refer to the divinity. This *force* is unknown, *strange* to the human being. For that reason, the UDV participant seeks to be prepared for entering into contact with the *burracheira* during the sessions. And it is the Mestre who leads him in this experience.

Master and disciple

Certainly, the most pronounced word in a UDV session is Mestre. Above all, it is the word most used to denominate the Superior Force – a term equivalent to God for UDV members. Human beings are in this world to learn, that is, to evolve spiritually. Thus, God is, above all, the Master who teaches. Whom does he teach? Here appears the correlate of the category of Master: that of disciple. The latter is not a word as frequently used as Mestre, however, it is in a way implicit in the speech of the one who summons the Master and who puts himself in the position of learning. To learn what? Here arises the third element of this relationship: knowledge. The Master transmits the knowledge of spiritual things. Now, one can perceive the fundamental role that is attributed to knowledge in the UDV. And so, just like life, the ritual is also an apprenticeship; UDV is a school where one learns the teachings of the Master. And the Master has his messengers who convey his teachings. José Gabriel da Costa is one of them, like Solomon and Jesus. The position of UDV regards Jesus, according to the above mentioned book, is as follows:

> The União do Vegetal professes the fundamentals of Christianity, and integrates them in their purity and original integrity, free of the distortions that human hands imprinted on them through the centuries... The doctrine of União do Vegetal is Christian because it holds that Jesus Christ, Son of God, is the expression of Divinity and His Word points to the path of Salvation for mankind. The União do Vegetal believes in the Virgin Mary, Our Lady Immaculate, mother of Jesus (CEBUDV, 1989: 22–23).

Being a messenger of the Superior Force, the founder of UDV is, therefore, also called Mestre. According to one participant, he is 'Mestre who knows the way that a spirit needs to go through, so as to find the meaning of its own existence; and he knows, because he himself has gone through his own path; and he is Mestre because he is ready to help'.[11] I asked all the people that I interviewed the following question: 'Who is, for you, José Gabriel da Costa?' There was a great variety of answers. *Denise*, who is in the Membership Body, answered: 'Mestre Gabriel is a mystery to me. I still don't know what I feel, he is an interesting little old man; it is difficult to think he is a Master, not a conventional Master. It is easier to think of a Tibetan lama.'[12] The difficulty here appears to be of someone with a graduate education in accepting as Master a semi-illiterate rubber tapper. In reality, a Tibetan lama would certainly be more palatable in a first contact. However, as people remain longer in the UDV, the mystery of that person involves them more and more. *Renato*, who has been with the UDV for 18 years, says the following with regard to José Gabriel da Costa: 'It is a mystery; he is fascinating, he is the light. It is something like having to describe what humility is. It is essential to feel.'[13] Answers such as this, which appear repeatedly with much utilized words like 'light' and 'mystery', are recurrent in UDV. Also frequently seen is the indication of feeling as a means to access self-knowledge. Another aspect pointed out by *Alice*, who has known UDV for ten years, is the proximity of José Gabriel da Costa:

> A great friend, someone who, although I haven't even met personally, is someone very near. And more, he is a friend who is present in the important moments of my life. I even think of giving up but he always brings me back in an intelligent way.[14]

This feeling of proximity is also mentioned by *Clarice*, an old lady with little academic study, who has gone through a lot of suffering and can see these difficulties in the life of José Gabriel da Costa:

---

11. Interview with *Nelson* in Campinas, on September 30, 1998. A cultural producer, in his forties.
12. Interview with *Denise* in Campinas, on October 19, 1998. A doctor, in her thirties.
13. Interview with *Renato* in São Paulo, on October 21, 1998. *Renato* is in his forties.
14. Interview with *Alice* in Campinas, on September 17, 1998. A lawyer, in her thirties.

It is a person who didn't have formal study. But, why did he suffer so much? He lived in a poor place, a rubber tapper, had a mentally deficient son. Why didn't he come in a better life, without so many financial problems? Mestre Gabriel is an awakened[15] man.[16]

This empathic view, which sees the Mestre as a mirror of one's own self and simultaneously as someone with a high spiritual 'degree', is also observed in the interview with Mestre *Décio*, a psychotherapist: 'he is an internal therapist. To me, today, Mestre Gabriel is a light that permits the unraveling of my true self; when my true self is fully lapidated, his mission with me will be concluded.'[17]

The polysemy of José Gabriel da Costa's life is, primarily, related to the polysemic character of all human existence. However, due to the density and diversity of the experiences he lived, and by the sacred scope in which is given the knowledge and the identification with the Mestre, one sometimes observes a process that could be read in a hermeneutic perspective, from this text of Ricoeur:

> When he understands himself in and by the sacred signs, man operates the most radical dispossession of himself that we can possibly conceive... An archeology and a teleology reveal still an *arché* and a *télos* which the subject can dispose of when understanding them. The same does not occur with the sacred... Of this *alpha* and of this *omega* the subject cannot dispose. The sacred questions man, and with this questioning disposes of man's existence because it places his existence in an absolute manner, as effort and desire of being (Ricoeur, 1978: 23).

The *arché* – a Greek term that refers to the beginning, the origin, to the rooting in the past – is unveiled in *experience of the limit* in the lives of *Clarice* and José Gabriel da Costa. Now, the *télos* – which designates the end, the goal, the dynamism facing the future – is but perceived in the *overcoming of the limits* by Mestre Gabriel and in the desires of *Décio* of a 'self fully lapidated'. Therefore, *arché* and *télos* are experienced by these people as a radical interpellation of the sacred, sacred that disposes of human existence, imprinting on it a dynamic of search.

The leaders of União do Vegetal, as I stated above, are also designated with the name of Mestre. So, there are three levels of application of the word Mestre in a UDV session: the divine, the one relating to Mestre Gabriel, and another referring to those who have the *star of Mestre*[18] in the CEBUDV, that is, its directors. These multiple meanings of the word Mestre in a UDV session may cause ambiguities, but they will probably result in productive misunderstandings for the cohesion of the group, since it outlines a correlation high-low which ratifies the hierarchic authority and makes the divine feel nearer. At every moment the Mestre is called, and the Mestre directing the session promptly replies. In the statutes, for example, it is stated that 'the session will be directed by the Mestre and by whomever be appointed to represent him', that is, all the sessions have as director

---

15. *Clarice* used the expression 'recordado', which means, for UDV participants, someone who attained the spiritual degree to remember all his previous lives.

16. Interview with *Clarice*, in Campinas, on September 15, 1998. A housewife, in her seventies.

17. Interview with *Décio*, in Campinas on October 15, 1998. A psychiatrist and psychotherapist, in his fifties.

18. The Mestres wear on their uniform, during sessions, a shirt with a star embroidered at the height of the chest.

Mestre Gabriel; the person who occupies the place of 'director Mestre of the session' will be his representative. This aspect of the place is highlighted so that the 'Mestre of União do Vegetal' in the strict meaning of the term, actually, is Mestre Gabriel, the other Mestres being disciples who have a task: to transmit the doctrine of UDV and, together with the man-counsellors and women-counsellors, direct the UDV nucleus.

The disciple is, as I have stated above, someone who places himself in the position of learning. And the session is the most adequate space for that. Thus, in the UDV ritual time is strongly marked as a time for the exercise of the word. The game of asking and answering fills the major part of the session. And the question is asked to the Mestre directing the session, who answers in the quality of Mestre, that is, as someone who teaches. By calling this game 'exercise of the word', I hereby refer to a strong meaning of the term exercise. Just as a physical intense and ordained activity is an exercise, in the same manner the use of the word in the UDV sessions many times requires of him who uses it an effort, attention and precision that make of such an activity a demanding exercise. When facing the force of the *burracheira*, a great effort may be necessary simply to rise and articulate a question. In the whirlwind of sensations caused by the *burracheira*, a lot of concentration and attention may be necessary to focus on a subject and elaborate a pertinent question. And in this game, precision is demanded, since one cannot use any word in any manner. There is a whole series of prescriptions that aim at excluding from the sessions inadequate words, since the *burracheira* is perceived as something that is plastically molded by the word. So, just as speech regarding the beauties of nature may lead the listeners to experience beautiful and luminous *mirações*, in the same way, a communication referring to fear and personal conflicts, may lead some in the audience to feel uncomfortable too, in their *burracheira*, to the point of physical discomfort like nausea, or emotionally anguished. This plasticity of the *burracheira* requires thorough attention when speaking, so that the people are not led to difficult situations due to words uttered carelessly. In this way, there is a marked preoccupation with the form, with the choice of the words, which makes this exercise something very demanding. Some Mestres correct disciples when they employ a word or an inadequate expression. When, for instance, one asks a question saying: 'I wanted to know...' he may hear the Mestre: 'You wanted, now you don't want any more'. Therefore, a certain docility on the part of the disciple is necessary, so that he may let himself be corrected by the Mestre. All this constitutes a proper rhetoric style, formed by short, clear and slowly pronounced phrases and, above all, an assertive speech expressing conviction and firmness. The disposition to learn and to participate in the sessions, mainly by asking as well as the earnestness in taking part in the works and activities of the nucleus make it possible for the disciple to be summoned for the Instructive Body. All this value attributed to the word leads the UDV disciple to conclude that, not only during the sessions, but also in the daily life, the word is filled with efficacy.

Knowledge

The relevance of knowledge in the worldview of UDV may be observed by considering the requests made in the ritual and by the fruits which one is taught to expect of the *bur-*

racheira: to receive from Hoasca light to know and to receive, from the *mariri*, strength to apply the knowledge in life. This emphasis on the search of knowledge is similar to that taught by the Gnostics of the early centuries of the Christian era. However, such an element in the UDV is balanced by the accent equally given to the need for that which Mestre Gabriel called 'the faithful practice of good'.

When asked if the UDV is a kind of gnosis, a Mestre answered:

> In the meaning of the word, yes. It is difficult to say what the Gnostics were for it is a name used for so many different things, something very difficult... But, in the aspect of knowledge, of the spiritual value of knowledge, of the realization through knowledge, I think that there is a lot to do with it. Because there are a lot of things normally associated with what was used to be called Gnostic that have nothing to do with UDV as, for example, a division between those elected and those not elected; this aspect does not exist. However, there are some aspects of teaching which are literal things, even written with the same words. So, it has something to do with it. Mestre Gabriel never placed himself as an exclusive possessor of knowledge. Knowledge is in the heights, whoever gets there reaches it.[19]

This relation with gnosis can be inferred from the statement of *Luísa,* a Counsellor and psychologist, in her fifties: 'the line of the Vegetal, this more direct line to the heirs of Saint Thomas; their faith needs the columns of feeling and of knowledge'.[20] In this aspect, it is possible to think of an analogy with the belief of ancient Romans who did not accept theological and metaphysical assertions before submitting them to critique. Linder and Scheid affirm that 'from this point of view, Romans were Thomasses, but Thomas models of faith and not of disbelief' (Linder and Scheid, 1993: 55). And in the related note: 'The best proof being that of the eyes' (Linder and Scheid, 1993: 60 n. 46). Now, the exercise of belief in UDV may perhaps be defined as that of 'Saint Thomas' heirs', as *Luísa* stated, to the extent that faith is not required *a priori*, but is figured as the result of an experience – in which, by the way, vision has a role of substantial importance – of the faculties of feeling and of knowing. As pointed out by Otávio Velho:

> Now, it is as if St Thomas were the apostle of the new era. An era that would require a religiosity of direct experience, where knowledge subsumes affectivity and is placed in lieu of transmission exclusively by way of tradition, which has no value except when it is convincingly reinvented (Velho, 1998: 38).

Mestre Gabriel himself said: 'do not believe what I say; examine!...to see that I am right'. This phrase is often remembered in and out of sessions, and brings to UDV a flexibility regarding the different degrees of acceptance of the doctrine, to the extent that this *examination* remains open. *Luís,* a professor in his fifties, stated:

> Religions require conformity and consensus, but not UDV. Although it apparently requires, it shelters a lot of people such as me. We learn what we can speak and what we cannot. It is interesting if you look at Rajneesh. He used to say: 'the only thing I

---

19. Interview with *Mestre Paulo*, in Campinas, October 16, 1998. An engineer, in his forties.
20. Interview with Counsellor Luísa , in Campinas, October 20, 1998.

demand of you is that you do the meditations'. UDV says: 'drink the Vegetal and pay the month's due'. It has no creed.[21]

However, such a statement should be understood in context, taking into account that Luís belongs to the Membership Body, although he has drunk the Vegetal for over four years. As he realizes himself: 'I do not belong to the Instructive. You have to show that you belong to UDV, that you ask the right questions... I would even like to, but I have to go through all this. In a way, I do not belong to UDV'.[22] Luís knows that the call for the Instructive Body requires a degree of adhesion that he does not yet have, which in a way makes him feel an outsider. On the other hand, the Membership Body is quite flexible. However, a greater engagement is expected from those of the Instructive Body, even regarding this doctrinal aspect, as one of the bulletins states: 'Only he who accepts the doctrines of the Instructive Session may remain in it'.[23] But there does not appear in detail what such an acceptance means, so there still remains a significant margin for a variety of comprehensions. Surely, the ascension to the degrees of the hierarchy is related to the degree of adhesion to the doctrine of Mestre Gabriel, but not in a univocal manner.

Feeling

UDV is a religion of oral tradition in which the portion of the doctrine considered by the group itself as fundamental – the stories and the *chamadas*[24] – is not written and may not even be registered as such, since it is prescribed that the teachings be transmitted 'from mouth to ear'. This raises a certain perplexity in its new members: what is the criterion to know if the knowledge is true? Mestre *Paulo*, approaching the question of José Gabriel da Costa's identity, says that 'there is a risk of each one of us, today, calling "Mestre" a series of things, of sensations regarding one's self. People sometimes say: "I spoke to the Mestre", "the Mestre told me, right".'[25] But, subsequently, *Paulo* talks of certain occasions when he could perceive an 'intelligent force' acting in União do Vegetal:

In a lot of cases it is quite perceptible this intentionality, this manner in which things keep happening which, if they happened differently, would have a different result. When I mention an intelligent force, I mean it is something I feel that has a purpose, a reason, it is not a force like that of a tempest, which we feel is a force whose direction cannot be perceived. But in the case of União do Vegetal there is this intelligent aspect and in my personal experience I see as if it were a strategy, a strategy of how to reach me. Then, to me, this José Gabriel da Costa, besides being the man he was,

---

21. Interview with *Luís,* in Campinas, November 6, 1998.
22. Interview with *Luís,* in Campinas, November 6, 1998.
23. Bulletin of the Conscience Conserving the Tranquility of the Center's Affiliates, fourth part (CEBUDV, 1994: 58).
24. *Chamadas* (in English, *calls* or *beckonings*) are ritual chants, like *mantras,* performed to open and to close the session and to *call* or *beckon* light and force for it.
25. Interview with Mestre *Paulo,* in Campinas, October 16, 1998.

with the example, which I find very important, Brazilian, near in time, in the way of living, in the space, geographical location, language, besides being this man, I identify Mestre Gabriel as that intelligent force in the União do Vegetal.[26]

Next, I ask him what the criterion is to perceive what is truly action of this 'intelligent force' so as not 'to personalize individual sensations' and call them 'Mestre Gabriel'. And he answers:

> We are going back to the *feeling*, right? I once asked a very spiritualized, very nice lady. But she read books that I thought had nothing to do with anything. Then, I asked her: 'Gosh, I don't understand…why do you read such things there?' She said the following: 'I read, read everything now, I only keep what touches my heart'. And it is more or less so, see? You *know, when it is* you *know*.[27]

This legitimate status of knowledge that feeling has in UDV has also been clearly manifested in a session in Rio de Janeiro. One talked about the truth. When a disciple asked how one can be sure that something one sees in the *burracheira* is true and not an illusion, the Mestre directing the session answered: 'when something you see is really the truth you *feel*; the *feeling* shows you that it is the truth'.

There is, certainly, the authority of Mestre Gabriel, the founder, which is accepted as that from someone who is the '*Mestre dos Mestres*'.[28] However, in the interpretation of his words or in those points on which he did not comment, feeling is a fundamental criterion, especially the feeling during the *burracheira*. It is true that during the same session mentioned above, another Mestre pointed out that there is the Council of the Memory of the Teachings of Mestre Gabriel, which gathers approximately 12 people from the beginnings of the União do Vegetal, those who received the star of Mestre from Mestre Gabriel's hands. Although in specific controversies that Council has supreme authority to define a consensus on the legitimate doctrine, in the daily life of the disciples of UDV, a basic criterion is that one given by Mestre Gabriel: 'examine!' Such an examination by the disciple of UDV should certainly not be guided only by rationality, but by the *feeling* illuminated by the 'Hoasca light' as well; that is, feeling sharpened and deepened by the experience of the *burracheira*.

In 1981, a cover story was published by the magazine *Planeta* with the title: 'Oasca and the religion of feeling'[29] (Araripe, 1981: 34–41). The author, Flamínio de Alencar Araripe is a disciple of UDV to this date. In this article, he stated that 'it is an unforgettable experience to *feel* the energy of this tea acting in the human organism' (p. 36). Describing the effect of the tea, he writes that 'in the innermost of the person it acts as something that clears the real sensibility of the organism' (p. 36). Talking about the 'transformative power' of the Vegetal, he says that 'true changes are operated among the people who continue to drink this tea':

---

26. Interview with Mestre *Paulo*, in Campinas, October 16, 1998.
27. Interview with Mestre *Paulo*, in Campinas, October 16, 1998.
28. Master of Masters. Words present in *Mistérios do Vegetal* (Mysteries of the Vegetal), a text read in the beginning of the sessions.
29. The spelling of the word 'Oasca', without 'H' in the beginning, was a lapse of the article's author, since well before its publication, the spelling of 'Hoasca' with initial 'H' had already been established among UDV members.

'*sensibility is increased* and along with it, discernment' (p. 40). This report had ample reper-
cussion among the disciples of UDV, in such a way that until today references are frequently
made to União do Vegetal as *the religion of feeling*. Answering my question about the origin
of this expression, Araripe told me that it came from Mestre Mário Piacentini, a Mestre
from São Paulo who was a Protestant pastor before entering UDV.

So, in my interviews I asked the question: 'Some people call União do Vegetal *the religion of feeling*. Do you consider this expression appropriate?' Approximately two-thirds of
the 50 interviewed answered this question affirmatively. The rest qualified their answer,
saying yes in various ways. And only three of them responded negatively, seeing this affirmation only as a 'found phrase, a slogan'.[30]

According to *Augusto*, an architect in his thirties, belonging to the Instructive Body, 'the
knowledge we have in the *burracheira* comes in a direct form. It is as if knowledge were a
sphere, with feeling and intuition forming the volume of this sphere. It is the power that
the *burracheira* gives you of the direct knowledge by the heart'.[31]

As to those who have disagreed with the affirmation that UDV is *the religion of feeling*,
Antonio, in his forties and a UDV participant for 21 years, of the Instructive Body, when
questioned, shook his head and said: 'I value more and more my rational side. In the *burracheira* there is this *feeling*, but there is thinking too. There is this thing of *studying*, and
this is more than the *feeling*.'[32]

However, *Claudia*, a therapist in her fifties, said:

In my experience it is *the religion of feeling*. Almost all is feeling. Besides, I don't
have linear reasoning, I feel one thing and feel another and switch another, and *puff*,
another springs up…as if it were a big mandala which goes on configuring and all of
a sudden, *ploff*! Everything fits! And it is something that is integrated in an ampler
meaning to understand certain things, and then comes that sensation of peace, of
well-being. There is the linear reasoning and the rhizomic one, like rhizomes, mine
functions like this: one thing comes, *tuc-tuc-tuc*, and all of a sudden *tuff*! it makes a
configuration…and I have integrated an idea.[33]

By these words, one can see that to *Claudia*, this *feeling* does not refer to the emotional
plan only, but also encompasses an exercise of thinking differently than logical reasoning,
a *rhizomic* thinking in which a series of insights lead to an integration and to a 'sensation
of peace'. All this seems to be similar to the synthetic answer of Counsellor *Lidia*, a teacher
in her forties: 'União do Vegetal is the religion of the discovery of *consciousness*, emerging
from *feeling*'.[34]

---

30. Interview with Counsellor *Waldir*, in São Paulo, on October 22, 1998. A designer, in his seventies. For him,
   the UDV is 'the religion of consciouness'.
31. Interview with *Augusto*, in Campinas, on October 19, 1998.
32. Interview with *Antonio*, in Campinas, on September 7, 1998.
33. Interview with *Claudia*, in Campinas, on October 16, 1998.
34. Interview with *Lidia*, in Campinas, on October 28, 1998.

Memory

Related to knowledge is the theme of *memory*. Within the reincarnationist cosmovision of União do Vegetal, memory has a significant role insofar as the process of knowledge is a process of recollection. Thus, José Gabriel da Costa is seen as a *recordado*, someone who reached the condition of remembering his past incarnations, and he is a Master who teaches to remember. So, in the UDV one talks about *degree of memory*. The *Bulletin of the Conscience in Reform* states that 'the disciples who follow the Instructive Session can only be chosen by the Representative Mestre, in accordance with the degrees of memory'.[35] The *degree of memory* is related to the capacity of comprehension of the spiritual teachings. But not only this, it is also something that is inferred from someone's practice. It is just like having the need for the *faithful practice of good* in the memory all the time.

Asked about the influence of his religious experience in his daily life, Mestre *Paulo* said:

> To believe in reincarnation is something that isn't easy. Nor is it obvious, right? I have the experience of this moment, that's my reference. So, I don't find it so simple to believe in reincarnation. But it is something for which I have sufficient reasons today for having it as a reference in my life. This changes the way of seeing things. I don't think it comes to the point of falling in *karmic* fatalism: 'the world is like this', 'I am here going through things which are the result'... In the UDV it is quite interesting that the major responsibility is in this incarnation. According to the word of Mestre Gabriel, very little passes from one incarnation to another. This is something quite different from a vision of *karma*, for which everything now is a direct consequence of the entire past. It is not exactly so that União do Vegetal sees it. The focus is this incarnation.[36]

So, to the extent that the focus of main attention is placed on the present incarnation, during sessions, disciples are called to *exercise the memory* through an ethical daily practice.

Faithful practice of good

The UDV disciples are exhorted in the sessions to experience certain values that are pointed out by Mestres and Counsellors as fundamental. There is a great emphasis on the cultivation of the monogamous family as the nuclear space for the experience of spirituality. Marriage is of great value to the members of UDV, and Mestre Gabriel himself is presented as an example of a man who earnestly dedicated himself to his wife and children. One of the requisites to reach the status of Mestre in the UDV is to be married. If, later on, he separates from his wife, he has to quit the Body of Mestres. Therefore, one can see that the hierarchical grades in UDV are not lifelong conquests but *places* where the disciples are called to occupy, and where they stay as long as they do not commit acts that

35. *Bulletin of the Conscience in Reform* (CEBUDV, 1994: 71). The 'bulletins' are documents which make up the UDV legislation, many of which are read in the beginning of the sessions.
36. Interview with Mestre *Paulo*, in Campinas, on October 16, 1998.

are incompatible with the position held, such as adultery, which may count as a reason for *removal from the communion of the Vegetal*. Another aspect frequently emphasized is the importance of leading a healthy way of living, without the use of tobacco, alcoholic drinks, and illicit drugs. And one can see a significant number of UDV members who, after starting to drink hoasca, have quit drug and alcohol abuse. Other values linked to *order*, like honesty and respect for the laws and the authorities of the country are also held in high regard.

The ritual of UDV expresses the importance of *order* in the cosmovision of the group. The ritual is simple but with some well-defined details that transmit a notion of precision. In the middle of the 'time of *burracheira*', he who directs the session must be attentive to the sequence of the *chamadas*, the subjects, the questions and the music, so that everything occurs 'in harmony'. The ritual space is austere: naked walls, with only the photo of Mestre Gabriel. And on the table, an arch of wood. In contrast to the Santo Daime, where a dance takes place on the days of hymnal 'works' (*hinários*), the corporal posture of UDV participants in the session is simply to sit. It is necessary to ask for permission from the Directing Mestre of the session to leave the room; likewise for making a *chamada*, speaking, and asking questions.

Order is also emphasized in the ritual by the prominence given to the hierarchy of those participating. At the beginning of the session, the tea is served by the Directing Mestre first to himself and to the Representative, then to the other Mestres present, to the Counsellors, to the disciples of the Instructive Body and, finally, to other members. The use of a uniform with different badges for each degree marks the importance of hierarchy. The *chamadas* with their precise succession of verses, which are repeated with slight modifications, as in an ascending scale and which must be faithfully memorized by him who makes them, express the presence of an objective order, exterior and greater, which surpasses the subjectivity of the participants, even when interacting with it. It is as if at every moment the message of the existence of an ordained cosmos were transmitted, which precedes and sustains the individual experience emanated from the Superior Force itself. So, in the austerity of the space, in the attention to the words, in the exercise of asking and answering, during the *chamadas*; finally, in each aspect of the ritual, there appears an Apollonian order that is proposed as an exemplary model to be followed by the disciple in his daily life.

Such an emphasis on order and its related values is reiterated especially in the beginning of each session when the UDV laws are read. Beginning with the *Internal Regiment* various documents are read, among which are *Bulletins of Conscience* with titles such as: *Bulletin of Conscience in Fulfillment of the Law*; *Bulletin of Conscience Recommending the Faithful Allegiance to the Law*; *Bulletin of Conscience in Defense of the Fidelity and Harmony of the Center's Affiliate*; and *Bulletin of Conscience Recommending the Preservation of the Moral and of the Family*. By the titles of the bulletins one can infer that in this context the word 'conscience' [*consciência*] is understood and utilized in its moral connotation as the faculty to pass moral judgments on the acts practised. All this emphasis on the moral aspects gives some people the impression of a legalistic exteriority, a morality that is summarized in 'good behavior', according to the rules of a wider society. I think, however, that a deeper analysis may lead to the observation of other elements that point to an ethic more demanding than this morality of 'good behavior'. At a certain point of the

147

reading of the documents, one hears the following words of Mestre Gabriel: 'we may be judged by all, but we cannot judge anybody; we may have enemies, but we cannot be anybody's enemies'.[37] And in the *Bulletin of the Conscience on Firmness*: 'the disciple should love his neighbor as he loves himself to be worthy of receiving the symbol of União'. By these assertions the sphere of knowledge is linked to the sphere of praxis, requiring from the disciple that his spiritual experience be reflected in a practice according to the Christian ethical principles of universal love, of non-violence and forgiveness to one's enemies.

In the speech of the participants of the Nucleus *Alto das Cordilheiras*, I was often able to detect an effort to affirm repercussions in daily life from belonging to UDV; 'reports of conversion' were offered, which compared contrasting aspects of someone's way of acting before and after joining UDV. If in the reports of some, such changes are more explicit, such as overcoming alcoholism, in others there are small changes of attitude detected in daily life. I consider it relevant that, in the speech of the majority of UDV participants, one finds abundant links between ritual experience and daily life, and that such a link is seen as indicative of *spiritual evolution*.

Spiritual evolution

In accordance with Article 1 of the *Internal Regiment*, read in all regular sessions, the CEBUDV 'has as objectives: a) to work for the evolution of the human being aiming at his spiritual development; b) to gather socially in its Spiritist temple and extraordinarily at the criterion of the Mestre'.[38] These initial words establish the fundamental existence of UDV upon the vision of *spiritual evolution*. And continually, in the words of members during sessions, there is some reference to evolution, in that 'we are here – on Earth and in this religion – to evolve spiritually'.

Denise, of the Instructive Body, a systems analyst in her twenties, when asked if the religious experience of UDV has had any impact on her daily activities, answered:

It surely has. In general, I feel it brings more direction, more equilibrium, mainly, simply the fact of having an objective, which is spiritual evolution, this already completely modifies your life. Because it's one thing to live with an objective and another thing to live with no orientation, right? Principally, the fact that you have an objective in life; this totally changes your life.[39]

This teleological focus is present in the speech of many disciples of UDV. It shares the same semantic province of the doctrine's emphasis on themes such as righteousness, firmness of thinking, and simplicity. It is as if an image of life being like a straight line prevailed, at the end of which there is a well-defined goal that is important to know and to sustain within your sight, in order to reach the goal more quickly. In the early days of UDV, in the rubber plantations and in Porto Velho, this teleological focus of life was understood in

---

37. *Mestre's Conviction*, article published in the newspaper *Alto Madeira*.
38. *Internal Regiment* of CEBUDV, article 1 (CEBUDV, 1994: 92).
39. Interview with *Denise*, in Campinas, on September 7, 1998.

eminently spiritual terms – it was important to have quite present that the objective to be reached by the disciple was 'spiritual evolution'. However, this same focus will be re-read by the urban participants of the Brazilian southeast, not only regards the spiritual aspect but as a tendency to search for efficacy, too. This, surely, is an element highly valued by many of the urban UDV participants: efficacy in personal life, efficacy in the organization of the Centro Espírita Beneficente União do Vegetal – an attitude that ties in with the values of modernity.

Besides endowing the UDV with a horizon oriented by spiritual evolution, Mestre Gabriel has imprinted on it the vision that affirms that a human being receives in life what is deserved, according to the acts that he or she practices. *Merit*, a category also present in the universe of Santo Daime, is one of the pillars of UDV doctrine. So, the theodicy of União do Vegetal, that is, its philosophical resolution for the problem of evil, is quite near the ideal type of theodicy present in the belief of transmigration of souls, as pointed out by Weber in his Sociology of Religion (1974: 412–17), and summarized by Colin Campbell as follows:

> the Indian doctrine of *karma*… 'the most complete formal solution of the problem of theodicy', since the world is regarded as a completely connected and self-contained cosmos of ethical retribution in which each individual forges his own destiny, with guilt and merit in this world unfailingly compensated for in the succeeding incarnation (Campbell, 1997: 106).

As Campbell subsequently observes, the three ideal types of solution exposed by Weber – the eschatological messianic, the dualism of the Zoroastrianism and the karmic Hinduism – are not sufficient to cope with certain traditions of thinking. Thus, Campbell presents one more type of theodicy, which is the philosophical theology of optimism of the eighteenth century. I consider that the UDV theodicy also has elements of this other ideal type to the extent that its reincarnationism deviates from the hinduism, which is not necessarily ascending in the sequence of incarnations and is closer to the vision of Allan Kardec, which has in its conception the expectation proper to the nineteenth century (rooted in the previous century), of a continuous overcoming of limits by the irresistible evolution of mankind. So, reincarnation for UDV has an optimistic and evolutionist character.

Peia

However, in this universe of optimism not all is flowers. People are, once in a while, involved in a wave of difficulties called *peia*, a colloquial Brazilian expression that means 'beating'. The statutes of UDV emphasize that 'the Hoasca tea is proven to be harmless to health', which has also been supported by recent scientific researches.[40] Even so, the experience of the *peia*, although momentary, can be intense: a strong physical indisposition, characterized by nausea, vomiting and dizziness may happen after drinking the tea.

---

40. Cf. Grob *et al.*, 1996; Callaway *et al.*, 1999; McKenna, 2004.

Sometimes this indisposition is not only physical: one may feel oppressed by remorse or by fear. All this physical, psychic and spiritual 'probation' is usually interpreted by the disciples as 'payment' for some erroneous moral conduct. So, *peia* is understood within the vision of *merit*. It is regarded as a pedagogical moment, necessary for the process of purification that leads to salvation.

Despite the fact of the *peia* being extremely unpleasant, it is an experience of very strong emotions, which reminds us of Campbell's observation, that 'one could say that the Puritans, or those who inherited their mentality, had become addicted to the stimulation of powerful emotions' (Campbell, 1997: 134). *Peia* is a tempest of emotions, an experience one lives in the mind and in the bowels, the whole body being shaken by the 'tempest of the *burracheira*'. Although extremely painful, it may have a certain 'charm' for those seeking intense feelings. The *burracheira* can be inscribed in the fourth type of play defined by Roger Caillois: vertigo or *ilinx* (Caillois, 1967: 169–72). The author identifies this type of play as 'an attempt to destroy for a moment the stability of perception' (Caillois, 1967: 169). And Caillois mentions the example of the dervish sufis, who seek ecstasy by spinning around themselves. Now, this search for ecstasy reminds us of the sensations provoked by the use of hoasca. The *burracheira*, the strange force of the vegetal, may also appear as a *play of vertigo*. The effect of hoasca is always surprising: before the beginning of the session, one cannot say whether it will be frightening or wonderful. In contrast with other rituals, perfectly foreseen and repetitive, each UDV session is unique and each *burracheira* unforeseeable.

Fernando de la Rocque Couto, in his anthropology Master's thesis on Santo Daime, when studying the phenomenon of *peia* in that other religious group, considers that 'this process is cathartic and psychotherapeutic'. Like the opinion of Lévi-Strauss when referring to the shamanic cure (Lévi-Strauss, 1975: 209) in which an abreaction would be the decisive moment:

> To ask for pardon, the sick one must bring to consciousness emotional and/or trau-matic remembrances which had been repressed. To achieve this, he has to get out of the conflict and solve his inner contradictions. In psychoanalytical terms, he has to ab-react, living and reliving intensely the initial situation which is in the origin of his disturbance, so as to be able to surpass it definitively (Couto, 1989: 179).

On the other hand, Luiz Eduardo Soares sees *peia* as an occasion for release from *hubris*,[41] transcending the inflated *ego* which had been placed at the center of the universe. The driving force of the tempest dislodges that *ego* from the summits of pride and throws it to the plains of humility, a virtue frequently praised by UDV:

> The sacred tea of the Daime, the sacred vegetal of UDV, as well as other religious, psychological, cultural resources ritualized all over the world, instructs us, quickly and efficiently, that *hubris* is the original sin, as we were taught by the Judeo-Christian tradition… This is what I infer from my own sensation: after all, if I could, without resorting to religious language and without experiencing mystic ecstasy, have a

---

41. The classical Greek term for the 'non-measure' of the man who puts himself in the place of gods; as the example of Prometheus, who steals fire from the gods and brings it to Earth.

glimpse of the finitude brought by the fetishism of the ego; what would they think of *hubris*, those mystics charmed by the emotion of the surpassable? The deduction is confirmed by testimonies (Soares, 1994: 229).

The *peia*, this complex experience that can be interpreted as the harvest of the Law of *Merit*, therapeutic catharsis, teaching and way to humility, is, surely, an intense emotional experience that is framed in an optimistic perspective. I propose we deal with these two aspects – intensity of feelings and optimism – and proceed to compare them with another nuclear experience of UDV: the *mirações*.

Mirações

If a member of UDV knows that he or she is liable to face a *peia*, on the other hand, he or she also knows that it is possible that 'the session will continue full of light, peace and love', as it is often mentioned by disciples when concluding their speeches during the ritual. The *mirações*, that is, the visual perceptions during the *burracheira*, during a tranquil session may be the occasion to experiment a feeling of beatitude, of harmony with the whole universe.

Roberto, a young man whose statement was cited above, told me about a remarkable *miração*[42] he had:

> The Mestre appeared to me, in his house, in a squatting position. That was remark-able. Suddenly, he spoke: 'look, here is my house'. All of a sudden, I saw a wooden house, fastened with rope and thatch, like this, that was on the top of a hill; behind the house there was a forest and at the front you had a view that you were able to see everything, from the sea to the pyramids and... everything there was on earth, like this, you know? Suddenly, you saw a dolphin out there in the sea, far away, but you could only see the eye of the dolphin. Then, suddenly, it was a question that you were able to see everything like this... And he spoke to me like this: 'Ah! From my house here you can see all the beauties of the earth!' And it was quite a nice house, you know? And I said: 'Gosh, quite good!' And he gave me some tips. Then, that is that, it is one of the things well impressed on my mind, Mestre Gabriel's house from where you could see all the beauties of the Earth, him squatting there. And then my father tells me that he really used to sit squatting, traditionally, but I did not know that.[43]

It is quite significant that, in Roberto's *miração*, from Mestre Gabriel's house, one could see 'all the beauties of the Earth'. This aesthetic dimension of beauty, which is unexpectedly presented as a gift, was many times evoked by the people I interviewed. There is a relevance of aesthetic dimension in the symbolic experiences of the UDV disciples.

Beauty can be related to other perceptions, not only the visual ones. In addition to the 'calls' *(chamadas)*, playing recorded music during the sessions is a part of the UDV

---

42. *Miração*, in Portuguese, is the singular form of *mirações*.
43. Interview with *Roberto*, in Campinas, on October 26, 1998. His father is a UDV Mestre.

ritual. This custom comes from the days when Mestre Gabriel authorized the first disciples of Manaus to play records in the sessions. The reason for the introduction of music is the beauty of the *mirações* that it propitiates, according to Mestre Geraldo Carvalho, a disciple since the first days of UDV in Manaus, who was present the first time music was played in a session (Da Rós, 1995: 11). Today instrumental music, such as New Age, Andean, or Classical, is frequently played at the beginning of UDV rituals. Later in the session, songs from Brazilian Popular Music are played, the lyrics of which are carefully chosen, in accordance with the subject advanced by the Directing Mestre. Themes related to love, friendship, and other virtues emphasized by the doctrine, are often heard. It is interesting to observe, above all, the importance of the *aesthetic feeling* in the valorization of music that was not composed for sacred use.

This important role of music in the ritual – in addition to the *chamadas*, which channel the experience of the *burracheira* – shows us that a *miração* is not simply a sequence of visions: it is a *synesthetic* experience that touches the sensibility of the participants of the session in *aesthetic* and *affective-sentimental* dimensions. This totalizing experience which, in addition to vision and hearing, may also mobilize the senses of touch, smell and taste, deeply impresses those who go through it and also motivates a pleasant intensity of feelings. Similar to the dream for the Romantics, the *mirações* have a revealing character for the UDV disciple, considering that an

insight into the real nature of the world can only be achieved through powerful and imaginative experience of an essentially aesthetic character... Romantics placed such importance on dreams – whether of the day or night variety – seeing them as essentially revelatory experiences (Campbell, 1987: 186).

Regarding *mirações,* we can also find the trace of optimism quite present. The *burracheira* – when 'plentiful of light' – creates an atmosphere of delight, harmony, and 'sympathy among the brothers and sisters', which places all things in an optimistic light.

The arch: portal to the high

In this section, I will deal with an element that is not regarded as a category of native speech, but it is a recurrent image in UDV, thus deserving reflection. The *arch* is present quite visibly in the ritual space of UDV, where it marks the sacred place *par excellence* at the head of the table, where the glass pitcher containing hoasca is placed, and where the Directing Mestre of the session sits, since he is, during the session, in lieu of Mestre Gabriel. The arch is painted green, with the words: 'Estrela Divina Universal UDV',[44] and on it there are two big stars and several smaller yellow stars. It is the most outstanding object in the *Salão do Vegetal*,[45] the place where the sessions are held. And on the wall, behind it, there is an element of utmost importance in the ritual space: the photo of Mestre Gabriel, also under an arch. The arch is a symbol connecting heaven and earth,

---

44. Universal Divine Star UDV.
45. Vegetal Room (or Hall).

like the rainbow in the narrative of Genesis.[46] The *mariri*, the vine itself, can be seen as a rope binding Earth and Heaven. One observes that in the UDV session there is an accented valorization of 'binding': there is the moment of 'binding of the *burracheira*' when the Directing Mestre goes on asking each participant whether he or she has attained *burracheira* and light; there is also an accented presence of the adjective 'linked' and the verb 'to link' in the speech of the participants during the sessions: for example, one talks about the importance of 'being linked to the Superior Force'.

Here, I approach the vision of Ramírez de Jara and Pinzón Castaño who see shaman- ism (and specifically that which utilizes the preparations of *Banisteriopsis*) as an open system that mediates indigenous categories and colonial categories; a system which incorporates Catholic notions, as well as Western pharmaceutical knowledge, to indig- enous religious conceptions and to their therapeutic techniques. The shaman is seen as a 'mediator between the supernatural world and the real world' (Ramírez de Jara and Pinzón Castaño, 1992: 287–303). And, really, the experience with hoasca has an accented aspect of mediation. This can be better understood if we observe the arch not only as a 'binding link' but as a 'threshold' as well.

The arch may be interpreted as the image of a portal through which the disciple is invited to pass. Van Gennep had already observed the

> identity of the passage through various social situations with the *material passage...* That is why, so often, to pass from an age, from a class, etc. to another is expressed ritually by the passage under a porch or by the 'opening of doors' (van Gennep, 1978: 159).

Mestre Gabriel himself is called: 'door that when open transports us'. Here, we have the notion of the threshold that the disciple approaches and, sometimes, even passes beyond. In the reports of *mirações*, references to portals, doorways, arches, and thresholds are frequent.

This leads me to infer that the *burracheira* is a marked liminal experience. An altered state of consciousness is reached, in which the person often feels present in 'another place', or in the threshold of another place. This makes possible a contact with the 'here' and the 'beyond', the daily and the strange, the normal and the altered. The ritual actually empha- sizes clearly the frontiers of the 'time of *burracheira*', the entrance and the exit, a sacred time, qualitatively distinct from the day-to-day. On reflecting upon liminality in rites of passage, Victor Turner observes that it:

> implies that the high could not be high unless the low existed, and he who is high must experience what it is like to be low... [S]ocial life is a type of dialectical process that which encompasses the successive experience of high and low, *communitas* and structure, homogeneity and differentiation, equality and inequality. The passage from lower to higher status is through a limbo of statuslessness. In such a process, the opposites, as it were, constitute one another and are mutually indispensable (Turner, 1969: 97).

---

46. Genesis 9.8–17

The *burracheira* is often felt as this 'limbo of statuslessness' that makes possible, for those who experience it, contact with the high and with the low, with an experience of brotherhood and with a hierarchical structure. For disciples, the *miração* and the *peia* are mutually indispensable. The humility imparted by the latter is fundamental, so that the transcendence offered by the former does not lead to *hubris* but to 'faithful practice'. And the *burracheira* is the connecting arch between these opposites.

Therefore, experiences with the hoasca altered state of consciousness are occasions to deal with frontiers; and the tea performs the role of mediator in these cases, whether the mediation is between different levels of reality or between distinct cultural universes. For this reason, I argue that the religious experience of UDV enables the urban participants to articulate dimensions of their lives and dimensions of UDV's worldview that were previously experienced as ruptured or incommunicable. The dilemmas of the contemporary urban individual, as well as oppositions faced by the human being (body/spirit; dictates of Heaven/dictates of Earth; individual/community; self-knowledge/knowledge of God) are in a way 'linked', conveyed in relationship, in the acute and dense experience of the *burracheira*. In this manner, UDV disciples find, in their search for *spiritual evolution*, the need to transpose the arches present in life and in the *burracheira*. By having the boldness to cross the unknown ground of the liminal, they advance in the articulation of what was previously broken in their lives, directing themselves towards the *Union*.

Encompassment in the force of the *burracheira*

Reflection on the discourse of UDV disciples referring to their symbolic experience led me to consider the *burracheira* as an accented liminal experience where there may be an experience of mediation through which the individual articulates elements of his or her life and of the worldview of UDV which were previously experienced as broken. By approaching the conceptions and representations of actual participants of the Nucleus *Alto das Cordilheiras*, in Campinas, it was possible to apprehend how certain aspects of those participants' lives interact with such religious ideas and are articulated with them. Now, I inquire with regard to the nature of this articulation: Could it be considered as syncretism? Or is this concept inadequate for this reality?

The existence in the UDV doctrine of traces that are clearly present in other religious traditions suggests the idea of syncretism. In the UDV, there are elements of popular Catholicism and the Spiritism of Alan Kardec, as well as Amazonian shamanism and Afro-Brazilian religions.[47] We know that the concept of syncretism is problematic, and it can be understood in several ways. Some understandings include a certain value-load expressing depreciation of the syncretic in relation to the 'pure' or conversely exalting 'Brazilian syncretism' as a mark of pacific multicultural conviviality.

With regard to the experience of UDV disciples, it is necessary to discern among the diversity of experiences. Some could, certainly, be well understood under the prism of the notion of syncretism. It may be observed in the speech of some participants experiences

---

47. See the article by Sandra Goulart, this volume.

of superposition of heteroclite elements that are quite near to contemporary trajectories of those who recognize themselves in the New Age Movement – which combined, according to Leila Amaral Luz,

> the heirs of the counterculture with their propositions of alternative communities; the speech of self-development on the basis of therapeutic propositions attracted by mystic experiences and holistic philosophies; the curious of the occult, informed by esoteric movements of the XIX century; the ecological speech of sacralization of nature and of the cosmic encounter of the individual with his essence and the *yuppie* reinterpretation of this spirituality centered on the interior perfection (Luz, 1999: 57).

However, in a series of other narratives of UDV disciples, I was able to identify experiences in which the category of syncretism is insufficient for adequate comprehension. I will quote below a report which, due to its density, seems paradigmatic to me. It is the speech of *Renato*, in his forties, of the *Membership Body*, but having already belonged to the *Body of Mestres*, referring to a *burracheira* he experienced in a critical moment of his life.

> To know how to venerate the presence of God, be grateful for being alive, makes me feel happy. I have gone through very difficult situations in my life and I have felt the presence of the Divine in crucial moments. To some people it can't even be explained. I was once in a situation when the mother of my children was pregnant of our first child, whom we lost; she had a case of eclampsia in the beginning of the sixth month. And it was a turmoil because I was in the *Council Body* and she in the *Instructive Body*, and we were sort of a model couple, everybody thought we were cute, all very nice, all in the right places, well organized, obedient, that standard sort of thing. And all was quite all right, everybody very happy about our marriage, our pregnancy. And then, all of a sudden, right after the 22nd July she started to feel very badly, a very difficult situation, and she didn't die thanks to the Vegetal, I'm sure.
>
> It was a very difficult situation and it was decided that she had to have a cesarean, she had to abort because it was the only way to save the mother, by removing the child and the placenta. And I drank the Vegetal, I was in the waiting room of the Maternity Nove de Julho, here in São Paulo, there were about 40 people of UDV there with me, and I drank the Vegetal, and stayed sitting, with a very strong *burracheira* and she was there, going through the abortion, and the chances of the child coming out alive were minimal; it was a baby in the beginning of the sixth month, there wasn't any chance. But Mestre Alberto [who is a doctor] gave her the Vegetal (a very small amount, about what would fit in a bottle cap) before the cesarean, in the Intensive Care Unit; she drank. A sister of ours was chief-nurse at the maternity, and they stayed with her during the cesarean, he on one side and she on the other, and the doctor, marvelous, was a Spiritist, a very nice person, and he did the cesarean. The child was born alive, as incredible as it may seem, it lived for 13 hours, and Vera not only survived but had no aftereffects: no convulsion, no lesion on the kidneys, nerves, or liver.

And during the cesarean I was in a very strong situation and there was a moment that… In my grandmother's house there was a picture of the Sacred Heart of Jesus, quite big, in the living-room. And in the *burracheira* there was that picture and I saw the image distinctly, his face, the hands coming out, one giving and the other receiving, and he has in the middle of the chest a light that shines at the outside, and at the front of this light there is a heart, that heart with a crown of thorns around it and some little drops of blood dripping, on top of the heart there is a little crown with a flame and on top of the flame the cross. And that image appeared before me in the *miração*, very clearly, as if I were facing the picture, and I understood that the Creator is really the Savior. The Creator creates pain, what for? So that we are open to him and then he brings love and light and he saves the pain. It was something like that… you know? It is a gift, a knowledge he brought to me which is something invaluable, understand? A wonderful thing because I saw that image and understood, like this: 'this suffering you are experiencing is opening the way for you and I am coming inside you'; then it is a balm, that light in the *burracheira*. I was in the living flesh but I was in peace, all was well, I was not rebellious, all was right. And when the situation presented itself, what was I going to do? Punch the air, on God's nose, and say I didn't want that? I had no alternative. I lowered my head and said 'yes, Lord, your will be done', what could I say? Then, by this acceptance he gave me knowledge in the flesh, in the skin, in the blood, in the gut, understand? You have no idea what it means to lose a child, you have no idea. I have two wonderful sons… but that girl I lost is irreplaceable, it is a bit of me that isn't there, understand? I saw, it was my daughter, man! You know, I saw God's perfection there, the wonder that life is. I, in the Intensive Care Unit, seeing the baby being cared for as if it were the most important baby in the universe, with all the chances and having none, and my wife in the adult Intensive Care Unit, the opposite pole… I had the opportunity to travel in a stage of pain, of misery of the human condition, in two directions at the same time, absolutely in peace with what was going on, comforting people, perfectly balanced. For ten days, I felt as if I were a robot remote-controlled by the Superior Force: I didn't make a peep. I stood by my family, friends, the Mestres, I held on, I stood by Vera, I lived something like that… This is religion to me, understand? Religion is not to go there and drink the Vegetal, go to the mass once in a while, go to the Sunday service. I think that to live the presence of God is in life, all the time. I had this grace several times, in moments of pain like this and in moments of joy as well.

This strong narrative shows the intensity of certain experiences with hoasca tea and the entwining of such experiences with ample aspects of the actor's life. I offer it here to better understand what I will call 'encompassment in the force of the *burracheira*'. I observe that contemporary anthropology has utilized the concept of 'encompassment' in various and distinct contexts, but here I will use this term aiming at a very specific application, therefore, I named it: 'in the force of the *burracheira*'.

The symbol of the Sacred Heart of Jesus does not belong to the symbolic ensemble of UDV doctrine. It is a symbol of Catholicism, with a very clear historical delimitation, and whose presence in the Brazilian Catholic iconography is mainly due to the activities of the Apostolate of Prayer, a movement introduced in Brazil by the Jesuits in the nineteenth century. Well, *Renato's* grandmother, from Minas Gerais, a fervent Catholic, had in her house a picture of the Sacred Heart of Jesus, which *Renato* had seen since infancy. Before entering the UDV, he had already withdrawn from Catholicism and taken part in Spiritism and in *Candomblé*.[48] Certainly, the Sacred Heart was but a faraway remembrance of his childhood and of his grandmother's faith, without a special significance in his adult religious life. However, one day, *Renato* has an intense existential experience, as a man, husband and father. And such a human experience, extremely significant by itself, is enveloped with a special meaning, density and coloring since it happened during a *burracheira* time. After drinking the Vegetal, at the moment he is waiting in the hall of the hospital for the result of the surgery his wife is undergoing, *Renato* is faced with the image of the Sacred Heart that emerges from his *memory* in a clear and revealing *miração*. As we have seen, the category of *memory* is highly valued in UDV, the Vegetal being perceived as the vehicle for remembering. So, in that moment, the symbol of the Sacred Heart is *encompassed* in the whole of his UDV religious cosmovision.

The *encompassment* experienced by *Renato* is quite distinct from a *bricolage* of a hypothetical subject who, in his or her modern individualism, chooses at will from among items exposed on the shelves of the religious supermarket, building his or her own 'do-it-yourself' religion. For *Renato*, this new element that is incorporated to his universe of convictions, illuminating it and expanding its range of meanings, is looked upon as 'a gift', 'an invaluable thing', 'a wonderful thing', 'a balm', 'light', 'presence of God', finally, 'grace'. Therefore, the element of specificity in this *encompassment*, which I identify as belonging to the experience of UDV disciples, is that it occurs 'in the force of the *burracheira*'. This force appears as a cyclone that, in the force of its centripetal movement, approaches a distinct symbolic province and includes it in its whirlwind. In utilizing this image, I seek to express the force of the self-generated dynamism of this incorporation and, in this case, even the speed it acquires amid the intensity of the altered state of consciousness conveyed by the ingestion of hoasca. And the emphasis that the narrative attributes to light, present in the image of the Sacred Heart and in the *burracheira*, indicates that this *encompassment* has as unifying principle the actual UDV cosmovision, where light has a fundamental role.

However, the singularity of the event that took place in *Roberto's* life could be taken as an argument to assert its uselessness for providing a greater comprehension of the experience of UDV disciples. Wouldn't *Renato's* experience be of a very accented existential intensity, which would differentiate it from the experiences of the majority of UDV disciples, nearer to the *bricolage* that is so present in the post-modern panorama of contemporary religiosity? Certainly, what *Renato* experienced has a special density and, as I said above, one can observe experiences among the participants of UDV that are less profound, from an existential viewpoint. But what I postulate here is that the *miração* of the Sacred Heart is a significant expression of something that occurs in an broader manner than that in *Renato's* life only. This is because intensity is one of the recurring characteristics of the *burracheira*. Certain extremely strong and significant experiences in the trajectory of the individual who lived them were frequently observed and fully documented in my field research, throughout the 50 interviews I conducted. Therefore,

---

48. Afro-Brazilian religion.

I consider that this 'encompassment in the force of the *burracheira*' may be a productive concept for the comprehension of the *démarche* of appropriations of religious contents undertaken by UDV disciples.

Another approach one can take is to perceive this 'encompassment in the force of the *burracheira*' in the actual trajectory of the founder of UDV, José Gabriel da Costa. As we were able to observe in the history of his life, Mestre Gabriel took part in various, quite specific Brazilian cultural configurations, starting with his childhood in the interior of Bahia, in a context permeated by popular Catholicism. Afterwards, he participates, in Salvador, in the environment of *capoeira*[49] groups, in addition to participating in houses of *Candomblé* and in Spiritist sessions. Going to the north of Brazil, he integrates the human crowds of the *Rubber Army*.[50] In Porto Velho, he participates in a house of Afro-Brazilian religion, and in the rubber plantation he acts in Amazonian cults of *caboclo*[51] shamanism. When, finally, in 1959, he drinks hoasca for the first time, José Gabriel seems to have had a very intense experience from the very beginning. Thus, according to his son Jair, on that first session he addresses the vegetalist who gave him the tea and tells him: 'Chico Lourenço, a person does not know everything. You told me you went to the end of the enchantments. Things are infinite.'[52] Before the second session, he is supposed to have said, 'We are going to drink the tea of Chico Lourenço and nobody is going to feel anything', and so it is said to have happened. The third time, his son Jair, then nine years old, in accordance with his own statement, he had a very strong *burracheira*. He started to scream and was called by his father, who told him: 'Sit down'. And Jair told his father: 'Daddy is a Mestre, he is a king, made by God'. Still according to today's Mestre Jair, after that session José Gabriel takes the *mariri* and the *chacrona* to his house, and dialogues with his wife: 'Pequenina, I am Mestre'. And she answers: 'But Gabriel, for God's sake, Chico Lourenço has been Mestre for so long, I don't know how long, we and everybody almost went crazy and you now say you are Mestre?' And he: 'I am Mestre, Pequenina, and I will prepare the *mariri*'. The intensity of the experience of José Gabriel, who is soon recognized as bearer of a mission as Mestre in the Vegetal, and the speed with which this experience assimilates his prior trajectory, submitting it to a new comprehension, are two aspects that support the interpretation of this process as 'encompassment in the force of the *burracheira*'.

In the symbolic universe of UDV many traces of the cultural configurations with which José Gabriel had had contact may be detected. So, for instance, there are northeastern popular religious songs referring to Saint Anne, mother of the Virgin Mary, which are extremely similar to the UDV's *chamada* of Saint Anne. The frequent invocations of Jesus and of the Virgin of Conception, in many *chamadas*, also express this profound mark of popular Catholicism in the symbolic universe of Mestre Gabriel. In the same way, indigenous conceptions that permeated the Amazonian *caboclo* shamanism may be identified

---

49. *Capoeira* is an Afro-Brazilian martial art and dance that was born in Bahia.
50. The *Rubber Army* was the name given to the thousands of workers from differents parts of Brazil, who were sent by the governement to the Amazon rubber plantations during World War II.
51. *Mestizo.*
52. Interview with Mestre Pequenina and Mestre Jair. Newspaper *Alto Falante*, Brasília, Aug–Sept 1995: 8.

in the UDV cosmovision, such as the belief that certain plants have a spirit.[53] Likewise, elements related to Afro-Brazilian religions can be found in *chamadas* and stories of UDV. In this way, one can see the 'encompassment in the force of the *burracheira*' as something constitutive of UDV, to the extent that it characterizes the foundational experience of José Gabriel da Costa. Such experience may be replicated in an original and always new manner by disciples, who, departing from their singular individual trajectories and from the specificity of their contact with the *burracheira*, live a similar movement, constituting different configurations which, however, find an articulate interpretative axis in the experience of Mestre Gabriel.

Finally, it is important to show that, in reality, although having its singularity, the 'encompassment in the force of the *burracheira*' has a similarity with the movement that can be observed in the mystic experience. What, from a more objective perspective could be seen as distinct, and even conflicting, religious comprehensions may suddenly begin to to be contemplated as a new unity that does not dilute the differences, but integrates them in something new. Something perhaps similar to what Otávio Velho indicated as present in Zen illumination and in the dialogic relation according to Buber, or in the resolution of opposition between Apollo and Dionysius 'in favor of a new Dionysius who includes Apollo' (Velho, 1995: 59). This movement can be understood, in the axis of the hermeneutic tradition, as the comings and goings of the *pre-understanding* and of the *understanding* constituting the *circle of interpretation*. This dense existential experience, which is 'deciphering of life in the mirror of the text' and 'reading of the occult meaning in the text of apparent meaning' (Ricoeur, 1978: 23) have a powerful expression in the re-reading of the image of the Sacred Heart of Jesus that *Renato* makes, in the light of Hoasca.

References

Araripe, Flamínio de Alencar. 1981. 'União do Vegetal: a oasca e a religião do sentir. Planeta magazine'. *São Paulo* 105 (June 1981): 34–41.

Brissac, Sérgio. 1999. 'A Estrela do Norte iluminando até o Sul: uma etnografia da União do Vegetal em um contexto urbano'. Master's thesis in Social Anthropology, National Museum, Federal University of Rio de Janeiro.

Brissac, Sérgio. 2002. 'José Gabriel da Costa: trajetória de um brasileiro, mestre e autor da União do Vegetal'. In Beatriz Labate and Wladimyr Sena Araújo, eds, *O uso ritual da ayahuasca*, 525–41. Campinas: Mercado de Letras.

Caillois, Roger. 1967. 'Jeux des adultes: Definitions'. In Roger Callois, *Jeux et sports, Encyclopédie de la Pléiade*, 150–79. Paris: Gallimard, 1967.

Callaway, J. C., D. J. McKenna, C. S. Grob, G. S. Brito, L. P. Raymon, R. E. Poland, E. N. Andrade, E. O. Andrade and D. C. Mash. 1999. 'Pharmacokinetics of Hoasca Alkaloids in Healthy Humans'. *Journal of Ethnopharmacology* 65: 243–56.

Campbell, Colin. 1987. *The Romantic Ethic and the Spirit of Modern Consumerism*. Oxford: Blackwell.

---

53. Cf. the words of the Peruvian shaman Pablo Amaringo, who utilized ayahuasca: 'Every tree, every plant, has a spirit. People may say that a plant has no mind. I tell them that a plant is alive and conscious. A plant may not talk, but there is a spirit in it that is conscious, that sees everything, which is the soul of the plant, its essence, what makes it alive' (Luna and Amaringo, 1991: 33).

Campbell, Colin. 1997. 'A orientalização do ocidente: reflexões sobre uma nova teodicéia para um novo milênio. Religião e sociedade'. *CER – ISER* 18(1) (August 1997): 5–22.

CEBUDV (Centro Espírita Beneficente União do Vegetal). 1989. *União do Vegetal: Hoasca, Fundamentos e objetivos.* Brasília: Sede Geral UDV.

CEBUDV (Centro Espírita Beneficente União do Vegetal). 1994. *Consolidação das Leis do Centro Espírita Beneficente União do Vegetal.* 3rd edn. Brasília: Sede Geral UDV (Centro de Memória e Documentação da União do Vegetal).

CEBUDV (Centro Espírita Beneficente União do Vegetal). 1995. *Alto Falante* Newspaper. Brasília: Sede Geral UDV. August–September–October.

CEBUDV (Centro Espírita Beneficente União do Vegetal). 2005. Official Site of the CEBUDV. Available on internet at http://www.udv.org.br. Archive consulted in 2005.

Couto, Fernando de la Rocque. 1989. 'Santos e xamãs: Estudos do uso ritualizado da ayahuasca por caboclos da Amazônia, e, em particular, no que concerne sua utilização sócio-terapêutica na doutrina do Santo Daime'. Master's thesis in Cultural Anthropology, Pontifical Catholic University of Brasilia.

Da Rós, Márcio. 1995. 'A origem da música nas sessões da UDV'. *Alto Falante* Newspaper. Brasília: Sede Geral UDV. August-September-October.

Grob, Charles S., D. J. McKenna, J. C. Callaway, G. S. Brito, E. S. Neves, G. Oberlander, O. L. Saide, E. Labigalini, C. Tacla, C. T. Miranda, R. J. Strassman and K. B. Boone. 1996. 'Human Pharmacology of Hoasca, a Plant Hallucinogen Used in Ritual Context in Brazil'. *Journal of Nervous and Mental Disease* 184(2): 86–94.

Lévi-Strauss, Claude. 1975. 'O feiticeiro e sua magia'. In *Antropologia Estrutural.* Rio de Janeiro: Tempo Brasileiro.

Linder, M., and John Scheid. 1993. 'Quand croire c'est faire: Le problème de la croyance dans la Rome ancienne'. *Archives des Sciences Sociales des Religions* 81 (January–March).

Luna, Luis Eduardo, and Pablo Amaringo. 1991. *Ayahuasca Visions: The Religious Iconography of a Peruvian Shaman.* Berkeley, CA: North Atlantic Books.

Luz, Leila Amaral. 1999. 'Carnaval da alma: comunidade, essência e sincretismo na Nova Era'. Doctoral dissertation in Social Anthropology, National Museum, Federal University of Rio de Janeiro.

McKenna, Dennis J. 2004 'Clinical Investigations of the Therapeutic Potential of Ayahuasca: Rationale and Regulatory Challenges'. *Pharmacology & Therapeutics* 102 (2004): 111–29.

Ramírez de Jara, María, and Castaño Pinzón. 1992. 'Sibundoy Shamanism and Popular Culture'. In E. Jean Langdon and Gerhard Baer (eds.), *Portals of Power: Shamanism in South America,* 287–303. Albuquerque, NM: University of New Mexico Press.

Ricoeur, Paul. 1978. *O conflito das interpretações: ensaios de hermenêutica.* Rio de Janeiro: Imago Editora.

Soares, Luiz Eduardo. 1989. 'Religioso por natureza: cultura alternativa e misticismo ecológico no Brasil'. In Leilah Landim, ed, *Sinais dos tempos: Tradições religiosas no Brasil,* 121–44. Rio de Janeiro: ISER.

Soares, Luiz Eduardo. 1994.'Misticismo e reflexão'. In *O rigor da indisciplina,* 223–31. Rio de Janeiro: Relume-Dumará.

Turner, Victor. 1969. *The Ritual Process: Structure and Anti-Structure.* Chicago, IL: Aldine.

van Gennep, Arnold. 1978. *Os ritos de passagem: estudo sistemático dos ritos da porta e da soleira, da hospitalidade, da adoção, gravidez e parto, nascimento, infância, puberdade, iniciação, coroação, noivado, casamento, funerais, estações, etc.* Petrópolis: Vozes.

Velho, Otávio. 1995. *Besta-fera: recriação do mundo. Ensaios críticos de antropologia.* Rio de Janeiro: Relume-Dumará

Velho, Otávio. 1998. 'Ensaio herético sobre a atualidade da gnose'. *Horizontes antropológicos* 4(8) (June): 34–52.

Weber, Max. 1974. *Economia y sociedad: Esbozo de sociologia comprensiva.* Mexico: Fondo de Cultura Económica.

8

Ayahuasca: the consciousness of expansion*

Domingos Bernardo Gialluisi da Silva Sá

Translated by Christian Frenopoulo, revised by Matthew Meyer

This article refers to the findings that I presented to the Brazilian Federal Narcotics Board (*Conselho Federal de Entorpecentes* – *CONFEN*) concerning the brew called ayahuasca, known more commonly in Brazil by the names 'Daime', 'Santo Daime' or 'Vegetal'.

For more than ten years, CONFEN – without a prohibitionist approach – has closely followed the use of ayahuasca by a variety of communities which, if one were to add up the number of people involved in the several ayahuasca-using organizations across Brazil, would amount to roughly 10,000 users at most.[1]

My purpose in this article is to evaluate a decade of non-policing government monitoring of ayahuasca use, in order to promote, from this pioneer experience, the adoption or modification of just public policies that are directed to the question of drugs, ordinarily subject to multiple peculiarities. Accordingly, this text does not have the objective of simply presenting a chemical or pharmacological analysis of ayahuasca, if only because this is not my field of specialization. When it became necessary to approach such matters, in the course of the preparation of my report, I consulted with renowned professors and specialists in those areas of scientific knowledge.

---

* Article translated from: Silva Sá, Domingos Bernardo G. 'Ayahuasca, a consciência da expansão'. *Discursos sediciosos. Crime, Direito e Sociedade*. Rio de Janeiro: Instituto Carioca de Criminologia. Ano 1, N° 2, 2° sem. 1996, pp. 145–74. Used with permission of Instituto Carioca de Criminologia.

1. cf. more recent approximates for membership numbers: 'Alto Santo: 600 (source: Sandra Goulart, March 2002); Barquinha: 500 (Sandra Goulart In: Labate, Beatriz and Wladimyr Sena Araújo, *O Uso Ritual da Ayahuasca*, Campinas: Mercado de Letras, 2004, p. 619); União do Vegetal: 15000 (source: Edson Lodi, Coordinator of Institutional Relations for the UDV, via Beatriz Labate, pers. comm., April 2006); Cefluris: 4000 (source: Enio Staub, National Secretary of Cefluris, via Beatriz Labate, pers. Comm., May 2006). Beatriz Labate (pers. comm.) suggests that an estimate of the total number of people currently involved in the several ayahuasca-using organizations across Brazil would also need to include figures on new forms of urban use and on new independent groups that although claiming a symbolic affiliation to the major matrices, have developed new rituals and spiritual doctrines – trans.

I am convinced that the cost-benefit analysis of the drug problem is fundamentally resolved on the cultural level. Otherwise, how can merely medical or pharmacological scrutiny explain the integral assimilation of the use of alcohol and tobacco in our society, for example? Moreover, how else can one understand the 'health and safety risks to consumers' admitted in the Consumer's Code itself to be 'considered normal and predictable, resulting from [the substances'] nature and use' (8th art.)?

However, it is must be recognized that ayahuasca, a brew made from the decoction of the Amazonian vine called *Banisteriopsis caapi* with the leaves of *Psychotria viridis*, is scientifically classified as a drug, displaying a specific pharmacological action of the kind shared by hallucinogens.

Consequently, this is a substance that, from a purely technical point of view, is classed as a hallucinogen. I think that this is the most pressing matter that I wish to develop in this article: can the strictly chemical or pharmacological classification of a substance suffice to exhaust the question of the viability of accepting or not accepting its use? After all, what is a hallucinogen? And, what is a hallucination?

Ayahuasca in Brazil

The use of ayahuasca is, in some way, always ritual. In Brazil, there are two main clusters of users, that of the 'Santo Daime' and that of the 'União do Vegetal' (UDV).

The União do Vegetal, or simply UDV, has some differences with the Santo Daime, though they both share the same essential use of the brew. The UDV is a Spiritist centre that uses ayahuasca. The União do Vegetal was created on July 22, 1961 in Porto Velho, Rondônia state, and has has José Gabriel da Costa as its founding *mestre* (master or teacher). The Santo Daime Doctrine has Raimundo Irineu Serra (or 'General Juramidam', according to followers) as its founding *mestre*.

In 1992, the UDV claimed that it had 'almost five thousand members across Brazil'. It is the organization with the largest number of ayahuasca-using centers, which they classify into 'nucleus', 'pre-nucleus', 'pre-nucleus and distribution center' and 'authorized distribution center of Vegetal'.

The other group – the Santo Daime – has the largest single community, called Céu do Mapiá, which lies in the municipality of Pauiní, in the state of Amazonas. At the time [of CONFEN's research], about 450 people were living there. If this figure is added to that of the other centers that also call the brew 'Daime' (i.e., CICLU-I, CICLU-II, other CEFLURIS centres, *Centro Espírita e Culto de Oração Jesus Fonte de Luz, Centro Espírita Daniel Pereira de Mattos* and *Centro Espírita Fé, Luz, Amor e Caridade – Terreiro de Maria Bahiana*), the sum would reach about 1,800 members. Therefore, the total number of active participants in the ayahuasca religions is about 6,800 people for all of Brazil.

Some of the ayahuasca-using centers are close to celebrating 70 years of existence, according to the Clodomir Monteiro, who states that:

> Alto Santo began on March 26th, 1931, with Irineu Serra, José Neves (an Acrean, from Xapuri) and some people from Brasiléia. It was officialized on May 21st,

1962, as an esoteric center, and on December 23rd, 1971, it disengaged from the Esoteric Circle for the Communion of Thought in São Paulo, and became known as the Universal Light Christian Enlightenment Center (*Centro de Iluminação Cristã Luz Universal*). The church was established on land that had been donated by the governor Guiomard Santos. Not far from there, in 1942, Daniel Pereira de Mattos, advised by Irineu Serra, organized his own center in Vila Ivonete, following his own 'initiatory vision'.[2]

It is essential, therefore, to recognize that the ritual use of ayahuasca is not a passing trend or a novelty, such as often excite personal and, frequently, irresponsible interventions by those who are momentarily in positions of power. The unreflexive and catastrophic actions of those who are temporarily in power generate violence, chaos and revolt.

To this effect, it is germane to ponder the words of the anthropologist, Professor Edward MacRae, whose research on this matter was invaluable at the time that I prepared the latest report for the CONFEN:

> With regard to the cultural interest in the urban ritual use of ayahuasca in Brazil over the past seventy years, consider that this is approximately the same time that Umbanda has been in existence. Like the latter, the religious use of the psychoactive brew stimulated the creation of institutions that provide numerous people with ethical, social and cultural guidelines for building their lives.
>
> The numerous anthropological and historical studies of the use of the brew have highlighted the pacific and orderly lives led by the followers of the religions, in accordance with the same values considered emblematic of Western Christian society. Far from engaging in an abusive and destructive use of psychoactive substances, the most notable tendency of such people is the promotion of austere and restrained life-styles that are oriented to the development of spirituality and to family and community values.[3]

It is indispensable to recognize their social and political integration, and family connections, with the rest of the urban population of Acre. For example, Raimundo Irineu Serra was highly regarded. The Alto Santo church provided me with two documents that exemplify, not only the kind of activities that Mestre Irineu engaged in, but also the high esteem in which local political authorities held him. The first of these reveals the cordial relations and trust that the governor of Acre, Major José Guiomard Santos, sustained with Irineu Serra in requesting some wood and materials to give to Francisco Gabriel Ferreira. This was in January 1948, by which time Mestre Irineu had been leading ayahuasca rituals in Rio Branco for 17 years. The second document recommends Raimundo Irineu Serra to 'fulfill functions as a forest ranger' in the famous rubber settlement Seringal Empresa in December 1950. Lastly, the center in Vila Ivonete referred to by Clodomir Monteiro was established by Daniel Pereira de Mattos more than half a century ago, in 1942, and

---

2. 'La Cuestión de la Realidad de la Amazônia', *Revista Amazônia Peruana*. AAAp, Vol. VI, No. 11, p. 92 – Lima, Peru.
3. Reply to request concerning the report issued by Dr Alberto Furtado Rahde, 20 March 1992.

now accommodates the *Centro Espírita 'Casa de Jesus – Fonte de Luz'* on the same spot. It is led by Manuel Hipólito de Araújo, who is one of Daniel Pereira de Mattos' successors, and who participated in the founding of the center in 1945.[4] Manuel Hipólito de Araújo signed an agreement with the state's ministry of education and culture in July 1991 for the maintenance of the St Francis of Assisi elementary school, which is connected with the center.

The anthropologist Regina Abreu, researcher of the *Muséu Histórico Nacional* (Rio de Janeiro) and professor at the State University of Rio de Janeiro, has provided descriptions of the basic doctrinal and ritual elements that characterize Padrinho Sebastião's community (currently the rubber settlement Céu do Mapiá, located in the Amazon rainforest). Padrinho Sebastião is the leader of the 'Doctrine' – as the followers of the Santo Daime call their unique liturgical complex. The latter embraces the gathering of raw plant products, the preparation of the brew (called *feitio*), and ceremonial sessions (called *trabalhos*, i.e. 'works') during which hymns (the core of the doctrine) are sung and prayers are recited according to a liturgical calendar that is largely Christian. The same arrangement is followed in churches and smaller congregations elsewhere, in Rio de Janeiro and in other locations around Brazil and abroad (Spain, The Netherlands, Japan, the United States, etc.).

Professor Regina Abreu has stated that:

Everyone respects the *Padrinho* and [his wife,] the *Madrinha*. They are acknowledged as the community's father and mother, representing on Earth the heavenly Father and Mother ... Generally speaking, the well-being of the group, of the community as a whole, is what matters, rather than individuals or isolated family units. In this sense, the Santo Daime community resembles the French anthropologist Louis Dumont's model of a 'holistic' society.

According to their spiritual understanding, in the astral plane, 'the paramount foundation is the Daime', declares the eldest son of the Padrinho, who has been designated by him to occupy the future leadership of the church and who already directs the administration of the community, 'because the Daime is the Master (*Mestre*). [In healing ceremonies,] the sick person needs only approach the Master, because He already knows what will ensue'.

The Master is Juramidam, commander of the entire universe and spiritual entity identified with Jesus Christ and the Eternal Father (the Christian 'God, the Father'). 'In the spiritual world, the Daime is called Juramidam,' he adds, 'The Daime is the brew, but within the brew is the divine being that emanates from the forest [...] The presence within the Daime is the presence of Christ'.[5]

The proof of Padrinho Sebastião's fundamental relevance within the Santo Daime doctrine is revealed by the fact that no church in Brazil or abroad may function legitimately unless the interested party has visited the rubber settlement Céu do Mapiá in the Amazonian rainforest and directly obtained the Padrinho's authorization in person.

Here follow some brief reports concerning Padrinho Sebastião and the settlement Céu

---

4. This center is now presided by Araújo's son, Francisco Hipólito de Araújo – trans.
5. Report by Prof. Regina Abreu, CONFEN committee consultant.

do Mapiá, taken from Vera Fróes' book, *História do povo Juramidam* ('History of the People of Juramidam').[6]

Sebastião Mota de Melo was born in Eirunepé, in the state of Amazonas, on October 7th, 1920. Members of the Santo Daime rural community have been calling him *'padrinho'* (godfather) since 1975. This designation expresses the respect and recognition of his qualities as a spiritual leader, and also indicates the deferential position in which those who consider themselves 'godchildren' to him place themselves, seeking his spiritual protection and guidance.

Padrinho Sebastião recounts that he has suffered health problems since birth and that, as a child, he would hear voices from the spiritual world, as well as having visions and dreams of future events. When he was eight years old, he had a dream that he interprets as a sign of his mission in the Santo Daime that would come many years later:

'I was in the middle of the forest, with a straw hat on my head and dark clothes. Then, a fire erupted and I heard that disturbing droning sound; and I saw tongues of fire all around me, burning everything. Nothing was left, only the spot where I stood … My life for the next fifteen years, there in Amazonas, was just vision after vision: visions of the waters, of the forest, of the heavens. But I was unable to understand them. They were like dreams … I didn't give them much attention. I was stubborn. But things would happen, and I would see for myself. The vision subsided and I began to fly. I was flying, seeing the heavens, seeing the forest, the waters, and seeing these visions. Eventually, I began engaging with spiritism. A voice called me "Bastião!" I responded, "Yea!" Then, the brightness would fade and the voice would go silent. Some time later, I flew on a spiritual aeroplane and landed in Acre. Not too long after that, I came here, I came materially.'

For Padrinho Sebastião, there is a difference between dream, vision and *miração*. A healer must be able to distinguish these events.

Don't think that a *miração* is dream, or that a vision is a *miração*. When you receive a *miração*, you are left doubting, you saw something but you didn't quite see. When you have a vision, you are left feeling that it was a dream, but it wasn't. It was the truth. You see everything, you hear and perceive everything. A dream, on the other hand, is hazier. A fellow rolls out, walks along a narrow path, and journeys. But when he wakes up, he doesn't recall. In a vision, you retain full consciousness, you never go beyond…

Just like Mestre Irineu, Padrinho Sebastião was initiated by a shaman – in his case, mestre Osvaldo, who was a black man from São Paulo. They also called him 'cumpade' ['co-godparent'] Osvaldo, because he was the godfather of Pedro Mota, one of Padrinho Sebastião's sons.

Padrinho Sebastião apprenticed to mestre Osvaldo for one year in the forests of the river Juruá, carrying out Spiritist séances in which he would receive the surgeon medium

---

6. Vera Fróes, *História de Povo Juramidam (A Cultura do Santo Daime)*, Manaus, Prêmio Suframa de História, 1983, pp. 41–42.

Dr Bezerra de Menezes. During that time, mestre Osvaldo would sometimes redirect sick people to Padrinho Sebastião for healing.

Céu do Mapiá currently hosts the head office of the CEFLURIS – *Centro Eclético da Fluente Luz Universal Raimundo Irineu Serra* (Eclectic Centre of the Universal Flowing Light – Raimundo Irineu Serra). The Colônia Cinco Mil, located nearly 9 km along the road to Porto Acre, had been the CEFLURIS headquarters before. The community is called 'Cinco Mil' ('Five Thousand') because the plots of land were sold for five thousand old cruzeiros when the rubber settlement was dismantled and the land divided up for sale.[7]

After this, Padrinho Sebastião and 'his people' – as the community that adheres to his spiritual leadership is referred to – moved to the rubber settlement 'Rio do Ouro,' in the Endimari river region, on the banks of the Trena tributary. Vera Froés says of that time:

> To everyone's surprise, Padrinho announced in 1981 that that wasn't the spiritually determined location where the New Jerusalem was to be built. Simultaneously, a group of people interested in the land that the community had cleared began to exert pressure through the discovery of an irregular land deed, dated from the beginning of the century, which granted the property to a southern rancher.

The regional INCRA office, despite having authorized the community to establish itself in Rio do Ouro, now informed them that there was some vacant untitled land close to the Mapiá river – a tributary of the Purús river – in the Pauiní municipality (Amazonas state) where they could move to. This land was some 150 km distant from Rio do Ouro.

The community began the process of moving once again to a new settlement, Céu do Mapiá, facing numerous difficulties, and leaving behind the budding profits of the agricultural and rubber production that they had launched, without receiving any form of indemnity from the alleged lawful owners of the land.

The relocation of the Colônia Cinco Mil community into the depths of the Amazonian rainforest held strong significance in ways both material and spiritual. The Daime would protect its children ('Midan') who had heeded the call to return to their origins, to the rubber settlement life in which so many of them had been born and raised. It was also a return to the days when Mestre Irineu first came into contact with the Daime, during his work as a rubber-tapper.[8]

The situation of the ritual use of ayahuasca calls to mind similarities with the legitimation process of Afro-Brazilian cults. The latter were subject to brutal police repression at the turn of the century, such as the case of the Gantois *terreiro* (ceremonial site) of Mãe Menininha, who was only able to avoid police repression after an alliance with contemporaneous intellectuals.[9]

History repeats itself, though obviously with differences, in the communities of the Santo Daime and the União do Vegetal. Yet, both place strong emphasis on the symbolic content of their rituals, so appreciated by them, for the benefit of others and for God.

The historical expression of these cults is intimately tied to a particular culture, that

---

7. Vera Fróes, op. cit., pp. 43–4.
8. Vera Fróes, op. cit., pp. 120–1.
9. Denise Ferreira da Silva, *Comunicações do ISER*, Year 5, No. 1, pp. 70–1.

of Brazil; or more specifically, of the Indian, of the *caboclo*, of Amazonia. This vital fact should not go unnoticed.

In their first official document, the União do Vegetal confirms what I have expressed above:

> The União do Vegetal, currently undergoing a process of expansion and institution-alization, exhibits a solid presence in urban milieux, counting within its membership a diversity of professionals, including highly regarded scientists and intellectuals.
>
> Even so, the União do Vegetal preserves and cultivates its *caboclo* origins, upholding the purity of teaching and sustaining the testimony that spiritual degree is not always related to erudition or academic rank.[10]

Similarly, the Santo Daime community also includes current or former followers who are or were famous intellectuals and artists, and who equally exalt their reunion with Nature and with the primordial. For example, in a report in the *Manchete* magazine, the deceased actor Carlos Augusto Strazzer declared that he had discovered an 'eminently "Brazilian" path of internal development' in a 'ritual as old as South America'. He passion-ately reveals that: 'It was the first time that a musical ritual with dancing and lyrics had made me feel completely integrated to my country, my culture, and, by extension, allowed me to comprehend the whole planet. What is more, it was gratifying to know that it was the Amazon rainforest that was giving us all this.'[11]

As MacRae has noted:

> the use of ayahuasca has been considered legitimate until now, and numerous people have invested their whole lives in these cults, which have become central to their social, individual and spiritual identities. ... The history of humanity is rife with examples of the insanity of intolerance and religious persecution, whose primary effect has often been the exacerbation of fanaticism on one side and abuse of power on the other.

After explaining how the repression of Afro-Brazilian cults in Brazil caused serious social damage, as I exemplified above with the case of the Gantois *terreiro*, MacRae goes on to add that:

> the Christian tradition is itself rich with models of martyrdom for the faith, which could easily serve as examples for the followers of the ayahuasca religions in protest of a prohibition of their rites. Considering the importance of the socially integrative aspects of these religions, it follows that the weakening of them would contribute to the enervation of social cohesion, the harboring of feelings of revolt and the return of some to the state of anomie from whence the religions had offered them a meaning for their lives.[12]

The UDV has emphasized the administrative bureaucratization of the organization in its process of institutionalization. They have released publications, such as the *Consolidation*

---

10. *União do Vegetal – Hoasca – Fundamentos e Objetivos*, p. 36.
11. *Manchete*, No. 1 1941, 1 July 1989, p. 46.
12. Reply to request, cit.

of UDV Norms (*Consolidação das Leis da UDV*) and *União do Vegetal - HOASCA - Objectives and Fundamentals* (*União do Vegetal - HOASCA - Fundamentos e Objetivos*); they have organized a Center for Memory and Documentation (*Centro de Memória e documentação*), which publishes the association's journal, *Alto Falante* ('Loud Speaker'). They have also established the Center for Medical Studies (*Centro de Estudos Médicos*),[13] which has organized three scientific congresses, the last of which was held in Rio de Janeiro simultaneously with the International Conference on Hoasca Studies.

Moreover, the UDV has implemented medicinal plant gardens and extractivist production enterprises in the *Novo Encanto* ('New Enchantment') ranch in Acre, managed by the Novo Encanto Ecological Development Association (*Associação Novo Encanto de Desenvolvimento Ecológico*).

Preserving its own characteristics and communitarian tendencies, the Santo Daime has also sought institutionalization. This is particularly the case of the CEFLURIS branch, which congregates the largest number of Santo Daime affiliates (about one thousand people). They founded the National Cefluris, based in Céu do Mapiá, which includes within its commission the regulation of the establishment of new churches and the observance of ritual unity.

The CEFLURIS has also resolutely invested in environmental projects, honoring the presidential decree No. 98.051 (August 14, 1989) that created the Mapiá-Inaunini National Forest Reserve, which occupies 311,000 hectares, in the state of Amazonas.

They also established an association that represents the residents of Céu do Mapiá (*Associação dos Moradores da Vila Céu do Mapiá*), which signed an agreement in August 1989 with the IBAMA federal environmental agency pledging mutual collaboration in the efforts to protect the Forest Reserve's natural resources.

The residents of Céu do Mapiá also constituted the COPEAMA, the Amazonian Extrativist Cooperative (*Cooperativa Extrativista da Amazônia*), which endeavors to implement sustainable development projects in the Mapiá-Inaunini National Forest Reserve.

The ritual use of ayahuasca

A rite is a means, an instrument. Its rules must aid the participant to accomplish a desired objective. Religious rites always strive to be vehicles or means of communication between humans and the Absolute, the Astral, God, or whatever other name is given to the Transcendental Reality that human beings cannot ordinarily perceive, especially in our current Western civilization. Religious rituals comprise the notion of limitation, or the ordering of the 'here' to realize the 'there.' Thus, their magnitude as discipline, but also, as generators of force; similar to the current of a river that produces energy only when dammed – the cost of electrical energy.

In order to arrive at a serene evaluation of the significance of the ritual use of ayahuasca, one must first reflect upon contemporary liturgies, especially those practiced in the West. A ritual is not justified by the ritual itself, but inasmuch it is pregnant with

---

13. Now called the Medical-Scientific Department or DEMEC (source: www.udv.org.br) – trans.

symbolic content. Otherwise, it would be no more than mechanical repetitions, frustrating and alienating

The meaning of 'symbol' traces back to Greek antiquity when a guest, on leaving his host, would break an object in two, with each keeping one half. If, one day, their descendants joined the two pieces, they would reveal the pact of friendship that had been established, and they would harmonize with each other. The unity of the two parts was a testimony or sacrament of the precedent hospitality. A symbol, therefore, necessarily unifies. It seeks to overcome a separation and reunite the parts back into the whole.

Nowadays, we live a generalized and obvious crisis regarding the symbolic value of numerous rites that prevail in our society (if we even participate in them; perhaps those that accompany life cycle events, such as birth, marriage, and death). Habitually, in the West we experience rituals as vacuous, repetitive, and intellectualized. We find them remote from our cultural roots and language.

Leonardo Boff rightly states that, when the symbolic dimension is realized in sacred rites, 'the intense moments of life become mysterious vehicles of Divine Grace. If this were not so, they would be merely empty and mechanical ceremonies, ultimately ridiculous'.[14] He stresses the importance of comprehending religion as a 'symbolic complex that permanently expresses and nurtures faith, within the bounds of a particular culture'.[15] The interest in the ritual use of ayahuasca appears in major urban centers at a time of emptiness, meaninglessness and exasperated consumerism, while it has been in use in the backwaters of Brazil since the beginning of the twentieth century.

It is worth noting that the brew is conceived of as vehicle or means, and *not an end*. The UDV has expressed that they 'do not see the brew as an end in itself, but as a vehicle in a path of much sacrifice and austerity'.[16] Nevertheless, ayahuasca is itself an important element for the communities that use it, since it is an instrument for achieving spiritual goals. In the absence of the plants, these religious forms probably would not continue.

The numerous centers that compose the Santo Daime cluster carry out similar rituals. Men wear a white suit with blue trimmings on the legs and a blue tie. Some bear a round golden medal, engraved with a star and a moon. Women wear a white dress with green embellishments and a tiara on their heads. This clothing is called the 'uniform' (*farda*) and is worn by those who have committed to the 'doctrine'. Santo Daime churches are similar to those of other Christian denominations: candles, crosses, rosaries, statues of St Mary, Jesus Christ and St John the Baptist. There is a small room in rear of the temple where the Daime is kept and is served during the ceremony from two small windows.

Ceremonies last from six to twelve hours, depending on the kind of 'work' that is being undertaken. They begin with the recitation of Christian prayers, specifically the Our Father (*Pai Nosso*), rosary (*terço*), Hail Holy Queen (*Salve Rainha*), and jaculatory prayers. After this, men and women form two lines in front of the windows where Daime is served; on a table between them are candles, crosses, water, crystals and rosaries. Each participant contritely makes the sign of the cross and is given between 100 ml to 150 ml of Santo Daime. They then return to their positions in the dancing rows. Throughout the

---

14. *Os Sacramentos da Vida e a Vida dos Sacramentos*, 2nd edn, Vozes, p. 100.
15. Idem, p. 75,
16. op. cit., p. 34.

liturgy, hymns are sung and played on instruments, such as the guitar and accordion, in step with the cadence of the *maracás* (metal rattles). Everyone dances following a single uniform and repetitive lateral step.

Vomiting and diarrhea (less frequent) are regarded unaffectedly. They are considered a manner of purifying spiritual and corporal ills. Designated members of the community are always entrusted with the task of assisting participants that might be undergoing a purge. Churches are always equipped to accommodate these genuine 'expiatory rites' (that is, vomiting, diarrhea, or both). A 'work', therefore, includes foreseeing the conditions for purging 'expiatory rites' and providing for the suffering participant. The hymns evoke the forces of Nature, the power of God, of the Virgin Mary and all the saints. They praise human virtues, exhorting people to love, to be humble and to repent. They proclaim the joy and strength of those who place their faith in the Divine and do good. During small pauses, between hymns, *vivas* are exclaimed that praise the Divine Eternal Father, the authors of the hymns, and guests. The brew is served twice more, in the same manner (two solemn lines of men and women behind the small windows), much like the distribution of the Holy Communion among Catholics. Participants drink less Daime in the last serving, in order to bring to a close their contemplative experiences and return to daily life. The 'work' is formally concluded with the recitation of prayers and expressions of gratitude to God. After this, participants cordially and peacefully greet one another and return home.

Another important ritual of the Santo Daime movements containing particular ceremonials, and that has prominent symbolic and religious significance, is the *feitio*, which is the preparation and brewing of the beverage. For this, the women pick, clean and assemble the leaf ingredients, while the men carefully scrape the vine stalks that are then pounded. The ingredients are boiled in large pots, alternating layers of *Banisteriopsis* sinews with layers of fresh *Psychotria* leaves. This task is carried out by skilled specialists, who monitor the flavor, visual aspects, and effects of the drink. Usually, the same liquid is boiled three times, together with fresh raw plant materials on each occasion. This produces a thick dark liquid that is then filtered through a cloth sieve. Depending on the stage of brewing, the Daime is classified as 'first', 'second', or 'third degree'. The strongest type is 'first degree', having boiled three times. The quality of the brew is further regulated through the selective use of raw plant materials – in terms of quantity or of the specific parts of the plant (e.g. the branches of the vine are not as strong as the roots). Some samples can be stored successfully for several years, fully preserving their properties.

The UDV ritual is different from that of the Santo Daime. A 'session', as the ritual is called, lasts for about four hours. Men wear a uniform composed of white pants and a green shirt, while women use a yellow skirt or pants with the green shirt. Lower-ranking *mestres* use a green shirt with a yellow star, but the *mestre representante* ('representative *mestre*') wears a blue shirt. They do not dance, but always remain seated after drinking the brew. A 'session' is led by a *mestre* who recites melodies called '*chamadas*', which open, close or orient the session, variably summoning or dismissing the Force and Light of the Vegetal. Throughout a session, any participant may recite a *chamada*, which they have learned from the oral tradition passed among *mestres*. Instrumental music and songs that evoke Nature or values are also played [on stereo equipment – trans.] during a session. The same purification processes of vomiting and diarrhea also occur frequently. During the session, participants may also raise questions concerning a wide variety of issues for which they seek advice. The *mestre* then responds to them. The vines used in a *'preparo'* – as they call the brewing process – are transported from the Amazonian rainforest.

Ayahuasca and the CONFEN

The federal narcotics board, CONFEN (*Conselho Federal de Entorpecentes*), was asked to provide a determination concerning the inclusion of *Banisteriopsis caapi* in the list of scheduled illegal drug products in July of 1985. I was designated president of the commission that was commended to study the production and consumption of the brew ('Daime' or 'Vegetal').

Two members of the commission, Isac Germano Kamiol and Sérgio Daria Seibel, psychiatrists, traveled to Rio Branco, the capital of Acre state, where several ayahuasca-using communities are located. They sought to obtain more information that would support the commission's resolution. In October 1985, they visited three places where ayahuasca rituals are held regularly, all in Rio Branco, the capital of Acre state: the União do Vegetal, Colônia Cinco Mil, and Alto Santo.

I wish to bring to light some points that are mentioned in their report, due to their relevance to the current presentation.

We have observed among the several sects moral and ethical behavior patterns that are identical to those that our society shares and recommends; at times, even stricter. Obedience of mores is frequently underscored.

The effect is probably not only due to the brew alone, but also to the setting as a whole, that is, the melodies, the dancing, and so on.

After the ceremony, all appear to return naturally to their homes, composed.

The members of the sects emerge as peaceful and happy people. They claim to have obtained family reunion, interest in work, and to have found themselves and God in these religions and through the brew.

Previously, the vine and the *chacrona* leaf were obtained directly from the virgin forest. Nowadays, some of the sects have been attempting to cultivate the plants, with a good deal of success. The production of the brew is rather difficult and long, entailing the use of an ancient technology and following a set ritual. It seems improbable to us that a larger quantity of the beverage than is needed for the cults' internal use could be produced using these methods of production. That is, it seems very unlikely that the beverage could be produced in such quantities that some amount could be diverted for non-ritual use in the society at large.

We visited ayahuasca-using communities five more times. Sergio Dario Seibel, psychiatrist, and I visited the Céu do Mar community (at Estrada das Canoas 3036, south of Rio de Janeiro) in April, 1986, to arrange a formal observation in the future. We were received by the community's spiritual leader, Paulo Roberto Silva e Souza, a psychologist, who escorted us to the church where 'works' were carried out. There, we met six more followers of the Doctrine.

It is worth pointing out that Paulo Roberto had been in Cape Cod, Boston, USA, where he conducted 'works' at the request of a group of American psychotherapists who, we were told, were considering opening a church in Boston. Dr Paulo Roberto also informed us that he had received invitations to conduct 'works' in Madrid, on Maui, in London, Brisbane, and Oslo. We agreed to attend the 'work' that was scheduled for the following day, in which we indeed participated, and which lasted some six hours.

Both of us drank the tea three times (a smaller quantity for the last serving). The liquid has a brown nutty color, with a bitter, repulsive and nauseous taste. We suffered the expected vomiting and diarrhea. We experienced perceptions that were not obviously related to external objects when we had our eye-lids closed or partially closed, and in variable states of stupor, as if in a sleep-like state. These are what conventional science would consider hallucinations. I shall return to this matter below. Slightly quivering closed or half-closed eyelids were observed during the moments that participants experienced visions.

The legal name of the community we visited is CEFLUSMME – Sebastião Mota de Melo Eclectic Center of the Universal Flowing Light (*Centro Eclético de Fluente Luz Universal Sebastião Mota de Melo*), which is the legal owner of the property. Though in the midst of the city of Rio de Janeiro, the location is a 200,000 m² dense forest reserve (of which 20,000 m² can be built on). At the time, the church had a following of about 200 people. Approximately 30 people lived on the land as a co-residential community. They held employments elsewhere (the community had university professors, journalists, physicians, and even a state deputy), and shared maintenance expenses. The contribution to the church provided by other 'uniformed' followers depended on their assets, according to informants. ('Uniformed' members have opted to belong to the Doctrine).

Together with the psychiatrists Isac Germano Karniol and Sérgio Dario Seibel, we conducted our fourth visit in June 1986 to the CEFLURG community – Rita Gregório Eclectic Center of the Universal Flowing Light (*Centro Eclético de Fluente Luz Universal Rita Gregório*), located in the Fazenda Nova Redenção, in Visconde de Mauá-Rezende, in the state of Rio de Janeiro. The leader of the center is Alex Polari de Alverga, a journalist, author and former political prisoner during the last military dictatorship in Brazil. The basic characteristics of the ritual and doctrinal elements in the CEFLURG were identical to those of the CEFLUSMME, in the capital of Rio de Janeiro.

We all participated in the 'work'. We noted some insignificant differences in regards to the service held in Rio de Janeiro, which would be analogous to the differences between Catholic masses held in different parishes. Just as in Rio de Janeiro, we all drank the beverage during the 'work', and once again suffered nausea and vomiting. Though only visitors, we seemed to grasp that the profoundly emetic effects of the beverage are attenuated with the active participation in the dancing and singing.

Special consideration should be given to a 'work' that is offered on Sunday mornings called 'Children's Daime' (*Daime das crianças*), in which children are given very modest doses of Daime (small babies receive Daime from a teaspoon). Some pregnant women in the Sunday 'work' had also been there the night before. Other women shared positive experiences regarding the use of Daime during childbirth. As an example, one woman narrated the understanding she achieved regards the event of birth and the profound love that she felt for her emerging son. She added that her relationship with that son had always been more intense and positive than with his senior sibling.

Our fifth visit was to the headquarters of the Santo Daime Doctrine, Céu do Mapiá, located in the Amazon rainforest. To reach it, one must travel from Rio Branco, capital of Acre state, to Boca do Acre, a locality in Amazonas state. Paulo Roberto, a psychologist, accompanied us to Céu do Mapiá, departing from Rio de Janeiro international airport. Given his experience with the route, we planned together the stages and requirements of the trip: flights, land and river transportation (including for small watercourses), night stopovers, meals and drinking water for the river segment, medications (including anti-malaria and anti-variola vaccines), hammocks, ropes, mosquito nets, etc.

We arrived in Rio Branco on 14 July 1986, and immediately caught a 30 minute flight to Boca do Acre. The population of Boca do Acre, built on the banks of the Purus River, is rather poor. A Santo Daime 'first aid' primary care unit ('*Pronto Socorro*'), authorized by Padrinho Sebastião, operates there. Followers of the religion provide emergency treatment to people experiencing physical or spiritual suffering. We learned of this and other matters from various members of the Doctrine, some local residents and others travelers.

The Céu do Mapiá community, located in the midst of the dense Amazon rainforest, has established a commercial station in Boca do Acre that offers a restaurant service. We observed how the neighborhood is also a market for goods that are produced in Céu do Mapiá, such as rubber, raw sugar, and a diversity of horticultural products – goods that also supply the restaurant. Similarly, the residents of Céu do Mapiá stock a variety of supplies from Boca do Acre, such as clothing, medications, tools, utensils, house items, etc.

We embarked on a boat owned by the INCRA, named 'Tucuxi,' the following morning. We followed the course of the Purus river, from Boca do Acre all the way to the junction with the Mapiá river, after which we could only continue on canoes. We spent the night on hammocks strewn across an uninhabited shack that lay on the banks of the Mapiá River. It is not feasible to travel by canoe during the night, due to visibility difficulties and the sinuous winding of the river, which is loaded with floating logs and branches, of which you must steer clear. We were persistently alerted to take care when stepping on the shore or base of the river, to avoid being stung by a ray.

This brief narration of the difficulties and adversities faced by travelers to Céu do Mapiá – the community of Padrinho Sebastião and Madrinha Rita – is relevant. We encountered numerous people, from all parts of Brazil (Brasília, Bahia, Rio de Janeiro, Visconde de Mauá), traversing the route with us. We were impressed by the mark of a true pilgrimage toward the core of the Santo Daime Doctrine. Many of them were true pilgrims sacredly seeking contact with the apostolic old bearded man, Padrinho Sebastião. Overcoming difficulties and discomforts were acceptable to them. Together with the yearning for integration with Nature, this phenomenon will surely provide rich material for future social scientists.

We arrived in Céu do Mapiá on July 16, 1986, and departed on the 19th. It was a small village, with about 250 inhabitants, embedded and developed in the bosom of the Amazon rainforest. As said before, there were many people from several regions of Brazil, and also foreigners.

We visited the place where the leaf ingredients of the brew (called '*Rainha*,' or also '*chacrona*') are stored for the *feitio* (the process of preparing Santo Daime). The new construction for carrying out *feitios* (the '*feitio* house') was almost finished. It had a large furnace for boiling the liquid in 120 liter pots, and two rows of seven stumps each, facing one another, with stools, where the members of the Doctrine pound the vine in a procedure called *bateção* ('pounding'). The vine is pounded in synchronized blows, using special mallets that they fabricate themselves. We also visited the locations where they grind sugarcane, manufacture raw sugar, and store the produce. Gardens provide the community with its subsistence needs, requiring only the acquistion of salt from outside (Boca do Acre). The extraction and sale of rubber latex is also an important economic venue for the community. Lastly, we visited the '*casa de cura*' construction, where they carry out healing rites for alleviating the physical or spiritual suffering of those who seek the Doctrine.

We participated in another 'work' that evening, which we noted was also similar to those of Rio de Janeiro and of Visconde de Mauá. Once again, our participation in the ritual was complete, including ingestion of the beverage, singing and dancing.

We also participated in a ceremony during the *feitio*, which included the ingestion of newly made Santo Daime. Unlike the other 'works', this time we drank the beverage inside the *feitio* construction, located in a clearing in the forest, some distance from the houses. When it is new, the taste is less acrid and repulsive. Even so, several participants vomited. We remained seated while melodies were sung. The perceptions and manifestations experienced by participants are forcefully influenced by the setting, the contact with the Amazonian rainforest under the full moon, and by the lyrics of hymns that evoke the force of the elementals and the Divine Power, as well as the mutual aspiration to encounter the other and the sacred. On our outbound journey, we met yet another canoe coming upstream with about six more pilgrims, from Brasília, Bahia and Rio de Janeiro, on their way to discover the sacred that Céu do Mapiá has to offer them.

For our sixth review, Isac Germano Karniol, Sérgio Dario Seibel, Clara Lucia Inem (a psychologist), and I, visited the Centro Espírita Beneficente União do Vegetal nucleus of Jacarepaguá, on the Estrada do Carretão, Rio de Janeiro. The visit lasted from September 12 to 13, 1986. Just as we had done elsewhere, we participated in a 'session' (i.e. 'work', for the Santo Daime) that lasted about four hours, and also in a *preparo* (analogous to the *feitio* in the Santo Daime).

The UDV is the official owner of the land in Rio de Janeiro, approximately 6,000 square meters. At the time, there were 117 members in Rio de Janeiro and about 2,000 in all of Brazil. Members that are in a position to disburse a monthly fee, pay an amount equivalent to 10 percent of the minimum wage. Poor people, if unable to pay a contribution, are not charged. Some people, following their own judgment, pay more.

It is worthwhile to recall why ayahuasca was banned and placed on the list of prohibited substances, as it was this that led to the involvement of the CONFEN (the federal narcotics board). The incident that triggered the flow of events was the arrest of Eder Candido Silva, a 22–year-old lad, in Rio Branco, capital of Acre state, on September 30, 1981. The report on his arrest describes him carrying a green backpack. He drew the attention of the driver and nearby police, who decided to search him and found '*maconha*' (*Cannabis sp.*) in his bag. He was living in the Colônia Cinco Mil, where some people were growing hemp. The next day (October 1, 1981), the Federal Police went to the Colônia Cinco Mil and confiscated hemp plants, seeds and leaves. Therefore, the inclusion of *Banisteriopsis* in the DIMED's list of forbidden substances occurred as a result of the use of *maconha* in Colônia Cinco Mil, which was only one of about ten other communities that, instead, exclusively used ayahuasca. The inquiries conducted into the several ayahuasca-using groups, and in particular to those under the leadership of Padrinho Sebastião, were initiated as a consequence of the imprisonment of Eder.

I draw attention to this episode because the narcotics board commission did not verify any unequivocal evidence of social harm that could be attributed to the use of ayahuasca. The commission did not set out to study the use of hemp, cocaine or any other drug, and instead, only problems that could be directly derived from the use of ayahuasca and that require consideration.

The CONFEN concluded its tasks, inquiries, and reports in 1986, determining the exclusion of *Banisteriopsis caapi* from the Health Ministry's Medication Division's (DIMEP) list of prohibited substances. However, in 1989, an unidentified accusation launched another examination into the use of ayahuasca in Brazil. I would like to point out some themes in the accusation, as they express recurrent unfounded fantasies that I have observed through the years:

(a) Membership is 'estimated to be more than ten million fanatics in the large urban centers'.

(b) The leaders are all 'drug addicts and former guerrilla fighters'.

(c) People who drink the brew 'abandon everyday life ... the extensive singing wears members into a mental stupor that induces them to abandon everyday life, their families ...'.

(d) 'Participants collapse from exhaustion, and then, with doors and windows closed, they burn leaves and herbs under the pretext of incense, which confidants say is *maconha*'.

(e) 'At the time of serving, LSD or a similar drug is added to the Vegetal, without anyone noticing'.

(f) Members are 'induced into slave working conditions' and to offer copious donations.

(g) 'Several *mestres* are solicitors for the Central Bank, the banker's union, professors, and so on'.

(h) 'Participants feel a motivation to help one another, it is not known if due to the drug or to suggestive induction'.

(i) 'Isn't this a national security risk?'

(j) The unidentified author of the accusation lists a series of 'unsuccessful measures' she or he had taken previously. For example, a file was handed to Cardinal Eugênio Salles and to a 'high Presbyterian authority' in 1982; 'presentation was made in person to the Federal Police' in 1984, and also to the court for minors on Av. Presidente Vargas in the same year, where the judge personally notified her or him that taking measures would compromise his appointment, since his superior was a friend from Law School that was a drug addict and had liberated that drug.

(k) The accuser added some remarks to a photograph of one of the leaders of an ayahuasca-using community – Padrinho Sebastião – that included the following, 'the representative for the Divine on our planet, utterly illiterate, leader of a community of more than ten million followers in all of Brazil. In Acre state alone, 80% of the population uses the brew continuously'.

(l) 'The poor children ... are kept awake for more than 72 hours, completely anguished from horrifying visions.'

(m) 'Who is to blame for this situation? Undoubtedly, the counter-offensive of urban guerrilla groups. I believe this is the most reasonable explanation.'

Dr Ester Kosovki, then president of the CONFEN, assigned me to examine the accusation, especially requesting me to 'make use of the information gathered in preceding reports, engaging in local corroboration as necessary'. I consulted with prestigious experts and professors from the fields of anthropology, psychopharmacology and psychiatry – especially with track records of research on ayahuasca – to complement my own knowledge of the matter, informed by juridical and philosophical perspectives.

I resumed contact with the leaders of the ayahuasca-using communities – particularly from the União do Vegetal and Santo Daime clusters – in order to organize further visits that would provide fresh data and documents about their activities and development, with the purpose of updating the information that had been obtained for our earlier reports. I returned to several communities and arranged a meeting in the Rio Branco town hall with the delegates of the numerous ayahuasca-using groups in the country. They provided me with abundant documents and materials about their centers, their activities, cases of healing, family reunion, and positive modifications of life.

It is worthwhile to probe the potential background for the accusation. Until the most recent claim, the identified accusers, in the few accusations registered since July 1985, when the CONFEN began to take charge of the matter, were parents who were unhappy about their children's religious and lifestyle preferences. In all cases, the children – one young woman and two young men – were middle-to-high-class urban Rio de Janeiro residents, beyond the legal adult age. I held interviews with the young woman and young men from all three cases, as well as with the parents of two of them (in one case, with both parents, in the other, with the mother). In these three factual situations, I plainly realized that the problem they faced was the radical divergence between the life-projects of parents and children, and of models for the latter, much more than repercussions related to the ritual consumption of ayahuasca on the young person's central nervous system. These alleged 'repercussions' were, nonetheless, always used for carrying the weight of the accusations. It is telling that the problem was overcome with time, as the parents and children came to live with their differences, as I was later informed. One more piece of information is worth noting: the three young people involved in the accusations were all young adults seeking a communitarian life experience, which was radically different from the one they had broken from. This project of communitarian lifestyle is characteristic of the Santo Daime, to which all three of them belonged.

The unidentified accuser refers to a state of dependency – that which Anastácio Morgano observes is 'characterized by a complete investment in what is only a fraction of reality'[17] – as the 'abandonment of everyday life' and 'of the family'. Consequently, these 'fanatics' would be completely focused on matters of spiritual life, disregarding family and everyday domains.

---

17. *Revista da Associação Brasileira de Psiquiatria*, Vol. 7, No. 26, p. 100.

Yet, a number of facts that I have confirmed over the past decade of involvement in this matter utterly refute the unidentified accuser. The analysis of this affair would be even more difficult if there were only one type of ayahuasca-using community, either the UDV or the Santo Daime. When I mentioned that the three young people had left behind their urban lives to live in the country or the jungle, I anticipated the relevance of contemplating the different types of ayahuasca-using groups, because this evens the terms of the debate. Numerous individuals have chosen to leave their urban lives and the proximity of their families to go and live in the country, in the jungle, or in a community. All of these cases occur in relation to the Santo Daime faction that is under the leadership of Sebastião Mota de Melo (Padrinho Sebastião) – who, in the early 1980s, attracted a new class of follower: 'middle class [youth] from the large south-eastern metropoli', according to MacRae. Many of them were hippies or backpackers, features that inherently 'identify', or better said, stigmatize a distinct generation.

It is worth examining the prejudice that informs the allegation of 'abandonment of everyday life [and] family. We need to reflect and reconsider how our society readily classifies some people as mad or alienated when, with or without ayahuasca, they choose unconventional lifestyles or processes of personal realization or knowledge acquisition.[18] In actual fact, what society rejects is madness that is not shared, 'abnormal' madness, madness that escapes regular insanity. Behaviors many times classified as mad have often been no more than unintegrated or unrecognized cultural differences. Maria José de Queiroz explains that 'the definition of what counts as madness varies not only from locality to locality, but also from family to family, according to behavior norms that codify "the regular way to be mad"'. She recalls that Michel Foucault suggested that 'every culture makes sickness an image drawn by the anthropological virtues that it neglects or represses'. She concludes that 'for all places, there is a convenient or acceptable way to be mad'.[19]

The União do Vegetal presents an entirely different scenario, currently exhibiting a markedly urban character. Members are employed in common city jobs. Though UDV associates consume ayahuasca, they sustain the same professions, lifestyles and habits that other urban citizens do. It is probably due to their fairly unremarkable standard civic semblance that families, and society, do not signal young people's involvement in the UDV as ruptures. I am not implying that participation in the Santo Daime necessarily entails rupture. In fact, this is probably not the case in most circumstances. However, inevitably, some individuals find it 'madness' or an 'abandonment of everyday life' (according to the unidentified accuser) when others choose to leave the city and prefer, instead, a quiet community life in the countryside or in the midst of the Amazon rainforest – which, I insist, is only the situation of a small minority. This is a parallel situation to that confronted by the parents of children who opted for a monastic or cloistered life, of which abundant illustrations can be found through history.

Clearly, the accusation sought to cause alarm by claiming that 'millions' of fanatical followers (in fact, not even 10,000) were dropping out of 'everyday life' due to their ingestion of the brew. Paradoxically, it was claimed that they were simultaneously being 'induced into slave labor', which can hardly be the case of people dreamily disengaged

---

18. Final Report, p. 30.
19. *A literatura Alucinada 'Atheneu Cultura'*, p. 71.

from daily life. The claim to 'abandonment of everyday life' is plainly incompatible with the kind of professions that the accuser had concomitantly listed. Numerous accounts that I gathered from different centers of the UDV were provided by people engaged in the following professions: physician, civil employee, lawyer, military, entrepreneur, psychologist, ombudsman, university professor, architect, engineer, economist, publicist, author, banker, cocoa producer, tax collector, federal police cashier supervisor, and student.[20] In regards to the Santo Daime, people are employed in practically the same professions mentioned above, in addition to attracting popular television actors and actressess.

In the presence of this apocalyptic scenario in which 'poor children' are, literally, 'anguished by horrifying visions' and the ayahuasca-using communities are being led by 'drug-addicts and former guerrilla fighters', one is compelled to agree with the accuser that all this can only be the result of a 'counter-offensive of urban guerrilla groups. I believe this is the most reasonable explanation.'

Indeed, this incident might even be humorous, if it had not involved many grave and onerous measures that had to be taken, such as police inquiries and the upsetting of numerous families who, every time the narcotics board is recomposed with new members, once again are unfairly and illegally subjected to the suspicion of criminal activity, pending sudden accusations (whether identified or anonymous) that contain whatever unsound fanciful depictions, and requiring the execution of exhaustive and costly reviews, as has been the case.

It is the author of the accusation who deserves to be criminally charged for submitting such unwarranted serious allegations. The most shocking demonstration of the accuser's dangerous insanity is the assertion that the acting judge in the Rio de Janeiro's Minor's Court literally expressed fear of losing his position and would not take action because his hierarchical superior was a drug addict. The nonsense of this statement dismisses giving it more consideration, except in order to illustrate the inconsistency and frivolity of the accusation.

A number of other assertions were also branded as delirious, such as the claims of 'slave labor', 'national security risk', 'counter-offensive of urban guerilla', blending of the brew with 'LSD or a similar drug', burning of *maconha* (*Cannabis sp.*) as an incense 'with temple doors and windows closed' and 'children [...] completely anguished from horrifying visions'.

The allegation of adding LSD to ayahuasca, 'without anyone noticing' is ludicrous. Let's first consider the terms of this nonsense. The brew has been used for more than 70 years in rituals in Brazil. I ask the accuser, when did LSD begin to be added to ayahuasca? Upon whose advice? The rubber-tappers and their religious leaders, Mestre Irineu of the Santo Daime or Mestre Gabriel of the UDV? Perhaps the suggestion is recent and came from the Santo Daime headquarters in midst of the Amazon rainforest? Or from the UDV authorities? And, why the blend? Is the brew a placebo?

Additionally, we know that the effects of LSD last a lot longer than those of ayahuasca (which is around two hours). Imagine them combined!

Furthermore, the unique 'expiation rite' inherent to ayahuasca (i.e. vomiting and diarrhea), with its natural and non-synthetic quality that makes it radically different from LSD, deserves some emphasis. The distinctive features of ayahuasca impose requirements for

---

20. Final Report, p. 22, item 29.

achieving the desired benefit. These requirements are related to multiple ritual uses and adhesion to the doctrine, and oblige the participant to embrace certain behavior patterns in daily life. Pharmacology alone provides an insufficient basis for evaluating the 'effects' or 'causes' that relate to the use of substances that are indistinctly defined as 'drugs'.

Since Socrates' maieutics, one of the finest instruments for arriving at the truth is to ask questions. The truth to be revealed, in this case, is the patent impropriety of the unidentified accuser's allegations.

The photographic records of our visits to the ayahuasca-using communities likewise reveal that, in a number of the locations used for services, there is no way to close doors and windows with the purpose of 'better intoxicating participants' when burning incense or *maconha*. This is, simply, because many places do not have doors and windows, while others are so large that it is not viable to smoke the entire room in a manner that could have noticeable psychoactive consequences, as the accuser implies.

The story about 'children … completely anguished from horrifying visions' is flatly denied on the basis of my visits to practically all of the major communities. In particular, children would not be able to conceal 'complete anguish' caused by 'horrifying visions'.

In regards to the children who live in Céu do Mapiá, the journalist Elias Fajardo (in *Jornal do Brasil*, environmental supplement, January 13, 1991) reported that 'the children of Mapiá swim in the river, surrendering to the loving movement of those who believe in the doctrine that preaches the union of the sun, the moon and the stars'.[21] The photographs of Céu do Mapiá corroborate the journalist's testimony.

To wrap up the analysis of the anonymous accusation, albeit discarding the accuser's hysterical condemnation of the rituals, it is interesting that she or he also literally declares that, 'participants feel a motivation to help one another'. This motivation 'to help one another' is fundamental, and reveals the social and ritual dimension of ayahuasca. As Clodomir Monteiro has explained, 'the use of Santo Daime is almost exclusively social, which implies that there is always a sequence of acts or rites that must be observed'.[22] Perhaps this is the only, and crucial, segment of truth that the anonymous accuser offers: the discovery of the 'motivation to help one another'.

The accusation lacked any kind of consistency or minimal degree of seriousness that would have justified our reconsideration of the matter. It involved a great degree of unease for the individuals and for the families living in the communities, who are entitled to exercise their right of freedom of religion within the bounds of public order and the law.

The final decision of the narcotics board, CONFEN, also considered the following reflections.

The chemistry of Ayahuasca

In 1992, in addition to the anonymous accusation that prompted the reexamination of ayahuasca use in Brazil, the distinguished Dr Alberto Furtado Rahde (a CONFEN board

---

21. *Jornal do Brasil*, 13 January 1991.
22. Annals of the *45° Congreso Internacional de Americanistas*, Bogotá, 1985, fl. 9.

member, at the time) pronounced some views concerning the brew. It is worthwhile to reflect on some of his observations.

(a)   the consumption of the brew 'together with foods that are rich in tyramines' 'can produce harmful reactions in the body';

(b)   'severe personality modifications may occur';

(c)   'altered states of perception, mood and behavior';

(d)   The 'use of "daime" all over the country has surpassed the original local use in the Amazon rainforest';

(e)   'a ritual and restricted use of daime' needs 'to be specified'.

From his field of expertise, Isac Karniol, a professor at Unicamp (State University of Campinas) provided a strictly technical reply to my request for advice. He concluded that the combination of *Banisteriopsis caapi* and *Psychotria viridis* contains betacarbolines, such as harmine, harmaline, and tetrahydroharmine, as well as N-dimethyltryptamine. Dimethyl-tryptamime is more active than the other constituents. Nevertheless, it has limited action when ingested orally because monoaminoxidase enzymes metabolize it rapidly in periph-eral tissues. Betacarbolines inhibit these enzymes, allowing the N-dimethyltryptamines to have a prolonged action. This mechanism has been studied by McKenna and colleagues.

Regardless of the chemical constituents that compose ayahuasca, it is indisputable that, in conjunction, they produce hallucinogenic effects (according to conventional drug cate-gories). The preparation, as such, produces hallucinogenic effects in the organism, besides other possible peripheral actions, such as vomiting and diarrhea.

Having briefly reviewed Professor Karniol's explanation concerning the chemical structure of ayahuasca, I wish to emphasize that a developed and mature understanding with reference to drugs cannot accept a simple mechanistic point of view, like that of pharmacological determinism. It is precisely for this reason that a holistic perspective is necessary. We all know that a balanced analysis considers three elements: the individual, the context, and their interaction (in this sequence, I would add). If this were not the case, all that would be necessary to determine whether a certain substance should be banned or not, is a knowledgeable technician's identification of its chemical components.

In such a mechanistic analysis, the person is a secondary element, rather than the central one. Using the example of the accusation presented above, a simplistic view would consider that 'DMT + individual human being = abandonment of everyday life', or 'indi-vidual + harmine = cerebral vascular arrest'.

This unidirectional and mechanistic model, which conceives the human being as a machine, is to a holistic perspective on drugs just like classical Newtonian physics is to quantum physics, after which the structure of matter could no longer be thought of as immutable, at rest and occupying absolute space. In the words of Fritjof Capra, a physi-cist, 'the mechanical view of nature is intimately bound to rigorous determinism. The great cosmic machinery was viewed as fully causal and determined. All events possessed a distinct cause, which generated a distinct effect.'[23]

I insist that adherence to pharmacological determinism would render the CONFEN narcotics board superfluous and imply its dissolution, since a simple technician could

---

23. Fritjof Capra, *O Tao da Física*, Cultrix, p. 50.

be hired instead. Still, pharmacological and psychiatric particulars are obviously invaluable, so long as they are not foremost. Rather, researchers should appraise them within the complex multidisciplinary perspective that the matter obliges. Our inquest included opinions of great scientific merit and unmatched import (since they approach the issue from highly specific disciplinary niches), yet we never lost sight of the wider scenario, which embraces other domains of knowledge and the inevitable mutual interactions between them.

The following are excerpts from the responses to our enquiries provided by professors E. A. Carlini and Isac Karniol, both of which were quite similar.

RE: a) The use of ayahuasca in Brazil

b) The report issued by Dr Alberto Furtado Rahde – then boardmember of the CONFEN – on January 20th, 1989. (A copy of which is attached to this letter).

Dear Professor,

Following our previous conversations, this letter requests your precious and invaluable assistance to provide the board with your expert opinion on the matter at hand, particularly in regards to the items mentioned below, which appear repeatedly in the aforementioned report and which require further clarification. We would appreciate if you could provide a response before March 31st.

a) What are the 'occasional very harmful effects on the body' (see report, item 6ff)?

b) What are 'severe personality modifications' that have been observed (see report, item 8)?

c) Are the 'altered states of perception, mood and behavior' (see report, item 8) necessarily negative, harmful or pathological conditions?

Additionally, I implore you to provide us with any other clarification that you might deem pertinent, in order to thoroughly elucidate the matters raised by the attached report, which the president of the CONFEN board has entrusted me to accomplish.

Please bear in mind that the use of ayahuasca is legitimate in this country, in accordance with CONFEN resolution #6 (February 4th, 1986).

I reaffirm the highest esteem and special consideration that I hold for you.

Briefly, Professor Carlini responded with the following remarks:

(a) possible damage to the body (a hypertension crisis that could lead to cerebral vascular injury) might occur from, *verbatim*, 'mass release' of noradrenaline; 'tyramine is its most well-known liberating agent'. However, such a release would occur to the ayahuasca user in the case of, literally, 'consuming extremely fermented cheeses or high quantities of some wines';

(b) alterations in the ayahuasca user's mind, *verbatim*, 'do not imply personality transformations, but rather temporary sensorial changes';

(c) The distinguished professor added that, 'the aforementioned mind alterations can be positively "channeled" in social and individual life'.

He quotes from an article on 'psycho-socio-therapeutic functions of ayahuasca' and concludes that 'There are also examples of other hallucinogenic plants or preparations that are used in religious rituals without causing impairment for the population of users (sometimes, quite the opposite)?

In response to the concern whether altered states of perception, mood and behavior necessarily imply negative, harmful or pathological conditions, he concludes, *verbatim*, 'my response to this third item is negative'.

The views of Professor Isac Karniol are similarly presented summarized below.

I have become convinced that, given our current knowledge, prohibiting the religious sects from using this plant would be a much greater act of violence than might occur as side effects of use.

In response to our questions,

(a) he declares that possible 'harmful reactions in the body' are 'not proven';

(b) he also adds that, there are 'no scientifically proven severe personality modifications' occurring as a result of consumption of the brew. Even so, the sensory-perceptual alterations are steered by the *mestre*, who puts a check on the amount of brew ingested.

(c) 'In no way do I consider that "altered states of perception, mood and behavior necessarily imply negative, harmful or pathological conditions". It may be worth monitoring these sects, but in no way should they be censured beforehand.'

The use of ayahuasca has been legitimate in Brazil for more than ten years. Since the ban imposed in 1985, and subsequently lifted in 1986, there has been no scientifically proven case of mental problems that were genuinely caused or generated from such use. There has been no news of abuse or of other socially disturbing behavior, either.

There are, of course, cases of individuals who already had problems, and also some who did not display an obvious pathology, who consumed the brew and engaged in self-harming or anti-social behavior. First, they are a very small number of cases, less than a handful. Besides that, it is absurd to mistake the institution for the individual actions of its members. For example, highly esteemed and traditional educational institutions have had the misfortune of having suicidal students, or have been accused of tolerating torture or murder. Individual deviant behaviors can be identified in most, if not all, types of human institutions. What counts is that they persistently and uncompromisingly attempt to attain integrity and perfection.

With respect to the groups that use the brew, the development of adequate mechanisms of control should be the object of persevering and rigorous concern for their leaders; which, in fact, likely occurs in accordance with the singularities of each group. The fact is that, before 1985, the brew had been used in rituals for several decades without anomalies. On the contrary, these practices exerted, and continue to exert, an integrative function among users with their surroundings, underscoring 'the peaceful and orderly behavior of the members of the several sects' (see MacRae). This is the strongest evidence that the community possesses the best controls for the brew's use, and is more competent to implement them. As an aside, a society usually does organize more adequately its own control mechanisms against excesses that arise in the midst of private, family or social relationships, speaking in general terms, not just with regard to the brew.

The brew's use has always been ritual – perhaps even owing to the brew's effect – which makes its use 'almost exclusively social', as indicated by Clodomir Monteiro, with the consistency of a liturgy that is always observed. Furthermore, the control exerted by the leaders of the several communities is extremely efficient, as mentioned above.

There is no logical or scientific basis to explain why the ritual practices are confined to the city of Rio Branco. On the one hand, simply walking through the streets of Rio Branco, sitting in a restaurant, or turning on the radio or television, is sufficient to realize that the programs, fashions and patterns that are put forth (or rather, imposed) are identical to those in the other states. There is no reciprocity, as unique regional characteristics are not influential, which is regrettable. It would certainly be beneficial to inject southern and southeastern Brazilians with a larger dose of the Amazonian forest, than to contaminate the latter with the consumerism and vacuity of the megalopolises. On the other hand, even if an exclusively pharmacological stance was taken, there is no obvious reason to distinguish the physiology of northern Brazilians from the southerners.

Feitios or *preparos* (the ritual complex for making the brew) are now being carried out in a variety of centers. The constitution of the brew is identical among the different groups. Centers that do not make their own brew receive it, mostly, from the North. MacRae's opinion with respect to the significance of restricting ayahuasca ritual practices to interior of the forest is notable:

> Such a restriction would be equivalent to the proscription of the most important religious services of the several ayahuasca sects which, as explained, are, and always have been, predominantly urban. This proscription would be counterproductive, because it would lead to a weakening of the centralizing and hierarchical structures of the sects, which exercise a fundamental role in the control over the brew's use. This control has shown itself to be exceedingly efficacious, until now, given the orderly and socially innocuous proceedings of the several sects.[24]

The holistic approach to Ayahuasca

Considering the data obtained from the fields of psychiatry and psychopharmacology, it follows that adherence solely to detached scientific categories and nomenclature is incapable of addressing the kinds of issues raised by the Brazilian and, especially, the urban use of ayahuasca. We must reconsider the commonly accepted order of things. There are unquestioned – but not unquestionable – concepts which, in fact, are constituted in large part by preconceptions, and often are the result of ideas simply received and accepted, without ever undergoing any critical analysis. One example of this is the concept of hallucinogen and hallucination. If you define hallucination as a perception in the absence of the object, you tread on an extremely thorny conceptual ground. 'To perceive' is a transitive verb that always requires an object. The nature of such an object cannot be restricted in accordance to a single social standard. During the 43rd Annual Meeting of the SBPC, I

---

24. Reply to request concerning the report issued by Dr Alberto Furtado Rahde, March 20, 1992.

had a chance to articulate how there are numerous histories of human perception. What may have once been defined as mad, absurd, heretical or fantastic (and, for this reason even worthy of death or burning at the stake), now often comprises erudite doctrinal or scientific formulations. The perceiver apprehends one part of reality, only a sliver in its infinite unfolding. The history of perceptions is a history of struggle, passion and censure. We are easily drawn to exalt that which we also perceive; and we are profuse to condemn as mad those who perceive what we do not.

The 'insanity of the Cross' is an example of a disparaging paroxysm that has divided time and revolutionized History. What would we think today of someone who, like St Francis, abandons all material comforts and begins to wear sack-cloth, aiding the sick and poor? Or of Bernadette Soubirous, the mystic of Lourdes, who hollowed out the mud with her bare hands where the miraculous water would spring, according to accounts? Would they be 'diagnosed' as anything other than crazy?

All perception has, consequently, an object. Madness is the incapacity to integrate the different levels or forms of perception of the challenging reality. Mircea Eliade has written about the images, symbols and myths that are, precisely, the object of ecstatic, transcendent or metaphysical experiences. Adjectives are scarce for defining such experiences (which may occur spontaneously or be induced through various means), recorded throughout human history. Eliade contends that 'these images, symbols and myths are not irresponsible creations of the psyche; instead, they respond to a need and fulfill a function: to reveal the most secret "modes of being"'.[25] Demonstrating the fallibility of conceptual expressions in this matter, the mellow Romanian historian of religion continues, 'if the spirit uses images to capture the profound reality of things, this is exactly because this reality manifests itself in contradictory ways, and consequently, cannot be expressed through concepts'.[26] 'Images have the power and mission to show what remains refractory to concepts'.[27]

The opinion of Stanislav Grof, recapitulated by Fritjof Capra, is pertinent:

> Grof concludes that a common fault in contemporary psychiatry is to diagnose someone as psychotic on the basis of the contents of his or her experiences. My observations have convinced me that the idea of what is normal and what is pathological should not be based on the content or nature of uncommon individual experiences, but instead on the way in which the individual is able to deal with them, and the degree with which such experiences are integrated into the individual's life. The harmonious integration of transpersonal experiences is decisive for mental health.[28]

Capra also recalls Bateson in order to express that one of his main objectives for studying epistemology was to 'point out the inadequacy of logic for describing biological patterns'.[29] He concludes that, 'it is extremely difficult, if not impossible, to describe

---

25. M. Eliade, *Imagens e Símbolos*, Martins Fontes, p. 8.
26. Idem, p. 11.
27. Ibidem, p. 16.
28. F. Capra, *Sabedoria incomum*, Cultrix, p. 100.
29. F. Capra, op. cit., p. 66.

the transpersonal mode of consciousness and intellectual analysis by using concrete language'.[30]

It is imperative to establish that the concepts of hallucination, delirium, illusion, anxiety and panic during the ecstatic experience 'only possess a limited range of applicability, however unambiguous they appear to be', as expressed by Werner Heisenberg.[31] This conceptual weakness is fully comprehensible when referring to ecstatic experience, and for this reason it is impossible to define its being. A concept is always limited by our rational models and circumscribed by the linguistic universe to which we are bound. As the being is the whole, it is possible only to talk about it in a way that never fully encloses it within the limits of definitions.

Thus, concepts such as hallucination and panic are far from translating the reality of these spiritual states. Panic is integral to the lives of all of us, just like our universe of fantasies, deliriums and illusions. These experiences are traversed by that well-known 'giant of the soul': Fear. Panic is simply being afraid and feeling that there's no way out. But the way out can be learned. This learning – or initiation – is progress. The path is always ahead of us, with all its anxieties. We must learn to vanquish them, because they are unavoidable. By fleeing we are not advancing. Progress is achieved by passing them, by breaking through.

With respect to this breakthrough, Eliade tells us that 'the depiction of such images should not surprise us. Every symbol of transcendence is paradoxical and impossible to comprehend on the profane level. The symbol that is most used to express the rupture of levels and penetration into the "other world" the supra-sensorial world (whether the kingdom of the dead or of the gods), is the "difficult passageway", the blade of the knife.'[32] Recalling other similar situations that appear to have no way out, Eliade evokes the Gospel according to Matthew (7:14), 'Because strait is the gate, and narrow is the way, which leadeth unto life, and few be there that find it.'

This brings to mind the short film *Ô Xente Pois Não* (directed by Joaquim Assis and produced in Salgadinho, in the rustic countryside of Pernambuco), in which the poor peasants interpret their universe. In his unique manner of speaking, one of them talks about the last topic: a dream.

> I had a dream, and I understood my life. Because sometimes you dream things that are … just things. Stuff goes on, but its just amusement. But then, there are dreams that you know are real. And this was one of them real dreams. It was so real that I understood that it was a … a message that was being given to me. It was a message about what was going to happen in my life. And I kept on dreaming it, again and again. And then, I didn't have the dream ever again.
>
> When I was young, I always dreamt that I was traveling through strange lands. Wandering those lands, I entered a large house, the largest one. Yep, it was a really big house. I entered the house straight away, along the way I was going. I think that it was night time. And then, I just kept struggling to find a way out. I kept jumping about,

---

30. Idem, p. 83.
31. In F. Capra, *O Tao da Física*, cit., p. 30.
32. M. Eliade, op. cit., p. 80.

without finding a way out. I didn't know how to go back. But I'd never give up. I'd try a door, then another one, find it closed ... then another one ... I struggled ... ahh ... And then, finally, I'd always find a door that would lead me out. I was always able to get out and not stay locked in. I always found a way out. I could pass through.[33]

That which has been called 'hallucination' is often a convenient rationale for excommunicating those who have dared to find a 'door' and to pass through.

Meanwhile, Contenau notes that 'all these plants which have the objective of increasing the subject's metanomic potential are hallucinogenic'.[34] This renders a dispassionate scrutiny of the matter very difficult, given that the term 'hallucination' is emotionally-laden and practically impossible to translate conceptually.

The assortment of juridical, pharmacological, botanical or psychiatric terms, and chemical formulae, are concepts. Wisdom has shown that life is beyond concepts. The 70 years of ritual practice with ayahuasca in Brazil – orderly, socially integrated – are life itself. To paraphrase the biblical question of the Sabbath, forms and concepts were made for life, life was not made for them. The words of Michel Foucault, in *The Archaeology of Knowledge*, are germane:

> discourse is not life: its time is not yours; in it, you haven't reconciled with death; it's possible that you may have killed God with the weight of everything that you have said; but don't think that, with all that you say, you can make a man live longer than he.[35]

We know that people have always sought continual transcendence of the limits of their capacity for understanding. Not just hippies, but even Thomas Aquinas, when he discusses the soul (which, it should be noted, means here the human capacity for understanding), alludes to circumstances that allow the soul to retract from the body, to retire from matter, and which enable its intrinsic understanding to arise. Professor João Manoel de Albuquerque Lins, of the Catholic University of Rio de Janeiro, says about them:

> These are all moments in which 'sensory activities' cease to overwhelm our consciousness, allowing us, thus, to take distance from the immediacy of our surrounding external world. So, in *De Anima*, he refers to the *'dormientibus'* – those who sleep, and so, dream – ; and to the *'alienatis a sensibus'* – those who do not use their senses, who for some reason are alien to their senses – ; in *Suma Contra Gentiles*, again we find the *'dormientes'* – those who sleep – ; the *'syncopizantibus'* – those who suffer from strokes, fainting – ; and *'extasim passis'* – those who experience ecstasy – ; and, in *IV Sententiarum* he again refers to sleep, *'in dormiendo,'* in ecstasy, or better said, in trance.

> These are, consequently, the same conditions that modern parapsychology recognizes as favorable for ESP[36] manifestations, or Psi-Gamma Faculty.[37]

---

33. *O Xente, Pois Não*, FASE: Federação de Órgãos para Assistência Social e Educacional, Rio de Janeiro.

34. G. Contenau, *La Divination Chez Lês Assiriens et Les Babyloniens*, Paris: Payot, 1940.

35. M. Foucault, *Arqueologia do Saber*, Vozes, p. 256.

36. ESP: extra-sensory perception.

37. *Revista Verbum*, tome XXIV, fasc. June 2, 1967. Catholic University of Rio de Janeiro, p. 221.

The references to Thomas Aquinas intend to promote reflection on various human states of perception that would not qualify as madness or mental insanity, or even timidly as illusion, fancy or fantasy. It is extremely perverse to condemn transpersonal experiences with the stigma of insanity. Obviously, the comments on Thomas Aquinas do not themselves offer reasons whether ayahuasca should be used or not. Instead, they aim to illustrate that we often hastily classify as 'hallucination' the use of faculties that 'all of us possess, at least in core'.[38] Concepts that have remained undisputed, unmodified and settled with the passing of decades hamper the issue's evaluation. This is especially the case for concepts 'necessarily' associated with the 'full-blown war on drugs' – as identified by Anthony Richard Henman – itself 'based on the prohibitionist hysteria promoted by the American Drug Enforcement Administration in the local mass media'.[39]

In fact, the general public's questioning of the use of ayahuasca reflects the prohibitionist bias, prompted by the seditious 'war' that Henman talks about. These questions really conceal a censuring prejudice, revolving on two words: *hallucinogen* and *cultures*. Is ayahuasca a hallucinogen? Is it possible to admit the use of ayahuasca by urban residents, given the differences between urban and rural 'cultures'?

Régis Jolivert, honorary professor of the Faculty of Philosophy of the Catholic University of Lyon, specifies that 'culture' in sociology refers to 'the collection of institutions, traditions, customs and collective representations, belief and value systems that characterize a certain society'.[40] Yet, how can one conceive of the existing 'cultures' of Céu do Mapiá, Rio Branco, Rio de Janeiro, or Visconde de Mauá, stagnantly, when 'pilgrims' from diverse regions of Brazil travel several times a year to spend a while in the Amazonian rainforest in Céu do Mapiá? And what about the notion of an 'impermeability' of cultures, knowing that Padrinho Sebastião (deceased) and his whole family also spent long periods of time in the Céu do Mar community in São Conrado, in the city of Rio de Janeiro. Reflection on the 'pilgrimages' to Céu do Mapiá is also relevant to the matter at hand.

It is worth bringing to mind the words of Professor Regina Abreu in relation to the eventual clash or incompatibility of 'cultures'.

I want to add some more comments regarding the topic discussed previously (fl. 14, this report), the conversion to the Doctrine of people from urban-industrial society. This matter generates anxiety in religious groups, civic and military authorities, and members of civil society. The embracing of the Santo Daime Doctrine in cities obviously exhibits characteristics that are particular to urban life. You obviously won't find people engaging in rural economic exploits, such as hunting or agriculture. Even so, the conversion to the Doctrine may lead some people to adopt ritual and lifestyle practices that are characteristic of rural religious communities. There is a similar project in both cases. In each, as the anthropologist Dumont, cited before, has said, 'the emphasis is placed on the society as a whole, as a collective man. The ideal is defined by the social organization in view of its ends (and not according to personal gains). Above all, there is hierarchy. Every individual man must contribute

---

38. Albuquerque Lins, op. cit. p. 211.
39. *América Indígena*, Instituto Indigenista Interamericano, Vol XLVI, Jan–Mar, 1986, p. 221.
40. 'Jolivet', in *Vocabulário de Filosofia*, 1975, AGIR, p. 60.

to the global order. Justice consists of proportioning social functions in relation to the whole' (Louis Dumont, *Homo Hierarchicus – Lê Systeme dês Castes et Sés Implications*, Paris: Tel Gallimard, 1996, p. 23). Thus, in the cities, the communities are structured to provide for spiritual needs (they adopt the Doctrine as a rural practice) and material needs. These material needs are satisfied by a wide variety of urban employments (liberal professionals, employees in the public and private sector, politicians, professors, intellectuals, etc.).

In all, the communities that embrace the Santo Daime Doctrine, from country to city, may appear exotic to many. However, living with this diversity can only be enriching, for individuals and for society as a whole.[41]

The comments of Claude Lévi-Strauss wrap up this matter excellently:

No culture is alone. It is always capable of binding with other cultures, and this is what allows it to construct cumulative series. The chance that a longer one should appear among these series naturally depends on the extension, duration and variability of the binding system. … The sole fatality, the only obstacle that can afflict a group and thwart it from fully developing its nature, is to be the only one.[42]

If today, the proposal to exclude the issue of ayahuasca from penal law and not schedule it as a prohibited substance is so polemical, imagine what it was like 11 years ago. That more than a decade has passed without the formation of traffic or cartels and without the proliferation of violence that could have developed from an abuse of the brew, notwithstanding the aloofness of police repression, constitutes a powerfully persuasive argument in favor of the orientation that the CONFEN board took.

The serene handling of the matter, on the other hand, provided opportunity for exercising freedom of academic inquiry. We already have the first results of the biomedical investigation, conducted by a multinational team, published in 1996, in the official journal of psychiatry and psychopathology of the State University of Rio de Janeiro, *Informação Psiquiátrica*, with the title, 'Human Pharmacology of Hoasca, hallucinogenic plant used in a ritual context in Brazil; I. Psychological effects'[43] Researchers who participated in the study, conducted during the summer of 1993, came from the UCLA Medical Center (USA), the University of Kuopio (Finland), Centro de Estudos Médicos (São Paulo), Escola Paulista de Medicina and the University of New Mexico. Unfortunately, it is not possible to provide a thorough analysis of this immensely valuable contribution, born from an initiative of the UDV. I fully agree that, as remarked in the journal, 'the results of an objective, unbiased scientific study may offer a protective value in the future, if the political direction in Brazil were to change'.[44]

The study worked with 15 individuals who had been members of the ayahuasca-using institution for 15 years, and a control group of 15 people with no history of ayahuasca consumption. The report says that, 'the current analysis of the data is, nevertheless, an indication that the long-term consumption of hoasca in the structured ceremonial

---

41. Consultant's report to the CONFEN, cit. pp. 16–17.
42. Claude Lévi Strauss, 'Raça e História', in *Raça e Ciência I*, São Paulo: Ed. Perspectiva, 1970, pp. 262–63.
43. *Informação Psiquiátrica*, trimestral journal, Vol. 15, No. 2, pp. 39–45.
44. Op. cit., p. 40.

context of the UDV does not exert a toxic or degenerative effect on neuropsychological functions'.[45] The abstract of the article reads, 'there was no evidence of cognitive or personality deterioration among hoasca users. In fact, the overall results revealed an elevated functional status, which the individuals claimed was due to the ritual use of the psychoactive sacrament, hoasca'.[46]

Finally, Dr. Osvaldo Luiz Saide, illustrious professor at the State University of Rio de Janeiro and member of the research team, reminds us that the use of ayahuasca is a constitutive element of the rituals of religions (the UDV and the Santo Daime) that are authentically Brazilian, 'even in their syncretism (a trait of our culture, as Darcy Ribeiro would say)'.[47]

I affirm with serene conviction that the search for the particular form of perception that ayahuasca users engage in during their 'sessions' or 'works' must not be defined, unreflectively, as hallucinations, in the sense of mental insanity or deviation. I did, however, corroborate one feature, rigorously shared by all: the consciousness to expand their individual and communitarian virtues, in search of self-knowledge and the sacred.[48]

Children of a future age,
Reading this indignant page,
Know that in a former time
A path to god was thought a crime.[49]

---

45. Op. cit., p. 45.
46. Op. cit., p. 39.
47. Op. cit., editorial.
48. The author's works included in this text were organized by his son, Filipe Gialluisi da Silva Sá.
49. Adapted from William Blake, in *Religion and Psychoactive Sacraments: A Bibliographic Guide*, Thomas B. Roberts and Paula Jo Hruby, 1995.

9

The development of Brazilian public policies on the religious use of Ayahuasca[*]

Edward MacRae

The 'scientific control' of the African-Brazilian religious groups – A precedent

Since the mid 1980s there has been a an expansion in many parts of Brazil of a number of new religious groups that use in their liturgy the psychoactive brew known as ayahuasca. Although this brew has long been used in certain parts of the Amazon, mainly in Indian and mestizo or 'caboclo' shamanic rites, once its use began to reach other parts of the country, and eventually even to be exported abroad, authorities came to view it as another potential drug of abuse and calls were made for its control and even for its banning. The followers of these religions are frequently represented in the press and by the police, as people whose alleged religious convictions are mere excuses for drug use. So in recent decades there have been a series public and official discussions on the matter, in which considerations of a medical nature have often overshadowed those pertaining to the preservation of religious freedom.

Thus it seems that an understanding of the current discussions in Brazil over official measures to control or regulate the activities of these religious groups might benefit from comparisons to those raised by the constraints imposed in that country on the possession cults at the end of the nineteenth century and beginning of the twentieth. Both situations have much in common, reflecting the long history of official intervention in the activities of Brazilian religious 'minorities'.

Until 1976, African-Indian-Brazilian religious centres were still legally obliged to register and to submit to police supervision, with all the arbitrariness this entailed. At the time this law was passed, such police supervision was clearly intended as a means of

---

[*] A first version of this article was originally published as 'A elaboração das políticas públicas brasileiras em relação ao uso religioso da ayahuasca' in the book *Drogas e Cultura: novas perspectivas*, edited by B. C. Labate, S. Goulart, M. Fiore, E. MacRae and H. Carneiro, Salvador, Edufba, 2008.

fostering the surveillance and control of the black members of the population, who were perceived as a potential threat by the elite after the abolition of slavery in 1888. The arguments favouring these measures were originally presented in medical terms and enjoyed all the prestige that was beginning to be accorded to scientific thought in Brazil at the end of the nineteenth century. Significantly, this was a period when there was much rivalry and disagreement between lawyers who favoured more universal and egalitarian approaches to social policies and doctors who believed in innate racial and sexual hierarchies that should not be ignored. These doctors argued that science and rationality demanded that Brazilian society ought to be viewed as a sick organism and that in dealing with social problems it was best to take a clinical or epidemiological approach and that 'evolutionary' differences had to be taken into account if a cure for the social ills of Brazil was to be found. Disease and racial degeneration had to be eliminated and the juridical notions based on the respect for equal rights and freedom of choice should receive little credit, since they lacked scientific grounding (Schwarcz 1993: 213).

Thus, the first republican penal code, which was passed in 1890, considered 'witch-doctory', as African religiosity was then generically labelled, to be a crime, linking religious issues to the illicit practice of medicine. In its Article 157, the new Code established penalties for those who 'practice spiritism, sorcery and witchcraft, use charms and cartomancy to arouse feelings of hatred or love, promote cures for curable or incurable diseases or, in other words, prey on public credulity'. The penalties ranged from one to six months' imprisonment, to be increased if the crimes committed led to 'a temporary or permanent alteration of the victim's mental faculties' (Dantas 1988: 165).

At a time when biomedicine was still largely concerned with self-legitimization and with ensuring for itself the monopoly of therapeutic procedures, this law also served to discredit and stigmatize folk medicine and its practitioners. At the time, medical science associated madness and possession trances in a simplistic manner, considering the African-Brazilian religious cults, alongside syphilis, alcoholism and contagious diseases, to be an important source of mental illness. Black religious leaders were accused of exploiting the gullible and casting defenceless girls into debauchery. Alongside the mention of orgies, were charges of 'states of dementia due to … initiation into things of witchcraft' (Dantas 1988: 166).

According to the then highly respected coroner Nina Rodrigues and his followers, possession trances, the core of 'witchcraft', were pathological states of hysteria, caused by organic lesions. Black people were equated to the sick or abnormal and medical science joined in with the, then current, anthropological discourse on race, to demand a more sophisticated form of control, substituting legal considerations for 'scientific' ones. But, due to the strong political rivalry existing between the legal and medical establishments, the 'scientific controls' advocated by Nina Rodrigues did not succeed in fully taking over from the legal controls and a new penal code, enacted in 1932, maintained the articles relating to the exercise of witchcraft and magic. Thus African-Brazilian cults were classified as both criminal and pathological.

In the 1930s, Brazilian intellectuals still sought to understand these religious cults from a perspective which was mainly medical. This is well illustrated by the psychiatrist Ulysses Pernambucano de Melo, a follower of Nina Rodrigues, who, in 1931, started the Office of Mental Hygiene, a division of the Pernambuco State Assistance to Psychopaths. There studies were carried out on African-Brazilian religious cult members, adopting what was purported to be a wide ranging approach that accepted that, in some cases, the factors that might influence the production of disease or trances might, apart from their biological bases, also have a social nature. Yet, despite his interest in multidisciplinary approaches, Ulysses Pernambucano de Melo was not willing to accept certain sociological concepts, such as those put forward by his collaborator Gilberto Freyre, who disagreed with the idea that possession trances were pathological syndromes and conceived of them as an expression of a cultural past that erupted in certain circumstances, favouring a reflex action (Dantas 1988: 176).

In the Office of Mental Hygiene, the followers of trance cults were subjected to 'strict observation' and 'mental tests', which sought to establish a form of 'scientific control' that might replace police action. There was, in turn, a tacit understanding on the part of the police that, once subjected to mental examination, the practitioners of these religious cults should be granted permission to perform their ceremonies of worship, as long as they kept to previously approved times and schedules. This medicalization of the studies of the African-Brazilian cults was also to be found in other states of Brazil (Dantas 1988: 176–7).

In an intellectual climate which was still heavily influenced by scientific theories on racism and cultural evolution, many of the discussions on the subject revolved around the question of the nature of the cults. Were they magic or religion? There was a prevailing notion that the cults of Jeje-Nagô origin were purer and more evolved than those of Bantu origin, which, due to the simplicity of their rituals, were considered to be more prone to falsifications, quackery and witch-doctory. This opened the way to fierce arguments over the relative degrees of 'purity' of the various cults and to frequent accusations of 'evil practices' and 'of the abuse of African names and traditions for the furtherance of mere entertainment and exploitation'. These alleged distinctions were adopted and maintained by the followers of the African-Brazilian cults themselves, who wished to ensure their individual legitimacy by endorsing the differences between what should be seen as religion (their own forms of worship) and what should be considered as mere exploitation of public credulity (that of the other groups) (Dantas 1988: 178–9).

In 1934, a law was passed requiring the African-Brazilian centres of worship to be registered at the police. Since there was no legal charter to guarantee a legal backing to the existence of these centres of worship, this law exposed them to frequent police arbitrariness and abuse. In order to counter this injunction and to neutralize the stigmatization they suffered, many of these groups began to seek registration as civil associations and, subsequently, to form larger and more powerful organizations or federations under which they might congregate. In 1934 and 1937, two very important Afro-Brazilian Congresses were held in Recife and Salvador, with a considerable participation of anthropologists and physicians. The two conferences were concerned with a search for African 'authenticity' and with a 'popular presence', in the hope of spreading new ideas and promoting a more tolerant vision of the African Candomblé, which was still commonly identified with witchcraft, sorcery and evil. They also marked the beginning of a long process which, in more recent times has led to the final public and official acceptance of these cults as legitimate religions of great cultural significance to Brazilian national identity. At present the police surveillance and persecution they were once subjected to are generally regarded as shameful episodes in Brazilian history and as remnants of the slave system.

Institutionalization and official controls of the ayahuasca religions

Currently, similar threats to the freedom of religious organization and worship loom over the followers of the Brazilian ayahuasca religions, which are also of popular origin and display many African and Indian traits. Despite the major doctrinal and liturgical differences separating them, they have been labelled under the generic name 'ayahuasca religions' owing to the central role played by the use of ayahuasca in most of their ceremonies. This is a brew containing the beta carboline alkaloids: harmine, harmaline, tetrahidroharmine (present in the *Bannesteriopsis caapi* vine) and N-dimethyltryptamine (DMT) (present in the *Psychotria viridis* leaves), the ritual ingestion of which leads the participants to enter into a trance state generally known in anthropological literature of 'shamanic flight' (MacRae 1992: 45).

These religions were originally developed by members of the poorer strata of Brazilian society and their use of Ayahuasca harks back to ancient indigenous traditions, particularly in regions of the south-western Amazon. Since the 1930s, this sacred brew has played a central role in the rituals of three religions: the Santo Daime (including the so-called 'line of Padrinho Sebastião' or CEFLURIS), Barquinha and União do Vegetal (UDV), whose followers use it as a sacrament to trigger off 'shamanic flights' (MacRae 2004a: 493). These three major Brazilian ayahuasca religions are now considered by anthropologists to be different developments of a particular complex of beliefs and practices, making up a tradition that is common to them and by which they are all inspired (Goulart, 2004 and 2008). Their doctrines blend elements of Catholicism, Kardec spiritism, European and Eastern esotericism, Amazonian 'encantaria' or magical lore and African-Brazilian traditions. In many ways Santo Daime and Barquinha are similar to Umbanda, a very popular African-Brazilian possession trance religion which was consolidated at roughly the same time, combining similar traits from much the same religious traditions, although eliciting a different type of trance (Camargo 1973).

These ayahuasca religions give great emphasis in their rituals to physical or spiritual healing. In the States of Acre and Rondônia these religions, with their conservative hierarchical and patriarchal structure, have played an important role in the urban integration of poverty stricken rubber tappers who were displaced from their forest habitats after the end of the rubber boom (Monteiro da Silva 1983). In a manner which is similar to other recent Brazilian religious movements, such as Umbanda and Neo-Pentecostalism, the doctrines, rituals and organizational structures of the ayahuasca religions are still undergoing many changes and there are frequent splits leading to the emergence of new groups with their own doctrines and rituals. In this environment it is difficult to avoid sectarianism and the claims of certain doctrines to greater 'purity' or 'authenticity'. Moreover, some, like CEFLURIS[1] and the União do Vegetal (UDV), are more expansionist, while others are jealous of their exclusiveness, making a point of maintaining their regional character and criticizing the expansion of others.

---

1. Centro Eclético Fluente Luz Universal-CEFLURIS is the name of the biggest and most expansionist of the Santo Daime groups. It gathers the followers of Padrinho Sebastião and is often considered to be unorthodox with regard to the liturgy and doctrine originally instituted by Mestre Irineu the founder of the Santo Daime.

Most of these religions were originally developed in the rural outskirts of the city of Rio Branco, but other towns such as Brasiléia and Cruzeiro do Sul, in Acre, and Porto Velho, in Rondônia, have also witnessed significant ayahuasca religious activity. In the rubber estates there has also been a considerable use of the 'vine'[2] on the part of local folk healers (Pantoja and Conceição, in this volume, pp. 21–38). Since the 1980s, the expansion of religious ayahuasca groups such as CEFLURIS and UDV and the emergence of urban neo-ayahuasqueiro[3] groups has led most of the use of ayahuasca to now take place outside the Amazon, mainly in the outskirts of urban centres in other regions of Brazil and even abroad.

Now once again, medical and police concerns intertwine, while scholars from different branches of science try to mediate between the followers of the religions and the official agencies of social control. Although Brazil has become more democratic and scientists, ayahuasqueiros[4] and those responsible for developing public policies on the subject are aware of the dangers involved and seem genuinely intent on avoiding injustice, the risk still remains that official interventions and regulations may end by establishing new paradigms for outside interference in these religious activities. Once again, instead of doing away with police controls, there is the risk of overlapping them with new ones, of a medical nature, such as occurred in the case of the African-Brazilian religions.

Ever since their beginnings, these religions have suffered much opposition, primarily due to the widespread prejudice against the social strata most of their members came from. After all, most of them were poor, black or mestizo, social groups that, at different times in Brazilian history, have been seen as threats to civilization and to law and order; in the names of which they have been repeatedly subjected to different forms of repression. Thus, as in the case of other religions of African or Indian origin, prejudices were vented in accusations of sorcery or witchdoctory. More recently, they came to be accused primarily of 'drug use' (MacRae 1998, 2001; Goulart 2004, 2008). The very expression 'ayahuasca religions' is evidence of the medical-pharmacological lens through which they are seen to this day.

In 1985, ayahuasca was placed on the Brazilian list of proscribed substances, where it remained for six months, owing to a series of questions raised about its psychoactive properties. After a number of legal and political moves, undertaken mainly due to pressure from members of one of these religious groups, the União do Vegetal, the Federal Council of Narcotics-CONFEN[5] was called to rule on the matter. This led to the setting up of an official Working Group charged with the study of the religious use of ayahuasca.[6]

---

2. 'Cipó' (meaning 'vine' in Portuguese) is one of the traditional names used for the brew among those who are not regular followers of any of the established ayahuasca religions.

3. These are new ayahuasca groups that usually draw their members from the middle class and who often mix New Age concepts with the more traditional teachings derived from the Santo Daime, União do Vegetal or Barquinha traditions.

4. 'Ayahuasqueiros' is a Brazilian neologism used to refer to those who take ayahuasca regularly in a ritual manner.

5. This institution, which used to be responsible for drug control and enforcement, came to be substituted by the National Anti-Drug System, directly linked to the Presidency and comprising the National Anti-Drugs Office (or SENAD) and the National Drug Policy Council (or CONAD).

6. CONFEN Resolution No. 04/85.

This Working Group, after issuing an initial recommendation for a temporary suspension of the ban, spent two years carrying out research and paying several visits to ayahuasca using communities in various states of Brazil, mainly Acre, Amazonas and Rio de Janeiro. In September 1987, it finally presented a comprehensive report recommending that the plant species that were used in the preparation of the Ayahuasca beverage should be excluded from the official list of proscribed substances. The document was approved by CONFEN and, on the following February, CONFEN issued Resolution No. 06, which definitively excluded from the list of proscribed substances not only ayahuasca, but also the plant species used in its making.

The 1987 report also concluded that the ayahuasca religions contributed to the strengthening of values considered to be emblematic of Western societies influenced by Christianity, and promoted sentiments leading to social cohesion such as discipline, generosity, familial love, communality and respect for nature. More recent anthropological research has corroborated this view and shown that these religions should be seen as 'rites of order' (Couto 2004: 385) and the religious use of ayahuasca as a good example of harm reduction[7] for the use of psychoactive substances, since they provide a framework of rules, values and rituals, both religious and social, for their use, life structure for their followers and control over the availability of the substance (Couto 1989, 2004; MacRae 2004b, 2009; Labate 2005).

But, besides social persecution, the ayahuasca religions face further difficulties due to the discord and rivalry that prevails among their followers. As commonly happens among religions in general, there are frequent power struggles among the ayahuasqueiros and each religion tends to believe its doctrines and rituals to be the only correct and legitimate ones. Just as the different African-Brazilian religions often seek to disqualify each other, so the followers of different ayahuasca doctrines commonly allege that, through a series of spurious doctrinal alterations and inventions, the others deviate from the purity of the traditions established by their founders.

Demonstrating intolerance and a paradoxical adherence to anti-drug and drug-traffic paradigms, some of these ayahuasqueiros frequently accuse the followers of the other ayahuasca religions of doing commerce in ayahuasca and of also using other, illicit, entheogens[8] in their rituals. They also criticize each other for, in some cases, allowing the occurrence of possession trances, considered to be foreign to the original doctrines which only admitted 'shamanic flights' (MacRae 2004a: 493; Goulart 2004; Labate 2004). It seems significant that followers of the ayahuasca religions should be the authors of most of the complaints against ill-usage of the brew which are brought to the attention of government authorities who, left to themselves, would usually prefer to turn a blind eye and avoid entanglements in religious disputes.

---

7. Harm reduction is a public health policy that is currently being applied in many countries, including Brazil, in order to deal with the negative consequences of drug use. It is based on the idea that drug effects depend on set and setting as well as the pharmacological properties of a given substance and that, rather than trying to forbid drug use, it is better to ensure that it occurs in positive, less harmful ways.

8. Entheogens are substances, usually of a botanical origin, that are used ritually to produce altered states of consciousness. This neologism which means 'that which generates the divine within' is often used by ayahuasqueiros and social scientists as an alternative to 'hallucinogen', which is considered to be pejorative.

Such accusations and the prevailing repressive social attitudes in Brazil towards anything that might be regarded as 'drug taking', make it difficult to reach a final settlement for the ayahuasca question, since new problems keep cropping up. In 1991, for instance, an anonymous complaint led to another call for a review of the matter and once again CONFEN had to commission studies on the context of production and consumption of the beverage which further confirmed the appropriateness of the 1987 decision to allow the religious use of ayahuasca. (CONAD 2006; MacRae 1994, p. 31; Sá, in this volume, pp. 161–90).

Further difficulties arise due to the expansion abroad of the UDV and CEFLURIS groups, which brought in its wake questions regarding the export of the brew and the subsequent involvement of the Brazilian Foreign Office in the discussions. Followers of ayahuasca religions faced a series of legal charges in the USA, France, Spain and the Netherlands. In some countries, such as Spain, the Netherlands and the USA, Santo Daime and União do Vegetal followers were acquitted and awarded, in 2000, 2001 and 2006 respectively, official recognition of the legitimacy of their religious rituals involving the use of ayahuasca. In others, official positions are still ambiguous and the ayahuasca rituals are carried out in varying degrees of secrecy.

Currently, given the increasing social integration and institutionalization of the ayahuasca religions in Brazil, those who still take a prejudiced view of their practices seek other, more indirect, ways of curbing their activities and expansion. Thus, for example, there may be bureaucratic hindrances to the production and transportation of the brew, under the pretext of the need to supervise the management and preservation of the *Banisteriopsis caapi* and *Psychotria viridis* species. However justifiable this may seem environmentally, the ayahuasqueiros argue that the controls they are subjected to are much more severe than those which are applied to the big landowners, who regularly destroy large expanses of the forest where these species grow naturally, in order to sell the timber and use the land for raising cattle. As for the international distribution of the brew, even after the establishment of the legitimacy of its production and religious use at home, the Brazilian customs authorities continue to be reluctant to issue international documentation making this clear, thereby rendering it almost impossible for foreign religious groups to legally import the brew into their countries.

Finally, echoing the doctors of the first half of the twentieth century who equated possession trances to insanity, there are frequent articles in the press that cast ridicule on the ayahuasca religions and their followers or manifest concern about supposed health risks to users of the drink, regardless of all the scientific research backing the official positions. Much is also made of the risks to users that might be young, pregnant, suffer from mental illness or use certain medicines. Even in the absence of strong scientific confirmation for many of these fears, medical concepts and values are invoked as conclusive arguments to predominate over religious conviction and freedom.

New official provisions concerning the religious use of ayahuasca

The growth and internationalization of some ayahuasca religions continued to foster accusations of improper use of the brew and, in some cases, these were given much publicity by the press and taken to the notice of government agencies, notably the National Drug Policy Council (CONAD), the Federal Police and public prosecutors. This ended up by leading, in 2002,[9] to another CONAD resolution which set up yet another Working Group to look into the matter. However, due to a change of government this resolution remained ignored until, March 2004, when CONAD requested its Technical and Scientific Advisory Board (CATC) to carry out a new study and produce yet another scientific and technical report on the religious use of ayahuasca. This board, which was made up of scientists and academics from different fields, including myself, as anthropologist, held several discussions on the subject and produced another report which, once again, reaffirmed the importance of respecting the religious rights of the followers of the ayahuasca religions. In November 2004, a new CONAD resolution[10] was issued, emphasizing the importance of ensuring the free exercise of religious worship. It also carried a reminder that the United Nations International Narcotics Control Board[11] had declared that 'no plant (natural material) containing DMT is currently controlled by the 1971 Convention on Psychotropic Substances. Consequently, preparations (for ex. decoctions) made from these plants, including ayahuasca, are not under international control and therefore not subject to any of the articles of the 1971 Convention.'[12]

The resolution also dealt with the religious use of ayahuasca by children and pregnant women, leaving the decision up to the children's parents and to the women themselves. It further established the creation of another Multidisciplinary Working Group (GMT Ayahuasca) commissioned to survey and monitor the religious use of the brew, and to carry out research on its possible medical use. It was determined that this working group should consist of 12 members: six chosen from the fields of anthropology, pharmacology/biochemistry, social work, psychology, psychiatry and law, to be indicated by CONAD, and six to be nominated by the religious groups as their representatives. This working group was commanded to draw up a plan of action to be submitted to CONAD within 180 days, with a view to producing a document on the 'deontology'[13] of its use. It was also instructed to begin its activities by organizing a national register of all the religious institutions that used ayahuasca in their rituals.

The scientific and academic members of the Ayahuasca Working Group were selected from researchers who had previously provided advice to government offices dealing with drug use such as CONAD and its predecessor CONFEN. Some had already acted in previous official enquiries on ayahuasca. The religious representatives were chosen during a seminar held by CONAD in Rio Branco in March 2006.

During this event, the deep rivalry and animosity reigning among the different ayahuasca groups became specially evident, in a manner that was strongly reminiscent of the quarrels among the African-Brazilian religious groups when their legal status was still

---

9. CONAD Resolution No. 26, 31 December 2002.
10. CONAD Resolution No. 4, later corrected and reissued as Resolution No. 5 of 4 November 2004.
11. The International Narcotics Control Board – INBC is the board charged by the Vienna Convention with providing norms and supervision for the control and prohibition of certain drugs.
12. INCB-UNO, 17/01/2001–01/2001-Ref: INCB-PSY10/01-File: 14/1NET. This is the author's attempt at translating a reference taken from a text in Portuguese (CONAD 2004).
13. This expression, most commonly used in Medicine and Law, is defined by Dictionary.com as: 'Ethics sp. That branch dealing with duty, moral obligation and right action'.

uncertain and there was a felt need to establish their respective degrees of 'African purity' so as to ensure their legitimacy. Thus, members of the more orthodox branches of the Santo Daime and of the Barquinha religions wanted to exclude from the discussions the CEFLURIS group. This is by far the biggest, most expansionist and best known of the Santo Daime groups (MacRae 1992). Consequently it is also the most controversial and the main object of most of the accusations raised against the ayahuasca religions regarding doctrinal deviation, commercial exploitation of their sacrament and use of Cannabis in their rituals, in a way in which one cannot help being reminded of the accusations of 'impurity' and 'exploitation' raised against some of the African-Brazilian groups in the first half of the twentieth century. The quarrels even led to the Barquinha groups refusing to take part in the working group and being replaced by another member of one of the smaller but more orthodox Santo Daime groups. Alongside the members of the more established religions, there were also two representatives of the so-called 'neo-ayahuasqueiros',[14] a label covering a wide range of independent groups whose doctrines and liturgy are still undergoing a process of formation and consolidation (Labate 2004).

During these discussions, the representatives of the União do Vegetal, the biggest and best organized of the ayahuasca religions, maintained a discrete and fraternal conduct with regard to the other doctrines, which was very helpful in ensuring that the working group was a success. In fact, throughout the procedures, the general goodwill on the part of most of CONAD, CATC and Ayahuasca Working Group members was quite noticeable and it was clear that most of them were genuinely committed to defending the religious rights of the different religions and to establishing sensible standards for the ritual use of the sacramental brew. This became especially evident in the unprecedented suggestion, originally presented by the CATC, that religious representatives be included in the debates on an equal basis with the scientific experts.

Despite the historic rivalry between the different organizations they represented, the religious members of the working group also tried to avoid exchanging accusations, and, when this was not possible, the charges brought forward found little echo in the other members and did not prosper. The formality of the Presidential Palace, where the discussions were held, and the presence of the Minister in Chief for the Office of Institutional Security, General Jorge Armando Felix, alongside the National Anti-Drug Secretary, General Paulo Roberto Yog de Miranda Uchoa, presiding over the proceedings, seem to have driven home, to all those taking part, the importance of the occasion. It also became clear that it would be folly to oppose the official intentions of establishing a generally agreed code of conduct which would provide further legitimacy for the ayahuasca religions.

So as to ensure that the registration of ayahuasca groups did not affect their religious freedom, as had previously happened in the case of the African-Brazilian religions, it was stressed that the aim of such registration should be the improvement of communication between the different religious organizations and government offices, in order to strengthen their institutional and social legitimacy. It was also to be done on a voluntary basis.

---

14. These are new ayahuasca groups whose members are usually drawn from the middle class and who often mix New Age concepts with the more traditional teachings derived from the Santo Daime, União do Vegetal or Barquinha traditions.

During the working group discussions many points were raised. These revolved mainly around the fears, expressed by some religious representatives, that the sacramental brew might be treated by some as yet another commercial commodity. Thus, much was said about the need to devise adequate rules for the cultivation of the plant species used in making the brew, so as to ensure their preservation, and to prohibit the sale of ayahuasca to people with little commitment to the traditional rituals.

There was also much debate about an 'ayahuasca tourism', promoted for profit by Brazilian and foreign organizations that advertised unproven medical and spiritual healing properties for the 'workshops' they held in remote parts of Brazil. On the other hand, the CEFLURIS representative stressed the need to establish a difference between such predominantly commercial activities and those of parties, made up of members of the religious groups from different parts of Brazil or from abroad, who regularly undertake spiritual pilgrimages to certain ayahuasca centres in the Amazon, like Vila Céu do Mapiá, the CEFLURIS headquarters. This representative also called for official regulations for the export of ayahuasca to foreign religious groups.

In contemporary Brazil, the discussions concerning the use of psychoactive substances in general have been taking place under the aegis of a moral panic[15] linking young shanty-town dwellers to drug addiction, trafficking and violence. The feelings over this issue seem comparable to those which existed after the abolition of slavery, in 1888, when the Brazilian elite went in fear of Black disorder and violence, leading to draconian measures aimed at controlling African cultural movements, especially religious ones.

The pervading public suspicion of psychoactive substance use, and the political limitations it imposed, certainly acted as a restraining influence on some of the working group and CONAD members who would have liked to be even more liberal in regulating ayahuasca use. However, others, usually the representatives of the more orthodox groups, invoked the perceived social threats to argue in favour of stricter controls over the use of the brew, its distribution and the recruitment of new followers.

The Final Report of the Ayahuasca Working Group

On 23 November 2006, the Ayahuasca Working Group submitted its final report to the President of CONAD, General Felix. The overall tone of this report was one of tolerance and respect for constitutional safeguards regarding religious freedom and the rights to privacy, family life and self image. Thus, it was made clear that the National Register of Ayahuasca Using Groups should not be used as a means of state control and that it should be left to the different groups whether or not they decided to register or not.

In its conclusion, the report listed ten deontological principles by which it sought to define what was meant by ayahuasca and the purposes and locations that should be

---

15. 'Moral panic' is a concept developed by the sociologist Stanley Cohen (1972: 9) to refer to events that tend to happen in times of social change or upheaval, when moral standards are challenged and the community tries to reaffirm its values, redefining the frontiers between what is to be considered good and evil and the mass media invent new 'demons' to be used as scapegoats.

considered appropriate for its religious use, while stressing the unacceptability of its consumption in conjunction with illicit substances. Moreover, it clarified issues related to the cultivation of the species used in making ayahuasca and to the production and distribution of the brew. It also rejected any kind of commerce involving the sale of ayahuasca or the promotion of profit-making events related to its use. There was also a rejection of quackery and a recommendation that ayahuasca should not be given to people suffering from mental disorders or who were under the influence of alcohol or other psychoactive substances. There was also a call for multidisciplinary research on ayahuasca and a suggestion that CONAD might give institutional support to the creation of representative institutions of the religious organizations with the aim of supervising the maintenance of the agreed deontological principles.

Although the issue of ayahuasca exports was not directly dealt with in the report, since foreign trade was considered to be outside the Council's concerns, the subject was raised orally by the representative of CEFLURIS when the document was officially delivered to General Felix. On the following day it was informally disclosed that the matter had been referred to the National Sanitary Surveillance Agency (ANVISA), which had been charged with settling the necessary legal niceties involved.

On 6 November 2006, a general meeting of the CONAD members gave the final approval to the document. In February, 2008, another meeting of the Ayahuasca Working Group was convened to discuss the steps that had been taken to put into practice the CONAD decisions. Alongside the regulation of religious ayahuasca use, other subjects were also broached, such as a call for research projects on the medicinal use of ayahuasca, as well as questions related to environmental issues and to the transportation of the brew and its component species.

When environmental issues were raised, there was a call for more publicity to be given to the CONAD decisions, since police and official agents continued to hinder the free transportation and distribution of ayahuasca among different religious groups around the country. In response, the Anti-Drug Office (SENAD) representative undertook to supervise more closely the manner in which the government agencies carried out the CONAD recommendations. Once again religious representatives tried to raise the discussion of the supposed need for a representative body charged with enforcing the deontological principles that had been agreed upon, but the representative of SENAD offered little encouragement on the subject.

Conclusion

As has been emphasized here, the current attempts to regulate the religious use of ayahuasca share many points in common with the past process of legitimating the African-Brazilian religions (now seen as such and no longer as deviant cults or sects). One of the points in common is the important role played by sympathetic scientists and other intellectuals interested in the subject. Doctors and anthropologists, with varying degrees of involvement in the actual practice of the religions in question, have played crucial roles in the process. In the past, important Brazilian intellectuals like Nina Rodrigues,

Arthur Ramos, Edison Carneiro, Gilberto Freyre, Jorge Amado and others were of great importance in promoting the legitimacy of the African-Brazilian religions. Through their support for important political and scientific events like the Afro-Brazilian Congresses held in Salvador and Recife during the 1930s, they helped make this a legitimate field of social organization and research.

In more recent times, the ritual use of ayahuasca has also benefited from the attention of many important contemporary Brazilian medical and social scientists who have helped promote the expansion and dissemination of knowledge on the subject, providing important contributions to the reduction of the persisting prejudices that stigmatize the ayahuasca religions and their followers. A few of these scientists took an active part in the Ayahuasca Working Group, others have organized important scientific events or produced significant reflections on the subject.

Another point in common is the atmosphere of rivalry and suspicion that often seems to prevail among the different religious groups, be they African-Brazilian, be they ayahuasca users. This is something one must bear in mind when appraising the efforts made by some members of the Ayahuasca Working Group (GMT Ayahuasca) to supervise the way the different religions use the sacramental brew and to punish those who deviate from the accorded rules. The suggestion that a board of representatives of the different groups should be constituted for this purpose was frequently brought up in the Ayahuasca Working Group discussions and, although the idea seemed to meet with little official favour, the final report presented to CONAD left open a possibility that it might come to be created in the future, should this be deemed necessary.

One of the main reasons for the controversy around this issue is that the creation of such a board would open the way for the different groups, whose longstanding rivalry seems to be a structural element at the very basis of ayahuasca religious field (MacRae 2001; Goulart 2004), to meddle in each other's affairs. Here CEFLURIS would be especially vulnerable, since it is the object of most antagonism. Returning once again to the efforts made in the past by the African-Brazilian religions in their bid for social legitimacy, it may be remembered that one of the strategies adopted in the past to meet police repression was to join forces in creating larger umbrella organizations which claimed to promote the maintenance of the purity of the traditions and prevent their abuse. Since most of the African-Brazilian groups were not particularly orthodox in following the original models from Africa and were fiercely committed to defending their individual autonomy, the various umbrella organizations that came to be created were generally short-lived (Braga 1995: 168–77; Santos 2005: 159–60).

During the working group discussions, such past examples were remembered and it was pointed out that the very processes of fragmentation and stigmatization at work in the ayahuasca religious field, attested to the many differences separating the various religious groups that make ritual use of the brew. These had become particularly apparent during a not very successful attempt, carried out in Rio Branco in 1991, to establish a Charter of Principles to be implemented by all the ayahuasca religious groups functioning at the time. Now again, it was said, there was little to encourage optimism about the possible success of a new board with similar intentions. The SENAD representative also showed little enthusiasm for the idea, reminding the group that it would be constitutionally impossible for a government body to create a board of religious representatives and extend to it sanctioning powers to supervise the use made of ayahuasca by the different religions and thus the final report dealt very briefly with the subject.

In spite of the apparent lack of political will to create a board endowed with sanctioning powers, one should not underestimate the symbolic weight of the support offered by SENAD and CONAD to the establishment of principles and aims that might help guide the relations between ayahuasqueiro religious groups and state institutions in Brazil. The task of enforcing the new principles was finally left to the different informal agents of social control that are usually quite efficient in controlling daily life in society, alongside the more formal legal sanctions that govern the conduct of citizens in general.

In Brazilian society, medicine continues to be held in great prestige in the discussion of religious 'minorities', and the predominance of its supposedly 'rational' positions over those tainted by 'religious irrationalism' is still fiercely defended. But times have changed and the example of the unsuccessful attempts to control African-Brazilian religions, as well as other social developments, seem to have led CONAD to consider it important to consult the different social groups involved, before developing new official policies on the religious use of ayahuasca. One must also consider the groundbreaking importance of the inclusion of the 'independent', neo-ayahuasqueiro groups, which helped to establish that the use of ayahuasca, although restricted to a religious context, should not be seen as a monopoly of certain already established religions, leaving room for the acceptance of future ritual and doctrinal innovations. Thus, although the task of devising and imposing some kind of regulation for the religious use of the brew is a difficult one, due to the wide diversity to be found in this religious field, the attempts being made by the Brazilian government seem like a good and rare example of public policy making, regulating the use of a psychoactive substance that takes into account wider considerations of a sociocultural nature and avoids the usual pharmacological reductionism. In the international scene, this Brazilian approach appears as a pioneering example with wide implications for the general issue of drug control.

Bibliography

Braga, Julio. 1995. *Na gamela do feitiço: repressão e resistência nos candomblés da Bahia*. Salvador: EDUFBA.

Camargo, Cândido Procópio Ferreira. 1973. *Católicos, protestantes, espíritas*. Petrópolis: Ed. Vozes.

Cohen, Stanley. 1972. *Folk Devils and Moral Panics*. London: MacGibbon & Kee Ltd.

Couto, Fernando de La Rocque. 1989. 'Santos e xamãs: estudo do uso ritualizado da ayahuasca por caboclos da Amazônia, e, em particular, no que concerne sua utilização sócio-terapêutica na doutrina do Santo Daime'. Master Thesis in Anthropology, UNB.

Couto, Fernando de La Rocque. 2004. 'Santo Daime: Rito da Ordem'. In B. C. Labate and W. S. Araújo, eds, *O uso ritual da ayahuasca*. Campinas: Mercado das Letras, 2nd edn, pp. 385–411.

Dantas, Beatriz Góis. 1988. *Vovó Nagô e Papai Branco: usos e abusos da África no Brasil*. Rio de Janeiro: Graal.

Goulart, Sandra Lucia. 2004. 'Contrastes e continuidades em uma tradição amazônica: as religiões da ayahuasca'. PhD Thesis in Social Sciences, Unicamp.

Goulart, Sandra Lucia. 2008. 'Estigmas de cultos ayahuasqueiros'. In B. Labate, S. Goulart, M. Fiore, E. MacRae and H. Carneiro (eds.). *Drogas e cultura: novas perspectivas*. Salvador: EDUFBA, pp. 251–88.

Labate, Beatriz. 2004. *A reinvenção do uso da ayahuasca nos centros urbanos*. Campinas: Mercado das Letras.

Labate, Beatriz. 2005. 'Dimensões legais, éticas e políticas da expansão do consumo da ayahuasca'. In B. C.

Labate and S. L. Goulart (eds), *O uso ritual das plantas de poder*. Campinas: Mercado de Letras, 2005, pp. 397, 457.

Labate, Beatriz. 2006. 'Brazilian literature on ayahuasca religions'. In B. C. Labate and E. MacRae, eds, *The Light from the Forest: The Ritual use of Ayahuasca in Brazil. Journal Fieldwork in Religion* 2.3 (published 2008), pp. 200–34.

MacRae, Edward. 1992. *Guiado Pela Lua: xamanismo e uso da ayahuasca no culto do Santo Daime*. São Paulo: Editora Brasiliense. [An English on-line version was published as: *Guided by the Moon: Shamanism and the Ritual Use of Ayahuasca in the Santo Daime Religion in Brazil*. Interdisciplinary Group for Psychoactive Studies – Neip, available at: http://www.neip.info/downloads/edward/ebook.htm]

MacRae, Edward. 1994. 'A importância dos fatores socioculturais na determinação da política oficial sobre o uso ritual da ayahuasca'. In A. Zaluar (ed.). *Drogas e cidadania*. São Paulo: Editora Brasiliense, pp. 31–46.

MacRae, Edward. 1998. 'L'utilisation religieuse de l'Ayahuasca dans le Brésil contemporain'. In *Cahiers du Brésil Contemporain – Religions: Orthodoxie, Heterodoxie et Mysticisme*. Paris: Maison des Sciences de l'Homme, pp. 247–54.

MacRae, Edward. 2001. 'Un llamado por la tolerancia entre las diferentes líneas ayahuasqueras a partir de una visión brasileña'. In *Memoria del segundo Foro interamericano sobre espiritualidad indígena*. Peru: CISEI, pp. 91–98.

MacRae, Edward. 2004a. 'Um pleito pela tolerância entre as diferentes linhas ayahuasqueiras'. In B. C. Labate and W. S. Araújo, eds, *O uso ritual da ayahuasca*. Campinas: Mercado das Letras, 2nd edn, pp. 493–505.

MacRae, Edward. 2004b. 'The ritual use of ayahuasca in three Brazilian religions'. In R. Coomber and N. South, eds, *Drug Use and Cultural Contexts: Beyond the West*. London: Free Association Books, pp. 27–45.

MacRae, Edward. 2009. 'O uso ritual de substâncias psicoativas na religião do Santo Daime como um exemplo de redução de danos'. In: A. Nery Filho, E. MacRae, L. A. Tavares, and M. Rego, eds, *Toxicomanias: Incidências clínicas e socioantropológicas*. Salvador: EDUFBA, pp. 23–36.

Monteiro da Silva, Clodomir. 1983. 'O palácio de Juramidam: Santo Daime um ritual de transcendência e despoluição'. Master Thesis in Cultural Anthropology, Universidade Federal de Pernambuco.

Pantoja, Mariana and Conceição, Osmildo. 2010. 'The use of ayahuasca among rubber tappers of the Alto Juruá'. In B. C. Labate and E. MacRae, eds, *Ayahuasca, Ritual and Religion in Brazil*. London: Equinox.

Sá, Domingos Bernardo Gialluisi da Silva. 2010. 'Ayahuasca: The consciousness of Expansion'. In B. C. Labate, and E. Macrae, eds, *Ayahuasca, Ritual and Religion in Brazil*. London: Equinox.

Santos, Jocélio Teles dos. 2005. *O poder da cultura e a cultura no poder: a disputa simbólica da herança da cultura negra no Brasil*. Salvador: EDUFBA.

Schwarcz, Lilia Moritz. 1993. *O espetáculo das raças: cientistas, instituições e questão racial no Brasil*. São Paulo: Companhia das Letras.

Official Documents

Conselho Nacional Antidrogras. 2004. Resolução No. 5, November 4th 2004. Diário Oficial da União, 8/11/2004, Seção 1, Brasília.

Conselho Nacional Antidrogras. 2006. Relatório Final do Grupo Multidisciplinar de Trabalho: GMT Ayahuasca. Brasília. (An English translation is available at: http://www.bialabate.net/pdf/texts/gmt_conad_english.pdf)

10

The treatment and handling of substance dependence with ayahuasca: reflections on current and future research

Beatriz Caiuby Labate, Rafael Guimarães dos Santos, Brian Anderson,
Marcelo Mercante and Paulo César Ribeiro Barbosa

This text presents a series of reflections on the therapeutic potential of the ritual use of ayahuasca in the treatment and handling of substance dependence problems. Anthropological and psychiatric data on the ritual use of ayahuasca for 'healing' dependence in psychotherapeutic centers (in Peru and Brazil), as well as in ayahuasca religions (in Brazil), are reviewed and critiqued. Methodological, ethical and political considerations for current and future research in this area are then discussed, and an interdisciplinary agenda for studies on the use of ayahuasca to treat or handle substance dependence is proposed.

Introduction

Problems related to dependence[1] on psychoactive substances, both legal and illegal, pose serious challenges for international public health. According to the World Health Organization (WHO), tobacco not only has a high dependence potential, but it is also the cause of one in ten adult deaths worldwide (WHO 2008). Also, the use of many illegal substances with significant dependence potential, such as cocaine, heroin and methamphetamine, carries risks such as overdose, the transmission of HIV, and the exacerbation of other medical and psychiatric conditions (UNODC 2007).

---

1. The concept of 'dependence' can be critiqued from various points of view (for a discussion from a social sciences perspective, see Fiore 2007). We have decided to use this term, however, because of its wide circulation in the specialized biomedical literature and because it is a relevant category in the native discourses discussed here. In these latter discourses there frequently appears also the term 'addict' [*viciado*], which evokes images of moral deviance, perversion and illness, as well as often functioning as an accusatory category (Velho 1987), and was therefore left aside here.

A number of different pharmacological and psychotherapeutic interventions are used by health professionals in the treatment of substance dependence (Sadock and Sadock 2005). Self-help groups, such as Alcoholics Anonymous and Narcotics Anonymous, as well as therapeutic communities and religious groups, are dedicated to reducing the harmful use of psychoactive substances (Galanter 2006; Silveira and Moreira 2006; Sanchez and Nappo 2007).

A particularly interesting (and today relatively unknown) chapter in the treatment of dependence was formed around the use of psychedelics[2] as adjuncts to psychotherapy during the 1950s and 1960s (Grinspoon and Bakalar 1979).[3] Halpern, in careful reviews of the subject (1996, 2007), argues that the imprecise criteria for defining dependence and recovery, as well as the diversity of the procedures adopted in the various clinical trials, make it difficult to reach definitive conclusions about the efficacy of the psychedelic-assisted treatments developed in that era. He suggests, however, that the forced interruption of these studies in the beginning of the 1970s prevented the appropriate follow-up of promising initial evidence. Due to the limitations of current strategies for dependence treatment (Silveira and Moreira 2006) and contemporary rethinking of the War on Drugs, there has been a slow but growing resurgence of interest in the use of psychedelics as therapeutic agents in the treatment of dependence on psychoactive substances.

For example, ketamine, which has psychedelic properties at sub-anesthetic doses, has been used with promising, although preliminary, results in clinical trials for the treatment of heroin and alcohol dependence (Krupitsky and Kolp 2007). There is also growing evidence of substantial effects of ibogaine – a psychedelic extracted from the African shrub *Tabernanthe iboga* – in the relief of craving associated with heroin and other

---

2 The term 'psychedelic' denotes an agent that provokes the 'manifestation of the mind' (Osmond 1957); in this article we have chosen to use the term 'psychedelic' in place of 'hallucinogen' to designate this class of psychoactive substances for reasons rooted in both the biomedical and social sciences. On the one hand, restricting oneself to the domain of perceptual alterations, 'hallucinogen' suggests detrimental effects to the wide range of affective and cognitive functions known to be influenced by this type of substance (Graeff 1984). The term 'hallucinogen' is also questionable because psychedelic perceptual alterations are normally distinguished from ordinary reality and attributed to the effects of the psychoactive substance, which thus does not fit the classic meaning of hallucinations as 'perceptions that the perceiver himself firmly believes indicate the existence of a corresponding object or event, but for which other observers can find no objective basis' (Barron *et al.* 1964: 29). On the other hand, the term 'hallucinogen' is not adequate from a native point of view because, classically, 'hallucination' suggests that the affective and cognitive alterations caused by this type of substance are of a detrimental or pathological nature (Goulart *et al.* 2005), whereas many ayahuasca users would claim that their mental faculties are enhanced, rather than hampered, by ayahuasca. Finally, to complicate matters further, the distinction between 'illusion', a perceptual alteration that is distinguished from reality, and 'hallucination', a perceptual alteration that is not distinguished from reality, is not always applicable in the case of ayahuasca, as many ayahuasca users believe that their perceptions while under the influence of ayahuasca are indeed real, if not more than real.

3 In the 1950s Osmond and Hoffer, working in Saskatchewan, Canada, developed psychedelic therapies for the treatment of alcoholism with LSD (Hoffer 1967). Stanislav Grof, in turn, adopted the use of LSD to treat heroin dependent individuals in Prague, and later in the United States. Psychedelic therapies were characterized by the ingestion of a large dose of a psychedelic substance with the goal of provoking a 'peak experience', a profound mystical experience capable of generating a radical transformation (Grof 2001). Psycholytic therapy, another model, used primarily in Europe, was marked by the use of ordinary psychoanalytic techniques (in group or individual sessions) in conjunction with the consumption of small doses of LSD or psilocybin (Grinspoon and Bakalar 1979; Grob 2002; Passie 2007).

opiates (Alper and Lotsof 2007). The ritual consumption of peyote in the Native American Church, and of ayahuasca in various contexts, have also attracted the attention of specialists as potential tools for the treatment of alcoholism and problems resulting from the dependence on numerous other substances (Albaugh and Anderson 1974; Dobkin de Rios *et al.* 2002).

The aim of this article is to consider the therapeutic potential of the ritual use of ayahuasca – a dimethyltryptamine (DMT) containing a decoction originating among the indigenous peoples of the western Amazon basin – in the treatment and handling of problems related to dependence on psychoactive substances. 'Treatment' is here defined as a systematic intervention for substance dependence; the 'handling' of substance dependence is considered to comprise non-systematic interventions carried out secondary to a religious practice. We bring together evidence from the specialist literature and from our field observations of two types of institutions engaged in treating or handling substance dependence: psychotherapeutic centers that combine elements of biomedicine with the ceremonial use of ayahuasca, such as Takiwasi (in Peru) and IDEAA (in Brazil); and Brazilian ayahuasca religions, namely Santo Daime and the União do Vegetal. As it will be seen, it is no simple task to analyze the therapeutic potentials of ayahuasca, particularly for mental health problems. We summarize and critique the available evidence and we conclude by presenting several methodological, ethical and political considerations, which we feel are essential for the development of future interdisciplinary research into the question of how ayahuasca may be used to ameliorate substance dependence.

Two psychotherapeutic centers for the complementary treatment of substance dependence with ayahuasca

There are currently two main substance dependence treatment centers that use ayahuasca: the Takiwasi Center for the Treatment of Drug and Alcohol Addiction and the Research of Traditional Medicines,[4] in Tarapoto, Peru, and the Institute of Applied Amazonian Ethnopsychology [Instituto de Etnopsicología Amazónica Aplicada] (IDEAA), located on the banks of the Prato Raso creek, a tributary of the Igarapé Mapiá, near the Santo Daime community Céu do Mapiá in the municipality of Pauini, Amazonas state, Brazil. There are reports of other centers, groups, and individuals who treat substance dependence with ayahuasca, although this is not their central focus. Both Takiwasi and IDEAA practice particular forms of complementary medicine and neither has an institutional alliance with biomedical dependence treatment centers.

Takiwasi

Takiwasi was co-founded in 1992 by Jacques Mabit, a French doctor and naturalized Peruvian. The local *curanderos*, doctors, psychologists and therapists who work there explore

---

4. www.takiwasi.com

the curative potentials of Western therapies together with techniques from traditional Amazonian therapies, using ayahuasca, herbal emetics, *dietas* (isolation in the forest with fasting and the ingestion of various plants), *sopladas* (blowing tobacco smoke or *agua florida* [perfumed water]), *chupadas* (the sucking out of a pathogenic object),[5] communitarian life, manual and artistic activities, and psychotherapy. The primary emphasis is on the treatment of dependence on cocaine paste, an intermediary in the cocaine manufacturing process, which is cheap and thus widely consumed in the region. Dependence on alcohol and heroin, among other substances, is also attended to (Mabit 1996a, 1996b; Mabit *et al.* 1996; Mabit, 2002, 2004, 2007).

According to Mabit (personal communication, March 2009), since its foundation Takiwasi has treated more than 700 patients. In one of his various writings Mabit presents the results of an uncontrolled pilot study, conducted by Giove (2002), of the center's first seven years of activity (1992–8); these results were that, of a sample of 211 patients, after treatment 31 percent were feeling 'well' and 23 percent 'better', while 23 percent were 'the same or worse', and the condition of the remaining 23 percent was unknown.[6] Mabit adds that if only the patients who completed the entire program are considered, the rate of positive results increases to 67 percent. Although Mabit's various writings indicate beneficial effects of Takiwasi's treatments, so far no investigator has elaborated a research protocol which would permit the collection of data with sufficient scientific credibility to verify these claims. Paradoxically, while the center largely works in the style of the local *curanderos* who do not consider such studies to be necessary for proving their therapies to be efficacious, Takiwasi would need to utilize such studies in order to gain the legitimacy it seeks within the realm of international academic debates about the utility of using ayahuasca in the treatment of substance dependence.

IDEAA

Another psychotherapeutic center, similar to Takiwasi, is the Institute of Applied Amazonian Ethnopsychology (IDEAA), created by the Spanish psychiatrist Josep María Fábregas. IDEAA combines therapeutic techniques derived from Amerindian shamanic traditions, the Santo Daime religion (see below), Gestalt therapy, and humanistic and transpersonal psychology (Villaescusa, 2007; Fernandez, in press). While IDEAA is chiefly concerned with problems related to dependence, the center also receives patients with psychological and physical disorders, as well as otherwise healthy clients in search of self-awareness or personal development. The Institute's therapists and 'users' (as the clients are known within the institution) live together in a small communitarian group.

IDEAA's therapeutic program includes manual labor, sessions with ayahuasca, and

---

5. These features are characteristic of Peruvian *vegetalismo*. For an overview of the subject see Luna (1986).

6. These terms are defined by Mabit to mean the following: 'well' – 'satisfactory development, with the problems apparently resolved thanks to a true structural change at various levels in the patient's life'; 'better' – 'satisfactory development with structural changes evident, but vestiges of the original problem remain'; 'the same or worse' – 'a return to using the substance(s), albeit in a more discreet form, without a convincing structural change, and frequent exchange of previous substances for alcohol' (2002: 31).

group integration sessions, as well as interactions with the neighboring Santo Daime community Céu do Mapiá. According to one of the resident therapists, Xavier Fernandez (in press), the principal objective of IDEAA is to engage the individual in a process of introspection and self-awareness. Thus, the program also includes individual sessions with ayahuasca, as well as Eastern contemplative practices, such as Zen meditation and yoga. No quantitative measures of IDEAA's dependence treatment efforts have been divulged so far. Recently, however, a qualitative research project on the institution has been started, based primarily on user narratives of their experiences, with a follow-up on their condition one year after the end of their treatment. These data are currently being processed (Villaescusa, 2007; Fernandez, in press).

Although both Takiwasi and IDEAA treat Western patients suffering from substance dependence by using complementary approaches centered on the ritual use of ayahuasca, several differences between the two centers deserve mention. Takiwasi is older, more established and has generated more visibility and publications (see Presser-Velder 2000; Denys 2005; Sieber 2007; Bustos, 2008; among others) than IDEAA, which maintains a lower international profile. The Takiwasi program is relatively long, obliging their patients to stay for nine months, whereas that of IDEAA can vary from a few weeks to several months; and while Takiwasi's activities are almost exclusively directed at dependence treatment, the same cannot be said of IDEAA. Furthermore, the Takiwasi model follows more closely that of a biomedical addiction treatment clinic, utilizing isolation, rigid discipline and a stern atmosphere, while the IDEAA model is more reminiscent of a spiritual retreat and has a freer and more flexible ambiance. At Takiwasi, ayahuasca sessions are conducted weekly and are based on the Peruvian *vegetalismo ayahuasquero* healing tradition, with strong elements of Catholicism (including exorcist prayer); IDEAA, on the other hand, offers rather simple ayahuasca ceremonies that appear to be influenced by the Santo Daime religion as well as the Western psychedelic and psycholytic therapy styles that emerged in the 1950–70s. While neither Takiwasi nor IDEAA has produced reliable quantitative data on their treatment success rates, people continue to seek out these centers for a complementary approach to dealing with substance dependence. Future research on the work of these and other such psychotherapeutic centers needs not only to include quantitative measures of abstinence and remission, but also to explore how distinct beliefs and ritual styles reflect and influence the process of dependence, its conceptualization as a 'problem' or 'disease', and the resultant strategies used to treat it.

Two ayahuasca religions and the handling of dependence

The Brazilian ayahuasca religions comprise three principal traditions: Santo Daime (with two main branches, Alto Santo and CEFLURIS), Barquinha, and the União do Vegetal (UDV).[7] In general, these groups are all heirs to a single religious and cultural complex

---

7. For general information on these three groups, see Goulart (2004), Labate and Araújo (2004), Labate and MacRae (2006) and Labate et al. (2009), among others. For information on smaller, neo-ayahuasquero

which includes Amerindian shamanism, Christianity (above all the folk Catholic expressions of Brazil's northeast), the Afro-Brazilian religions, esoteric currents of European origin (such as Kardecist spiritism), and, importantly, a general culture of 'spiritual healing' and 'spiritual evolution' centered around the use of ayahuasca and the religious teachings of the groups' founders. Here we discuss Santo Daime (specifically the CEFLURIS branch) and the UDV – the two largest ayahuasca religions, with around 4000 and 15,000 members respectively (Labate *et al.* 2009). It is important to note that these religions do not follow formal protocols when dealing with dependence problems, and hence participation in their ceremonies should not be seen as constituting a substance dependence treatment. They are, however, often engaged in the informal handling of substance abuse and dependence issues, due to the fact that (according to their members) their organizations are frequently sought out by people suffering from such afflictions. Given these similarities, Santo Daime and the UDV nevertheless have quite different drug cultures, or different styles of dealing with problematic and non-problematic drug uses; these cultural differences will be touched upon below. The existing academic studies on the handling of substance dependence in Santo Daime and the UDV are here presented in chronological order, by religion, so that the reader can follow how this field of investigation has developed over time.

Santo Daime

Santo Daime was founded by Raimundo Irineu Serra, or Mestre Irineu (1892–1971), in the early 1930s in the Brazilian state of Acre. It encompasses two principal religious denominations: the set of groups generically identified as the 'Alto Santo line' and the set commonly called the 'Santo Daime or Padrinho Sebastião (Mota de Melo) line', with most groups in the latter line being linked to the Raimundo Irineu Serra Eclectic Center of the Universal Flowing Light [Centro Eclético da Fluente Luz Universal Raimundo Irineu Serra] (CEFLURIS), recently renamed the Church of the Eclectic Cult of the Universal Flowing Light Patron Sebastião Mota de Melo [Igreja do Culto Eclético da Fluente Luz Universal Patrono Sebastião Mota de Melo].[8] CEFLURIS has spread to several countries around the world, and its centers are generally characterized by a rather loose structural organization and a high rate of membership turnover. This group is also characterized by the quite eclectic and dynamic nature of its cosmology.

In our fieldwork over the past decade we have observed that in Santo Daime, especially in the lineage of Padrinho Sebastião, the consumption of illegal psychoactive substances

---

groups located in urban areas, many of whom have splintered off of one of these three main traditions and now function autonomously, see Labate (2004). One of these groups, the Associação Beneficente Luz de Salomão (ABLUSA), in Mogi das Cruzes (São Paulo) is known to have run a small social program with ayahuasca rituals for homeless individuals, including those with substance dependence problems (see Labate 2004; Mercante 2007); this program started in 1999 but has since ceased to exist according to reports collected by us in 2007–8.

8. In this text, however, we continue to use 'CEFLURIS' because in practice this denomination continues to predominate among both members and academics despite the official change. For more information about this group, see MacRae (1992), Goulart (1996), Groisman (1999), Cemin (2001) and http://www.santo-daime.org among others.

and the problematic or dependent use of alcohol are looked upon with disapproval. In general, the majority of Daimistas (Santo Daime members) do not drink alcohol; some say it is 'incompatible with Daime' to do so. However, moderate drinking is not forbidden, just as there is no official ideology forbidding the use of cigarettes. Within the Daime groups, there is a kind of common sense notion that 'Daime cures addiction to drugs and alcohol'.

The topic of handling substance dependence in a Santo Daime community is touched upon briefly by Isabel Santana de Rose (2005) in her master's thesis in anthropology on Céu da Mantiqueira, a Daimista church in Camanducaia (Minas Gerais state). According to Rose, this group has developed practices particularly focused on the recovery from substance dependence. Various psychiatrists and other health professionals participate in this church, which is known in the region and in the Daimista community at large as a healing center.[9] A few initial 'successes' stimulated the group to create a specialized clinic in concert with the center's ritual space in order to elaborate their substance dependence work. Accounts collected indicate that the clinic only operated for a short time before it was abandoned.

Only one explicit study of recovery from substance dependence in Santo Daime exists thus far (Labate et al., in press). In this preliminary study, conducted with 83 members of CEFLURIS between the ages of 18 and 40 (41 men and 42 women), 90 percent of the individuals identified as dependent according to DSM-IV criteria self-reported abandoning their dependence on one or more psychoactive substances after a period of participating in Daime rituals. These rates of 'recovery' should, however, be viewed with caution, since the study has important limitations, as the authors themselves note. These limitations include: the lack of a control group to compare to the surveyed Daimistas; the absence of subjects who tried unsuccessfully to treat their dependence and subsequently left the church; the very broad definition of 'recovery' used in the study, which included those individuals who had discontinued the use of merely one substance even though they had reported initially being dependent on two or more substances; and the exclusion of Cannabis consumption from the analysis of substance use patterns (we return to the particular issue of Cannabis below).

União do Vegetal

The Union of the Vegetal Beneficent Spiritist Center [Centro Espírita Beneficente União do Vegetal] (CEBUDV), or União do Vegetal (UDV), was founded in 1961 in Porto Velho, Rondônia state, by José Gabriel da Costa (1922–71), also known as Mestre Gabriel.[10] The UDV is the largest of the three ayahuasca religions, with about 15,000 'disciples' (members) in Brazil, the United States, and Spain, in addition to other countries where it is just

---

9. The Céu de Maria church, in São Paulo, is also known within the Daimista ranks as a place that often receives drug dependent individuals from various social strata. In this group, the local comandante (religious leader) is known to speak of having been 'cured' of cocaine addiction through Daime. It is also said that a lot of poor 'junkies' from São Paulo show up there looking for help. No formal investigations of this church have been carried out so far.

10. For more information, see: Andrade (1995); Brissac (1999); Goulart (2004); Labate and Pacheco (in press), among others.

establishing a presence (Labate *et al.* 2009). The UDV is the most hierarchical, organized and bureaucratic of the ayahuasca religions; it also has demonstrated the greatest interest in legitimizing the use of ayahuasca from a scientific and biomedical perspective (ibid.).

In the União do Vegetal, the use of all psychoactive substances, including legal ones such as alcohol and tobacco, is strongly discouraged.[11] As stated in an official publication of the religion, 'The União do Vegetal categorically condemns the use of drugs, alcoholic drinks, and other vices. It considers them incompatible with spiritual evolution' (CEBUDV 1989: 2, our translation). In general its members neither smoke nor drink, and the consumption of all illegal drugs is sternly condemned. There is a strong emphasis on the idea that the use of Vegetal (ayahuasca) in the UDV 'helps in recovering from vices' and that it is important to 'help addicts'. During sessions, disciples commonly ask permission to speak on various topics, including personal problems such as their difficulty in quitting smoking or stopping using illegal substances. On these occasions they are advised by the *mestres* (high-ranking members) and encouraged by the group. A document entitled the *Regimento Interno* (Internal Regiment), and which is read aloud at each ritual session, states that should a disciple be seen in a drunken state, he or she will be warned by the center's leadership, and if the incident is repeated they may receive a 'punishment' – the gravest of these being the revocation of the right to communion of the Vegetal. A disciple may also be punished for the use of illegal psychoactive substances, though in practice this occurs less frequently. If a disciple smokes, drinks, or consumes illegal substances, he or she will likely not advance within the group's internal hierarchy.

There currently exist four small studies that have analyzed, directly or indirectly, the issue of handling substance dependence in the União do Vegetal: the Hoasca Project by Grob *et al.* (1996, 2004); a master's thesis in mental health by Labigalini (1998); a study of UDV adolescents led by Doering-Silveira *et al.* (2005); and a master's thesis in social sciences by Ricciardi (2008). The study by Grob *et al.* (1996) was conducted with 15 members of the UDV who had drunk ayahuasca ritually for at least ten years. According to the authors, five of the UDV members had histories of excessive consumption of alcohol under the criteria of the International Statistical Classification of Diseases and Related Health Problems (ICD-10) and the Diagnostic and Statistical Manual of Mental Disorders (DSM-III-R). In addition, 11 members reported a history of moderate to serious use of alcohol before joining the UDV, and five of these described incidents of violent behavior (two of them had been arrested as a result of their violence). The research also revealed that four individuals reported abuse of other psychoactive substances, including cocaine and amphetamines, and that eight of the 11 with histories of moderate to serious alcohol use and abuse of other psychoactives were dependent on nicotine at the time of their first encounter with the UDV. All of the cases of substance abuse and dependence, however, were reported to have resolved without relapse after these individuals joined the UDV (Grob *et al.*, 1996, 2004).

Building on the work of Grob *et al.*, psychiatrist Eliseu Labigalini, Jr. (1998) developed a qualitative study of the subjective experiences of four individuals who had presented with serious alcohol dependence, two of whom were also dependent on cocaine, before

---

11. This does not include the psychoactive substances prescribed legally by physicians, such as antidepressants or other such medications.

joining the UDV. According to Labigalini, the four stopped consuming the psychoactive substances a few months after beginning to attend UDV rituals. Among the study's conclusions is the claim of the author that the interviewees did not substitute their dependence on alcohol for dependence on ayahuasca or the religious group – an idea likely to be suggested in the world of dependence research. Indeed, Labigalini affirms that the use of ayahuasca in which the UDV members came to periodically engage through the rituals did not present the psychopathological features of a 'compulsion'. Because it is based on short-term fieldwork, however, this study should be viewed with caution.

In the study led by Doering-Silveira *et al.* (2005), 40 adolescents who used ayahuasca in the UDV were compared with a group of 40 controls across various parameters, including the use of psychoactive substances over their lifetime, the previous year, and the previous month. No differences were found between the groups with respect to lifetime use. In the year prior to the study, significantly less use of alcohol was reported by the UDV adolescents than by those in the control group. Reported use of alcohol was also significantly lower among the UDV adolescents in the month preceding the study, as was the use of amphetamines. In the discussion, the authors indicate that despite their early exposure to the consumption of a psychoactive substance (ayahuasca), the UDV adolescents did not seem to be predisposed to a greater incidence of psychoactive substance abuse; on the contrary, the authors argue that their participation in a religious organization may offer the adolescents protection against the problematic consumption of psychoactive substances. They note, however, that the limitations resulting from the study's sample size did not permit the investigators to assess the impact that 'dimensions of religiousness' might have on the results. They emphasize, moreover, that the study's retrospective design can only establish correlations between the events studied, and not relationships of cause and effect.

Ricciardi (2008) conducted an ethnographic study of experiences of transformation, relief, and healing in the UDV. The study addresses the question of dependence, arguing that the context of the UDV is important in its prevention. According to Ricciardi, five of the 11 people she interviewed (each with between two and 13 years' experience with the UDV) reported having had, at some point in their lives, problems related to the use of psychoactive substances. All of them claimed that their participation in the UDV led to some improvement in their situation and reported having been 'cured' of dependence (p. 116). Although the interview reports collected by Ricciardi were not verified with standardized diagnostic questionnaires,[12] thus making her qualitative findings difficult to generalize, they do nevertheless provide an intimate glimpse of this phenomenon that may serve as a lead for more standardized studies in the future.

---

12. While standardized questionnaires are among the most widely used and informative tools employed in scientific studies within the fields of psychiatry and epidemiology, the validity of these instruments for measuring and assessing complex behavioral patterns, such as problematic substance use, is the object of continual discussion and debate. We will not take up this issue here, rather we merely wish to draw attention to the fact that the criteria of psychiatric diagnoses are complex, and not static; they must be reevaluated and updated constantly. For a discussion of the DSM-IV and epidemiological studies of drugs, see MacRae and Vidal (2006).

We have presented here two religions whose members regularly consume ayahuasca in a ritual setting and many of whom report spiritual and physical health benefits, including a decrease in use of, and even the cessation of dependence on, psychoactive substances that they view to be harmful. Only a few academic studies have been conducted on the recovery experiences of these groups' members, and the methodologies used include participant-observation, interviews and surveys. Importantly, all quantitative data collected has been derived from exploratory studies with small sample sizes, and control groups were not always used. In general, these studies report that among Santo Daime and UDV members there exists a common culture of 'spiritual healing' and 'spiritual evolution' that includes discouraging the abuse of psychoactive substances and attending to people seeking relief from dependence. At the same time, there are important differences between these two groups regarding how they deal with psychoactive substance use. The CEFLURIS Santo Daime line has an entheogenic spirit, being more interested in experimenting and exchanging knowledge with other psychoactive sacrament-using groups in the Americas and elsewhere; some members also had previously used, or currently use but in an extra-official manner, *Cannabis* as a sacrament (see below). The UDV condemns the use of any psychoactive substance other than ayahuasca, illegal or not. Another major difference is that in CEFLURIS there is a general healing culture where Daime is seen as a supernatural and powerful remedy for all sorts of diseases – a true panacea. The UDV, on the other hand, maintains a view of the Vegetal as a substance to be more strictly used to 'promote mental concentration and spiritual evolution'; the official discourse of the UDV states that Hoasca is not for the healing of the body. The institution represents itself as a Spiritist-Christian doctrine rather than as a popular healing or shamanic-curanderistic tradition, and it openly seeks legitimacy from the medical and scientific community (see Labate *et al.* 2009).

Ultimately, and despite their differences, both Santo Daime and the UDV endorse a distinction between the labels 'sacrament' (i.e., ayahuasca) and 'drug' (i.e., other psychoactive substances), their members differentiate themselves from drug users, and they employ a discourse of 'curing drug addiction' as a means of self-legitimization (see section below). Given the complex elements at play in these two Brazilian ayahuasca religions' practices of handling dependence problems, future investigations into this phenomenon need to consider several methodological, ethical and political questions such as those addressed in next two sections of this text.

Scientific research and legality: the case of Santa Maria in CEFLURIS

The relationship between research and legality is a question that must be confronted by scientific studies in this area. Investigations whose objective is to analyze the effectiveness of practices involving ayahuasca consumption in the treatment and handling of dependence must take into account the history of persecution of ayahuasca users in Brazil (MacRae 1992; Goulart 2004; Labate 2005; MacRae 2008, among others). This historical legacy may influence the statements offered by the members of these religions, since the fear that their highly valued practices could become prohibited or socially stigmatized still weighs heavily upon these groups. The question of ayahuasca's therapeutic efficacy is particularly relevant to the field of ayahuasca studies and practices, not only because of its strong presence in the very cosmologies of some of the groups, but also because this could potentially allow for the differentiation of ayahuasca from other psychoactive substances (i.e., 'Ayahuasca is not a hallucinogen, but a sacrament that cures addicts').

An especially important issue to be considered for future investigations on the effects of ayahuasca use on psychoactive substance consumption is the use of *Cannabis sativa* within the CEFLURIS branch of Santo Daime, where it is known as Santa Maria. The political and ethical difficulties inherent in our broaching this subject here are problems shared by many studies involving the use of illegal substances (MacRae and Vidal 2006). During a certain period, Santa Maria was used regularly in the rituals of the Padrinho Sebastião lineage as a religious sacrament, above all in the Amazon forest (Monteiro da Silva 1985; MacRae 1998, 2008, among others). However, as CEFLURIS and groups identified with the spiritual teachings of Padrinho Sebastião spread to Brazil's major cities, the use of ayahuasca in Brazil became institutionalized and regulated within a legal framework while *Cannabis sativa* remained illegal. Eventually, CEFLURIS's national leadership decided to prohibit religious rituals with the plant.

The highest leader of CEFLURIS, Padrinho Alfredo Gregório de Melo, told us the following in a 2008 interview at the Céu de Maria church in São Paulo:

> We did a study of Santa Maria to cure the addictions [*des-viciar*] of people who used marijuana. Papa [that is, Padrinho Sebastião, his father] received [divine] instructions and we began to take this plant back from its worldly use ... we began to learn to use it as a spiritual sacrament ... a power plant ... Using it with respect, Santa Maria can heal, too ... This was during the time of [CEFLURIS communities at] Colônia Cinco Mil and Rio do Ouro ... When the law clarified that its use was illegal [around 1982], we stopped doing our study. That's why we say we didn't 'close' Santa Maria, because the truth is that it was never 'open' ... It was just an experimental period ... Now, in this time of legalization, of normalization [of ayahuasca], we make a point of not permitting its use.

Other informants we spoke with, however, indicated that Santa Maria was still used frequently at Céu do Mapiá in the years following the termination of the 'study'. Whatever the case may be, the important thing to highlight here is that, as a consequence of an internal prohibition on the use of Santa Maria, the substance came to be consumed in an irregular, personal, and extra-official fashion (outside the context of ritual) by some members because it was already deeply rooted in the group's religious imaginary. This kind of use has promoted the social stigmatization of this Daimista denomination within the Brazilian ayahuasca field (Goulart 2004; Labate 2004; MacRae 2008).

Owing to the dynamic, ambivalent and partly conflicted nature of CEFLURIS's relationship with Santa Maria, and all the difficulties associated with the consumption of an illegal substance, the authors of the above-mentioned study on 'recovery' in CEFLURIS decided not to include *Cannabis sativa* in the survey of substance use administered in their study (Labate *et al.*, in press). However, despite the possibility of offending the group's religious sensibilities, a more incisive study would involve an investigation of members' patterns of Santa Maria consumption – be they therapeutic, recreational, or abusive in nature. Such a study could also attempt a contextualized analysis of what said categories of consumption patterns mean – an issue that is not always sufficiently problematized in the specialist literature.

In the discourse of Padrinho Alfredo cited above, there is a distinction between 'sacrament' (Santa Maria) and 'drug' (marijuana), extending to this substance a significance derived from several of the ayahuasca religions' central argument about ayahuasca – that its proper ritual use is as a tool for humankind's salvation and healing. We suggest, as a hypothesis to be tested in future research, that the use of Santa Maria in conjunction with Daime within CEFLURIS might serve to help Daimistas recover from dependence on other psychoactive substances (e.g., crack or alcohol), perhaps even in a synergistic manner. Some incipient studies, including one of Brazilians who reported using *Cannabis* to overcome their dependence on crack, and another study of heroin users in the Netherlands who substituted the use of *Cannabis* for heroin, suggest that *Cannabis* may potentially be used with some success in the recovery from dependence on certain psychoactive substances (Sifaneck and Kaplan 1995; Grinspoon and Bakalar 1997; Labigalini *et al.* 1999; Lenza 2007). These studies, though far from providing a definitive judgment on the utility of *Cannabis* for alleviating dependence on other substances, do provide theoretical leads in support of our hypothesis.

On the other hand, it should be asked also whether some Daimistas have abandoned a problematic pattern of use of one psychoactive substance, but maintain problematic use patterns of *Cannabis*. The possibility that this occurs in at least some individuals, and whether there exists a noticeable trend towards this behavior, may be verified through future investigations. Such research should also take into account the specific psychoactive properties of ayahuasca and of *Cannabis*, and the implications of this interaction for lived experience and for the treatment of dependence in particular, as well as the effects perceived and attributed by Daimistas to each of these plants, and their understanding of possible problems stemming from their use. The question of the interaction of ayahuasca and *Cannabis* also allows us to consider the close theoretical relationship between the consumption of supposedly recreational psychoactive substances used in an un-structured way, and the consumption of substances held to be sacred in ways described as structured. Building on the work of Edward MacRae (2008), our field observations also suggest that, in effect, the illegality of *Cannabis* and the legality of ayahuasca in Brazil influence the consumption patterns of these substances. The fact that *Cannabis* use is prohibited prevents the development and stabilization of a particular set of sacred symbols around this substance and prevents the establishment of ritual controls for its use, unlike what occurred in the case of Daime, where the religious pantheon was creatively developed and highly ritualized forms of cultivation, distribution and consumption were consolidated.

This question might also be analyzed through a systematic comparison between CEFLURIS's use of Santa Maria in Brazil and in the Netherlands, where the substance enjoys relative legal freedom. Groisman (2000), in an unpublished dissertation, discusses Santo Daime's expansion to the Netherlands, arguing that in the European context Santa Maria was taken to be an integral part of the Daimista tradition, with a status on a par with that of Daime. Although he treats the use of Santa Maria in the Netherlands as, in large measure, equivalent to its use in the Brazilian context (which, in our view, is imprecise), his observations do allow us a glimpse into the very dynamic processes of transformation and reinvention that the use of Santa Maria is undergoing in the Dutch Daime churches.

In this context of greater legal liberty there seems to be the beginnings of both a spontaneous development of strong mechanisms of symbolization and of strategies for establishing efficient controls over the use of Santa Maria. According to Groisman (2000), the Santa Maria used in Dutch Daimista rituals generally comes from personal gardens and its preparation for consumption involves a ritualized effort on the part of the church members. Moreover, Groisman points to innovations such as holding introductory meetings with Santa Maria for novices (before they drink Daime), and the custom of smoking officially at intervals during the religious ceremonies. We have not done fieldwork in the Netherlands, but we speculate that in the Dutch Daimista context the patterns of *Cannabis* use and abuse vary significantly from those present in Brazil partly due to the plant's different legal status in the two countries. Despite the many legal and methodological challenges posed by such a design, we believe that a natural experiment comparing CEFLURIS members' use of Santa Maria in a ritual/semi-legal context (e.g., the Netherlands) versus in a non-ritual/illegal context (e.g., Brazil) could help clarify empirically the relationship between drug prohibition and the degree to which more integrated, less problematic cultures of psychoactive substance consumption can develop. CEFLURIS would seem to provide a privileged setting for such an investigation. The importance of the legality of a substance's use should not, however, be over-estimated as it is just one variable among many others that can influence how a substance is used. Within Brazil, as within the Netherlands, there of course exist different patterns of Santa Maria consumption among CEFLURIS members. The legal status of a psychoactive substance certainly cannot explain all aspects of how it comes to be handled and consumed, but this factor nevertheless needs to be paid close attention in investigations of substance use.

Considerations for an interdisciplinary research agenda

As greater numbers of people seek out ayahuasca-using psychotherapeutic centers and religious groups because of problems with psychoactive substance dependence, investigators in the health sciences will likely soon feel the necessity to weigh in more formally on the debates about such uses of ayahuasca. New scientific studies may arise which attempt to investigate the claims of these groups about the efficacy and safety of their practices. Hypothetically, this could eventually lead to larger, more clinically significant studies that include, for example, randomized double-blind experimental protocols with control groups. Should such research be conducted within the context of religious, shamanic, psychotherapeutic, and/or other non-strictly medical practices? Or should they be carried out in the secular laboratories and procedure rooms of modern hospitals? We propose that future studies of the therapeutic potentials of ayahuasca would benefit greatly from an interdisciplinary approach that makes use of the available anthropological data on the ritual uses of ayahuasca when dealing with the necessary methodological and practical considerations that such research would demand. We will not enter here into a detailed discussion of contemporary biomedical experimental methodologies; rather we will outline broad interdisciplinary questions that we argue should be considered for an agenda for future research into the use of ayahuasca in the treatment and handling of dependence problems.[13]

A basic challenge for biomedical research in this area is to try to establish the degree to which the influence of the therapist or religious group can be separated from a possible pharmacological role of ayahuasca, if it is indeed possible to separate and speak of such an autonomous entity. This is an especially intriguing question given the potential importance of the patient-therapist relationship for general treatment outcomes, or more specifically, the degree to which participation in a religious community is thought to be positively associated with recovery from psychoactive substance dependence (Sanchez and Nappo 2007). In order to attempt to isolate the 'religious variables' or the 'psychotherapeutic variables' from the 'pharmacological variables'[14] at play in healing uses of ayahuasca, one might, as some investigators have done, measure the effects of administering active or placebo ayahuasca to a group of volunteers in a single setting, such as a religious setting (Santos *et al.* 2007), or a laboratory setting (Riba 2003; Riba and Barbanoj 2005). Alternatively, one could administer the same active ayahuasca preparation to groups of volunteers in different settings, such as a religious context, a psychotherapeutic context and a recreational context. Even it if is not possible to discuss this topic in sufficient detail here, it is nevertheless important to note that these attempts to isolate the 'pharmacological variables' of the ayahuasca experience are quite complicated, and that artificially constructed research settings are never free of their own effects on the subject of study (for further discussion, see Labate *et al.* 2009).

It would be interesting to go beyond traditional pharmacological research models to design studies of a truly interdisciplinary nature by, for instance, utilizing the qualitative methods of anthropology and psychology to take into account, in conjunction with variables like dosage and genetics, the cultural and life history factors that can influence an individual's ayahuasca experiences. While it is widely recognized that set and setting are important factors in determining the actions of psychoactive substances in general, and especially psychedelics (see Winkelman and Roberts, 2007a), biomedical studies rarely address the important role of symbolic efficacy in the production of healing – a phenomenon shaped by the expectations of the patient, the healer, and the community (Lévi-Strauss 1963). Native conceptions about health, illness, and healing should therefore surely be considered in evaluating the therapeutic uses of ayahuasca and their outcomes.[15]

---

13. A common example of such a methodological critique is that the double-blind experimental design is overly difficult to rigorously implement when using psychedelic substances because of the challenge of camouflaging the unique and powerful effects of these substances (see Halpern 2007; Winkelman and Roberts 2007b). For further discussion of the challenges and future potentials of using conventional psychopharmacological methods to study ayahuasca and other psychedelics, see O'Brien and Jones 1994; Strassman 1995; Gouzoulis-Mayfrank *et al.* 1998; Grob 1998; Doblin 2000; McKenna 2004; Riba and Barbanoj 2005; Frecska 2007; Winkelman and Roberts 2007a; and Johnson *et al.* 2008.

14. The complex and limiting attempts of science to separate or purify the realms of nature and culture in human experience have been and continue to be analyzed under the rubric of the anthropology of science. See, for example, Latour (1993), among others.

15. For example, according to Daimistas, some afflicted spirits [*espíritos sofredores*] may seek out Santo Daime in search of light [*luz*] and should be indoctrinated [*doutrinados*]. Sometimes such spirits might incorporate in the apparatus [*aparelho*] (that is, the physical body) of a medium and drink Daime through him or her.

Individual and group conceptions of drugs are especially important for any analysis of what constitutes the treatment or handling of substance dependence. As we saw in the case of Santa Maria, a substance may figure into certain contexts as a remedy and in others as a vice.[16] Another good example of the ways the ideological and moral prescriptions of a group can influence substance consumption patterns may be found in the fact that in the UDV, as far as we could determine from our observations, almost no one seems to smoke tobacco, although many members tell of having been smokers before joining the group. As is well known, nicotine dependence is one of the most difficult dependencies to treat, which suggests that the situation found in the UDV regarding tobacco use could hardly be attributed solely to the pharmacological properties of ayahuasca.

The comparison of groups that use ayahuasca in the treatment or handling of dependence with religiously-oriented organizations, like Alcoholics Anonymous, that serve a similar population but without the use of psychoactive substances should also be considered. This sort of analysis might also help to tease apart the effects of 'religious variables' and 'pharmacological variables'. Such a comparison also draws into relief an important fact that should not be forgotten: in Brazil, non-ayahuasca religious groups can practice many different forms of healing, and the religious uses of ayahuasca are legal, but its therapeutic uses outside of conventional medical contexts are prohibited (Goulart 2004; Labate 2005; Rose 2005; MacRae 2008). In Brazil, the topic of the healings performed by the many religious and therapeutic communities and centers is often controversial because of the low degree of medical professionalism that some exhibit[17] and the lack of official monitoring of these groups' activities. This controversy is only exacerbated by the addition of the therapeutic use of ayahuasca into the equation. Issues like this semantic and almost arbitrary distinction between 'religious' and 'therapeutic' call for serious

---

From the point of view of an observer, the individual drinks the Daime, but from the emic perspective, it is the spirit itself who consumes the substance to become enlightened (Alves 2007; on Daimista concepts of illness and healing see also Peláez (1994) and Rose (2005)). On the other hand, according to reports that we collected during our field research, in some cases certain obsessing spirits [*espíritos obsessores*] may induce the 'addict' to consume certain 'drugs' to satisfy them. There may thus be variation, with the spirit said to be 'addicted' or the individual 'addicted' due to the external influence of the spirit. The latter possibility seems to be the case in the Barquinha, an ayahuasca religion which we do not discuss here, but which has generated a number of anecdotal reports of 'curing' substance dependence (Mercante 2006). In the Barquinha, spiritual work consists of, for example, removing the obsessing spirit from the company of the dependant during a session with a class of spirit known as *Preto Velho*. The *Preto Velho* may use techniques such as discharging herbal baths [*banhos de descarrego*], among others, to weaken the spirit – an action which would considerably diminish the desire of the individual to consume the psychoactive substance, making him or her more open to the treatment (ibid.).

16. We should not forget that ayahuasca itself, which is associated by all the groups described here with some notion of healing, in other contexts may sometimes be considered a 'drug' to be combated, as in the case of groups such as Narcotics Anonymous, where total abstinence from any use of psychoactive substances is suggested to be the only means of controlling the 'illness of addiction' (Loeck 2006).

17. This problem is clearly related to another, much wider, issue, which is the tension between conventional Western medicine and folk therapies and alternative healing practices (including here religions) in Western countries today. For critiques of mutual aid groups by medical professionals and others, see Burns and Labonia Filho (2006). On the relationship between Western medicine and folk healing practices and forms of knowledge in Brazilian history, and the former's attempts to constitute itself as a hegemonic healing practice, see Montero (1985).

reflection on the boundaries we place between psychotherapy, religion and healing, as well as the ethical and legal issues associated with the role of the State and medicine in shaping the health, body, and subjectivity of the individual.

Finally, current research into the use of ayahuasca in the treatment of substance dependence should be contextualized with respect to the interrupted tradition of psychedelic and psycholytic therapies that were developed from the 1950s to the 1970s. For example, it could be suggested that the first contact of people with ayahuasca in the context of Santo Daime might resemble the insight, revelation or awakening experiences of patients in the early psychedelic therapies with LSD aimed at treating alcoholism and other dependencies (Abramson 1967; Grinspoon and Bakalar 1979). Alternatively, one might in some sense interpret the UDV's religious ceremonies as having certain similarities with group therapy because of the emphasis placed on personal growth and group cohesiveness during the ceremonies. The most direct legacy of this decades-old research is probably to be found in the work of the Takiwasi and IDEAA centers, which explicitly adopt Western psychotherapeutic techniques, such as individual therapy and group sessions, to aid in integrating the ayahuasca experience after the rituals. As some scholars have noted, psycholytic therapies would frequently include shamanic elements in the therapeutic setting (Passie, 2007), thus providing another parallel between older psychotherapy research and the practices of current-day ayahuasca groups.[18]

One of the most promising results of clinical psychedelic research done in the 1950s and 1960s comes from the use of psychedelic agents in conjunction with psychotherapy – as opposed to the more reductionist psychedelic pharmacotherapy model, in which psychedelics are administered without any accompanying psychotherapy. The accumulated experience of psychedelic therapists suggests that the period of psychedelic 'afterglow'[19] is likely a source of important therapeutic benefit (Pahnke *et al.* 1970; Halpern 2007), seeing as how during this period the patient may experience 'increased openness and willingness to communicate' (Albaugh and Anderson 1974, cited in Calabrese 2007: 31). In view of the hypothesis that psychedelics have promising anti-addictive properties which last for an indeterminate, but finite period (Halpern 2007: 4), belonging to a religious community or psychotherapeutic group that uses ayahuasca on a regular basis may act as an efficacious form of substitution therapy. In fact, active participation in such groups might facilitate a 'prolonged afterglow' (Halpern 2007: 7) and increase the possibility of successful treat-

---

18. In our fieldwork we have noted an ever-greater proliferation, especially in Europe, of groups that use ayahuasca in psychotherapeutic contexts, which are not necessarily directed at the treatment of dependence, but occasionally address this type of need. Many of the leaders of these groups are people familiar with various psychedelic substances and with the techniques of psychedelic and psycholytic therapy. In this sense it is the psychedelic therapies that encounter ayahuasca, which is sometimes administered in workshops together with other psychedelics (simultaneously or on alternating days). According to López Pavillard (2008), in the context of Spanish neo-shamanism, ayahuasca analogs are frequently used. These are any of various combinations of pure chemical substances (e.g., harmine + DMT) and/or plants rich in such substances (e.g., *Peganum harmala* + *Mimosa hostilis*, or jurema – a combination known as juremahuasca). These preparations produce effects supposedly similar to those of ayahuasca (Ott 1994, 2004).

19. The 'afterglow' refers to the positive physical and mental effects that can sometimes remain with the individual for days or weeks after the use of psychedelics.

ment. Hopefully, future research into the therapeutic uses of ayahuasca can learn from the successes and failures of previous psychotherapeutic work done with other psychedelics and subsequently contribute new and significant findings to the extant body of knowledge.

Research into the different ways that ayahuasca is and may potentially be used in the treatment or handling of substance dependence problems requires that careful attention be paid to a broad set of interdisciplinary considerations. We have attempted to outline here only a few lines of inquiry to be pursued, including: the extent to which the effects of ayahuasca may be reduced to and modified by 'religious', 'therapeutic' or 'pharmacological' variables; the importance of anthropological methods, native concepts and social contextualization in understanding substance use and dependence; and the possibility of using historical comparisons to better understand past and present practices.

Final considerations

This text has reviewed the available evidence of how ritual ayahuasca use is employed in South America – specifically in complementary, psychotherapeutic Amazonian rehabilitation centers and urban Brazilian religions of folk origin – in the treatment and handling of psychoactive substance dependence. While the surveyed data was not always generated by studies with the greatest generalizability or methodological rigor, these studies offer preliminary evidence that the ritual use of ayahuasca may serve as an effective tool in the treatment, and religious handling, of substance dependence problems.

The general assumption that ayahuasca heals substance dependence has become a kind of self-evident truth within the ayahuasca field. Takiwasi plays an important role in the creation of this idea; the uses of ayahuasca within the Brazilian religions and IDEAA are also frequently cited as examples of ayahuasca's therapeutic value. This naive point of view has often been incorporated into descriptions of ayahuasca found in the Brazilian media and even in some scientific studies (which are frequently written by enthusiastic researchers from the ayahuasca field).

The uses of ayahuasca for treatment and healing can be understood within the diffuse tradition of using other psychedelic substances for the purpose of stimulating 'mystical-type' experiences that may have persisting positive effects (Griffiths *et al.* 2008), particularly for substance abuse and dependence (Dyck 2006). Many factors are expected to influence the success of different psychedelic treatments for different kinds of dependence problems. Such factors include, but are not limited to, the normative capacity shared by different ritual contexts, as well as the pharmacological nature of the substance and the mechanisms by which it acts (Callaway *et al.* 1994; Grob *et al.* 1996; McKenna *et al.* 1998; McKenna 2004; Barbosa *et al.* 2005; Santos *et al.* 2007; Labate *et al.*, in press).

Should future research provide substantial evidence that, beyond the mere pharmacology of ayahuasca, the cultivation of the therapeutic bond or a religious zeal plays a significant role in the health outcomes of ayahuasca-using centers and religions, there will be important implications for the formulation of public policies on the therapeutic uses of ayahuasca. For example, it would have to be decided whether physicians could openly refer their patients to centers and religious groups, such as those mentioned here, and if so whether health insurers or the government would finance such organizations to perform ayahuasca therapies. It should also be asked: who might be officially licensed by the State to conduct therapy sessions with ayahuasca, and how might such licensure be obtained? Would licenses be granted to psychiatrists, therapists, nurses, shamans, *padrinhos* and *mestres*, groups such as Alcoholics Anonymous, or priests? What sorts of didactics and self-experience with ayahuasca might such training and certification entail? Might medications be made from ayahuasca to be administered in clinical practice by physicians? What kinds of intellectual property considerations might be important, such as the protection of or compensation for using forms of traditional indigenous knowledge (UMIYAC 1999; Labate 2005; Tupper 2009)?

We have analyzed many of the challenges facing a research agenda concerned with the therapeutic potential of ayahuasca, in particular for substance dependence. While it is important to stimulate scientific research in this area, investigations of this nature should not be the only means of approaching the phenomenon, nor should they monopolize the 'proof' of the 'efficacy' of the different shamanic, psychotherapeutic, and religious uses of ayahuasca. It is worth pointing out that many practices of contemporary biomedicine – such as choosing which medications to use for which patients – are guided by tradition or institutional affiliation and are often not validated by the strictest criteria of medical science; also, clinical practice normally differs greatly from practice under experimental and laboratory conditions. That is to say, we are in danger of ethnocentrically applying certain demands on the 'medicine of others', but not on our own medicine (Winkelman and Roberts, 2007b). The pursuit by some ayahuasca users of a scientific seal of approval that could validate native claims of safety and therapeutic efficacy while shielding these users from accusations of charlatanism should not obviate the right of other ayahuasca users to be recognized as legitimate in their own terms.[20]

The apparent improvements in many anecdotal cases of psychoactive substance dependence reported by the various psychotherapeutic and religious groups that ritually use ayahuasca, as well as by anthropologists, psychologists, and psychiatrists who have studied this phenomenon, represents a promising lead for future research. The effects of such complex ritual practices will likely be best understood through systematic interdisciplinary studies that combine a quantitative approach with the subtleties of qualitative and ethnographic methods. Such an interdisciplinary effort must be accompanied by a sincere attempt at a dialogue with 'native', emic knowledge so that the understanding acquired over decades by the various groups that use ayahuasca in the treatment and handling of dependence and other physical and spiritual ailments may better inform the society at large, in which the use of ayahuasca is constantly growing and expanding. With this text we hope both to call attention to the importance of this intriguing cultural and mental health phenomenon, and to help stimulate and guide future research in this area.

---

20. For example, there are more orthodox ayahuasca groups (indigenous or Western) that are actively opposed to the use of ayahuasca in any secular context, whether in animal experiments, research with human subjects in clinical contexts, the creation of synthetic substances from the raw materials that make up ayahuasca, or even any kind of scientific approach to the subject.

Acknowledgments

An earlier version of this text was published in Portuguese as 'Considerações sobre o tratamento da dependência por meio da ayahuasca' (Considerations for the treatment of substance dependence with ayahuasca; available here: http://www.neip.info/upd_blob/0000/456.pdf) and translated to English by Matthew Meyer; the present text has been substantially revised since the translation. We are grateful for the comments from Henrik Jungaberle and Kenneth Tupper.

References

Abramson, H. A., ed. 1967. *The Use of LSD in Psychotherapy and Alcoholism.* New York: The Bobbs-Merrill Co.

Albaugh, B. J. and P. O Anderson. 1974. 'Peyote in the treatment of alcoholism among American Indians'. *American Journal of Psychiatry* 131: 1247–50.

Alper, J. R. and H. S. Lotsof. 2007. The use of ibogaine in the treatment of addictions. In M.J. Winkelman and T. B. Roberts, eds, *Psychedelic Medicine: New Evidence for Hallucinogenic Substances as Treatments,* vol. 2, 43–66. Westport, CT: Praeger.

Alves, A. M. 2007. 'Tambores para a Rainha da Floresta: a inserção da Umbanda no Santo Daime'. Master's thesis in Religious Studies, Pontifícia Universidade Católica de São Paulo.

Andrade, A. P. De. 2005. 'O fenômeno do chá e a religiosidade cabocla'. Master's thesis in Religious Studies, Instituto Metodista de Ensino Superior.

Barbosa, P. C. R., J. S. Giglio and P. Dalgalarrondo. 2005. 'Altered states of consciousness and short-term psychological after-effects induced by the first time ritual use of ayahuasca in an urban context in Brazil'. *Journal of Psychoactive Drugs* 37(2): 193–201.

Barron, F., M. E. Jarvik and S. Bunnel Jr. 1964. 'Hallucinogenic drugs'. *Scientific American* 210: 29–37.

Brissac, S. 1999. 'A Estrela do Norte iluminando até o sul: uma etnografia da União do Vegetal em um contexto urbano'. Master's thesis in Anthropology, Museu Nacional/Universidade Federal de Rio de Janeiro.

Burns, J. E. and Filho, W. Labonia. 2006. 'Grupos de ajuda-mútua no tratamento de pessoas dependentes de substâncias'. In SUPERA (Sistema para Detecção do Uso Abusivo e Dependência de Substâncias Psicoativas: Encaminhamento, Intervenção Breve, Reinserção Social e Acompanhamento), Módulo 5: Encaminhamento de pessoas dependentes de substâncias psicoativas, 24–26. Brasília: Secretaria Nacional Antidrogas.

Bustos, S. 2008. 'The healing power of the icaros: A phenomenological study of ayahuasca experiences'. Doctoral dissertation in Philosophy in East-West Psychology, California Institute of Integral Studies.

Calabrese, J. D., 2007, 'The therapeutic use of peyote in the Native American Church'. In M. J. Winkelman and T. B. Roberts, eds, *Psychedelic Medicine: New Evidence for Hallucinogenic Substances as Treatments,* vol. 2, 29–42. Westport, CT: Praeger.

Callaway, J. C., M. M. Airaksinen, D. J. McKenna, G. S. Brito, and C. S. Grob, 1994, 'Platelet serotonin uptake sites increased in drinkers of *ayahuasca*'. *Psychopharmacology* 116(3): 385–87.

Cemin, A. B. 2001. *O poder do Santo Daime - ordem, xamanismo e dádiva.* São Paulo: Terceira Margem.

Centro Espírita Beneficente União do Vegetal (CEBUDV). 1989. *Hoasca. Fundamentos e objetivos.* Brasília: Sede Geral.

Denys, A. 2005. 'Alliance des médecines occidentales et traditionnelles dans le traitement des addictions'. Master's thesis in Social and Public Health Sciences, Université Henri Poincaré Nancy I.

Dobkin de Rios, M., C. S. Grob and J. R. Baker. 2002. 'Hallucinogens and redemption'. *Journal of Psychoactive Drugs* 34(3): 239–48.

Doblin. R. 2000, 'Regulation of the medical use of psychedelics and marijuana'. Doctoral dissertation in Public Policy, Harvard University.

Doering-Silveira, E., C. S. Grob, M. D. Dobkin de Rios, E. Lopez, L. K. Alonso, C. D. Tacla, and D. X. Silveira. 2005. 'Report on psychoactive drug use among adolescents using ayahuasca within a religious context'. *Journal of Psychoactive Drugs* 37(2): 141–44.

Dyck, E. 2006. '"Hitting highs at rock bottom": LSD treatment for alcoholism, 1950–1970'. *Social History of Medicine* 19(2): 313–29.

Fernandez, X. in press. 'Experiencia de un tratamiento con ayahuasca para las drogodependencias en la Amazonia Brasileña'. In B. C. Labate and J. C. Bouso, eds, *Ayahuasca y salud*. Barcelona: Los Libros de La Liebre de Marzo.

Fiore, M. 2007. *Controvérsias médicas e o debate público sobre uso de 'drogas'*. Campinas: Mercado de Letras.

Frecska, E. 2007. 'Therapeutic guidelines: Dangers and contraindications in therapeutic applications of hallucinogens'. In M. J. Winkelman and T. B. Roberts, eds, *Psychedelic Medicine: New Evidence for Hallucinogenic Substances as Treatments*, vol. 1, 69–95. Westport, CT: Praeger.

Galanter, M. 2006. 'Spirituality and addiction: A research and clinical perspective'. *The American Journal on Addictions* 15: 286–92.

Giove, R. 2002. *La liana de los muertos al rescate de la vida: Medicina tradicional amazónica en el tratamiento de las toxicomanías*. Tapa Blanda.

Goulart, S. L. 1996. 'Raízes culturais do Santo Daime'. Master's thesis in Anthropology, Universidade de São Paulo.

Goulart, S.L. 2004. 'Contrastes e continuidades em uma tradição amazônica: as religiões da ayahuasca'. Doctoral dissertation in Social Anthropology, Unicamp.

Goulart, S. L., B. C. Labate and H. Carneiro. 2005. 'Introdução'. In B. C. Labate and S. L. Goulart, eds, *O uso ritual das plantas de poder*, 29–55. Campinas: Mercado de Letras.

Gouzoulis-Mayfrank, E., F. Schneider, J., Friedrich, M., Spitzer, B., Thelen and H. Sass. 1998. 'Methodological issues of human experimental research with hallucinogens'. *Pharmacopsychiatry* 31(Supplement): 114–18.

Graeff, F. G. 1984. *Drogas psicotrópicas e seu mecanismo de ação*. São Paulo: EPU-EDUSP-CNPq.

Griffiths, R. R., W. A. Richards, U. McCann and R. Jesse. 2008. 'Mystical-type experiences occasioned by psilocybin mediate the attribution of personal meaning and spiritual significance 14 months later. *Journal of Psychopharmacology* 22(6): 621–32.

Grinspoon, L. and J. B. Bakalar. 1979. *Psychedelic Drugs Reconsidered*. New York: Basic Books.

Grinspoon, L. and J. B. Bakalar. 1997. *Marihuana: The Forbidden Medicine*. New Haven, CT: Yale University Press.

Grob, C. S. 1998. 'Psychiatric research with hallucinogens: What have we learned?' *The Heffter Review of Psychedelic Research* 1: 8–20.

Grob, C. S. 2002. *Hallucinogens: a Reader*. New York: Tarcher/Putnam.

Grob, C. S., D. J. McKenna, J. C. Callaway, G. S. Brito, E. S. Neves, G. Oberlaender, O. L. Saide, E. Labigalini, C. Tacla, C. T. Miranda, R. J. Strassman and K. B. Boone. 1996. 'Human psychopharmacology of hoasca, a plant hallucinogen used in ritual context in Brazil'. *Journal of Nervous & Mental Disease* 184(2): 86–94.

Grob, C. S., D. J. McKenna, J. C. Callaway, G. S. Brito, E. S. Neves, G. Oberlaender, O. L. Saide, E. Labigalini, C. Tacla, C. T. Miranda, R. J. Strassman and K. B. Boone. 2004. 'Farmacologia humana da hoasca: efeitos psicológicos'. In B. C. Labate and W. S. Araújo (eds). *O uso ritual da ayahuasca*. 2nd edn, 653–69. Campinas: Mercado de Letras.

Grof, S. 2001. *LSD Psychotherapy*, 3rd edn. Sarasota, Florida: Multidisciplinary Association for Psychedelic Studies.

Groisman, A. 1999. *Eu venho da floresta. Um estudo sobre o contexto simbólico do uso do Santo Daime*. Florianópolis: Editora da Universidade Federal de Santa Catarina.

Groisman, A. 2000. 'Santo Daime in the Netherlands: An anthropological study of a new world religion in a European setting. Doctoral dissertation in Anthropology, University of London.

Halpern, J. 1996. 'The use of hallucinogens in the treatment of addiction'. *Addiction Research* 4(2): 177–89.

Halpern, J. 2007. 'Hallucinogens in the treatment of alcoholism and other addictions'. In M. J. Winkelman and T. B. Roberts, eds, *Psychedelic Medicine: New Evidence for Hallucinogenic Substances as Treatments*, vol. 2, 1–14. Westport, CT: Praeger.

Hoffer, A. 1967. 'A Program for the treatment of alcoholism: LSD, malvaria and nicotinic acid'. In H. Abramson, ed, *The use of LSD in Psychotherapy and Alcoholism*. Indianapolis, IN: Bobbs-Merrill.

Johnson, M. W., W. A. Richards and R. R. Griffiths. 2008. 'Human hallucinogen research: Guidelines for safety'. *Journal of Psychopharmacology* 22(6): 603–20.

Krupitsky, E. and E. Kolp. 2007. 'Ketamine psychedelic psychotherapy'. In M. J. Winkelmanand and T. B.

Roberts, eds, 2007, *Psychedelic Medicine: New Evidence for Hallucinogenic Substances as Treatments*, vol. 2, 67–85. Westport, CT: Praeger.

Labate, B. C. 2004. *A reinvenção do uso da ayahausca nos centros urbanos*. Campinas: Mercado de Letras.

Labate, B. C. 2005. 'Dimensões legais, éticas e políticas da expansão do consumo da ayahuasca'. In B. C. Labate and S. L. Goulart, eds, *O uso ritual das plantas de poder*, 397–457. Campinas: Mercado de Letras.

Labate, B. C. and W. S. Araújo, eds. 2004. *O uso ritual da ayahuasca*. 2nd edn. Campinas: Mercado de Letras.

Labate, B. C. and E. MacRae, eds. 2006 (published 2008). *The Light from the Forest: the Ritual use of Ayahuasca in Brazil*. Fieldwork in Religion 2.3.

Labate, B. C., I. S. Rose and R. G. Santos. 2009. *Ayahuasca Religions: A Comprehensive Bibliography and Critical Essays*. Santa Cruz (CA): Multidisciplinary Association for Psychedelic Studies.

Labate, B. C. and G. Pacheco. in press. *Música Brasileira de Ayahuasca*. Campinas, Mercado de Letras.

Labate, B. C., R. G. Santos, R. J. Strassman, B. Anderson and S. Mizumoto. in press. 'Efectos de la pertenencia al Santo Daime sobre la dependencia a sustancias psicoativas'. In B. C. Labate and J. C. Bouso, eds, *Ayahuasca y salud*. Barcelona: Los Libros de La Liebre de Marzo.

Labate, B. C., S. Goulart, M. Fiore, E. MacRae and H. Carneiro, eds. 2008. *Drogas e cultura: novas perspectivas*. Salvador: Edufba.

Labigalini, E. 1998. 'O uso de ayahuasca em um contexto religioso por ex-dependentes de álcool – um estudo qualitativo'. Master's thesis in Mental Health Sciences, Universidade Federal de São Paulo/Escola Paulista de Medicina.

Labigalini, E., L. R. Rodrigues and D. X. Silveira. 1999. 'Therapeutic use of Cannabis by crack addicts in Brazil'. *Journal of Psychoactive Drugs* 31(4): 451–5.

Latour, B. 1993. *We have Never been Modern*. Cambridge, MA: Harvard University Press.

Lenza, M. 2007. 'Toking their way sober: Alcoholics and marijuana as folk medicine'. *Contemporary Justice Review* 10(3): 307–22.

Lévi-Strauss, C. 1963. 'The effectiveness of symbols'. In C. Lévi-Strauss, *Structural Anthropology*. New York: Basic Books.

Loeck, J. F. 2006, 'Narcóticos Anônimos: um estudo sobre estigma e ritualidade'. *Núcleo de Estudos Interdisciplinares sobre Psicoativos*, NEIP. Available at: http://www.neip.info/downloads/jardel/jardel_01.pdf.

López Pavillard, S. 2008. 'Recepción de la ayahuasca en España'. Doctoral dissertation in Social Anthropology, Universidad Complutense de Madrid.

Luna, L. E. 1986. *Vegetalismo: Shamanism among the mestizo population of the Peruvian Amazon*. Stockholm: Almquist and Wiksell International.

Mabit, J. 1996a. 'Takiwasi: Ayahuasca and shamanism in addiction therapy'. *MAPS Newsletter*, 6 (3). Available at: http://www.maps.org/news-letters/v06n3/06324aya.html.

Mabit, J. 1996b. 'The Takiwasi patient's journey'. *MAPS Newsletter* 6 (3). Available at: http://www.maps.org/news-letters/v06n3/06327tak.html.

Mabit, J. 2002. 'Blending traditions – using indigenous medicinal knowledge to treat drug addiction. *MAPS Newsletter*, 12(2): 25–32. Available at: http://www.maps.org/news-letters/v12n2/12225mab.html.

Mabit, J. 2004. 'Produção visionária da ayahuasca no contexto dos curandeiros da Alta Amazônia Peruana'. In B. C. Labate and W. S. Araújo, eds, *O uso ritual da ayahuasca*. 2nd edn, 147–80. Campinas: Mercado de Letras.

Mabit, J. 2007. 'Ayahuasca in the treatment of addictions'. In M. J. Winkelman and T. B. Roberts, eds, *Psychedelic Medicine: New Evidence for Hallucinogenic Substances as Treatments*, vol. 2, 87–105. Westport, CT: Praeger.

Mabit, J., R. Giove and J. Veja. 1996. 'Takiwasi: The use of Amazonian shamanism to rehabilitate drug addicts'. *Yearbook of Cross-cultural Medicine and Psychotherapy* 6: 257–86.

MacRae, E. 1998. 'Santo Daime and Santa Maria: The licit ritual use of ayahuasca and the illicit use of Cannabis in a Brazilian Amazonian religion'. *International Journal of Drug Policy* 9: 325–38.

MacRae, E. 2006 [1992]. 'Guided by the moon: Shamanism and the ritual use of ayahuasca in the Santo Daime Religion in Brazil'. In *Núcleo de Estudos Interdisciplinares sobre Psicoativos*, NEIP. Available at: http://www.neip.info/downloads/edward/ebook.htm.

MacRae, E. 2006 (published 2008). 'The religious uses of licit and illicit psychoactive substances in a branch of the Santo Daime Religion'. In B. C. Labate and E. MacRae, eds, *The Light from the Forest: The Ritual use of Ayahuasca in Brazil*. Fieldwork in Religion 2.3: 393–414.

MacRae, E. 2008. 'A elaboração das políticas públicas brasileiras em relação ao uso religioso da ayahausca'. In

B. C. Labate, S. Goulart, M. Fiore, E. MacRae and H. Carneiro, eds, *Drogas e cultura: novas perspectivas*, 289–311. Salvador, Edufba.

MacRae, E. and S. Vidal. 2006. 'A resolução 196/96 e a imposição do modelo biomédico na pesquisa social: dilemas éticos e metodológicos do antropólogo pesquisando o uso de substâncias psicoativas'. *Revista de Antropologia da USP* 49: 35–47.

McKenna, D. J. 2004. 'Clinical investigations of the therapeutic potential of *ayahuasca*: rationale and regulatory challenges'. *Pharmacology & Therapeutics* 102(2): 111–29.

McKenna, D. J., J. C. Callaway and C. S. Grob. 1998. 'The scientific investigation of ayahuasca: A review of past and current research'. *The Heffter Review of Psychedelic Research* 1: 65–77.

Mercante, M. S. 2006. 'Images of healing: Spontaneous mental imagery and healing process of the Barquinha, a Brazilian ayahuasca religious system'. Doctoral dissertation in Social Sciences, Saybrook Graduate School and Research Center.

Mercante, M. S. 2007. *Estudo do uso terapêutico de ayahuasca entre moradores de rua na cidade de São Paulo.* Projeto de pesquisa de bolsa de Pós-Doutorado Junior, CNPq. Programa de Pós-Graduação em Antropologia Social, Universidade Federal de Santa Catarina.

Monteiro da Silva, C. 1985. 'Ritual de tratamento e cura'. *I Simpósio de Saúde Mental da Amazônia. Santarém.*

Montero, P. 1985. *Da doença à desordem: a magia na Umbanda.* Rio de Janeiro: Ed. Graal.

O'Brien, C. P. and R. T. Jones. 1994. 'Methodological issues in the evaluation of a medication for its potential benefits in enhancing psychotherapy'. In A. Pletscher and D. Ladewig, eds, *50 years of LSD: Current Status and Perspectives on Hallucinogens.* New York: Parthenon.

Osmond, H. 1957. 'A Review of the clinical effects of psychotomimetic agents'. *Annals of the New York Academy of Science* 66(3): 418–34.

Ott, J. 1994. *Ayahuasca analogues: Pangaean entheogens.* Kennewick, WA: Natural Products Co.

Ott, J. 2004. 'Farmahuasca, anahuasca e jurema preta: farmacologia humana da DMT oral combinada com a harmina. In B. C. Labate and W. S. Araújo, eds, *O uso ritual da ayahuasca.* 2nd edn, 711–36. Campinas: Mercado de Letras.

Pahnke, W. N., A. A. Kurland, S. Unger, C. Savage and S. Grof. 1970. 'The experimental use of psychedelic (LSD) psychotherapy'. *Journal of the American Medial Association* 212: 1856–63.

Passie, T. 2007. 'Contemporary psychedelic therapy: An overview'. In M. J. Winkelman and T. B. Roberts, eds, *Psychedelic Medicine: New Evidence for Hallucinogenic Substances as Treatments*, vol. 1, 45–68. Westport, CT: Praeger.

Peláez, M. C. 1994. *No mundo se cura tudo: interpretações sobre a 'cura espiritual' no Santo Daime.* Mestrado em Antropologia Social, Universidade Federal de Santa Catarina.

Presser-Velder, Anja. 2000. 'Das therapeutische Potential der rituellen Verwendung sakraler Heilpflanzen. Eine ethnopsychologische Studie'. Master's Thesis (Diplomarbeit) in Psychology. Universitaet Koblenz Landau 3.

Riba, J. 2003. 'Human pharmacology of ayahuasca'. Doctoral thesis in Pharmacology. Universitat Autònoma de Barcelona.

Riba, J. and M. J. Barbanoj. 2005. 'Bringing ayahuasca to the clinical research laboratory'. *Journal of Psychoactive Drugs* 37(2): 219–30.

Ricciardi, G. S. 2008. 'O uso da ayahuasca e a experiência de transformação, alívio e cura na União do Vegetal (UDV)'. Master's thesis in Social Sciences, Edufba.

Rose, I. S. 2005. 'Espiritualidade, terapia e cura. Um estudo sobre a expressão da experiência no Santo Daime'. Master's thesis in Social Anthropology, Universidade Federal de Santa Catarina.

Sadock, B. J. and V. A. Sadock, eds, *Kaplan & Sadock's comprehensive textbook of psychiatry.* Philadelphia, PA: Lippincott Williams & Wilkins.

Sanchez, Z. M. and S. A. Nappo. 2007. 'A religiosidade, a espiritualidade e o consumo de drogas'. *Revista de Psiquiatria Clínica* 34(suppl 1): 73–81.

Santos, R. G., J. Landeira-Fernandez, R. J. Strassman, V. Motta and A. P. M. Cruz. 2007. 'Effects of ayahuasca on psychometric measures of anxiety, panic-like and hopelessness in Santo Daime members'. *Journal of Ethnopharmacology* 112(3): 507–13.

Sieber, C. L. 2007. 'Enseñanzas y Mareaciones: Exploring Intercultural Health Through Experience and Interaction with Healers and Plant Teachers in San Martín, Peru'. Master's thesis in Anthropology, University of Victoria.

Sifaneck, S. J. and C. D. Kaplan. 1995. 'Keeping off, stepping on and stepping off: The stepping stone theory reevaluated in the context of the Dutch *cannabis* experience'. *Contemporary Drug Problems* 22(8): 483–512.

Silveira, D. X. and F. G. Moreira. 2006. 'Reflexões preliminares sobre a questão das substâncias psicoativas'. In D. X. Silveira and F. G. Moreira, eds, *Panorama atual de drogas e dependência*, 3–7. São Paulo: Atheneu.

Strassman, R. J. 1995. 'Hallucinogenic drugs in psychiatric research and treatment'. *The Journal of Nervous and Mental Disease* 183(3): 127–38.

Tupper, K. W. 2009. 'Ayahuasca healing beyond the Amazon: The globalization of a traditional indigenous entheogenic practice'. *Global Networks: A Journal of Transnational Affairs* 9(1), 117–36.

Unión de Médicos Indígenas Yageceros de Colombia (UMIYAC). 1999. *Encuentro de Taitas en la Amazonía colombiana: Ceremonias y reflexiones*. Caquetá, Colombia, 1–8 June.

United Nations Office on Drugs and Crime (UNODC). 2007. *2007 World Drug Report*. United Nations Publication. 2007. Available at: http://www.unodc.org/pdf/research/wdr07/WDR_2007.pdf.

Velho, G. 1987. 'Duas categorias de acusação na cultura brasileira contemporânea'. In G. Velho, *Individualismo e cultura: notas para uma antropologia da sociedade contemporânea*. 2nd edn, 55–64. Rio de Janeiro: Jorge Zahar Editor.

Villaescusa, M. 2007. 'Proyecto IDEAA: Terapia integrativa de sustancias visionarias y disciplinas psicoespirituales en el tratamiento de toxicomanías'. *Núcleo de Estudos Interdisciplinares sobre Psicoativos*, NEIP. Available at: http://www.neip.info/downloads/villaescusa/Proyecto%20IDEAA.pdf.

Winkelman, M. J. and T. B. Roberts, eds. 2007a. *Psychedelic Medicine: New Evidence for Hallucinogenic Substances as Treatments*, vols 1 and 2. Westport, CT: Praeger.

Winkelman, M. J. and T. B. Roberts, eds. 2007b. 'Conclusions: Guidelines for implementing the use of psychedelic medicines'. In M. J. Winkelman and T. B. Roberts, eds, *Psychedelic Medicine: New Evidence for Hallucinogenic Substances as Treatments*, vol. 1, 271–98. Westport, CT: Praeger.

World Health Organization (WHO). 2008. *The World Health Report on the Global Tobacco Epidemic, 2008: The MPOWER Package*. Geneva: World Health Organization.

Index

Religious leaders are entered under their name rather than their title – for example, Mestre Irineu is entered as Irineu, Mestre. Entries for illustrations are entered in italics – for example, *46*.

229

Breinigsville, PA USA
14 February 2011
255428BV00004B/23/P

9 781845 536794